Ethics of Maimonides

MODERN JEWISH PHILOSOPHY AND RELIGION
Translations and Critical Studies
Barbara E. Galli and Elliot R. Wolfson, SERIES EDITORS

Ethics of Maimonides

Hermann Cohen

Translated with commentary by

ALMUT SH. BRUCKSTEIN

Foreword by

ROBERT GIBBS

THE UNIVERSITY OF WISCONSIN PRESS

The University of Wisconsin Press
1930 Monroe Street
Madison, Wisconsin 53711

www.wisc.edu/wisconsinpress/

3 Henrietta Street
London WC2E 8LU, England

5 4 3 2 1

Printed in the United States of America

Library of Congress Cataloging-in-Publication Data

Cohen, Hermann, 1842–1918.
[Charakteristik der Ethik Maimunis. English]
Ethics of Maimonides / translation with commentary by Almut Sh. Bruckstein; foreword by Robert Gibbs.
p. cm.—(Modern Jewish philosophy and religion)
ISBN 0-299-17760-2 (Cloth: alk. paper)
ISBN 0-299-17764-5 (Paper: alk. paper)
1. Cohen, Hermann, 1842–1918. Charakteristik der ethik Maimunis. 2. Maimonides, Moses, 1135–1204—Contributions in Jewish ethics. 3. Ethics, Jewish. 4. Philosophy, Jewish. 5. Philosophy, Medieval. I. Bruckstein, Almut Sh. II. Title. III. Series.
BJ1287.M64 C64313 2002
296.3'6'092—dc21
2001005417

The upright blossom like a date-palm
They thrive like a cedar in Lebanon
...
In advanced age they still produce fruit
They are full of rigor and freshness
Psalm 92

For Zev

Contents

Foreword

Without students, there are no teachers. For about ten years, interest in Franz Rosenzweig has been growing, not only in Jewish studies, but indeed, in other contexts, including philosophy, theology, and German studies. Part of that interest arose in relation to Emmanuel Levinas, who, though never Rosenzweig's student, clearly expressed a deep debt to Rosenzweig, and especially to *The Star of Redemption*. Levinas, whose moment of fame in France is now being echoed in North America, represents a specifically Jewish inflection of postmodernism. Rosenzweig, on the other hand, lived in that fecund and difficult moment of Weimar Germany—the years before the Shoah—and died in 1929. Rosenzweig, however, is not the topic of the book that lies in your hands; this work is written by Rosenzweig's own teacher, Hermann Cohen. The book before you is a decisive refutation of Rosenzweig's view of his own teacher—and at the same time a vindication of the teacher, and even of the student.

Thus we are drawn from student to teacher, to learn from the teacher and become students. There are many lines back to Cohen, and were we ourselves not interested in becoming students, interested not in the teaching but only in the history of teachers, we would still need to study Cohen. Rosenzweig hails him as a Columbus (and I would, as a Copernicus), and claims that Cohen was the first truly Jewish philosopher who discovered a new route, a new thinking. Like a Columbus, it is Cohen who discovered the new possibility and exigency of thought, discovering a land for the voyages not only of Levinas and Rosenzweig, but also of Buber and Benjamin and, in different ways, of Scholem, Strauss, Pines, and many others.

Cohen is not merely the first, he is also the teacher of those who follow. His teaching, moreover, is one that reflects a decisive need in philosophy itself, a need to engage with Judaism. Judaism for Cohen is defined through its literary sources and so retains a certain kind of particularity even as it enters into conversation with, or better a correlation with, or still more clearly, even as it is translated into, philosophy. This disruption of the Greek/German philosophical tradition happens so seamlessly and so adroitly in Cohen, that even students like Rosenzweig could overlook Judaism's role in Cohen's systematic philosophical works. But what seems obvious to postmoderns, that an engagement with otherness should disrupt philosophy's authority, is developed in a complex and in its own way disturbing fashion in Cohen's work. For Cohen will not compromise on universality and on reason (and in this remains a modern, even a modernist), but at the same time he negotiates with the specificity of Jewish sources, and not merely as warehouses for properly philosophical ideas, but as texts and, indeed, as originary sources for a reasoning that knows ideas that are foreign to the Greek tradition. What happens when such ideas become translated into philosophy, when, for example, the messianic age becomes the idea of humanity, or when atonement becomes the way of individuating the self, is a reorientation for philosophy itself.

The 1908 essay "Charakteristik der Ethik Maimunis" (Ethics of Maimonides) is one of Cohen's central teachings of this new thinking. It is here translated into English for the first time, and the translator, Almut Sh. Bruckstein, has provided not only a translation and a commentary, but also an extremely valuable introduction, in which she explains why Cohen undertook to write this essay in 1908. She situates it not only in the Maimonides project of the German Jewish intellectuals, but also in Cohen's own career. Cohen's task is to listen again to Maimonides, but to listen in order to let him address Cohen's contemporary philosophical and religious scene. Cohen does make historical claims per se, that Maimonides innovated in relation to his philosophical context, or as biblical interpreter, but such claims are vastly overshadowed by Cohen's discovery of a full range of ethical insights, insights that almost leap across the generations to address Cohen and his contemporaries. The essay is a reframing of the histories of ethics, of philosophy, and of religion—starting with Socrates, and demanding a revisiting of the tension between Aristotle and Plato.

The essay makes its case with the Protestant philosophical and theological establishment of Cohen's time—arguing for the philosophical superiority of a rationalist theology—or, as Cohen would prefer, of a critical idealism. The possibility for a better philosophical position starting from the origin of the Good beyond Being, from an ethics arising in reason, is made to conform with a radical but legitimate reading of the Jewish tradition—Maimonides'. For Cohen understands the task in his time to be just this reorientation of philosophy.

Almut Bruckstein has produced a book that will allow us to become students of Cohen—a book that lets Cohen teach us. By finding ways to bring Cohen's argument into our intellectual world (a mere hundred year jump), Bruckstein is brilliantly imitating what Cohen does for Maimonides in his essay.

Such a text is not a simple one, nor is it an easy one to present today. Bruckstein had an immediate task of producing a translation of the essay. The problems of translation are explored in her introduction, but given the interplay between Hebrew, Aramaic, Greek, Latin, and then German, the target language of English has been pushed in decisive and important ways. To hear Cohen in English, to think with him in our philosophical vocabulary, and to hear the resonances in English of what he tried to do in his own German rendering of ideas and phrases, words, and technical jargon, requires an ear or an eye that is used to reading and thinking in disparate languages at the same time, and even more to going across the languages. What Bakhtin, a follower of Cohen, called polyglossia is all the more performed in the feat of translation here.

This book, moreover, is not only a translation: it is also a commentary. Cohen becomes our teacher due to the work of the commentary. Cohen struggled to find a way for Maimonides to teach Cohen, to teach his world. And Bruckstein has struggled to find a way for Cohen to become our teacher. What is this struggle? It happens on several levels all at once.

First, Cohen wants to teach us the history of philosophy, but for many readers the key philosophers are not familiar. Bruckstein has to provide not only citations but also explanations and her own readings of Cohen's readings to let us get close to the teaching about the history of philosophy. Second, Cohen also presumes a familiarity with medieval thought in the three religions—and such thought is technical. For many readers any technical thinking is off-putting, but even for those who are inclined to such rigorous thinking, the medieval version is still simply foreign. If we become bogged down or remain simply allergic to such technical discussions, we will not be able to learn from Cohen. Bruckstein manifests the sort of mastery of those texts that allows her to explain complex and technical materials clearly. But third, and most important, Cohen is a critical idealist. His philosophical convictions seem outdated to most readers. Cohen cannot teach us unless he is allowed to address us, and to escape from the pigeon-hole that reduces him to an antiquarian curiosity.

We are not, in general, prone to consider ourselves idealists, and yet Bruckstein offers in her reading of the Platonism of Cohen, as a critical idealism, a reach forward to some of the thinking that often characterizes postmodern thought. She draws deeply from the various texts of Cohen's system, pausing to explain the reasoning and the innovation of Cohen's logic. At the same time she does not compromise Cohen's claims: rationality, the centrality of the Good beyond Being, the ideas, and more, are all developed and explored in the commentary. The task is not to make Cohen say just what we want, but to make what he does say first intelligible and then even plausible.

Thus what we see in Cohen's own work is echoed in Bruckstein's commentary: an effort to let the historical background of the prior work (Maimonides in Cohen's case, and Cohen in Bruckstein's) fuel an interpretation that brings the prior work into our contemporary conversation. The teacher is looking for a student: and the commentator takes up this task. Bruckstein's book works by juxtaposing a translation of Cohen's effort and her commentary: a doubling of the reading and interpreting of Cohen. There are repetitions here, and more, there is recitation here. The problems of translation lead well beyond what I could describe, but the problems of commentary point in one deeper direction as well. The paradigmatic nature of Jewish textual tradition must be explored, and while Cohen depends on it in his essay, it is Bruckstein who best develops an analysis of it in her introduction and commentary.

For the task of citation is precisely in tension with reason, in a dialectic that speeds reason on its way, and which undergirds the claims that originate in a citation by building the reason up through it. The citation of Jewish texts in a philosophical essay, even the citation of philosophical texts, seems to hide the writer from the demanding call of reason in a thicket of authority. But for the text to exercise any role it must first be cited. And what happens then? Bruckstein, in the introduction to this volume, writes: "We render account of ourselves in facing an ancient text. But the ancient text, which has been trusted in such a way, is not really the issue when it is being cited. No ancient past, but rather the commentary in the very context of which the citation has been invoked, is defended by the citation. Nothing concerning the original narrative is signified by the citation other than that which the interpretation itself has constructed."

The text is introduced not to defend the past, but to take responsibility for giving an account, for providing a reason, to the reader—*of the commentary.* Jewish tradition discovered in its commentaries that the future readings and meanings are invoked and stand judgment over all traditional texts. What Cohen calls idealizing interpretation is framed precisely by the need to place the past under our judgment for the sake of the future. While the Jewish texts (and Cohen's genius is to extend the practice to philosophical texts as well) are cited as sources for reason, it is reason that will reconstrue the meanings, will cultivate the highest possible reading of these texts—the readings that find the tasks of ethics.

Cohen extended this process of citation and cultivation of the tradition, not as mythic, but as de-mythicizing, to the philosophical tradition, and so he began his essay with Socrates, and with the tension of Plato and Aristotle. He explored how the traditions of Greek and Arabic philosophy were tributaries to Maimonides' thought. His own rereading of the philosophical traditions refuses a reduction of their history to the victory of the dominant or surviving interpretations. Because the past is not a security for a commentary, Cohen's commentary discerns discontinuities and unrealized rationality in previous texts. To explore the tributary is to find rich backwaters, and even little streams that run more purely than the main river.

But Bruckstein has offered us insight into the main tributary that Cohen muted: the Jewish textual tradition. While Cohen cites the medieval Jewish philosophers, it is Bruckstein who provides extensive commentary on the talmudic and biblical materials that inform the medieval discussions. She explores that other tributary, offering careful and challenging readings of the Jewish pretexts to readers who often might be unaware of those texts. This is not merely a question of historical research, although it involves extensive research, but it is still more a reconstruction of the conflictual interpretative tradition, in direct parallel to what Cohen did for the other two tributaries of philosophy. She provides what is only hinted at in Cohen's essay, allowing this book to offer a full curriculum for Jewish philosophy.

Because the process of citation opens the text to the future, and makes the commentary give reasons, Bruckstein's exploration of the river leads beyond Cohen, too. It leads, indeed, and this is the final element of Bruckstein's commentary, to a discussion of the one hundred years of Jewish thought and Jewish existence that separates Cohen from her readers, his would-be students. The commentary leads on to Rosenzweig and to Levinas, even to Derrida. It finds its non-foundational ethics, its ethics of responsibility for the other, its new thinking of Judaism and philosophy, as a renewed source (spring or tributary) for the ongoing river of Jewish thought. Bruckstein examines the way that contemporary Maimonides scholarship takes a stand with or against Cohen's Platonizing reading of Maimonides. In discrete references, she links Cohen's messianism to contemporary debates in Israeli society about democracy and religion. She traces the river, thus, not only back, but also forward to our time, and lets Cohen's voice register in our contemporary scene.

The critical nature of these connections and river explorations is made clear in the very first citation by Bruckstein. For she cites Cohen's student, Rosenzweig, in fulsome praise of Cohen, and yet the fact of this book, with translation and commentary of an earlier essay by Cohen, is a refutation of Rosenzweig. It seems that no single factor has prevented us from reading Cohen, from studying him in order to learn his teaching, as much as Rosenzweig's reading of Cohen. Rosenzweig read Cohen as having exceeded his own philosophy in his last works on Judaism, particularly *Religion of Reason: Out of the Sources of Judaism.* Rosenzweig, therefore, refused to see, even in the volumes of Cohen's Jewish writings that include the essay "Charakteristik der Ethik Maimunis" (Ethics of Maimonides), volumes for which he (Rosenzweig) was writing the introduction, that Cohen had framed a philosophical Judaism and a Jewish philosophy as the center of his own system, and not as a belated effort at the end of his life.

Almut Bruckstein cites Franz Rosenzweig, then, in an ironic gesture at the very start of her book. And to reread the context of her citation from Rosenzweig will allow us to learn not only about citation and about the development of Jewish philosophy in the twentieth century, but also, or perhaps especially, about the task of commentary and letting a teacher teach.

I cite Rosenzweig's essay "Hermann Cohen's Nachlaßwerk" (1937, 294), with Bruckstein's own citation of Rosenzweig in italics:

> In order to write about Cohen's work and its meaning, one would perhaps have to actually write a new work from the same starting point. And someone *will* do that. Jewish books have not only their fate as do all books, rather they also have a special Jewish-book fate. *I envision Cohen's book printed in Hebrew folio-editions of the seventh millennia,* printed in Siberian and Fuegian, in New Guinean and Cameroon editions, *editions in which Cohen's word is drowning in a flood of* three, four *commentaries that surround it from all sides.*

First, the plain sense of this text: Rosenzweig claims that the ultimate meaning of Cohen's *Religion of Reason: Out of the Sources of Judaism* lies in the future, in a new book. One can hardly overlook that this piece was written and published in 1921, the very year of Rosenzweig's own new work: *The Star of Redemption.* But one might just as well consider Buber's *I and Thou,* or Levinas's *Totality and Infinity*—books that are new works but have the *same starting point.* But Jewish books have more than this relation to their successors, they have a special Jewish-book fate: to be commented upon. Thus Rosenzweig imagines an edition of Cohen in the next Jewish millennium (three hundred or so years out) surrounded by commentaries. Not rivers, now, but a sea, a flood—like a Talmud of its time. Rosenzweig, moreover, imagines translations into the most diverse and "un-Jewish" of places, in languages around the globe. Cohen's thought will be at home both among the Jews and amongst all the world—it will have achieved the true cosmopolitan readers, will further the development of knowledge and so of humanity that Cohen so esteemed.

What happens, then, in Bruckstein's citation? Bruckstein obviously chose this passage because it is a prophecy of her own work—a translation and a commentary on Cohen. Her work here is a fulfillment of Rosenzweig's prophecy. She is reluctant, however, to include the phrase that might link her own English translation (of a different Jewish writing by Cohen, but the point is all too similar) with the outlandish translations for non-European humanity—because this English translation is not in the realm of the exotic, but precisely directed to communities of readers who have already been fed by the various tributaries of thought flowing in the book.

This citation, moreover, also vindicates Cohen—for despite Rosenzweig's praise, Bruckstein, along with many others, has had to defend and reread the teacher's writings from Rosenzweig's too-dominant reading. She shows us that even a student's reading of a teacher's work *cannot merely be cited.* The commentary must reengage both the text and its interpretation. The study of the river of Jewish philosophy extends beyond the tributaries, through Cohen and then on to the course of the river in our day. But such study is not simply a historical study: reason calls us to interrogate the interpretations and the currents. Commentary serves not merely to name the linkages, but also to disrupt the course, and to heighten our responsibility for following the teachings that the previous students did not learn. Such a recourse to the text, and to the recovery of unlearned teachings, is the characteristic of the Jewish textual tradition—a characteristic that Cohen developed in the philosophical tradition, and that Bruckstein here develops in relation to modern Jewish philosophy. To let the teaching teach; to produce the students who will be able to learn. This foreword itself can only allude to this subtle and rich task that is Bruckstein's task in offering us Cohen's vital essay and was Cohen's task in teaching us the ethics of Maimonides.

Robert Gibbs

Preface

When I first came to the Hebrew University, Jerusalem, in 1986, I participated in Shalom Rosenberg's seminar, "Aristotle's Ethics in Medieval Jewish Thought." When the discussion turned to Hermann Cohen's radically Platonic reading of Maimonides, Shalom Rosenberg told us of the philosophical importance of Cohen's essay. He emphasized that the "Charakteristik der Ethik Maimunis" holds the key to a deeper understanding of the contemporary philosophical significance of Maimonides, warning us, however, that this essay is "among the most difficult texts of twentieth-century Jewish thought," and that it remains a riddle even for the initiated, despite the existence of a Hebrew translation.[1]

By then I had read and studied Cohen's essay several times. Cohen's language, after all, seemed familiar, and I admired the courageous teaching of humanism that spoke from every page of Cohen's work. The literary Jewish sources, however, which obviously constitute the very basis of this particular essay, were barely accessible to me at the time. Finding myself in Jerusalem for extended periods of time, I missed the scholarly presence of my teacher, Norbert Samuelson, whose competence and whose love for the critical tradition of the medieval Jewish thinkers had guided my studies of Jewish philosophy in Philadelphia. In Jerusalem I began to owe most of what I learned in reading Jewish texts to having been introduced to an eminent Jewish scholar, Zev Gotthold, whose resources in classical Greek and rabbinic literature seem inexhaustible, and whose scholarly ethos reflects the cultural *Bildungsideal* so typical of the European Jewish intellectual elite before the Shoah. The privilege of having been able to learn with this master of Jewish sources for over fifteen years—sometimes hours a day—is too great to be measured even in terms of gratefulness.

The very format of this book, the translation and commentary of Cohen's essay on Maimonides, tangibly reflects the *Sitz im Leben* of this privileged situation of learning. Often I would translate Cohen's text face-to-face with this teacher, and if there are traces of linguistic resourcefulness and intellectual creativity in the English translation, these are his and not mine. As we explored the very depth of the conceptual and historical issues involved, the room would pile up with volumes upon volumes of classical Jewish literature, all opened up at places where the master—from the well of his impeccable, photographic memory—would point out and teach me the living sources of Cohen's reading. *Zettelach* with numerous notes started to fill first my bags, later my desk, and finally my room, notes on subtexts and more subtexts, too numerous to be all remembered, with the result that only a small part of this flood of literary references found its way into my own commentary, which surrounds the work of translation.

My commentary elicits the fruits of those precious daily sessions of labor. Within that commentary I strive to situate the meaning of the classical Jewish sources within the philosophical context of a contemporary Jewish humanism that is inspired by Hermann Cohen, reaches back to Saadya Gaon, and finds forceful contemporary expression in the work of Emmanuel Levinas. A different reading of Jewish philosophy thus emerges, a reading in which the classical issues of medieval Jewish philosophy are folded into the margins of commentary, following the gravity of Cohen's essay, which I read as a canonical text in Jewish humanism. This reading of Jewish philosophy, inasmuch as it appears in the literary form of translation and commentary, makes itself deliberately subservient to a text whose critical humanism it aspires to transmit.

A project like this, which is the result of a decade of life and learning, is nourished and inspired by friends, colleagues, and teachers in ways that are difficult to retrieve. The following therefore will naturally fall short of its proper expression. I am grateful to Yechiel Greenbaum, who lent me his superb editing skills over many years, and whose patience and graciousness is beyond what can be expressed on paper. My friends, colleagues, and teachers, Dieter Adelmann, Annette Aronowicz, Hillel Fürstenberg, Robert Gibbs, Helmut Holzhey, John Reumann, Yossef Schwartz, Hartwig Wiedebach, and Michael Zank, shared their time with me during many hours of discussion, whether in Jerusalem, Zürich, or Boston. My understanding of Cohen's texts and philosophy would be nowhere near where it is now, if it were not for those countless hours of shared learning. Moreover, they all read the manuscript, either in parts, or in its entirety, and offered informed and critical suggestions. This is true in particular for my good friend and colleague Hartwig Wiedebach, one of the leading editors of Cohen's Werke edition, who gave the manuscript critical close reading toward the very end of the process, lending me his vast knowledge of Cohen's philosophy and its sources. He is presently engaged in preparing the forthcoming German critical and annotated edition of "Charakteristic der Ethik Maimums," to be included in the critical *Werke* edition, Volume 4 of *Kleinere Schriften* (Werke, vol. 15). I wish to express my profound gratitude to Michael Fishbane, whose critical reading of a former version of the introduction inspired me and whose personal and professional advice set in motion more than just the rewriting of the introduction.

I also thank Hilary Putnam, who found time to read the introduction, to meet, and to make valuable suggestions. My friends and fellow graduate students Jeff Israel, Christoph Noethlings, Or-Nistar Rose, and Tobias Tunkel spent time reading and commenting on the manuscript. I am indebted to them for their efforts and their keen and critical insights. My friend and colleague Dirk Westerkamp made valuable suggestions throughout the entire manuscript. And I express my deep gratitude to Nils Ederberg, who devoted his time, vast learning, scholarly competence, sense of precision, and patience to a relentless reworking of my bibliography and notes. Without him the manuscript would not have seen the light of the day. The Franz Rosenzweig Research Center for German-Jewish Literature and Culture, under its former and present directors, Stephane Moses, Gabriel Motzkin, and Paul Mendes-Flohr, granted me two generous scholarships toward the completion of this book. Without the graciousness of their support, the book would not even have had a beginning. I also wish to thank the Rothschild Foundation—Yad haNadiv, as well as Ruth Morris and David Braun, who generously supported the editing process.

To the most precious of all, Arnon, Noga, Renana, Immanuel, Sinai, and Adàm-Jair, my gratitude, not only for their generosity and understanding, but also for teaching me the depths of life with which the writing of any book cannot compete.

Introduction

I envision Cohen's book printed in Hebrew folio-editions of the seventh millennia . . . editions in which Cohen's word is drowning in a flood of commentary that surrounds it from all sides.

Franz Rosenzweig

This translation and commentary of Hermann Cohen's 1908 essay, "Charakteristik der Ethik Maimunis," is an introduction, of a unique sort, to medieval and modern Jewish philosophy. As a translation, it makes available in English for the first time this seminal work of Hermann Cohen—rigorous critic of Kant, passionate teacher of the prophetic Jewish tradition, philosopher, and cultural critic. As a commentary, partaking of both Cohen's philosophical and Jewish writings and of the author's own learning, this book guides readers along the path of reexamining Jewish philosophy and Jewish literary sources through the eyes of a thinker whose philosophy, whose interpretation of Jewish texts, and, in fact, whose entire life is committed both to the critical tradition of ethical reasoning and to the authority of the Jewish oral tradition.[1] The physical format of this book reflects the inspiration of that tradition, as the multilayered structure of text and commentary corresponds to the pedagogical setting that stood at its inception and that tradition calls *chavruta* (studying and dialogue).

Moses ben Maimon: Sein Leben, seine Werke und sein Einfluß (His Life, His Work, His Influence)

Cohen's essay "Charakteristik der Ethik Maimunis" appeared originally in the first of two volumes entitled *Moses ben Maimon: Sein Leben, seine Werke und sein Einfluß*· (His life, his work, his influence), published in 1908 by the Society for the Advancement of Jewish Studies on the occasion of the seven-hundredth commemoration of Maimonides' death.[2] The essays collected in these two volumes reflect an interdisciplinary cultural agenda in which Maimonides figures as an active and creative participant. He emerges here as a thoroughly acculturated intellectual and philosopher who interacts simultaneously with Christian scholasticism, Muslim culture, the work of Saadya Gaon, halakhic tradition, the world of Scripture and Haggada, rabbinic hermeneutics, Platonic Aristotelian philosophy and science, and Kabbala. The commanding breadth and depth of this multicultural portrayal of Maimonides reflects the scope of Jewish scholarship at the turn of the twentieth century; the most distinguished Jewish scholars from all over Europe and throughout all fields of textual scholarship (including philosophy, Arabic literary studies, rabbinic studies, the study of Midrash and Jewish liturgy) contributed to these volumes. Among them are Hermann Cohen, Jacob Guttmann, Ismar Elbogen, Adolf Schwarz, Israel Friedlaender, Eduard Baneth, Wilhelm Bacher, and Ludwig Blau.

A Long-Overdue Translation: The Importance of Cohen's Jewish Writings

Hermann Cohen (1842–1918), primarily known for his groundbreaking contribution to the critical idealism of the neo-Kantian school of Marburg,[3] published about seventy essays on matters related to Jewish studies and public Jewish life. In these essays, Cohen wrote about Jewish philosophy, Jewish history, Jewish biblical literature, Talmud, Jewish education, and Jewish contemporary political affairs. Most of these essays were published during Cohen's lifetime in various Jewish journals and newspapers; all of them were either reprinted (or first printed) in the three volumes of *Hermann Cohens Jüdische Schriften* (Hermann Cohen's Jewish writings), published posthumously in 1924, with a famous and influential introduction by Franz Rosenzweig.[4] Cohen's "Charakteristik der Ethik Maimunis" (Ethics of Maimonides) was included in this posthumous collection. Although studded with rabbinic learning and medieval Jewish literary references, this essay on Maimonides speaks the language of philosophy. Due to the strict, and unfortunate, editorial division between Cohen's "philosophical" essays and his "Jewish" writings, however, Cohen's essay on Maimonides was lost to the philosophical readers that it clearly wished to address.[5]

In order to understand the cultural agenda that was destroyed by this editorial division, the following background may prove instructive. After Cohen's death in 1918, Bruno Strauss, Albert Görland, and Ernst Cassirer took the initiative to compile collected volumes of Cohen's essays. These scholars distinguished systematically between Cohen's "Greek" writings and his "Jewish" writings.[6] Two separate posthumous collections of Cohen's essays subsequently appeared in Berlin within five years. The first collection contains Cohen's "Jewish" writings, edited by Bruno Strauss, published in three volumes under the title *Hermann Cohens Jüdische Schriften,* 1924, as mentioned above. The second includes Cohen's "philosophical" writings, including his dissertation, his early writings on Plato and on German Idealism, his work on mathematics (the infinitesimal method), and the much-cited, influential "Introduction with a Critical Note on Lange's *History of Materialism.*"[7]

A half-century later, scholars finally corrected this editorial policy. Inadvertently, it had created an abyss between European philosophers, who until a few years ago saw Cohen as mainly a neo-Kantian philosopher, and North American and Israeli Jewish scholars who read Cohen exclusively as a critical Jewish thinker. In the 1960s, Helmut Holzhey, the founder of the Cohen Archive in Zurich, and his friend and colleague, Steven Schwarzschild, came to the joint decision that the long-standing division between "Greek" and "Jewish" writings, in fact, undermines the entire gist of Cohen's philosophy; Cohen's reading of Western philosophical sources throughout reflects the promise of an ethics that draws its life from Jewish sources. The new *Werke* edition subsequently presents Cohen's work chronologically, foregoing the old division between matters "Greek" and "Jewish."

What is lost in chronologically compiling Cohen's work is the reader's focus on a "table of contents" in Jewish studies, whose scope and depth attests to the sovereignty and authority of a creative, philosophically assertive, and often polemical, mind steeped in the Jewish sources. Cohen's "Jewish" essays demonstrate in a masterful way how to make manifest what is truly humane in the Jewish literary tradition, and how to retrieve the humanity of this tradition even in cases where the phenotype, or outward appearance, of Jewish tradition and Jewish history has failed to do so.[8] Cohen's essay on Maimonides and his essay on Spinoza are the longest, most complex, and most influential of these "Jewish" writings.[9] The full translation of these and, indeed, of most other essays in this collection into English has long been a desideratum for Jewish scholarship.

Cohen's "Charakteristik der Ethik Maimunis"

Cohen's essay on Maimonides may be considered philosophically the most challenging among Cohen's "Jewish" writings as it provides a central nexus between Cohen's critical philosophy and his Jewish thought. In "Charakteristik der Ethik Maimunis" we find Cohen's most explicit attempt to hermeneutically unravel the mysteries of Cohen's own philosophy of origin and its concept of correlation: Cohen here develops the correlation between Greek and Jewish sources, between Plato's idea of the Good (which is prior to being) and Maimonides's concept of "lovingkindness, righteousness, and judgment," which is prior to Torah.[10] Here, Cohen also substantially explicates the hermeneutical correlation between human reasoning and traditional wisdom, between reader and text, and thus the ethical relationship between one person and another. Also emerging for the first time is Cohen's philosophy of "I and Thou," a philosophy of alterity, predicated upon the concepts of infinity, purity, and holiness—concepts that figure centrally in Jewish tradition. In this essay, Cohen—through a careful textual investigation of the traditional medieval theory of divine attributes—arrives at a full-fledged formulation of the correlation between the one God and mankind, and between this world and the world-to-come. In his "Charakteristik der Ethik Maimunis," Cohen most explicitly correlates his principle of origin, which I read as a self-critical method of interpretative thinking, with the traditional hermeneutics of the Jewish oral tradition. In this correlation, Moses Maimonides (1135–1204) is assigned an inspirational role: it is through the philosophical and rabbinical work of Maimonides that Cohen follows his own path toward the philosophical construction of a Jewish humanism that draws abundantly from Jewish literary sources.[11]

The influence on twentieth-century Jewish thought of Cohen's reading of Maimonides has been profound. Cohen's essay on Maimonides offers a radically Platonic reading of Maimonides, which runs counter to former Aristotelian interpretations. This reading has left a decisive philosophical and political impact upon such modern Jewish thinkers as Leo Strauss, Franz Rosenzweig, Steven Schwarzschild, and Emmanuel Levinas. It has also influenced an entire range of contemporary scholarship on Maimonides, which takes its cue from such a Platonic reading, often without knowing the *Urtext* of that position.

1904: Plato and Maimonides—a *Politicum*

European scholars of the early twentieth century aligned with the cultural agenda of the Wissenschaft des Judentums movement saw in Maimonides not only a towering figure in Jewish philosophy and Halakhah but also a means toward a rational, universalist, and ethical rethinking of the world of rabbinic sources. The work of Maimonides served as a window to these sources. It opened up the spiritual vista of a broad-minded, cultured, ethical, humane Judaism—a Judaism that was meant to serve as a "light unto the nations." It was none other than Hermann Cohen who in his Platonic reading of Maimonides, in his "Charakteristik der Ethik Maimunis," took the lead in the spiritual and intellectual reconstruction of the entire body of Jewish literary sources.[12]

That Cohen's Platonic reading of Maimonides was a political issue in the first place can be seen in the following. At the beginning of the twentieth century, a group of European Jewish scholars convened in Breslau, Germany, in order to discuss its scholarly projects. One of the projects was a comprehensive study on Maimonides, envisioning a new relationship to this great thinker—a relationship that would allow for a more critical, more socialist, more ethical, more political (more Platonic) Judaism. In short, they thought Jewish intellectuals in Europe deserved a more idealistic Maimonides than the Aristotelian epigone Jewish scholarship had been creating.[13] At the occasion of the seven-hundredth commemoration of Maimonides' death in 1904, European scholars involved in marking the occasion decided that the time had come to develop such a Platonic reading of Maimonides, both on philosophical and philological grounds. It was Hermann Cohen who actually delivered such a reading in the first of the two volumes that appeared in honor of Maimonides under the title *Moses ben Maimon: Sein Leben, seine Werke und sein Einfluß* in 1908.

What was at stake for the liberal Jews who turned to the sources of Judaism was public proof as to the ideality of humanity and universal justice as Jewish values. Such proof rested upon the conceptual framework of Platonic and Kantian ethics within which one could construct ethical ideals, such as the idea of the Good and ideas of justice and humanity, as a matter of universal knowledge rather than just of general agreement or convention. To read Maimonides as a Platonic thinker was therefore of paramount importance to those who hoped to prove the ideal of universal humanity to be inherent in the foundations of Jewish tradition and of Jewish traditional literature.

The Society for the Advancement of Jewish Studies and Its Scholarly Agenda

In October 1904, the scholarly board of the Gesellschaft zur Förderung der Wissenschaft des Judentums convened in Breslau. The society had been founded in 1902 with the aim of advancing the depth and scope of Jewish scholarship and education to the highest intellectual level. Its scholarly ambition—reflecting the presence and authority of people like Hermann Cohen and Jacob Guttmann—was dedicated to constructing a teaching of justice and humanity out of traditional Jewish literature. From as early as 1902, Hermann Cohen pushed for the advancement of a "Jewish humanism out of the sources of Judaism." He promoted a systematic and interdisciplinary approach to studying Jewish sources, under the connecting theme of "the ethical," over the classical agenda of mere historical and philological studies.[14] Cohen's aim for the society was to engage Jewish sources in a philosophical narrative committed to the ideal of *wahre Menschlichkeit.*

Cohen himself, together with Leopold Lucas, seems to have formulated the aims of the society. A flyer—entitled "An unsere Glaubensgenossen" (To our brethren in creed)—was sent out to Jewish institutions of higher learning and research, and to Jewish communities interested in discussing Jewish literary sources in the wider context of European culture. The most renowned Jewish scholars of the time—Wilhelm Bacher, Eduard Baneth, Hermann Cohen, Jacob Guttmann, Ignaz Goldziher, Louis Ginzberg, Salomon Buber, and Ismar Elbogen—collaborated in laying out a *Grundriss der gesamten Wissenschaft des Judentums* (Basic outline of encompassing science of Judaism).[15] The aim of this project was to systematically explore all aspects of Jewish culture and demonstrate the universal significance of traditional Jewish sources. The outline reads, indeed, like an adumbration of a most rigorous contemporary Jewish studies program. Its detailed scholarly agenda included Hebrew philology, biblical studies, talmudic studies, Jewish history, Jewish literature, poetry and folklore, Jewish mysticism, Jewish theology, ethics and philosophy, Jewish liturgy, Jewish music and art, Jewish education, and comparative religion.[16] Cohen's *Religion der Vernunft aus den Quellen des Judentums* was published in 1919 as volume 8 of this project. Parallel to this encyclopedic project, the society conceived of three additional scholarly projects no less impressive in scope: the *Corpus Tannaiticum,* the *Germania Judaica,* and the so-called *Maimonides-Biography.*[17]

The Maimonides Project

It is the latter of these projects—initiated by David Simonsen, Wilhelm Bacher, Markus Brann and Jacob Guttmann—that directly concerns our text.[18] A protocol of the October 1904 session shows a detailed outline of the envisioned project on Maimonides; its fourteen chapters or volumes were to be published in honor of the upcoming seven-hundredth *Jahrzeit* of Maimonides—commemoration of his death—as the protocol itself specifies.[19] Leading Jewish scholars from all over Europe had already given their consent and were working toward the publication of this project, among them Hermann Cohen, the Jewish philosopher of Marburg.[20] He was guiding the project in matters related to Jewish philosophy, and had agreed to take on a substantial part, namely the part on Maimonides' ethics. (In the appendix of the outlined project we find a programmatic paragraph entitled "Maimonides as a non-Aristotelian.")[21]

The scope of this agenda touched upon all aspects of Maimonides' teaching—from the discussion of Maimonides' commentary on the Mishna and his rabbinic masterwork, the *Mishneh Torah*, through a critical investigation of his philosophical thought and his hermeneutics as they emerge from *The Guide of the Perplexed;* a discussion of Maimonides' influence on later Jewish philosophy and on the Christian scholastics; an account of Maimonides' critics and of the polemics that his work evoked; and of course the long history of Maimonidean scholarship that had since emerged (not to mention a dozen other themes that the reader might wish to look up in the published protocol). With the notable exception of the two-volume *Moses ben Maimon: Sein Leben, seine Werke und sein Einfluß,* containing Cohen's "Charakteristik der Ethik Maimunis" and contributions by other well-known scholars, the full scope of the Maimonides project was not ever published.

Medieval Jewish Culture—A Project of Enlightenment

The society's placement of Maimonides, a cosmopolitan thinker of the highest order, as the authentic expression of Jewish tradition spoke to the very *Bildungsideal* and cultural identity of the European Jewish intellectual elite at the turn of the twentieth century. It was not by chance that the members of the society chose a *medieval* figure as the protagonist for their own interdisciplinary agenda of Jewish studies. In their belief in the universal significance of Jewish sources and in their faithfulness to a critical tradition of scientific thinking, European Jewish scholars did not have to revert to the ideals of the European Enlightenment. They, rather, intentionally made reference to rationalist medieval Jewish thinkers—Saadya Gaon and Maimonides—who viewed a conflict between faith and reason as blasphemous, and whose teaching of Torah is indebted to critical reasoning precisely in honor of God's divine teaching. This "enlightened" tradition of classical Jewish thought became a distinct inspiration for European Jewish intellectuals at the turn of the twentieth century. In this vein, Cohen accorded Maimonides the status of becoming the authentic measure of the primacy and privilege of German culture itself—a culture that, according to Cohen, derived its sublimity from its partial and, of course, temporary, fulfillment of the promise of enlightenment that Cohen saw rooted deeply in the Jewish sources.

The Present Book—A Medieval Commentary

The reader will note that, typographically speaking, by means of its translation-commentary format, this book assumes the appearance of a medieval commentary. It invokes the tradition of cross-cultural translation, wherein the book comes to speak in the linguistic and ideational context of the reader, reminding the reader that the very act of translation implies teaching and commentary. The sharing of any translator's learning—itself a sort of gift to the reader—situates the process of learning within the context of cross-cultural exchange, a sharing of literary traditions. This process stands at the inception of the great literary traditions of medieval translators of Greek, Hebrew, Syriac, Arabic, and Latin sources. The philosophical and cultural significance of this transcultural process provides a source of inspiration for my own translation of Cohen's essay on Maimonides. (Cohen and Levinas themselves are groundbreaking teachers of such an agenda: Cohen in his readings of medieval Jewish philosophy, and Levinas for his teachings of Talmud.) I shall be grateful if this translation and commentary convey something of their spirit.

Medieval Literary Features

On first view, the reader will realize that this book contains elements of traditional short, middle, and interlinear commentary. This reflects the understanding that any reading implies a translation, and that any translation amounts to a commentary. By offering a reading of Cohen in the medieval form of a line-by-line commentary, the author becomes the text's advocate, endorsing a definite standpoint, and providing an introduction to classical issues in medieval Jewish philosophy. This book thereby takes advantage of the nonlinear, associative, eclectic kind of discussion that the literary form of a line-by-line commentary permits—a literary form also indebted to the oral tradition of Jewish learning. These literary features, invoking the continuity of a traditional hermeneutical practice, permit me as the student and translator of Cohen's text to strictly heed the philosophical premises of Cohen's own readings of Jewish literature. These, in turn, are bound to the primacy of ethics as I wish to outline in the following excursus on Cohen's philosophical approach to literary sources.

On Textual Reasoning

Hermann Cohen's interpretation of Maimonides in his "Charakteristik der Ethik Maimunis" represents a masterful exposition of Jewish textual reasoning. In the following, I wish to say something about Cohen's hermeneutical approach to Jewish literary sources, which will enable the reader to situate Cohen's essay both within the context of his critical philosophy and within the contemporary philosophical debate on the significance of traditional religious hermeneutics.

At the conference "Textual Reasoning," held at Drew University in June 1997, Jewish and non-Jewish scholars explored the relevance of the traditional practice of Jewish hermeneutics and its methods of textual reasoning for the contemporary debate on postmodernity. At this and earlier conferences, I invoked the philosophy of Hermann Cohen as a helpful, indeed inspiring, source for the contemporary hermeneutical discussion among Jewish scholars. Cohen's philosophy of origin is grounded in an ethical lovingkindness and justice even before it sets out its first thought. Cohen calls this a non-foundational, anarchic thinking of origin, which he models on the Platonic Good beyond Being.[22] Cohen's reading of Plato, as well as his development of a critical idealism steeped in the concept of a transcendent Good in which the quest for justice originates, is intimately bound up with Cohen's reading of Jewish national literature, or classical Jewish literary sources.[23] Levinas's "Humanism and Anarchy" of 1968 may well be studied as the contemporary voice of a Jewish humanism that finds its most seminal modern expression in the philosophy of Hermann Cohen.[24]

Cohen's Philosophy of Origin—Translating "Jewish" into "Greek"

Cohen's work can be seen as conveying a neo-Kantian critical idealism, within a philosophical narrative deeply rooted in traditional Jewish hermeneutics and oral tradition.[25] Cohen's critical idealism resists the temptations of fundamental ontologies and metaphysical systems in the same way as the hermeneutical principles of Jewish oral tradition are meant to resist the temptations of religious dogmatism and textual literalism. Cohen's neo-Kantian philosophical system correlates with his Jewish writings in the strict philosophical sense of this term. Cohen constructs an interdependence between philosophy and Jewish tradition in which one set of concepts—such as Cohen's ethical idea of humanity or his logical principle of origin—receives its original meaning from another set of concepts, namely one that emerges from the messianic texts of the prophets, or from the biblical passages featuring the one, unique God who demands the Good of humankind. And vice versa: Cohen's reading of central concepts in Jewish tradition (such as messianism, creation, halakhic authority) receives its direction and significance from the transcendental principles of Cohen's own critical philosophy.

In an autobiographical statement Cohen discloses to what extent his general philosophy is bound up with Jewish tradition and with Jewish culture:

> My enthusiasm for Judaism is rooted in my conviction of the ethical validity implied in our idea of God. My understanding of Judaism stands within the context of my scholarly work. Hence I feel particularly fortunate that prior to my presentations of more extensive works on the ideas of Judaism I had the opportunity to demonstrate the place of Judaism within a philosophical system. I do not entrust the guidance of my Jewish consciousness to the instinct of loyalty, loyalty to one's own religious denomination or tribe, but to philosophical methodology, in as far as it is my share.[26]

We may then read Cohen's philosophy in its various stages and disciplines as a singular but multifaceted attempt to translate an Original Teaching (which is itself absent, not at hand) into the language required by the philosophical discourse at hand, be it logic, ethics, aesthetics, or philosophy of religion. As a result, all the different parts of Cohen's philosophy tell their readers—each in its own way—of the justice and humanity, of the lovingkindness, goodness, and peace, that he himself derives from the Original Teaching as a binding task for humankind, calling for a Kingdom of Humanity that none but ourselves can create.

Throughout my translation of Cohen, the reader will find textual synopses in square brackets, which I have inserted, drawn from the entire body of Cohen's work. Such a nonlinear reading of Cohen points to the almost midrashic manner in which Cohen cites himself. In the midst of an argument, he often brings to mind a philosophical theory carefully developed elsewhere, now being invoked while, so to speak, standing on one foot, whereby prior reasoning takes on a new direction. Moreover, Cohen's earlier works contain ideas that are often thought to have evolved later, such as the idea of developing a "religion of reason out of the sources of Judaism," which had been his own agenda for the Gesellschaft zur Förderung der Wissenschaft des Judentums since 1902.[27]

Granting primacy to the hermeneutical order (determined by the midrashic art of citation that underlies a continuous living oral discourse), over formal hierarchies of ethics established by written philosophical treatises, means that even the highest ideal of humanity itself must not remain an abstract dictum. Such an ideal, rather, receives its paramount *ethical* significance from being rooted in a living narrative, a narrative "as old as the world, a *messianic* narrative that captures our thinking from time immemorial, demanding that thought render account of its contents and actions before it even begins."[28] The subsequent discussion of text and commentary will prove this point while leaning closely on Cohen's texts.

The Original Teaching and Classical Jewish Sources

> "In the beginning is the sentence." However, "the question is the lever of origin." Hence the sentence relates to the question as commentary relates to the text or as reason relates to revelation.
>
> Revelation represents the nothing, that is: the question. Therefore, thinking must not shy away from any detour via nothingness.[29]

Cohen's essay on Maimonides demonstrates more than any of Cohen's other writings how Cohen's reading of classical texts—whether "Greek" or "Jewish"—is wedded to a relentless critical reasoning put at the service of what we could call the eternal task of unveiling the significance of the Original Ethical Teaching. The Original Teaching (which is *not* at hand) ideally carries forth and inspires the transformation of this world into a Kingdom of True Humanity. In his introduction to the *Religion of Reason,* Cohen claims that this teaching manifests itself particularly in classical Jewish sources.[30] According to Cohen, classical Jewish sources are texts whose immediate meaning is as absent as any immediate manifestation of God, yet whose presence is as commanding as the voice at Sinai. Cohen's principle of origin demands "there can be no givens at the inception of thinking" [*dem Ursprung darf nichts gegeben sein*].[31] The same is true for the peculiar hermeneutics of the Jewish oral tradition: nothing must restrict the process of interpretation and commentary, precisely for the sake of the holiness of the divine teaching. A medieval commentator, Shlomo ben Abraham Parchon says the following in his book *Machberet ha'Arukh:*

> When people who are uninitiated in the traditional ways of reading Jewish texts observe how the Jews extract all kinds of midrashic explanations from the words of the Sages, they refute them, saying: "you are twisting what we know to be written in scripture." They say that because they think that their particular translation of Scripture represents the literal meaning of the original text. Thus they have erased the "seventy faces of the Torah."[32]

On Text and Commentary

The meaning of the text, or, as Cohen would say, the meaning of the source, begins to speak and thus comes to life with commentary. Cohen advocates the simultaneity of text and commentary, and therewith an ahistorical, but highly traditional, hermeneutical method. He claims that classical Jewish sources *originate* in commentary, and that commentary means oral discourse, *Sprachdenken:* "Books tend to get sealed, whereas mouths and lips continue to speak."[33] It is in his introduction to the *Religion of Reason: Out of the Sources of Judaism,* which reads like a commentary on the very title of the book, that Cohen sets forth the hermeneutical agenda for any philosophical reading of Jewish sources, leading the reader to the conclusion that the presence of classical Jewish sources originates in future commentary in the same way as human history originates in the futuric vision of the prophets. In the Talmud Yerushalmi, "R.Yehoshua ben Levi teaches: 'Even what a learned student in the future shall expound before her teacher is part of the Torah as it has been taught to Moses on Sinai.'"[34]

Commentary and Oral Tradition

Due to the peculiarity of the claims of Jewish teaching (that it harbors an Original Teaching demanding the creation of mankind), Jewish commentary itself is bound to disseminate prophetic promises. Cohen systematically develops the political and ethical ramifications of these promises in his essay on Maimonides. Jewish commentary, then, would be charged with the ethical task of conveying the Original Teaching and its promise of humanity. The commentary, not the text, therefore continues the living word of God (*kol gadol velo yassaf*), that "great unceasing voice" which spoke out of the fire, out of thick darkness.[35] Onkelos translates *velo yassaf* as *velo passak* (the great voice that never ceases to command), and that demands justice and the good, traditionally speaking *Halakha leMoshe miSinai,* a principle that might well be rendered as "the sovereignty of the oral tradition."

The hermeneutical innovation in Cohen's *Religion of Reason* consists in identifying the originality or autonomy of the Jewish oral tradition with the originality or autonomy of human reasoning as such. In other words, the dynamics of Jewish oral tradition, in its claim of representing the originality of the Jewish teaching, demonstrates the primacy of what Cohen calls logic of origin. Cohen writes, "Originality—the true sign of creative reasoning—frees Jewish tradition from the enchantments of religious, dogmatic consciousness, and ideally purifies its teachings."[36] This kind of primacy, or *Ursprünglichkeit,* characterizes Jewish learning, drawing on sources that are privileged in that they yield the messianic promise of humanity. The living, oral tradition, which, according to Cohen, includes all teachings inspired by this promise, turns out to be the guarantor and heir of this primary source.

At first sight, Cohen seems to say that it is the oral and not the written tradition that constitutes the living well of Jewish learning.[37] According to Paul, the first great Christian, whom Daniel Boyarin reads as a creative Jewish cultural critic,"the letter is nothing," and the *pneuma* (the breath of the voice) that breathes vowels, and thus life, into the text is everything.[38] Medieval Jewish thinkers adamantly reiterate this hermeneutical point: the biblical scholar Abraham ibn Ezra maintains that interpretation relates to the written word as the soul relates to the body.[39] Judah ha-Levi claims the "breath" of the vowels relates to the "letter" of the consonants as the soul relates to the body.[40] Cohen emphasizes that "wherever the Talmud [the oral tradition] is taught, there the Torah is alive."[41] Repeating the Torah to his people, Moses said, "the Torah is not in heaven but very close to you, in your mouth and in your heart to do."[42] Cohen translates: "die Thora ist nicht im Himmel, sondern in deinem Herzen. . . . Sie ist in deinem Herzen und in deinem Munde; so muss . . . sie zur mündlichen Lehre werden" [the Torah is not in Heaven, but in your heart. . . . It is in your heart and in your mouth; thus it must become an oral teaching].[43]

The oral tradition teaches that even the written Torah is the result of an oral teaching—"Moshe kibbel Torah miSinai," [Moses receives the Torah from Sinai]. He *learns* Torah before he commits the divine teaching to writing. Jewish tradition has it that the written Torah was originally meant as a private, oral teaching for Moses alone, that it was conceived of in a strictly dialogical situation in which God spoke and Moses listened, and that Moses' very sharing of his Torah with the people of

Israel was a voluntary act, an act of personal kindness and generosity.[44] Early on, it was forbidden to capture the living word—which always reflects a pedagogical setting of teacher and student—in written script, an injunction that was suspended beginning at the time of the Mishna.[45] Even the Mishna, however, was written not for the sake of memorizing religious doctrine, but rather to keep alive debates among the Sages that remained unresolved (and here many sides of controversies were recorded as legitimate opinions).[46] The entire history of the Jewish oral tradition might thus be understood as one of learned disagreement. The Hebrew word *mishna* itself contains a threefold meaning, implying "to repeat, to learn, and to teach." It thus captures what Cohen means by the originality of the Jewish source, namely that even the repetition of an argument whose final implications have been suspended, must generate a new teaching. In this way, Jewish oral tradition calls for engaging in a discourse that, for the sake of the holiness of the living word of God, does *not* allow for human closure.

Philosophy Is Powerless: The Text Is Central

Despite the predominance of oral learning in Jewish tradition, Cohen surprisingly suggests in his essay on Maimonides that it is the *text,* the text in its physical embodiment, which is of vital importance for the continuity of Jewish learning. Paradoxically, it is the text, the book, the *chiffre,* that conceals rather than reveals its meaning, which is central to the Jewish hermeneutical tradition, a tradition that proclaims: *mipi soferim velo mipi sefarim* (we learn from the mouths of our teachers, and not from books).[47] One of the most important points that Cohen teaches us in his "Charakteristik der Ethik Maimunis" is that without the text as the communal core of learning, there can be no ethical teaching. "Philosophy is declared powerless," Cohen explains to the confounded reader of this essay, when it comes to the question of how to give further grounds to the ethical idea of the Good.[48] Cohen invokes Plato's solution of the *Ungrundlegung des Guten,* the non-foundation of the Good, when facing the aporia of a mere logical deduction of the "Good that is prior to Being."[49] But invoking Plato is only the first step in Cohen's philosophical solution to this hermeneutical problem, a solution so bold it required philosophies of Franz Rosenzweig and Emmanuel Levinas to teach it to the contemporary reader who now associates Cohen's teaching with Levinas's fundamentally Jewish critique of the Western ontological tradition. What is Cohen's point?

Philosophy's Impotence? How to Give Further Grounds to the Good

To give further ground to the idea of the Good, Cohen explicitly correlates Plato's *Ungrundlegung*—the concept through which Plato safeguards the idea of the Good beyond Being—with the original teaching of *rachamim* (compassion) and *chessed* (lovingkindness), which reside in classical Jewish sources. "It is revelation which posits these attributes," says Cohen in this essay on Maimonides, citing the biblical text "*rachum vechanun, erekh apayim, verav chessed ve 'emet*" [gracious and compassionate, long-suffering, full of lovingkindness and truthfulness].[50] Cohen maintains even in his "Charakteristik der Ethik Maimunis" that the Original Narrative, the text, revelation in short, "positive law"—specifies the ways of goodness.[51] "*Higgid lekha adam ma tov* . . ." [he has told you, O Man, what is good and what the Lord requires of you: only to do justice and to love goodness and to walk modestly with your God.[52]] Furthermore, the Sifre specifies, "As He is gracious, so you be gracious; as he is long-suffering, so you be long-suffering."[53]

Revelation Borders on Myth: The Rabbinic Art of Citation

At this point, of course, critical reasoning must protest, since wherever a traditional narrative informs a philosophical concept of crucial importance, we find ourselves on the grounds of myth and religious dogma—and not in the domain of critical philosophy. When discussing the relationship between the ethical teaching of the Good and the prophetic word of God, Cohen utters the elliptic sentence: "It is here that revelation itself borders on myth."[54] But what does it mean that a traditional narrative *informs* a philosophical concept, and that it therefore borders on myth? Jewish hermeneutics provides a crucial answer: the very citation of a text—where words are often quoted out of context—informs the content of a given reading. For Cohen, the midrashic art of citation thereby dispels all notions of mythical consciousness. The original narrative, revelation, borders on myth because for an infinitesimal moment—the very moment in which a text is being cited—the Original Teaching seems to affirm its meaning, just as in the case of all other mythical narratives. By being cited at the decisive moment in time at which reasoning reaches its impasse—the moment at which reasoning fails to give an account for the grounds of goodness—the text has become the original warrant for the priority of ethics over ontology. The text is trusted with a gesture of faith—which is precisely the significance of citation in rabbinic oral tradition. We render account of ourselves in facing an ancient text.

But the ancient text, which has been trusted in such a way, is not really the issue when it is being cited. "Oral tradition," Cohen says, "extends revelation to include tradition, a hermeneutical motion that amounts inevitably to the dissolution of revelation into cognition."[55] This is true despite the fact that the interpretation owes itself entirely to the Original Teaching that inspires it.

The Original Teaching defies mythification despite the fact that it is anchored in an immemorial past. It defies mythification, since its origin lies beyond memory. Thus, the first meaning, "older" than the first, lies in the future. We must pass through interpretation to surpass interpretation.[56] The meaning of the Original Teaching is deferred to commentary, as the past, the tradition itself, must be anticipated. "Anticipation is the fundamental activity of time . . . the past is predicated upon the future that is anticipated. It is not the past that is prior to one's thinking, but rather the future.[57]

Any idealization of the past is a hindrance to the messianic task, as the "past itself appears as . . . a continuous ejection of anticipation."[58] Time is grounded in futurity and only in futurity. Past and present vanish in the face of this temporal mode of futurity.

The Temptations of Citing an Ancient Text

Citing an ancient text carries with it the temptation of what Cohen calls "mythical consciousness"—invoking a revered tone in the hope of being granted special rights or privileges. However, Jewish tradition says that the Original Teaching must not be confined to such a mythical past. Even a doctrine as prone to mythical consciousness as *zechuth avoth,* "the merits of the fathers," is not intended to teach loyalty to ancient monuments, but rather faithfulness to the ideal of lovingkindness and justice, as Abraham instructed his children and all of posterity "to keep the way of God by doing what is just and right."[59] It is not the past but the future that decides whose commentary presents a true reading of the text. But such futurity—Levinas calls it the "*eschaton* by which the living are judged"—is not one that is brought about by politics (although the task of creating such a messianic future may result in political action). Cohen does not teach Jewish hermeneutics as the history of victorious interpretations. It is not any political future, but rather the extent to which one anticipates the promise of humanity, that provides the measure for an ultimate judgment on history. This is the reason why Maimonides so carefully distinguishes the world-to-come from messianic times. The world-to-come represents no utopian future, but rather the task of presently anticipating humanity, through the very act of engaging ourselves in the continuation of the Original Teaching: "*Lo achar kakh yavo oto ha'olam—ein hadavar ken! Ella hu matsui ve'omed*" [The world-to-come shall not come *after* this world has come to an end, but rather it must be presently anticipated].[60] The originality of classical Jewish sources demands that all citations—all interpretative human activity—be subsumed under the responsibility of our own ethical reasoning.

The Primacy of Ethics over Ontology: Faithfulness to a Hermeneutical Tradition

Cohen's proclamation of the priority of ethics over ontology demonstrates his faithfulness to a teaching whose messianic promise inspires the traditional interpretive methods of the Jewish oral tradition, setting forth ways of thinking that pervade Cohen's entire philosophy. The originality of Jewish teaching signifies to thought that which must not be given to it—namely the grounds for ever-interpretive versions of how to anticipate humanity. Humanity must be anticipated—this is the significance of the Original Teaching, and faithfulness to this teaching, according to Hermann Cohen, is the one and only gesture of faith that Jewish tradition permits and demands. Levinas expresses this point in a single sentence: "The confidence placed in the wisdom of the Sages is, if you like, a faith. But this form of faith which we proclaim is the only one that does not have to be kept discreetly to oneself."[61]

Cohen's Literary Style

Cohen's own voice reverberates with the ethical radicalism of the prophets. His voice is as clearly discernible in matters Jewish as it is in matters philosophical. Cohen's literary style is condensed, almost to the point of being elliptical, a language that is archaic, lapidary, a powerful prose in which conclusions are not reached but rather proclaimed: "Ezekiel *is the first to announce* . . . Jewish monotheism, ethical messianism is *nothing but* . . . *This is* the pantheism in monotheism" (emphasis mine).

Cohen's prose is poetic rather than scientific. It knows nothing of the academic constructs of scholarly research, does not follow the methodological schemes of thesis, antithesis, and one's own thesis; it does without expositions and conclusions, presents no theses or proofs thereof. Cohen's language recalls music rather than geometry. Rosenzweig calls it *Sprachdenken*, where one must listen to the last word before one understands what the beginning was all about. Cohen's is a "narrating philosophy," employing a philosophical language replete with metaphors, in which one single theme—the theme of true humanity, loving-kindness, justice, peace—is rehearsed and repeated throughout the entire body of the literary work as if we were dealing with an ever recurring refrain. It reads like a tractate on humanity which unfolds into a kaleidoscope of haggadic and halakhic teachings, the former in order to keep alive the soul of the teaching, the latter in order not to forget how to approach one's neighbor.

Out of the Translator's Workshop: To the Philologists

Given the density and the peculiarity of Cohen's literary style, it proves non-sensible to translate Cohen's texts in any interlinear way, word by word, or even sentence by sentence. In the translation of this text, I have taken to heart as methodological guideline the advice of the classical medieval translator of Jewish philosophical texts, Yehuda ibn Tibbon, who in the preface to his Hebrew translation of the Arabic *Duties of the Heart* proposes as follows:

> At times a translator will need to transfer an idiomatic expression which presents itself in one language, into a compatible idiom which resembles or approximates it in the language into which he is translating. At other times he will need to alter a parable or a referent that does not fit the cultural frame of reference in the second language, into a parable or a referent which is similar and which performs in the same manner.
>
> The most important principle is that the translator understands the idiomatic character both of the language from which he is translating and the language into which he is translating, and that thereby he understands the author's intentions in an accurate and fitting manner, so that the translation will reflect accurately both the author's emotional tenor and the concept he intends to convey. Once the translator has digested this basic principle, he can exercise some creativity in his manner of translation and his choice of parallelism, as long as he is faithful in capturing the "intent" of the author.[62]

Let us then draw an initial lesson from these opening remarks:

> There is no innocent translation. . . . To translate is already to interpret . . . the one thing that would be criticizable would be the naive claim of an exegesis that held itself to be without a history, as though it were possible to co-

> incide, without the mediation of a tradition of reading, with the original signification of a text, even with the presumed intention of its author.[63]

Translating means to introduce a text to an audience unfamiliar with its language, which means to repeat the teaching by saying it anew in a different cultural context.[64] Shmuel Ibn Tibbon developed so many ways of rendering into Hebrew, in his masterful translations of Judeo-Arabic philosophical works, that he felt the need to define *his* terminology in a separate glossary appended to his Hebrew translation, the *Moreh Nevukhim.* The tradition of Jewish translation—from the Septuagint, to Onkelos, to Mendelssohn, and up to Rosenzweig and Buber—is replete with *Nachdichtungen,* commentaries, innovations, "destructions of the original"; this, despite the insistence of Rosenzweig that translations ought not to "move the text closer to the reader" but rather "move the reader closer to the text."[65]

Rosenzweig himself, however, holds that "the book is subservient to the word."[66] Books are subservient to the word as texts are subservient to commentary. Such subservience, however, by no means characterizes the *initial* relationship between the text and the translator. To the contrary, such subservience is rather the very result of the translator's *faithfulness* to the original:

> When it is our concern to listen to "the person, her or his intonation, opinion, or heartbeat," any translation will indeed have to keep in mind the norm of exactitude, but that alone will not be sufficient; for the one language will have to vie immediately with the other—there exists no criterion outside their own bounds. . . . The two languages engage in a boundless game with each other and against each other. In fact, it is this very game . . . that creates the translation, a translation worthy of its name.[67]

The translator, probing the depths of a particular work, mediates between the text and the reader. In rabbinic tradition, the task of the translator (*ha-meturgeman*) is closely associated with the task of defending someone before a court of justice. In other words, the translator advocates a case. Translating means to become answerable for what the philosopher says.[68] In Rosenzweig's words: "The creative achievement of translating lies in the creative achievement of speaking itself. . . . Whoever has something to say will say it in a new way. The translator advances to being linguistically creative."[69]

Having said all this, I appeal to the reader's critical philosophical and linguistic sense, asking especially German-speaking readers to weigh this version graciously wherever they disagree with the translation. In order to demonstrate in what ways this translation transports the literal sense of the text, Table 1 featuring both Cohen's text in the original German and in my English translation may be illuminating.

TABLE 1. SYNOPSIS OF TRANSLATION

ORIGINAL GERMAN	*ENGLISH TRANSLATION*
Wenn die Ethik	If ethics is not to remain
nicht als eine Zufaelligkeit des Temperaments,	an accidental result of temperament
des Herkommens,	or background,
der geschichtlichen Gesetze der Trägheit und der Veränderungslust,	nor a result of historical inertia and of the urge for adjustment to fashionable changes,
nicht als das *Zuckerbrot oder die Peitsche* der Machthaber,	nor the *Carrot and Stick* of autocratic authority,
nicht als der Priesterbetrug des Aberglaubens,	nor the pious fraud of superstition;
nicht als Balsam für die unheilbaren Wunden des Menschenloses,	nor balm for the incurable wounds of human fate,
nicht als Tauschware des ästhetischen Verkehrs mit der Kunst;	nor barter of the aesthetic traffic with art;
wenn die Sittlichkeit ernsthaft und wahrhaft ein Problem des Wissens werden und bleiben soll,	but rather if ethics is to become and remain seriously and genuinely a problem of cognitive pursuit,
so darf sie nicht von allen anderen Gewissensfragen des Wissens abgetrennt und blossgestellt werden;	then the cognitive pursuit of ethics may not be separated from any other conscientious intellectual endeavor and may not be exposed disparately.
nur im Zusammenhange der Probleme des Wissens kann die Ethik als Wissenschaft gedeihen und aufkommen. (#3)	Only within the epistemological context can ethics flourish and advance as a science.

The translator has decided to clarify unspecified referents in Cohen's text, such as in a sentence like, "Therefore *this* signifies none other than *that*" (see Table 2). I resolved these unspecified referents in concrete and unambiguous ways, attempting a mediation that Cohen does not undertake, as he relies on the initiated reader whom he trusts will remember the intricacies of the argument all along. However, whereas German allows for the use of such unspecified referents, English does not. The repetition of these referents will clarify for the reader what I as a translator think the argument implies. The most decisive attempt at resolving unspecified referents is through the use of square brackets as exemplified in Table 3.

As Tables 2 and 3 demonstrate, attention has been paid to textual detail, especially in cases

TABLE 2. SYNOPSIS OF TRANSLATION

ORIGINAL GERMAN	*ENGLISH TRANSLATION*
Wenn nun aber die *Annährung* nur diesen klaren ethischen Sinn hat und haben kann, darf man dann nicht fragen, wie Maimuni der Versuchung widerstehen konnte, in *sie* die Glückseligkeit zu setzen und *diese* in *jener* wiederzukennen. (#116)	Now, if the concept of *drawing near to God* can and may only tolerate this clearly ethical connotation, are we then not entitled to ask how Maimonides could have resisted the temptation to translate "nearness" as eudaemonia, and to recognize *such nearness to God* as *personal bliss?*

TABLE 3. SYNOPSIS OF TRANSLATION

ORIGINAL GERMAN	*ENGLISH TRANSLATION*
Alle klassischen Religionsphilosophen des Judentums berufen sich auf Hiob (32:8): "Wahrlich Geist ist im Menschen, und die Seele des Allmaechtigen macht sie vernuenftig." Und schon Abraham ibn Daud's Erklaerung lautete: "der Geist ist der menschliche Geist, und die Seele des Allmaechtigen ist der heilige Geist." (# 39) *Das* ist der Pantheismus im Monotheismus.	*In this context* [Cohen closely connects this paragraph to the previous one, which ends with a note on the relationship between "these divine characteristics" and "the purposefulness of human ethics"], all classical philosophers of Judaism refer to Job 32:8: "But truly, it is spirit in man, the breath of Shaddai gives them reason." Abraham ibn Daud interprets thus: "The spirit refers to the human mind, the breath of Shaddai to the spirit of holiness." The correlation between God and man in ethical reasoning constitutes the pantheistic element within monotheism.

*The correlation between God and man in ethical reasoning constitutes the pantheistic element within monotheism.

where I opted for a translation and commentary that extend the boundaries of the text. Concerning Cohen's philosophical terminology, I tried to be consistent in my translation of technical terms (*Ungrundlegung,* for example, is always rendered as "non-foundation"), aiming at a translation that might prove compatible with future English translations of Cohen's philosophical works. The same consistency was also sought with respect to Cohen's usage of classical rabbinic terminology.

For the sake of clarity and structure, numbers were added to Cohen's unnumbered paragraphs, reminiscent of the practice in the edition of the *Religion of Reason: Out of the Sources of Judaism* in which all paragraphs, or sections, are numbered. Cohen's own transliteration system of Hebrew has not been made consistent with that used in my own text.

An Important Note to the Learner: How to Use This Book

This book is not one that the reader is supposed to read silently, alone, from cover to cover—as is the case with most books. This book, rather than being a text for mere "reading," provides the setting for an age-old pedagogical technique in which the living word is passed on from one learner to the other, and in which the act of translation provides only the first of many intermediary steps of disseminating the teaching among students. Learning Jewish philosophy with this book would therefore ideally happen in *chavruta*—a setting of two—whose reading would proceed from paragraph to paragraph, concentrating upon the issues at hand. The commentary itself, then, will serve as a sort of second, surrogate reader, as well as invite the student to explore the classical literature that underlies Cohen's text.

The living word of Cohen, Maimonides, philosophers, modern and premodern Jewish thinkers—as well as that of the translator and of the commentator—might be found here. It calls on the learner to create her own commentary. The book's multitextuality—with its two texts facing each other—calls for interaction in the same way as the traditional talmudic discussions of the rabbis call for interpretation and commentary, just as two or more voices arguing over a heartfelt issue might call one who was listening all along, if it concerns her too, to now open her own lips and speak. Similarly, a reader may decide to join in this study of Cohen. This book will provide a setting for an oral discourse, in which critical issues in Jewish reasoning are voiced by the reader herself in such a way that "every word becomes a spoken word" of her own.[70]

The Page

Where applicable, pages will contain my translation of Cohen's text and my commentary on them. The English translation of Cohen's text generally appears in the left column of each page, in an alternate font. Cohen's own notes appear in parentheses.

Within Cohen's text, you will find my interpolations, which are set in brackets. These contain textual references Cohen took for granted, as well as textual associations that are a result of my own reading. (However, not all paragraphs of the translation will be commented upon. Thus, some pages will contain simply my text in two-column format and some will contain simply Cohen's text in two-column format.)

The commentary follows the themes of Cohen's text in an associative manner, taking its cues from those passages in the text that, in my own first readings of the essay, called out for commentary. These passages, I felt, warranted commentary for three kinds of reasons. In some instances, the text was so difficult that I did not understand it at first sight—such as Cohen's idea of origin and non-foundation; his messianic epistemology,[71] which constructs the past from a temporal mode of futurity; or the historical genesis of issues in classical medieval Jewish philosophy. In other instances I decided to comment on a passage because I found it of great importance, so inspiring that I wished to emphasize it. In these cases, the commentary becomes an emphatic teaching, a repetition and enhancement—such as Cohen's teaching concerning the Platonic Good beyond Being; or the beautiful passages on alterity and shepherding; or those that radically challenge religious imagination, positing the world-to-come as a Kingdom of True Humanity.

Finally, I commented upon passages because I wanted to draw attention to their provocative nature—such as with Cohen's open polemic against Christianity, surely a surprise to the reader counting on the liberal, tolerant attitude of a German Jew who shies away from confrontation. I decided that it was not the function of my commentary to correct or even to apologize for Cohen's polemic against Christianity. Instead, I weave it into other texts of Cohen's philosophical and Jewish writings, distinguishing it from religious dogmatism, sharpening its position and deepening its claim. The same is true concerning Cohen's philosophical critique of Zionism, a biting polemic whose relevance for the contemporary debate on post-Zionism is hinted at without apology.

Subheads within Chapters: The Hidden Agenda of the Book

The subheads given within chapters of this book are not necessarily those one would give to the paragraphs of Cohen's essay itself. These subheads provide the reader with the hidden agenda of the book, pointing to the book within the book, the book "beneath" the commentary whose wholeness I could not retain as my reading became fractured in the pursuit of a strictly interlinear reading. Thus, only a reading all the way through the commentary will illuminate the beginning.

1

Socrates and Plato

Founders of Ethics

In this first chapter, Cohen provides the philosophical foundations for his Platonic, anti-Aristotelian reading of Maimonides: Plato establishes the Good as an idea, as an object of knowledge, whereas Aristotle reduces the good to the realm of economy and politics, ignoring the epistemological question concerning the interrelation between nature and goodness, which, according to Cohen, is central to Maimonides' thought. The idea of the Good, according to Plato, resembles a scientific hypothesis in that it must give an account of itself. The content *of the idea of the Good, however, exempts it from the relativity of all scientific hypotheses: in the idea of the Good* reason itself is grounded and comes to its end. *The Platonic concept of the "Good beyond Being" indicates a non-hypothesis or non-foundational origin of human knowledge that Cohen in the later parts of this essay equates with prophetic vision.*

Socrates, Founder of Ethics: What to Do with Socratic Irony

1. By proclaiming virtue as knowledge, Socrates became the founder of ethics; that is, concerning all other questions and pursuits of knowledge, he discovered and claimed the value of ethics as an object of cognition. Moreover, he demonstrated that only as knowledge and through cognition will the meaning of virtue become conceivable, its purpose and content applicable. With the enthusiasm of a discoverer—since here we are dealing with the discovery of terra incognita, the realm of ethics—and with the religious zeal of a prophet, Socrates made all Hellenic pursuits

(*See 1.*) *Socrates became the founder of ethics as a science.* Whereas pre-Socratic philosophers were primarily interested in nature, posing questions concerning the cosmos and its origins, Socrates rather focused upon the intricacies of human nature: Diogenes Laertius, in his ancient introduction to the lives of the philosophers, writes,

> Philosophy, the pursuit of wisdom, has had a twofold origin . . . [one leads] to Socrates, who introduced ethics or moral philosophy.[1]

of nature and natural sciences yield to the benefit of the human soul. Thus Socrates considered ethics not only as a science, but as the science par exellence. He proclaimed ethics as the core and focus of human cognition.

2. Socrates announced an agenda—the agenda of universal culture; understandably, his ethics bequeathed to us no record in writing. The whole value of this unique achievement is preparation, pioneering; a raising of the curtain, as it were, that had veiled the workshop of ethics. However, it was left to subsequent scholarly endeavor to clarify fully and to systematically present the meaning and purpose of the Socratic agenda. In this process, Socrates plays the role of the herald Elijah, and Plato that of the Messiah. [Malachi 3:23.]

3. Man's ethical stature is the loftiest and most relevant achievement of humanity. If our heart is to be pervaded by the powerful feeling attending this idea, then it must not be kept apart from and isolated from the mind and its own universal interests. If ethics is not to remain an accidental result of temperament or background, nor of historical inertia and of the urge for adjustment to fashionable changes, nor the carrot and stick of autocratic authority, nor the pious fraud of superstition, nor balm for the incurable wounds of human fate, nor barter of the aes-

Cohen elaborates:

> When Socrates founded ethics as a philosophical discipline he considered it to be the focus of all philosophy. . . . Ever since Socrates, ethics, the doctrine of man, becomes the center of philosophy.[2]

The Socratic emphasis on the study of man finds its renaissance in thinkers of the humanist tradition:

> *La vraie science et la vrai étude de l'homme, c'est l'homme.*[3]
> Know then thyself—presume not God to scan: The proper study of mankind is man.[4]

According to Cohen's Socrates, ethical knowledge expresses itself as the task of knowing one's self, an ideal transmitted to Socrates by the Delphic oracle "Know thyself" (γνωθι σεαυτον). Ironically, however, this task of self-knowledge constitutes a kind of not-knowing, for it has nothing to start with—cannot touch the grounds for which it searches. Cohen subsequently says:

> Socrates distinguished himself as the originator of scientific veracity. He was wont, however, to proclaim two intersecting axiomatic principles: "Know thyself" (γνωθι σεαυτον) alongside "I know that I don't know" (οιδα οτι ουκ οιδα). We may thus term Socrates the master of irony.[5]

thetic traffic with art—but rather if ethics is to become and remain seriously and genuinely a problem of cognitive pursuit—then ethics may not be separated from any other conscientious intellectual endeavor and may not be exposed disparately. Only within the epistemological context can ethics flourish and advance as a science. This epistemological challenge is wanting in Socrates.

4. Yet, the epistemological aspect is not altogether absent in Socrates; the discovery of virtue as knowledge represents an adumbration and a challenge, but it never matured into a full systematic presentation. Socrates threw down the gauntlet of conceptuality: he considered the concept to be the essence and the purpose of everything, of every object of nature, of human life and of every action. Aristotle, in fact, credited Socrates with the discovery of the concept. [Aristiotle 1945, NE 1144b, 371–73; Aristotle criticizes Plato's reading of Socrates' concept of virtue, however, for its scientific pretentiousness and for its nonpragmatic character. Aristotle 1981, *Eudemonian Ethics* 1217b–1218b, 225–33; 1945, NE 1096a–1097a, 17–25; 1145b, 379–81; 1147b, 393–95.] Anyone who directs enthusiasm for ethics toward scientific knowledge must comprehend the entire content and purpose of existence within the framework of conceptuality and as Concept; in order to solve the enigma of our

Socrates proclaims the maxim "Know that you know nothing" as the highest form of human knowledge. What had been the proclamation of an ironic paradox in Plato's Socrates, and what in popular literature has been depreciated as arrogant and ostentatious, becomes an innovative epistemological method in Cohen's reading.[6] In correspondence to his own philosophical method of origin, Cohen interprets the Socratic paradox as an "adventurous state of not-knowing,"[7] a privation that lies at the bottom of creative thinking. This kind of privation produces knowledge through an infinite generative process in which nothing is a given.[8]

In ethics, the Socratic privation of knowledge refers to the concept of the self, which—as Cohen says—exists only in terms of a task for ethical volition. The self is not "given to us" but rather has to be constructed anew at any moment in which a person is confronted with the demand to do good.[9] A leading Levinas scholar quite adequately sums up Cohen's reading of Socratic irony:

> Less than identical with itself, in deficit with regard to itself, unable to catch up with itself, unable to achieve presence and self-presence, the self cannot be conceived as an entity. . . . It is, in Levinas's telling expression, in exile in itself.[10]

world, one must acknowledge the universal nature of ideation, and thus establish the ethical charge exclusively within the realm of conceptuality. It is this conceptuality of ethics that separates it as ideation from the figments of myth and from mere aesthetic presentation.

Cohen's philosophy of origin converts Socratic irony into a critical method of ethical judgment—a method of critical thinking that ever distances itself from reality's status quo, that eternally binds the process of thinking under the yoke of ethical volition.

Concept and Idea: On Nominalists and Realists

5. Even conceptuality, however, is only a preliminary stage. The concept can do no more than indicate—it is an indication of what is relevant: the strict, exact meaning and value of ideation, of that which has been scientifically comprehended (the conceptual reality). But how do we validate this indication, and bring it to its conclusion, so that it does not remain a mere intimation? Indeed, a concept presents just an abstraction, if not just a word, a name. We recall the serious medieval controversy regarding the objective significance of the Universals.

(*See* 5.) *Indeed, a concept presents just an abstraction.* Cohen reads the medieval debate between realists and nominalists about the status of Universals, abstractions such as ideas and concepts, as a continuation of the debate between Plato and Aristotle about the very concept of the Good as an idea. Cohen seems to say that, in the context of science, nominalists are right when claiming that concepts are, indeed, just abstractions, although of central functional value. When discussing the "sublimity" of Plato's idea of the Good, however, Cohen sides with the realists: the idea of the Good is more than a mere abstraction; it is rather of constitutive significance in providing the fundamental grounds for human thought and human action.

The Platonic Bent: A Tradition within the Tradition

6. This controversy has remained, in fact, an ongoing discussion right up to the present: it is the controversy over the meaning of the Platonic idea. Whoever entertains even the slightest doubt that there exists a fundamental difference between Platon-

(*See* 6.) *The controversy over the meaning of the Platonic idea.* The renewed interest in Plato among Jewish neo-Kantian thinkers such as Cohen, Cassirer, and Levinas demonstrates the attempt to base ethical rationalism upon a transcendental method of

ic idea and Socratic conceptuality bears responsibility for the continuation of this undying controversy.

7. Plato did not stop short at the fascination that seized him when encountering the cognitive zeal of Socrates—nearly bordering on a cognitive creed. As if pledging the Sophist's advocate, he promoted critical doubt concerning naive faith in concepts and in the Socratic method of how to attain and clarify a concept. Plato demanded accountability for concepts. Thus he bestowed the validity and meaning of the concept upon this task, which he imposed upon the concept: to render an accounting of itself (λογον διδοναι). [Plato 1980, *Republic* 534b-c, 207; 531e, 195–96.] It is this accountability which distinguishes the idea (ιδεα) from the concept (ειδος). [Cohen's fundamental distinction between the Platonic idea and the Platonic concept is itself innovative. See *SPhZ* 60; differently, see Shorey in Plato 1980, 6:104; Shorey 1980, x–xi; 1965, 75. Plato uses the term ειδος less frequently, and nowhere with reference to the idea of the Good which "lies beyond the accountability of the concept." *LrE* 19, 73; Shorey 1965, 182–86.]

thought.[11] Both in Cohen's philosophy as well as in his interpretation of Judaism, the Platonic idea of the Good beyond Being is of creative, pivotal significance.[12] Accordingly, contemporary Jewish thinkers—in conscious or unconscious alliance with the decisively Platonic bent in Cohen's "new thinking"—align themselves with the Platonic tradition, emphasizing the "sublimity of the Good" in Jewish tradition.[13]

Vision and Idea: On Prophetic Hermeneutics

8. Two motifs converge in the development of the Platonic idea: first, the etymological element of vision, which early Jewish philosophers could not fail to acknowledge in spite of their addiction to Aristotle. The Platonic idea may surely be discerned in the biblical vision of the prophets. In this biblical context, we find the dual aspect of the prophetic act proper and its attending "objective vision," resulting in their reintegration. Hence, Fichte saw fit to translate the Platonic term *idea* as the

(*See 8.*) *The "Platonic Idea": the etymological meaning of "vision" and the "vision" of the prophets.* Note the etymological development of *video* (Ϝιδεα), "knowing or observing," from the ancient form of *eidos* (vision > *video* > Ϝειδος).[14] *Veidos* (compare the mishnaic *vadai*, ודאי, or "evident") signifies sense-perception. *Video* thus points to a process of abstraction in which truth—*Wahrheit*—means "having seen," and in which sense-perception, concretely perceived phenomena,

biblical "vision" [*Gesicht*]. [*ErW* 208–9; *SPhZ* 52–57.]

9. The second element appears to be more strictly scientific. Vision is not confined to scientific thinking, and within said thinking it does not yet bear the marks of requisite certainty and of methodical autonomy. For this certainty and methodological autonomy Plato searched, and these he discovered in the mathematical term *hypothesis.* [*SPhZ* 336–66; Plato 1980, *Republic* 511a b:112–15.]

are generalized. Sense-perception, indicated by the term *eidos,* represents the initial stage of conceptual knowledge, or of strictly scientific thinking. Cohen claims that prophetic imagination employs precisely this motif of vision-*eidos* in a peculiar hermeneutics that is based upon two factors, the first being a matter of personal experience and intuition, the latter of constructive reasoning. Whereas prophetic experience is a gift, and as such beyond the prophet's rational control, the prophetic message is an interpretive task entirely within the bounds of the prophet's own responsibility.

Cohen explains the phenomenon of prophetic knowledge initially within the context of Plato's theory of ideas. When asking about the subjective origins of Plato's theory of ideas, demanding to know how Plato was able to conceive of ideas that not only assume universal significance but that constitute entire worlds, Cohen describes a psychological process in which "Plato is being struck by a vision—by an *idea*—as by sudden flashes of lightning." To follow those "luminous traces" in which truth presents itself constitutes the infinite task of the Platonic thinker.[15] Cohen correlates this process of Platonic knowledge with prophetic vision. Maimonides' introduction to *The Guide of the Perplexed* thus resounds with Cohen's early essay on Plato. In a famous passage, Maimonides there describes prophetic imagination as an experience in which "truth flashes out" to the prophet in "lightning flashes time and time again."[16]

Prophetic imagination is based upon sense perception, upon a concrete vision that is translated into language, speech—those personal verbal associations and articulations, which constitute the prophetic message (*video*-idea). In other words, the prophetic message results from the prophet's attempt to decipher and decode the personally experienced divine word, translating the tangible, sensual vision (*eidos*) into a normative idea.[17] What characterizes prophetic vision is its *Gesamtschau,* the Mosaic view of the whole: a vision whose inclusivity and universality becomes an inspiration for the entire community of humankind.[18]

According to Cohen, Jewish oral tradition invokes precisely this kind of prophetic hermeneutics. In the same way as the prophet translates a personal experience into a coherent body of ideas, the community of listeners must first hear the words of the prophets before understanding the impact of their teaching. Cohen claims—and we may read this claim as a commentary on the biblical *na'asseh ve-nishmah*[19]—that the loftiest ideas of the prophets, their ethical vision of peace and of justice, and of a united humanity, originate with the tangible sound of speech and with the sensual movement of lips. "It was the prophets' lips, after all," says Cohen, "which announced the truth of God."[20]

Axioms

10. In keeping with his contemporary mathematical terminology, Plato saw in the hypothesis not just any premise at random, but the premise as a fundamental thesis, or even a fundamental concept. [*SPhZ* 358–64.] The term *axiom* was only later adopted for this specific purpose. The term *hypothesis* is applied even to the concept of the angle. [Plato 1980, 6:110–11.] The hypothesis then serves as the elementary methodological means of initiating an investigation. [Cohen claims that the terms *hypothesis, idea, nought of knowledge, question mark, angle, lever,* are all expressions to indicate the same, namely the creative ground—or—origin of the process of critical thinking. *LrE* 84.] It serves as a premise establishing the prerequisite for the exploration of any problem. The validity and fecundity of any such investigation is predicated upon congruence with the premise, which in turn constitutes its effective, continuous foundation.

(See 10.) The term axiom *was only later adopted.* The axioms of Euclidean geometry were considered self-evident truths, propositions for which no proof is required. In modern logic, an axiomatic theory is considered one in which all the claims of the theory are presented as theorems derivable from a specified set or system of axioms. Cohen himself criticizes the Aristotelian concept of the axiom in Euclidean geometry, contrasting it with the principles of modern natural sciences. The principles of modern sciences "cannot simply be deduced from theoretical doctrine and axiom, as these scientific principles are themselves predicated upon new insight, sense perception, and experiment."[21]

11. In mathematics, this clarification of each and every step, experiment, and premise of the investigation is concomitantly necessary and indispensable. Hence, the requirement of an initial presupposition (hypothesis) in mathematics arouses no suspicions. The premise cannot be mistaken here for a mere presumption, since mathematical cognition may not be relegated to the haziness of ingenious figment. Mathematical procedure moves along the lines of demonstration; in this case, it is only this procedural stringency which ensures free movement of cognition. The hypothesis in mathematics and in Renaissance astronomy thus initiated a new age: the modern era. The hypothesis became the foundation of the natural sciences. [Modern science and its emphasis on relativity and kinetic processes seems to correlate with Plato's theory of ideas, whereas Aristotle's view of truth as an eternal and static substance characteristically determines the entire medieval world of science. Frank 1945, 105n. 16.] Kepler himself recognized it as Plato's idea and credited him for it. [*LrE* 7, 430.]

12. Thus the idea constitutes the necessary premise, or grounding, for every scientific investigation. It contains the rationale, the basis and foundation—the account that cognition renders of itself. ["The idea is hypothesis. . . . Plato's determination of the idea as 'concept' . . . does not proceed beyond Socrates. Plato's original contribution lies in characterizing the idea as hypothesis." *ErW* 97 and *LrE* 30, 211. See also *JS* 1:308–9, and *RoR* 91; *RdV* 106; Lembeck 1994, 89–100.] There is no cognition without accountability, and no rendering of account without proper grounding. Science is nothing but the science of grounding.

13. This is evident, as long as we deal primarily with mathematics. Here this restriction to hypothetical thinking serves as an advantage. Mathematics does not move beyond ideas. Likeness, for example, is an idea, since it is a hypothesis. How else could it be defined but as a hypothesis? If we were not to accept "likeness" as an abstract idea, we might even mistake it for the result of a perceptual observation. The idea of likeness is not inferred from actual objects such as twigs and pebbles, but rather demonstrated by way of twigs and pebbles. [Plato 1982, 257, as cited in *LrE* 482–83. Cohen emphasizes that likeness cannot be inferred from the concept of number, since the concept of likeness implies the idea of relational magnitude. Ever since Georg Cantor's introduction of set theory, and, in particular, his idea of the one-to-one correspondence of members of two or more sets, the concept of number ceased to be fundamental for mathematical thinking.] Hence the concrete object merely serves as the perceptual stimulus for the cognitive idea of likeness. Cognition means grounding; the grounding of likeness is equivalent to the idea of likeness. It is the hypothesis that safeguards the idea against the appearance and suspicion of presenting merely an afterimage of perception.

14. How does this apply to the idea of ethics? How is it applicable to the idea of the Good, the supreme concept under which Socrates had classified and unified the virtues? Only as an idea will the Good constitute an object of cognition—but is the Good admissible as an idea? This is the grave problem of Plato's doctrine of ideas. [*RoR* 400–402; *RdV* 464–67. Cohen 1996, 36–38 (hereafter cited as *BdR*). *LrE* 88, and Plato 1980, *Republic* 505c–509b, 2:89–107.] It is this very question that serves as the testing ground for scientific idealism. Here we arrive at a crossroad which we feel prompted to compare to the prophetic metaphor: Heaven and Earth, nature and science, may pass away, if only God's word, if only ethics shall remain. [Isaiah 40:6–8.] On the other hand, if ethics itself must become a science, and nothing but a science—will it not thus become subject to the destiny of all natural sciences, by being submitted to scientific methodology? [The destiny of science is its inherent relativity: scientific inquiry constitutes a self-corrective process, in which relative truths are ever-changing.]

Scylla and Charybdis

15. This accountability, which threatens to put the axe to the tree of ethical cognition, exposes the idea of the Good as an idea, in contradistinction to the Good as a mere concept. It does not suffice to collect the various aspects of ethics as a conglomeration of separate concepts. The idea is not a concept, or rather, it is not merely a concept. Ethics is charged with accountability. This rendering of account is predicated upon proper conceptual procedure, which is grounding itself. We cannot help accepting that even the Good may gain recognition as and only as an idea. Whoever demands more will gain less, since one would thereby deprive ethics of its cognitive value. Thus Plato's doctrine of ideas is caught in the dilemma of Scylla and Charybdis.

(*See 15.*) *Scylla and Charybdis.* On the one hand, the idea of the Good must gain the cognitive status of all ideas—which is that of a hypothesis. On the other hand, defined as a hypothesis, the Good becomes subject to the self-corrective process that is the fate of all scientific hypotheses. Cohen seeks to avert the relativism implied in this development by introducing the term *non-hypothesis* in the next paragraph. Cohen, however, nonetheless insists upon the status of the Good as an idea. If the Good were conceived of as less than an idea, it would revert to being mere (dogmatic) opinion or doctrine, which is precisely the position of Aristotle in his critique of the ideality of the Good in Plato. In following Aristotle, one deprives the Platonic Good of its epistemological status, turning the Good into a social doctrine of cultural agreements without a critical cognitive function.

Metalogic: The Good Is Prior to Thinking

16. A solution to this dilemma may only be advanced by a change of terminology, provided

(*See 16.*) *"Hypothesis" and "non-hypothesis".* According to Cohen's *Logik*, the term *hypothesis* serves

that such a change does not lead to distortion. At this crossroad, the Platonic idea has eminently proven itself as hypothesis. The idea in itself, however, without reference to hypothesis, would not have provided Plato with a solution, since the idea of the Good is, qua idea, no different from the idea of likeness—just as, in fact, all mathematical ideas (τα μαθηματικα) belong to ideas. The idea as such does not allow for any transformational flexibility. Hypothesis, however, lends itself to the experiment of conversion in content: thus Plato converts the hypothesis into a matter of non-hypothesis (ανυποθετον), or non-foundation. [Plato 1980, *Republic* 507b, 2:107, 510b, 2:110–11, in Shorey's translation "a principle that transcends assumption."]

as a steppingstone for the concept non-hypothesis. A hypothesis (*hypo* meaning "under") is thus an underlying thesis; *an-hypothesis* signifies a thesis that is "beyond" the underlying thesis, one that is prior to rational deduction.[22] Introducing this Platonic, privative term *non-foundation* into his own *Logik,* Cohen creates the transcendental grounds for a knowledge that is prior to rational deduction. Accordingly, Cohen reads the Platonic Good as an idea that is prior to rational deduction—an idea that Plato himself terms an-hypothesis or non-foundation. Cohen's interpretation of Plato translates the privative proposition "the Good is a non-hypothesis" into a proposition of origin: "the Good is the origin of all ethical judgment." The commitment to the Good precedes one's own reasoning. Cohen's entire interpretation of Maimonides focuses, in a way, on the concept of the Good as the origin of ethical cognition. Cohen demonstrates that Maimonides' theory of negative attributes and his concept of Knowing God uphold the transcendental, epistemological function inherent in the concept of the Platonic Good. Following Plato's equation of the knowledge of the Good with the highest form of knowledge, Cohen terms Maimonides' ideal of Knowing God ethical.

Dogmatists and the Concept of the Absolute

17. Out of this predicament and its attempted disentanglement emerged the Unconditioned, the Absolute, which is employed to this day as the mainstay of dogmatism in its refutation of Idealism and the piecemeal of its human

(*See 17.*) *Out of this predicament emerged the Absolute.* The Platonic term *non-foundation* has been widely interpreted by religious dogmatists as the static concept of the Absolute. Cohen's own reading emphasizes the critical, regulative function of the Platonic Good with regard to all aspects of human life (ethical, political, or scientific), and rejects conceptions of the Good whose ontologies are steeped in mysticism. Cohen's contemporary, Paul Shorey, supports this reading:

> To call the ανυποθετον [an-hypothesis, non-foundation] the Unconditioned or the Absolute introduces metaphysical associations foreign to the passage.[25]

The concept of the Absolute or Unconditioned—illegitimately borrowed from Plato—continues to play a central role in attempts by religious dogmatists to defeat critical, non-foundational thinking. However, these defenders are unaware that it was philosophy that produced and stipulated the concept of the Unconditioned in the first place.

---

wits. The Absolute, however, is itself in truth nothing but the outgrowth of this defamed Idealism—a product of conscientious, daring cerebration, demanding accountability and rendering accountable, thus creating, grounding, and advancing toward conclusions, not without examining the validity of its premises and presuppositions all along. This is Idealism's feat.

18. Indeed, even the Good may not claim to exceed its status of idea, and hence of hypothesis. However, the content of ethics distinguishes the Good as idea from anything in the heavens above and on earth below. By virtue of this axiological distinctiveness, the Good deserves as hypothesis a preferential terminology. Thus we may term the idea of the Good a sufficient hypothesis (ικανον). [Plato 1982, Phaedo 1: 348; 1980, Republic 6:114n. c; Liddell and Scott 1968, ικανον 825a–b.] Whereas the idea in general merits the predicate "reliability" (το ασφαλες της υποθεσεως), the idea of the Good may be defined as that hypothesis which constitutes the telos or end of reason, and thus plainly terminates the report of its accountability.

19. The idea of the Good must remain an hypothesis. Ethics does not evolve from political constitutions, nor from the impulse of human nature, as manifested in the growth of trees, or the beasts' pursuit of enjoyment. The Good is a prophecy of wisdom; not as proclaimed by Plato in the dithyrambic style at the conclusion of his *Philebus,* but as the grounding of ethical cognition. Ethics is a mode of cognition. [*Philebus* 67b, 399]

20. Whereas all other scientific hypotheses are predicated upon prior hypothetical propositions, the hypothesis of the Good constitutes its own ultimate ground, closing the cycle of reason. The non-foundation must be considered the ultimate, rock-bottom ground of all grounding. Ethics is to be removed from any relativism, even from that which is part and parcel of the methodology of all scientific investigation. [*BdR* 36–38.] Having arrived at the idea of the Good, I am no longer justified in inquiring why and wherefore there ought to be ethics in the world, or whether such an ethical world might exist. If reasoning is to maintain meaning and validity at all, we have to admit on sufficient evidence that ethics must be an object of thought and cognition. The idea of ethics, in and of itself, constitutes its own foundation, its own grounding, its own accountability. It does not make sense to engage in yet more retrogressive reduction to find a root or provenance beyond and behind ethics. The Good constitutes the foundation of the world. [*Plato* 1942, *Timaeus* 29e, 55.]

"This Man Is Inhuman": Privations, Origins, and the Principle of Anticipation

21. In the light of more exacting scrutiny and conceptual analysis, we find that "hypothesis" takes the role not of an ultimate destination and telos, but rather of a point of origin and departure. Non-foundation turns out to be the origin of grounding. In this prominent example, the significance of the "infinite judgment" proves itself again to be the judgment of origin. [*LrE* 79–93.]

(*See 21.*) *"Infinite Judgment" and "Judgment of Origin"*. Cohen's logic of origin is based upon the logical function of the "infinite judgment."[24] Aristotle defines the infinite judgment as a proposition in which the predicate of a formally positive statement constitutes an indefinite term—such as in the proposition "Reuven is 'non-seeing,' or 'blind.'"[25] Cohen specifies that only those judgments ought to be called privative judgments whose formally positive predicate—blindness—denies a property that truly *ought* to be present in the subject—namely sight—creating a mental attitude of anticipation (namely that this person *ought* to be endowed with sight).[26] Cohen speaks of infinite and privative judgment interchangeably, implying that in both cases the property negated by the predicate is *anticipated* to be an attribute of the subject.[27]

Cohen's infinite or privative judgments are *affirmative* propositions—they formulate an ideal position precisely by means of a relational privation. If a man is blind, he ought to be seeing. Cohen invokes the negation-particle, μη, of Democritus in its relational syntactical function as the precedent for this form of privation.[28] The innovation in Cohen's reading of the privative judgment lies in his interpretation of it as an affirmative proposition of origin, anticipating and therewith *positing* that property which the privative proposition denies to the subject.

Let us take two examples in order to clarify Cohen's point: (a) "this world is unjust" and (b) "this man is inhuman." The privative wording of the predicative terms unjust and inhuman implies that the respective subjects—"this world," "this man"—lack the property denied in the predicates—"justice," "humanity." On the other hand, infinite judgments like "this world is unjust" or "this man is inhuman" create a horizon of expectation: in judging the world unjust, we imply that the world, indeed, ought to be just; in judging this man to be inhuman, we anticipate his humanity. Cohen's entire theory of messianism, in fact, follows this logic of anticipation.[29] Note that Cohen's relational interpretation of the privative judgment, based upon the pre-Socratics, Plato and Aristotle, breaks with the interpretation of the German Idealist tradition. Kant's example of "the soul that is non-mortal" does not propose that "the soul ought to be mortal," but rather affirms the existence of the soul by excluding mortality from its properties.[30] The Kantian example gave way to an interpretative history of the infinite judgment, contrary to Cohen, as Salomon Maimon, Hegel, and Schelling define the infinite judgment as a proposition in which there exists no reasonable relationship between subject and predicate at all.[31]

Motions of the Good

22. Hence, by employing the terminology of hypothesis, Plato combines the problem of ethics and ethical certainty with the problem of paradigmatic or mathematical cognition. Two points are important here: (a) the Good constitutes an idea, just as mathematics consists of ideas; and (b) the methodology of retrogressive reduction [as applied to the idea of the Good] differs radically from the methodology of other ideas. This difference obtains only in the reductive process backward; the methodology of forward motion applies equally to the cognitive process of all ideas. There is no other methodology for problems of ethics but that

(*See 22.*) *Retrogressive and progressive.* Cohen's differentiation between backward and forward motions in this paragraph seems somewhat confusing, since the fundamental difference with respect to the idea of the Good in comparison to other ideas refers both to its origin and its telos. The meaning of the statement that "the methodology of forward motion applies equally to . . . all ideas" lies in Cohen's claim that, formally speaking, all ideas represent regulative limits to human cognition. On the other hand, the idea of the Good is hypothetically excluded from the infinite process of scientific, conceptual deduction; thus, "retrogressively" (with respect to its own grounding) the idea of the Good distinguishes itself from any other idea.

implied in the idea of the Good *qua* idea; only with respect to its retrogressive motion of rendering account for its hypothesis, does the ethical idea differ from the accountability of other ideas. Herein lies the difference between ethics and mathematics: insofar as the latter is based upon the logic of ideation, it distinguishes ethics from logic. The *idea* is shared by ethics and logic; the idea of the Good separates ethics from logic.

23. With this dichotomy, Plato launches ethics as a science. The Socratic concept of the Good gave no premonition of the ambiguity that the idea of the Good would subsequently expose. There is no reason to suppose that Plato's contemporaries, for their part, understood that within this apparent dichotomy of the Good-as-idea was enveloped the innermost integrity and the most powerful harmony of the human spirit for the posterity of all mankind. It would mean skipping over medieval culture, however, if we should endeavor to look for precedents during the Renaissance and its enduring afterglow already in the teaching of the Platonic Academy, and if we were to expect and demand to find them there. We would deprive the Middle Ages of its innermost intellectual and historical significance, if we were to assume that Aristotle, foremost among epigons, ought to have understood his teacher. Crediting Aristotle with such comprehension of the idea of Plato would mean forestalling its medieval evolution. Or are we to appreciate this evolution merely as the outgrowth of Aristotelian interpretation? Whereas Plato far surpasses his generation and makes his contribution for all eternity, Aristotle rises after him as the harbinger of the Middle Ages. Aristotle becomes the apostle of an era that sought its purpose not in the giving account of its own reasoning and cognition, but instead in the concept of an Absolute. The recognition of the formation and significance of the Absolute as having derived from the hypothetical idea was, for medieval times, as unattainable as it was undesirable and unappealing.

Theoria and *Praxis:* Deconstruction of an Ancient Theme

24. Aristotle misinterprets, mocks the Platonic *idea* and holds it in contempt; and not the least of such treatment does he accord to the idea of the Good. [Aristotle 1945, *NE* 1096a, 17–27.] We may be justified in speculating that if he had properly

(*See 24.*) *Aristotle scorns the Platonic idea.* The interpretation of political history as the "struggle of human beings in the world for individual and social perfection" is predicated upon a Platonic pursuit of the Good, upon the commitment

appreciated the idea of the Good, he might have come to understand the theory of ideas in general. For that, however, he lacks not only Platonic capacity, but indeed is wanting even in the caliber of a Socrates. His heart is insensitive to the profound and sublime problems of ethics, its challenges, objectives, and aspirations. It does not drive him, like a discoverer, to set out and explore a distant terra incognita. He is not concerned about mankind's future emerging, as it were, from the Delphic *omphalos* of the universe. For him, every future is but the cyclic recurrence of the past and its ever-ascending, unexcelled wisdom. ["And so time is regarded as the rotation of the sphere. . . . And this is the reason of our habitual way of speaking; for we say that human affairs . . . seem to be in a way circular, because all these things . . . have their beginning and end as it were 'periodically.'" Aristotle 1980, *Physics* 223b, 425.] Aristotle is oblivious to ethics as a problem that demands ever-innovative rejuvenation, new questions posed unceasingly, and new challenges yielded with every new solution. This Good, to him, is not an idea, as the idea as such betokens to him, at best, a poetic metaphor. And if to Aristotle the Platonic idea itself does not warrant any scientific cognition, certainly the idea of the Good cannot serve any purpose in scientific discussion. Ethical cognition is the task of the statesman. For Aristotle, the ethicist as such is the politician. There are no further human tasks in Aristotelian ethics.

of society's members to act upon the idea of Goodness, which, in turn, is determined through an interpretative process of political reasoning.[32] Aristotle, to the contrary, considers ethics and politics to represent mere practical knowledge, in contrast to metaphysical speculation which he takes to be the highest form of human knowledge.[33]

Cohen's critique of Aristotle turns precisely on the latter's distinction between theory and praxis,[34] between contemplation as the highest Good and ethical practice. This is a distinction foreign to the active concept of ethical ideality assumed in Cohen's critical philosophy. Cohen allows neither for proclamations of pure theory nor for those of mere praxis. Rather, he constructs truth as the correlation of ideality and social action, committing praxis to the pursuit of the ideal, while demanding the responsibility of theory in the face of social misery.[35] This destruction of Aristotle's and Kant's distinction between theoretical and practical reason is of central significance to Cohen's entire interpretation of Maimonides. Historically speaking, this gave a Platonic direction to Jewish ethics, whose legacy—even among Maimonides scholars—had been strongly Aristotelian.

25. Perhaps we are doing injustice to Aristotle. In his ethics, he presents a discourse that not only transcends politics, but indeed represents the very climax and objective of his ethics, namely the pure theory of the philosopher, the theory of eudaemonia. [Aristotle 1945, *NE* 1177a–b, 613–19.]

26. This, however, displays one of the many contradictions in Aristotle's philosophy: he establishes cognition as the aim of ethics, yet he refuses to recognize ethics as a science. If eudaemonia serves him as the foundation of ethics, while, on the other hand, eudaemonia is excluded from all other civic activities, constituting merely the object of contemplative pleasure and the gratification of cognitive study—why then does he not arrive at the conclusion that it is cognition of ethics that constitutes the object of his eudaemonistic theory? Why does Aristotle insist that ethics does not enjoy the status of a science, such as mathematics, or—before all—even metaphysics, the cognition of Being as such? By what right may eudaemonia, if it is then the foundation of ethics, govern the realm of cognition—when keeping the problem of ethical cognition at bay as inferior?

27. We would miss the heart of the matter, if we were to typify Aristotle as the sober logician and Plato as the religious cogitator. [As in Zeller 1955, 185.] Had this been the case, we ought to have expected Aristotelian logic, which in this context means his metaphysics, to bear out that methodological sobriety and lucidity which characterizes, in profound contradistinction, Plato's discourse on his concept of ideas. In fact, none of Aristotle's present-day admirers would disagree that, even in his *Metaphysics,* he remains a dualist. His argumentation departs not only from perceptual and empirical notions, but no less emphatically from ultimate absolute principles conceived of as immediate propositions (αμεσα). [ἄμεσον: an "immediate proposition that cannot be proven syllogistically." Aristotle 1983a, 515.] In this way, as he is wont to do throughout, Aristotle adopts the previously rejected and misunderstood Unconditional, transformed into a dogmatic application. We wonder: To what purpose should these absolute first principles, and hence, the principle of eudaemonia, apply more urgently and more immediately than to the very purpose of ethics, especially since they converge in the dynamic cause of an absolute purpose? [See paragraph 26, this chapter.] Does not this purpose of ethics constitute the very purpose of all Being and of all thinking?

Misreadings: The Go[o]d, the Ineffable Name, and Blumenberg's *Work on Myth*

28. The interrelation between nature and ethics never dawned upon Aristotle. He remains ignorant of Plato's Helios Parable establishing the idea

(*See 28.*) *The Helios parable.* In his Helios Parable, positing the idea of the Good as foundation of all Being, Plato compares the sun—

of the Good as the foundation of all Being, and hence of cognition. [Plato 1980, Republic 100–107. "This superhuman hyperbole is the source of all so-called negative theologies and transcendental metaphysics from Philo and Plotinus to the present day"; cf. Shorey 1980, xxix.] Aristotle's *Metaphysics* fails to recognize this interrelation. As a result of this failure to correlate the ontological problem of nature with the teleological problem of ethics, Aristotle comes to deny cognitive validity for ethics. The target of his *Metaphysics* is the universe. All religious questions concerning the whys and wherefores of the terrestrial and supernatural world vacillate between physics and astronomy, on the one hand, and ontology, the cognition of Being "as such," on the other. Aristotle's ontology, however, relates exclusively to the being of nature. [Aristotle 1947, *Metaphysics* 1012b, 207; 1071b, 139–41.]

29. Plato, however, is dissatisfied with this Aristotelian universe. His teleology does not reflect upon a dynamic cause, a concept inherently attached to mechanics. Platonic teleology is viewed from the perspective of the Good beyond Being, the Good beyond the being of nature (επεκεινα της ουσιας). [Plato 1980, *Republic* 509b, 6:107; *LrE* 88; *ErW* 88; *BdR* 37.] By maintaining the interrelation between Being and that which lies beyond—which are two realms, distinct but not disparate—Plato postulates the cognitive approach that source of light which illuminates and exposes all objects to our visual faculty—to the idea of the Good, that source of knowledge without which our intellectual faculty would be shaded in darkness. Subsequently, true knowledge (from επιστημη, *episteme*) is based upon knowing the Good, whereas knowledge composed of mere opinions which remain unrelated to the foundational Good possess no clarity.

Cohen's interpretation of Maimonides is based upon Cohen's construction of a correlation between Plato's idea of the Good and Maimonides' theory of Knowing God. Cohen's reading thereby advances a non-foundational (anti-fundamentalist) interpretation which radicalizes the Jewish critical tradition of negative theology, maintaining the absence of the Absolute while claiming the idea of the Good to be the foundation for the ethical idealism prominent in Jewish tradition. Among contemporary thinkers, Hans Blumenberg's *Work on Myth* acknowledges the characteristic endeavor of neo-Kantianism to make Plato the founder of its own critical tradition (invoking the authority of Paul Natorp in this context).[36] Blumenberg, however, remains unaware of the critical bent of Cohen's philosophy and the Platonic reading of Jewish literary sources suggested therein. Subsequently, Blumenberg's concept of Jewish monotheism is one in which violence and jealousy prevails:

to ethics with no less urgency than he does to logic. Aristotle, on the contrary, could only disclaim the cognitive character of ethics, since the interrelation of nature and ethics did not present any problem to him; for him, Being completes itself within physical nature proper. What business does the Good have with nature? Nature pursues its good on the basis of its own inherent principles, and, accordingly, it operates within relative purposes of Being. [Aristotle's *causa finalis* denotes an immanent teleology, irrespective of the question of whether the final cause involves a conscious purpose or intention of will, or whether it simply refers to the end toward which something tends naturally to develop. Aristotle 1947, *Metaphysics* 1013a–b, 211–15; 1044a–b, 417.] The question of what constitutes the purpose of nature as such, and the response to this question, namely that it is ethics that constitutes the telos of nature, both lie beyond Aristotle's ken. Herein we grasp the difference between metaphysics and ethics.

> Only the God of monotheism, then, would be the God of Feuerbach . . . because He is like man. . . . His relationship to man has the character of the "narcissism of small differences," where a jealous attention is paid to dotting i's and crossing t's. This relationship of "being made in the image of . . . " is recognizably different from the beautiful anthropomorphousness of the Olympian gods. In them there is always a remainder of the *originally foreign element* . . . their taking on human form is a mere gesture of friendliness [emphasis added].[37]

Blumenberg's reading of the Jewish God as an anthropomorphic God and of the Greek gods as gods of transcendence remains oblivious to the fact that there is a Jewish critical tradition deriving its critique of ontology precisely from the concept of a transcendental Other, the presence of an absence, prominently exemplified by the God with the ineffable name.

Thales: On Monotheism and Pantheism and a Note to the (Postmodern) Critics of Reason

30. This difference explains why Aristotle's philosophy brought no satisfaction even in the decadent age of classical antiquity, and hence did not succeed in bringing the philosophy of that age under its exclusive control. At the incep-

(See 30.) On pantheism. Cohen reads Xenophanes as the beginning of both scientific thinking and pantheism.[38] He therewith hints at that irreducible pantheistic element that operates in all scientific and philosophic quests

tion of systematic speculation in Greece, pantheism had already evolved. [*SPhZ* 1:7; *RoR,* 40–41; *RdV* 47; also "Einheit oder Einzigkeit Gottes," *JS* 1:87–99.] It is significant that this development was preceded by the seed of monotheism. Monotheism has preserved this nexus with pantheism throughout its history. Monotheism's contact with pantheism is rooted in the ethical motif of teleology, hence it is poles apart from the mere mechanistic character of Aristotelian utilitarianism. Consequently, pantheism can be overcome philosophically only when ethics dispenses with pantheism's teleology, or with those of its motifs which have functioned as substitutes for teleology. It was not only Christianity that emerged in terms of speculation out of pantheism, in particular out of Philonic doctrines, finding its ever-recurring impetus for rejuvenation in this kind of speculation: even Judaism could not and would not altogether resist the temptation of pantheism's sweet poison. Philo lacks independent stature in his speculations, having been nurtured by the overwhelming power of Hellenic thinking, and therefore has no intimate effect on Jewish apologetics.

for unity—whether this unity is postulated with respect to nature or with respect to God. Even monotheism contains a hint of pantheism, simply due to its allowance that God becomes an *object* of thought. According to Cohen, monotheism proposes the unity of God and man in ethical reasoning.[39] Thus transcendence, or what was called "divine wisdom" in the Middle Ages, becomes immanent to thinking. To state this in Cohen's words: "Revelation is the creation of critical reasoning."[40] According to Cohen's principle of origin, transcendence and immanence—God and human beings, God's word and human knowledge—are relational positions in a logically immanent correlation of opposites in which God and human beings share the lawfulness of ethical reasoning.

When asked where the word of God first originated, Cohen gives us the following answer:

> It is God himself who announced Himself to man . . . not the human mind, not scientific reasoning. It is the concept of revelation in which prophetic Judaism itself borders on myth.[41]

Myth is storytelling, and so is revelation. Cohen claims that the very idea of the one, transcendent God is grounded in an act of speech—namely in the act of prophetic speech.[42] But speech that claims to contain the truth of God must mean more than what it says. The purity of God, God's transcendence and alterity, demands the task of exegesis, of interpreting His word which—for God's sake—must point beyond itself.

Transcendence in Cohen's sense is thus a "limit-concept," postulated by thinking itself in order to point to that which is prior to thinking. In other words, transcendence—perfection, fullness of time—may be anticipated infinitesimally in ephemeral, yet continuous, efforts of human will toward the actualization of the Good. In contradistinction to Hegel, Cohen's sense of "limit" does not limit the Absolute, as Hegel is wont to claim in his critique of Kant.[43] Rather, it ignites the activity of thinking, providing the grounds for a logic of anticipation, in which thought is infinitely open toward that which is other than itself.

(In)Justice Done to Philo: Logos and the Irony of History

Pantheism's sweet poison in philonic doctrine. When Cohen speaks of pantheism emerging out of Philonic doctrines, he makes reference in particular to Philo's doctrine of Logos that proved so influential to Christian theology, as evident in the interpretative history of John 1:1. Philonic doctrine obtains its pantheistic reading, according to Harry A. Wolfson, primarily within the context of Christian interpretation.[44] According to Harry A.Wolfson, however, it was none other than Philo who firmly established the doctrine of God's transcendence in his interpretation of the unique God as the "incorporeal, indivisible, and ineffable one" whose essence is beyond the reach of concepts.[45] The rejection of finite manifestations of the divine, which unites Jewish rationalists throughout history, and which lies at the bottom of Cohen's impassioned critique of all philosophies of totality or immanence as idolatrous and unethical, owes itself to Philonic doctrine. It is therefore ironic that, of all Jewish thinkers, Cohen accuses Philonic doctrine of having betrayed the spirit of ethical monotheism.[46]

Despite its transcendental bent, Philonic Logos has, ironically, lent itself hermeneutically to Christian scholastic tradition. This fact, according to Cohen, must be accredited squarely to Philo, who played no explicit role in the medieval debates where Jews defended (Philo's) doctrine of uniqueness and incorporeality against the Christian doctrine of the trinity.[47] Philo's contribution to the formulation of Jewish monotheism was not recognized until the dawn of Jewish Enlightenment and Zunz's Wissenschaft des Judentums, when modern Jewish scholarship became interested in the historicity of Jewish sources.

The Case of Shlomo ibn Gabirol

31. However, the stature within medieval philosophy of Avencebrol, the Wandering Jew Shlomo ibn Gabirol, presents quite a different case. It is noteworthy, in fact understandable, that traces of his authorship of *Fons Vitae* (מקור חיים) eventually fell into oblivion among Jews and Christians alike. We may attribute this not only to its lack of biblical references, nor even to his audacity in teaching the universal unity of matter and form throughout the entire realm of Being, [Heschel 1937, 68–77; 1938, 89–111] but perhaps mainly to his agenda of a metaphysics that assigns no exhaustive function to ethics as a subject for speculation. For this is characteristic of a life true to monotheism: that all speculation breathlessly advances in its pursuit of ethics. Any heresy may be absolved and even overlooked, as long as true teleology, the ethical convergence of nature and mind is being sought and attained. The history of philosophical speculation in Judaism may be developed in the light of this proposition.

(*See 31.*) *Avencebrol, the Wandering Jew.* Avencebrol, a linguistic corruption of the name ibn Gabirol, refers to Shlomo ibn Gabirol, the eleventh-century Jewish poet. He became known in the non-Jewish world primarily for his philosophical work *Fountain of Life*, whereas medieval Jewish thinkers cherished his Hebrew poetry, of which a poetic cosmology is entitled *The Royal Crown.*[48] His work *Fountain of Life* (Mekor Chayyim; *Fons Vitae*) lent itself for over nine centuries to Christian interpretation, with no reader even aware of its Jewish authorship.[49]

As in the case of Philo, the oblivion of *Fountain of Life* from Jewish tradition results from its Christian hermeneutical adoption. Ibn Gabirol interprets the concept of divine will in neo-Platonic fashion as an emanation from the first essence—from God. The emanation of divine will, however, had been interpreted by Christian readers of *Fountain of Life* as the divine Logos. Cohen holds ibn Gabirol responsible for such an *immanent* reading of divine volition, since ibn Gabirol interprets divine will in this work as an immanent link between God, the first essence, and the world composed of matter and form.[50] Thus the concept of divine will becomes primarily instrumental in an ontological theory of creation claiming that worldly matter and form were generated from divine non-matter and non-form.[51] For the sake of ethical reasoning, however, divine volition ought to remain independent of any ontic state of affairs. Cohen so emphasizes the transcendental character of divine will in Jewish medieval tradition that any definition which fails to represent divine will in terms of lawfulness and its ethical postulates excludes itself from the Jewish project of an ethical hermeneutics, or what Cohen calls prophetic monotheism.

2

Maimonides

A Radical Platonist

Ethics, not Aristotelian metaphysics, according to Cohen, constitutes the epitome of Maimonides' thought. Knowledge of God is inextricably linked to the cognition of the Good, which, according to the last chapters of Maimonides' Guide of the Perplexed, *corresponds to the cognition of "lovingkindness, justice, and true judgment." In this second chapter, Cohen investigates the relationship between ethical (autonomous) knowledge and religious tradition, between Written and Unwritten Law, reason and revelation. He discusses the question of what kind of response to the "Pauline polemic against the Law" emerges from Maimonides' ethics.*

Cohen's Reading of Maimonides: *Urtext* for a Contemporary Debate

32. There is no greater testimony to Maimonides as the most vital and most genuine representative of philosophy within Judaism than the fact that his ethics constitutes the core and effective center of his metaphysics. It would be fallacious to assume that by this homage we mean to imply that his metaphysics dissolves into disquisitions of morality, lacking the strict conceptuality of accepted metaphysical terminology; the first two parts of his *Guide of the Perplexed* clearly refute any such misapprehension. Here, neither the

(*See 32.*) *Maimonides: the most genuine representative of Jewish philosophy.* Cohen's reading of traditional Jewish literature, and of Maimonides, in particular, originates in a commitment prior to his understanding of any particular text: Cohen trusts that traditional Jewish texts will lend themselves to a distinctly ethical reading. The philosophical implications of the concepts of purity and holiness demand that ethics be paramount in Judaism. And by "ethics" Cohen does not mean "morality" in its

speculative structure of principles nor the astronomical underpinnings of a cosmic edifice of reason is wanting. However, it is the third part of this oeuvre that dispels any doubt about the meaning and purpose of wisdom: it is ethics. Even had he not authored the *Eight Chapters,* we would still be in possession of his ethical system in his concluding chapters of the *Guide;* they form the gravitational center of the entire exposition. [Maimonides *Eight Chapters* 1983b contains his introduction to the Mishna tractate of Avoth, providing a general introduction to the theme of ethics. Maimonides' Aristotelian terminology in the *Eight Chapters* led to the classical Aristotelian reading of Maimonides' ethics which Cohen opposes in this essay. See Rosin 1876, 6–7; as well as Gorfinkle in Maimonides 1912, 5.]

manifold manifestations of practical wisdom,[1] but rather the formulation of a theoretical maxim aiming at a fundamental critique of social reality.

Systematically exploring a correlation between the Platonic idea of the Good and the messianic vision of the prophets,[2] Cohen's reading of Maimonides (and his theory of divine attributes) commits the greatest authority of Jewish rabbinic thought to the cognitive pursuit of ethics. Maimonides' zeal in knowing God's actional attributes—represented in lovingkindness, justice, and true judgment—represents to Cohen what is genuinely humane in Judaism. As such, the ethical bent in Maimonides' thinking becomes imperative for any reading of Jewish literature.

The Characteristics of Maimonides' Ethics—*Urtext of a contemporary debate.* Ever since Leo Strauss's *Philosophy and Law,* a distinct tradition in contemporary Maimonidean scholarship inadvertently adopted Cohen's Platonic turn.[3] This is evident in a variety of readings: whether we take ethics to mean a commitment to political theory, as in Berman's "The Political Interpretation of the Maxim"; or to indicate human perfection, as in Kellner's *Maimonides on Human Perfection*; or to refer to the transcendental ideal in terms of halakic normativity, as in Twersky's *Introduction to the Code of Maimonides*; or in terms of a commitment to love and lovingkindness, as in Hartman's *Maimonides: Torah and Philosophic Quest;* or Harvey's "Maimonides on Human Perfection."[4] Classical expositions of Maimonides have stressed the Aristotelian character of his thought, evident in such interpretations as those by Harry A. Wolfson, Isaac Husik, Julius Guttmann, Shlomo Pines, Marvin Fox, Colette Sirat, and others. The translation of Cohen's philosophical essay "Charakteristik der Ethik Maimunis" provides the *Urtext* for the contemporary Platonic reading of Jewish philosophy in general, and of Maimonides' thought in particular.

Finis Coronat Opus

33. Even as competent an expert on Jewish philosophy as Manuel Joël missed the great historical significance of the magnificent climactic chapters of the *Guide.* His error of judgment is characteristically couched in these terms: "Maimonides himself indicated that they are but an appendix" (Joël 1876b, 1:16); זה הפרק . . . אינו כולל תוספת עניין על מה שכללו אותו פרקי זה המאמר, ואינו אלא כדמות חתימה; [*Guide* 3:51, 618. Cohen quotes the ibn Tibbon translation; cf. Maimonides 1987b, 577; and also Kafih in Maimonides 1972, 672.] Solomon Munk translates *"Le chapitre que nous allons produire maintenant n'ajoute aucun sujet nouveau. . . . Il n'est en quelque sorte qu'une conclusion."* [See *Guide* 3:51, 618.] The Hebrew term חתימה by no means connotes an appendix. On the contrary, it refers rather to a conclusion which, even though it does not add any new problem or subject matter, epitomizes all that has been dealt with in the foregoing discussions and chapters, which chapters actually serve only as a preparatory exposition for this deductive conclusion, focusing on the problem of love of God, or ethics. Not only according to its literal translation does the Hebrew term חתימה denote a signatory seal. (The background of this error is more profound and more general. Nobody can gain an insight into the unique character of Maimonides' ethics while being blocked by the insistence upon his dependence on Aristotle. And, in turn, one cannot properly assess Maimonides' relation to Aristotle without understanding the relationship between Aristotle and Plato differently than it is usually presented.)

(*See 33.*) *The signatory seal.* Maimonides employs the Arabic term *khatma,* corresponding to the Greek σφραγις meaning seal, mark, signet, signature. Designating the concluding chapters of the *Guide* as *khatma,* Maimonides presents them as the conclusion in the light of which the entire *Guide* is to be understood. According to a talmudic dictum, there is "a general rule in such cases: *hakol holekh achar hachitum*—everything is evaluated according to its conclusion."[5] Cohen would say that every reading of the *Guide* ought to originate in its concluding chapters—"*tchilath hamachshava vesof hama'ase*" [any original idea presents itself in the conclusion of its exposition].[6]

34. An additional question presents itself here. Maimonides teaches his ethics not only within the various discourses of his metaphysics, but even in his dogmatic magnum opus (יד החזקה). [Maimonides himself refers to his *Code* in Hebrew as *Mishneh Torah,* meaning *deuteronomy,* a repetition of the law, a teaching of the law by means of oral tradition. The *Mishneh Torah* has been traditionally transmitted under the title *Yad ha-Chazakah,* possibly due to the audaciousness of the original title. See Twersky 1980b, 105, 527.] But is philosophical ethics—and is there any other kind?—compatible with ethical norms that seem to be inherently religious, as they are an integral part of religious doctrine?

Natural Law: The Law in Our Bones

35. This problem is aggravated by the nature of Jewish tradition, which, much more than Christianity or Islam, is dominated and controlled by laws of Scripture, and even more by laws of oral transmission, regulating in detail the ethical conduct of all individual and social activity. It would seem that in such an authoritarian system, there is no room left for the autonomous exercise of ethical judgment, for moral law followed on the basis of pure principle. This principle of ethical judgment is conventionally accredited to the claim of the Unwritten Law [αγραφος νομος. Philo 1937, 101, 435; Wolfson 1947, 1:188–94; Heinemann 1927, 149–72, esp. 155; Husik 1925, 381–417], an ancient paradigm flexibly indeterminate to fit any human situation, and considered not to be predetermined to comply with any legal formulation and formality. The idea of living "under the yoke of the Law," on the other hand, has served since the polemics of the Apostle Paul as the dominant allegation with which to goad, tease, and heckle Judaism; intended as a stigma, it evokes the rebuttal: does not the sacramental rite of the Eucharist in this sense exceed the danger of legal ritualism attributed conventionally to

(*See 35.*) *The Unwritten Law.* In his *Ethik des reinen Willens* (Ethics of pure will), Cohen refers to the uncritical metaphysical prejudice that presents the foundations of ethics as natural law, as a "law in our bones."[7] Despite Cohen's recognition of the unwritten law as the foundation of any positive legislation, including that which in Jewish tradition is called revelation, he views the tradition of natural law with suspicion: like all uncritical metaphysics, the tradition of natural law remains attached to an empirical kind of naturalism, if it does not result in a juridical system in which the written law figures centrally.[8] Cohen's argument, in fact, invokes the association of Maimonides' much-cited discussion of the Noachite laws that so tantalized the modern Jewish Enlightenment.[9] Paradoxically, however, Maimonides' claim that the performance of the Seven Noachite Commandments by a non-Jew, based upon mere individual reasoning, is inferior to their observance based upon the authority of the written law of Moses, seems to find support in Cohen's own systematic, critical philosophy: Cohen demands that ethics, rather than

Jewish law? To be sure, our reservation related to the distinction between ethical judgment and ritual laws of religious worship remains. However, the former doubt weighs even more heavily: is ethics at all compatible with an ethical system based on religious service and on the awe and love of God?

leading us back to the natural, unwritten law, ought to motivate our study of the positive, written law.[10] Even Philo's doctrine of the Unwritten Law has been recently interpreted in this light—its generality and vagueness being contrasted to the "facticity" of the Jewish law in all its minutia.[11]

The Law and the Eucharist: Pauline Polemics and a Kantian Misreading

36. Let us start our discussion with this former doubt. The consensus of present-day Western culture sees in the autonomy of the human mind the main argument against the divine provenance of ethical judgment. This charge should not be taken too seriously, lest it lead one to the conclusion of atheism. As long as we wish to find autonomous ethics compatible with belief in God, it follows that God's relation to ethics can only be viewed as a problem of philosophical methodology. For the sake of the general religious and religio-ethical consciousness, we must not alienate God from ethics. What kind of a God would it be to whom merely nature, and in whom merely nature, would become manifest? Who would not explicitly and primarily heed the distinctions in so-called nature? And if we want to place the human above all beings known to us, it must follow that God would relate to this peculiar human nature in a particular way. [For Cohen's citations of Goethe in this and the following paragraphs, see Wiedebach's forthcoming critical edition.]

(*See 35.*) *Living under the "Yoke of the Law."* This polemic as Cohen understands it is predominantly reflected in Paul's Epistles to the Romans and Galatians.[12] The reception of Paul's criticism of a life under the "yoke of the Law" finds its traditional Protestant formulation in Luther's polemic of "pharisaic self-justification versus divine grace," a polemic whose anti-Jewish attitude is still reflected in some recent Lutheran commentaries.[13] Daniel Boyarin's *A Radical Jew: Paul and the Politics of Identity,* to the contrary, presents Paul's critique of the Law from a Jewish perspective, interpreting Paul as a Jewish cultural critic who, being "motivated by a hellenistic desire for the One," addresses the problem of "Jewish difference"—the problem of discrimination in the tradition of Jewish law.[14]

The sacramental rite of the Eucharist exceeds the danger of legal ritualism. We find Cohen's critique of the Eucharist in his

Religion of Reason: Out of the Sources of Judaism.[15] Paul's rejection of Jewish law—especially as it predicts Lutheran readings—not only targets so-called ritualistic law but rather aims at the very principle of lawfulness itself, and therewith fore and foremost at the principle of the *Sittengesetz* or moral law. "Lutheran" Paul rejects both, proclaiming Jesus to be the vicarious performer of that same law whose applicability to the Christian believer is suspended. The Law is fulfilled; the fulfillment, however, is being allocated exclusively to the realm of the divine. In other words, Christianity imposes upon Jesus the vicarious observance of the Law, and thus absolves the individual believer from that very obligation.

Cohen concludes that the one who absolves the believer in this way from the yoke of the Law by keeping it himself, acts, as a sacrifice for the sake of the Law, on God's behest. Such divinely ordained human sacrifice, however, cannot be reconciled with the Law in the first place. Jewish law, in the name of divine volition, abolished human sacrifice long ago—an abolition acclaimed by both Christians and Jews as a forward step in the evolution of humanitarian values. Ironically, divine will is resorted to by Christian tradition to propagate human sacrifice in order to abolish the applicability of that very Law. Cohen overtly alludes to the circumstance that Christianity, in its attempt to absolve its adherents from the Law, slides back into an affirmation of human sacrifice, transferred to the divine realm. The Eucharist seems then to suggest precisely that "man ingests God," signifying God's self-abandonment for the sake of man.[16] Even when interpreting the Old Covenant as a christological adumbration (Jeremiah 31:30–33), Christian tradition, in principle, recognizes the validity of Hebrew Scriptures. The Divine Law therefore cannot simply be dispensed with. It is transferred vicariously to God himself who atones for the absolution of the individual with the sacrifice of the only human being who could truly keep the Law.

The difference between Judaism and Christianity, according to Cohen, does not lie in their respective teachings about "the divine gift of Grace,"[17] as Lutheran tradition teaches, but in the question of who bears the responsibility for the commitment to the ethical commandment. Jews have traditionally maintained that they themselves are responsible for keeping that commitment, and the question of divine grace is thereby kept separate from the question whether or not someone actually keeps the Law to its letter. According to oral tradition, there can be no account of who in his pursuit of the Divine Law is deserving or nondeserving of divine grace, as grace, or rather "God's lovingkindness" *(chessed),* is precisely defined as that gift which comes utterly unexpected and undeserved.[18] Therefore, Cohen says with respect to Jewish tradition, "No special sacrificial arrangements involving God are necessary for the forgiveness of sin."[19]

The doctrine of vicarious fulfillment of the Law through the Son of God seems to suggest precisely what was rejected in Jewish oral tradition—namely, that there is a need for someone to be faultless in keeping with divine will in order to function as mediator of divine grace. According to Cohen, it is in the Lutheran-Pauline context that Divine Grace is predicated upon the performance of the Law—if only in form of the vicarious consummation of the Law through Christ. Cohen's interpretation of Law and Grace turns the traditional Christian reading of Paul's critique of the Law radically upon its head, invoking the argument concerning the undeserved nature of divine grace in the name of Jewish tradition against the core of Christian worship—the Eucharist.

The entire philosophy of Kant, of course, maintains the validity of moral Law in its legal function. Kant, according to Cohen, remains oblivious to the fact that his own upholding of the idea of lawfulness in the domain of practical reason clashes with Kant's own uncritical adoption of the Pauline-Lutheran polemic against Jewish law.

> God commands man, and man of his own free will takes upon himself the "yoke of the Law." The law remains a yoke. Even according to Kant's teaching, man does not voluntarily commit himself to the moral law, but has to subjugate himself to duty.[20]

Kant's misreading of Jewish law as an authoritarian system superimposed upon a passive, heteronomous individual, according to Cohen, has been sadly influential, as Kant's judgment was central in molding modern Western thought and culture. Rosenzweig in his introduction to Cohen's *Jüdische Schriften* indicates the loss of an important essay by Cohen criticizing Kant's uncritical adoption of Protestant prejudices against Judaism as a heteronomous religion.[21]

The Good God Is Impotent: Pantheism's Complaint

37. Nevertheless we wonder: what place is occupied by the autonomy of human reason, if we admit that its most precious achievement, the validity of ethics, is somehow predicated upon God? This question remains valid even if God were to function only as the

(*See 37.*) *Pantheism always succeeds in stigmatizing the transcendent God as an alien God.* Pantheism—advocating the idea that God pervades all Being—stigmatizes the transcendent God as impotent, claiming that such a God remains alienated from human

guarantor of ethics warranting its creative potentiality and perpetual validity in the face of all doubt. It is this crevice in our contemplation that at all times provides the entrance for pantheism: as we ponder the question of how God and the world should be related, pantheism always succeeds in stigmatizing the transcendent God as an alien God whose effect is only extraneous—although he is actually the innermost moving cause—as pantheism then proclaims. However, if we were to accept pantheism's notion of an immanent relationship between God and the world, we would have to conclude that there is simply no God at all; since God would then not only pervade the world, but lose himself in it, disintegrating and vanishing altogether. Dispense with ethics and God's intimate involvement with it, and the concept of God forfeits any claim to validity and meaning. However, we can avert this impasse: the autonomy of human reason is neither annihilated, nor even threatened, by the linkage between God and ethics. Monotheism has always absorbed pantheism to a certain extent, in order to save and preserve the autonomy of human reason despite the divine authorship of ethics.

beings since God's very transcendence allegedly does not allow for any relationship with the world. The philosophical position of such pantheism is reflected in the young Hegel's critique of Kant. According to Hegel, Kant's postulate of the transcendent God who guarantees justice in the moral world is merely an object of subjective faith; God remains alienated from history, and as such powerless and unredeemed.[22]

The defenders of dualist theology—such as Marcion and the Gnostics—on the other hand, convert the pantheist critique into positive doctrine. There is the truly good God, who does not mix with matters of the world; and then the Creator-God, the Jewish God, who due to his entanglement and concern with the world assumes the position of the evil demiurgus.[23] Steven Schwarzschild disqualifies both interpretations—that of pantheism as well as that of a radical dualism—as alien to the volitional character of Jewish thinking. Both interpretations visualize a transcendental Infinite in *spatial* terms rather defining it in terms of ethical volition, and therewith as an infinite obligation, as prevalent in the Jewish and neo-Kantian traditions.[24]

Dispense with ethics, and the concept of God forfeits any claim.

In his *Religion of Reason,* Cohen writes:

> There is no distinction in the Jewish consciousness between religion and ethics. Only where pantheism undermines the modern subconsciousness, skepticism with regard to the so-called existence of God is

entertained, and one then tries to recover at least moral teaching from an insolvent Judaism. This recovery is not even sufficient for the popular mind; for the latter, also, is affected by the pantheistic malaise. . . . Only pantheism is responsible for the fact that religion has crept into hiding behind moral teachings.[25]

Thus, ethics is anchored in the concept of the one, unique God, whereas pantheism leaves us with mere morality—expedient social behavior. Although Cohen later introduces a fundamental distinction between religion and ethics, this distinction does not affect his rejection of pantheism, developed prominently in his critique of Spinoza.[26]

The Doctrine of Free Will

38. The concept of free will serves to safeguard against reaching this impasse. This indeterminacy may be felt as a contradiction, or may even be challenged altogether. [Cohen has reference to the *Mutakallimun,* some of whom in their attempt to avoid the pitfalls of pantheism and to preserve the unimpaired autonomy of divine will, went so far as to deny human free will altogether. Wolfson 1976a, 605–12; Guttmann 1882, 133.] We are bound to search for a yet more fundamental principle warranting our assumption of freedom of will, a substratum without which the freedom of human volition would amount to a mere shallow thesis, denuded of any pristine vigor. Freedom of will always presupposes freedom of reason as its vital ground and premise. The philosophy of religion has always championed freedom of will in order to safeguard the exercise of reason. Hence, God can no more come into conflict with autonomous ethics than with human rationality altogether. If we call into question

(*See 38.*) *On free will.* Cohen claims that even the traditional presuppositions of medieval Jewish philosophy preserve autonomy of ethical will in the midst of their metaphysical constructions. Divine knowledge and divine will, according to the medieval theory of attributes, are to be identical so as to exclude plurality from the essence of God. Attributes of God's will, however, translate into "attributes of action," which, in turn, become ethical paradigms for human emulation: "As God is compassionate and gracious, you ought to be compassionate and gracious."[27] Emulation of God's actional attributes—"lovingkindness, righteousness, and judgment"[28]—is to be postulated as an act of free will in order to assume any meaning at all. A midrashic tradition insists that the Torah was given neither to animals, nor to angels, but rather to human beings who are uniquely capable, as well as fallible, of exercising free will and rational judgment.[29] Both

the compatibility of God's omniscience with human ethical autonomy, we may as well doubt the validity of cognitive reasoning, of scientific thinking, and of the methodical nature and resourcefulness of logic. Even with regard to these supreme achievements of rational activity, we could have assumed that God directly controls our rational judgments, inferences, and demonstrations. [Descartes 1986, 15, on *Deus malignus.*] If, however, we are to believe that divine omniscience and omnipotence do not restrict the diversity and uniform method of the human cognitive process, why should we then assume an embarrassing conflict between these divine characteristics and the autonomous methodology and cogent purposefulness of human ethics?

39. In this context, all classical philosophers of Judaism refer to Job (32:8): "But truly, it is spirit in man, the breath of Shaddai gives them reason" (אכן רוח היא באנוש ונשמת שדי תבינם). Abraham ibn Daud interprets

Cohen and Maimonides emphasize that without this fundamental human constitution of free volition, predicated upon an autonomous way of thinking, the commandment of knowing and loving God would be void of any significance.[30]

> If God had decreed that a person should be either righteous or wicked, or if there were some force inherent in his nature which irresistibly drew him to a particular course. . . . What room would there be for the whole of the Torah?[31]

thus: "The 'spirit' refers to the human mind, the breath of 'Shaddai' to the spirit of holiness" (Ibn Daud 1919, 58; רוח היא באנוש השכל האנושי ונשמת שדי תבינם רוח הקדש). [See also ibn Daud 1986, 143a, 160. *RoR* 87; *RdV* 101; also *JS* 3:176–96, esp. 180. Classical readings of Job 32:8 corroborate Cohen's reading: Midrash Tankhuma 1964, Mikkets 9; Saadya 1970, 20, on Job 32:8; 1976, 244.]

The Concept of Correlation: God Is Other to the World

40. The correlation between God and man in ethical reason constitutes the pantheistic element within monotheism. This ethical motif of pantheism did not escape the attention of Maimonides; he adopted it in spite of his basic aversion to intuitionism and mysticism. He has no objection to accepting the unity of reason,

(*See 40.*) *The correlation between God and man.* I am introducing the concept of correlation at this point as a referent for the indeterminate "*das ist der Pantheismus im Monotheismus*" in Cohen's text, interpreting and specifying "*das ist*" as the correlation of God and man in ethical cognition, in the cognition of the Good, of lov-

divine and human. [*Guide* 1:1, 23.] On the contrary, this unity lays the foundation for his theory of prophecy. [*Guide* 2: 7–14 32–48, 360–412; Maimonides 1992a, 143, 206–8.] Hence, the assertion of the autonomy of the human mind could not lead him astray in his proclamation of ethics as a way of serving God, or rather, as the one and only way of serving God.

ingkindness, and of justice. In *Religion of Reason* Cohen says, "We establish the correlation of man and God upon the theoretical grounds of reason. . . . Job expresses this relation even more specifically: 'But truly, it is spirit in man.'" Cohen holds that the transcendence of God "precludes the immanence of man and God. God's transcendence, however, includes the immanence implied in the *relationship* between God and man."[32] Ethical cognition, therefore, "does not signify identity, but rather correlation; the concept of correlation indicates 'identity' inasmuch as 'correlation' signifies 'cognition': the serpent calls it 'identity'; our philosophical language coined the term 'correlation.'"[33]

Cohen employs the term *correlation* consistently throughout his philosophical writings. It is in this essay about Maimonides' ethics, however, where Cohen specifically introduces and develops the idea of the ethical correlation between God and man, claiming that Maimonides' interpretation of divine attributes provides the theoretical grounds for such a concept.[34] Cohen works his idea of correlation carefully through the various stages of Maimonides' theory of knowing and emulating God, all the while drawing upon his own logic of origin, and thus maintaining an essential linkage between his reading of Jewish sources and his philosophical method.[35]

Ethical reasoning constitutes the pantheistic element within monotheism. Cohen admits that there is a pantheistic element in the idea of correlation. We may understand this claim with reference to Cohen's logic of origin which provides us with a theory of relativity for Maimonides' ethics. In this theory of relativity, God and human beings constitute relational positions in a logically immanent correlation, a correlation constituted by the *accessibility* of the divine commandment to human understanding:

> Thus reason lies at the root of the content of revelation. And no objection should be raised against this proposition, since the correlation of God and man, this correlation of the divine vis-à-vis the human spirit, necessarily entails a kind of identity of logical reasoning.[36]

However, God's transcendence is posited as a limit-concept exercising a critical function on any given socio-political context: Cohen's concept of *Deus necnon natura* (God is other to the world) demands *tikkun olam* (a mending of the world).[37] God's postulated otherness invokes an ever-critical attitude with respect to human reality. In order to maintain this critical perspective, Cohen contrasts his concept of God to all forms of pantheism: Judaism proclaims the *correlation* of God and man, whereas pantheism proclaims their identity.[38] (This correlation is "immanent" only in the sense that its own imperative nature must be advocated by means of ethical reasoning.) The concept of the transcendent God, according to Cohen, is not "given" to human consciousness (*gegeben*), but rather postulated by reason itself as a task (*aufgegeben*).[39]

The unity lays the foundation for his theory of prophecy. According to Maimonides, such unity of reason divine and human is realized de facto only by Moses who represents the highest form of knowing God, and whose prophetic knowledge therefore constitutes the authoritative teaching, the Torah.[40] Cohen's association of Maimonides' concept of Mosaic prophecy with lawfulness, ethics, and the Good provides the grounds for Maimonides' (otherwise triumphalist) halakhic claim that all humans are bound to acknowledge Mosaic tradition as the authoritative source of ethical conduct.[41] For the intellectually uninitiated, so Maimonides maintains, knowing God is therefore rightfully termed *mekkubaloth* (traditional knowledge).[42] Moses himself, the epitome of human perfection, knows God in a sovereign way, independent of the dictates from worldly, sensory images.[43] In this way Moses' sovereignty constitutes a paradigm for individual emulation, appealing to the initiated, whose rational capacity provides the grounds for such autonomous pursuit of divine wisdom.[44]

Ethics as the only and ultimate purpose of divine serivce. I find it important to remind the reader—even at the expense of repetitiousness—that Cohen's definition of ethics does not refer to any kind of practical morality but rather to the cognitive, normative interrelation of ideality and reality, an interrelation which is theologically termed Walking in God's Ways, or, more generally, *Imitatio Dei.* Ethics constitutes an epistemological function rather than a practical guide for moral action. According to Cohen, Maimonides defines the Torah and Jewish law through their *ethical* function insofar as they are instrumental in the ultimate human pursuit of Knowing God, a knowledge that translates into Walking in His Ways. For Maimonides, this knowing is bound up with a theoretical understanding of divine negative and actional attributes.[45]

Saadya on *Sikhlioth* and *Shim'ioth:* A Dichotomy in Legal Thinking

41. Early on, Saadya had made a fundamental distinction between the laws of the Torah: Some are based on rational truths (שכליות) while others require one to listen and obey (שמעיות). A tendency toward such a differentiation between the commandments can be detected already in the Talmud [Sifra on Leviticus 18:4; TB Yoma 67b; Numbers 19:2 and midrashic parallels; Heinemann 1993, 1:22–35]; and even though such a classification is not systematically developed there, the Sages made no attempt to homogenize these differences. Had they so attempted, they would not have singled out the tractate of Avoth as the compendium for ethical guidance.

(*See 41.*) *Radical commandments and those of obedience. Sikhlioth* (rational commandments) and *shim'ioth* (traditional commandments) are central to medieval Jewish thought and its systematic critique of Jewish tradition. Both terms are derived from the *Kalam,* and were introduced into Hebrew by the Tibbon family in their translations of Jewish philosophical works written in Judeo-Arabic. The term *sikhlioth* refers to rational laws whereas the term *shim'ioth* is derived from the Hebrew root **shm',* which in turn, has a threefold meaning—to perceive sound acoustically; to understand the meaning of a sound; and to accept an utterance as binding, to commit oneself to what is being signified.[46] The medieval term *shim'ioth* can accordingly have two connotations—to be informed by a voice, and to comply out of discipline.[47] The different readings and interpretations of the term *shim'ioth* are manifest in the variant translations into English, revealing the hermeneutical attitude of the respective translator.[48]

Cohen constructs an affinity between Saadya's distinction of *sikhlioth* and *shim'ioth,* on the one hand, and Maimonides' rationalization of the divine teaching (*ta'ame ha-mitsvoth*) on the other. Maimonides does express a distinction between those commandments that are spontaneously amenable to reason (such as the injunctions against murder and theft) and those whose rationale is hidden from human cognition (such as the injunction against wearing linen and wool woven together, or of consuming any combinations of meat and milk).[49] Maimonides insists, however, upon the *unity* of the entire halakhic corpus: "All the Laws have a rationale, though we ignore the rationale of some of them.[50]

Thus Maimonides himself does not employ the terminological distinction between *sikhlioth* and *shim'ioth.* He actually rejects this distinction, implicitly referring to

Saadya, when claiming that "some of our later sages, who were infected with the unsound principles of the *Mutakallimun,* called these [commandments amenable to reason] rational commandments [*sikhlioth*]."[51] Instead, he adheres to the biblical distinction between *chukkim* and *mishpatim* (Deuteronomy 4:8) or between *chukkim* and *mitsvoth*—a distinction Cohen explicitly adopts and endorses: "Those commandments whose purpose is clear to the multitude are called *mishpatim,* and those whose purpose is not clear to the multitude are called *chukkim.*"[52] In this sense, Maimonides classifies the entire group of ethical laws (*mishpatim*) as "social agreements by convention," or "those commandments whose utility is clear to the multitude" (*mefursamoth*).[53] Maimonides holds that only few commandments are truly *muskaloth,* "rational truths derived from reason." The most obvious case of those is the first directive commandment of Maimonides' *Book of Commandments* (Sefer ha-Mitzvot), demanding that all Jews "actively acknowledge that there is God."[54]

All things considered, let us note that Cohen's favorable exposition of Saadya's distinction between *sikhlioth* and *shim'ioth* in this paragraph does not provide us with his ultimate word on the matter, especially since Saadya's distinction indeed defeats the strategy of Cohen's own reading. The distinction between rational and traditional laws does a disservice to Cohen's Platonic reading of Maimonides. The unity of the entire body of law must be assumed in order to argue for the ethical function of the Jewish law. *The sages made no attempt to homogenize these differences.* Cohen induces an *argumentum ex silentium* which cannot be conclusively validated. The Talmud, in fact, cites the distinctions and divisions with regard to various groups of commandments under the names of different authors among the *tannaim* and *amoraim.* It is true that the Sages did not deal systematically with these distinctions, nor did they attempt to homogenize these differences. Cohen concludes that the Talmud, by means of silent consent, endorses a fundamental value-distinction among the commandments.

Ritual Law and Its Abolishment: The Pitfalls of Christian Liberation

42. Jewish tradition for the most part tends to ignore in practice any discrimination between ethical and ritual laws. This tendency may well have been motivated by the need to

(*See 42.*) *"Ritual Law" and its abolishment.* Cohen suggests that religious communities define themselves either by common (pedagogical) practice or by common re-

develop a defense mechanism against other religions which exempted themselves from the bonds of Law, a law which extends its regimentation to every detail of individual and communal modes of living. Yet, by this very act of liberation, they imposed upon themselves a stress of fiducial commitments which reaches far more deeply, imposing an even more burdensome charge. Despite this quandary of fiducial crisis, Christianity took advantage of its increasing political power to persecute Judaism. As a means of self-defense, Judaism saw its vindication in the indiscriminate validation of all laws, ritual and ethical, as the integral whole of Judaism. Christianity had abrogated the laws of the Old Covenant [Jeremiah 31:30–33] by establishing its own ritual in a polemical transformation and reinterpretation of Jewish tradition. Any denigration of the ritual laws on the part of the Jews would have meant recognition of Christian authority, exposing Judaism to its missionary influence. The historical judgment regarding the validity of ritual laws, and regarding Jewish persistence in validating them, seems ill-considered and self-righteous. The power of Christian dogma has proved effective not only with respect to the development of prominent political movements in world history but also by intermingling with cultural developments, not the least of which is philosophical speculation.

ligious dogma. Thus, Jewish tradition establishes specific directives and strictures concerning communal practice, but the range of its hermeneutic activitiy remain unbound by canonic dogma. According to Cohen, Christian freedom from the "yoke of the Law" is attained at the price of a bondage no less heavy than the original one—a new bondage which imposes itself on the individual by the very canonization of religious truth. Rabbinic thinking, on the other hand, allows for multiple ways of interpreting the tradition, as long as such interpretive action relates itself to the literary sources.[55] Cohen claims that Jewish tradition is privileged in that it constitutes a hermeneutical process of infinite creativity, whose very designation as oral tradition indicates the continuous enactment of the "living words of God":

> The "oral teaching" is not a finished product, but rather open-ended, one that always continues to be produced. The book gets sealed; mouth and lips continue to speak.[56]

Cohen's reading draws from the traditional sources:

> These words God spoke unto all your assembly at the mountain out of the midst of the fire, of the cloud, and of the thick cloud, with a great voice—*kol gadol ve lo yassaf.*[57]

Onkelos translates: *kol rav velo passak* (a great voice that did not cease), and Rashi comments: *kolo chazak vekayam le'olam* (for His voice continues to speak forever).

The Equal Validity of All Laws: Communal Ramifications

The emphasis put upon the validity of the entire corpus of rabbinic legislation is to be understood in the context of pressure exerted upon the Jewish diaspora by missionary activities of Christians endowed with political power. Maimonides' "validation of all laws" is by no means indiscriminate; he does distinguish between commandments pertaining to a person's traditional commitment, such as *tsitsith, tefillin, Shabbat,* and those relating to a person's social commitments, such as injunctions against stealing, adultery, groundless hatred, or bearing a grudge.[58] Maimonides, however, nonetheless stresses the equal validity of the entire body of rabbinic legislation. Maimonides interestingly relates the discussion concerning the "equal validity of the entire law" directly to the *hermeneutical* question of the "equal validity and indiscriminate status of all scriptural passages."[59] Both claims, according to Cohen, are directed against Christian canonization of Scripture and its preferential treatment of the most prominent directives of Jewish legislation—such as the Decalogue—at the expense of the validity of the Law—that is, the text—as a whole.

Maimonides himself illustrates the practical and communal ramifications of this debate in a responsum addressing the question of whether to listen to the public reading of the Decalogue while standing or sitting. In this responsum he strictly advises against any special homage to be paid to the Decalogue, opposing the opinions of Saadya and Nachmanides who treat the Decalogue as a central text, following the early Philonic attempt to structure the entire body of commandments as ramifications of the Decalogue.[60] Maimonides recalls that the Sages had abrogated an early custom during the times of the Second Temple to recite the Decalogue as part of the daily public services precisely in protest against the Christian preferential treatment of the Decalogue, as this "preferential treatment" epitomized the Pauline abrogation of Jewish law in all its detail.[61] It is in this context that Cohen evaluates the Jewish affirmation of "the indiscriminate validity of all laws as an integral whole of Judaism":

> The [equal validation of the] Jewish Law serves us as a legitimate means towards the isolation of Judaism. . . . Such

> isolation is undoubtedly necessary in order to preserve the undiminished [messianic] function of Jewish monotheism over against the two other forms of monotheism [Christianity and Islam].[62]

God Is Dying: The Bequeathing of a Testament

Christianity had abrogated the laws of the "old covenant". In Jeremiah we read, "Behold, a time is coming—declares the Lord—when I will make a new covenant [*berith*] with the House of Israel and the House of Judah."[63] The Septuagint translation of this passage applies the Greek term διαθηκη (testament, disposition of property by will) to the Hebrew term *berith,* which, in turn, signifies a contract between living partners.[64] Given the central significance that the concept of berith assumes in Jewish tradition and in Jewish identity, the etymological superimposition of the Greek term διαθηκη upon the Hebrew term *berith* plays a central role in the hermeneutical strategy of revoking the authority of the Old Covenant by reference to a greater authority, namely that of the διαθηκη (testament) of God himself. It takes the death of God to bequeath mankind a new formulation of God's will: invoking the διαθηκη of the dying God establishes the christological claim that in Christ the Law is no longer binding.[65]

Signs and Holy Objects: The Polemic against the Eucharist Continues

After having abrogated the Law, Christianity established its own ritual in a polemical transformation of Jewish tradition. Cohen turns the Pauline polemic against Christianity itself, to the effect that Paul's critique of Jewish statutory observance becomes a Jewish polemic against Christian dogma and the Eucharist.[66] At the same time, Cohen takes the Pauline critique seriously even in his own reading of Jewish sources. He deconstructs any dogmatic, statutory claim in Jewish tradition in favor of an ethical reading predicated upon the concept of purity—God's purity demands that there be no sacralization of immanence, of worldly things or sacred objects. Cohen's reading of Maimonides thus emphasizes the symbolic and educational character of the Halakhah, claiming that there are no holy objects in Judaism, and that not even a commandment can be legitimately called holy: each rather serves as a sign (*oth*) attesting to a person's relationship to the divine. Thus, *tefillin* or *mezuzah* are not holy objects, but rather reminders of a prior commitment.

> The entire ritual . . . presents itself explicitly as a system of symbols, designated by the technical term "sign" [*oth*] or "reminder" [*zikkaron*], imprinting the ritual with the seal of spirituality.[67]

Abraham Heschel echoes the tenor of Cohen's reading when maintaining that

> Things may be *instruments,* never *objects of worship. Matza* [unleavened bread, eaten on Passover], the *shofar* . . . , the *lulav* . . . are not things to be . . . paid homage to, but things to be used. Being instruments they have symbolic meaning, but they are not primarily regarded as [holy] symbols in themselves [emphasis added].[68]

Heschel, allying himself with Cohen's polemic, contrasts the functional character of religious objects in the Jewish tradition with the ontological character of religious objects in Christian theology, in which the symbol itself—the Cross, or the Grave—turns into a holy object of adoration and reverence. (Heschel's critique aims at Christianity, but the adoration of holy objects—holy stones and holy graves—is, of course, abundant among Jews.) In contrast, Jewish tradition, according to Cohen and Heschel, does not recognize the inherent holiness of religious objects. As such, the Jewish Pessach meal, the eating of the Pascal lamb together with bitter herbs and unleavened bread, and the drinking of four cups of wine,[69] signify personal freedom from bondage—exodus from Egypt—but not holy ritual. Cohen's polemic against the Eucharist charges the christological interpretation with turning these objects—wine, bread, and lamb—into "sacramental, ritual objects." Jesus *is* the Pascal lamb. Christ *becomes* the sacramental object represented in the transubstantiated host as *hoc est corpus meum,* and *hoc est sanguine meo.*

Cohen's critique fails to take into consideration the widely divergent opinions among Catholics, Lutherans, and Calvinists concerning the question whether the Eucharist ought to be understood ontologically or, in fact, rather symbolically.[70] (And we may observe that Cohen's polemical typology of Judaism and Christianity, indeed, amounts to a triumphalist inversion of the iconographic image of Church and Synagogue—one holding the light of truth, the other blindfolded; one representing a revolutionary mode of thinking predicated upon openness for alterity, the other characterized by the incarnation of what is holy, and by proclamations of salvational history, leading toward quietism and the political justification of the status quo.) But let us suggest that Cohen's anti-Christian polemic is primarily concerned with the dangers of totalitarian thought patterns. Totalitarian thinking invokes the holiness of things, proclaims holy history, works with fundamental ontologies. It is such an enchantment with being—whether in Christian, Jewish, or Greek terms—against which Cohen's critique is foremostly directed.

Axiological Distinctions in the Torah

43. In the light of this strenuous situation it is a sign of audacity and integrity of religious conviction that throughout the entire Middle Ages classical Jewish philosophy unchallenged and unabatedly advocated to make axiological distinctions within the content of Torah. [*RoR* 351–52; *RdV* 408–9; Kaufmann 1877, 105, 109; Saadya 1976, 1–3, 138–47; Judah ha-Levi 1997, 7, 11; ibn Daud 1986, 214a, 263; Bahya 1973, 85–108.] No one stated this with such lucidity, firmness, and cogency as the man who in his profound insight detected the grave danger latent within the philosophical speculations of ibn Gabirol despite all the goodwill and admiration he felt toward him personally. [Ibn Daud 1967, 100, 102.] Abraham ibn Daud did not become intoxicated by the pantheistic concept of prime matter nor by any of the other seductive charms of neo-Platonic fantasy. Proceeding carefully and thoroughly as he is wont to pursue his studies in logic and metaphysics, he proves himself as lucid a rationalist in ethics, and consequently also in dogmatics. He crowns his *Exalted Faith* with the proposition—not just as an aside, but in its full significance cited, demonstrated, and reiterated: "The various parts of the Torah are not all of equal value" (חלקי התורה . . . אינם כולם שווים במעלה Ibn Daud 1919, 102.); [1986, 214b, 263–64; also *RoR* 351–52; *RdV* 409; *RoR* 470.] The Torah is rooted in faith. [Ibn Daud 1986, 214a, 257 (see translator's note here), 263.] Next in importance to the commandments regarding faith are customs of universal convention, adopted by all people or

(*See 43.*) *Classical Jewish philosophy tends to make axiological distinctions within the Torah.* There are multiple ways—terminologically and conceptually—in which medieval Jewish thinkers distinguish between socially motivated or rational commandments on the one hand, and divinely revealed or traditional ones on the other. Throughout, Cohen interprets *sikhlioth* and *shim'ioth* as rational commandments, not versus traditional or disciplinary ones. He studiously avoids the attribute revealed (*offenbart*) with reference to *shim'ioth* in order not to suggest an antithesis between ethical reasoning and revelation, the unity of which provides the conceptual basis for his entire reading of Jewish literature.

approximated by them. "However, the commandments that are not rationally grounded, are of a very inferior grade in comparison to those rooted in faith" (מדרגתם מן הדת מדרגה חלושה מאוד Ibn Daud 1909, 102.); [1986, 214b, 263–64; *RoR* 351–52; *RdV* 409.] Prior to this statement, he bases his evaluation of rational commandments on the historical conventional agreement [*consensus gentium*] among all peoples concerning these commandments. [Ibn Daud 1986, 214a, 263; 1919, 102.] Hence he contends that the rational commandments are equivalent to the conventional ones (שכליות = מפורסמות). Their distinction is merely a terminological variation between logic and metaphysics. [According to ibn Daud 1986, 172 a–b, 204: "The logicians call the rational commandments *'mefursamoth,'* the *Mutakallimun* call them *'sikhlioth.'*"] Those commandments that are universally accepted he praises: "The dogmas of universal concurrence unite the hearts divided, they constitute the conventional agreement among the various nations. They unite people who otherwise differ in their professions of faith, and who contradict each other in their religious traditions, accusing one another of lying, and holding each other in contempt; the dogmas of universal concurrence, in turn, unite their reasoning as if incorporated within one state, within one body." [Ibn Daud 1986, 172b–73a, 204–5.] Therefore these universally accepted, and hence rational dogmas are not subject to any change or moderation, or to any doubt. [Ibn Daud 1986, 173b, 205. Reminiscent of Maimonides 1987a, chap. 8.] This then is the difference between the rational precepts and those that demand compliance and obedience (שמיעות = מקובלות). [Ibn Daud 1919, 75. See Guttmann 1879, 234.]

Ibn Daud: A Purist Critique of Neo-Platonism

"Ibn Daud did not become intoxicated by the pantheistic concept of prime matter, nor by any of the other seductive charms of neo-Platonic fantasy." Whereas ibn Gabirol at times identifies the concept of υλη (*hule* or prime matter) with divine will, jeopardizing the transcendental character of God's will as conceived by most medieval Jewish thinkers, Maimonides' older contemporary, Abraham ibn Daud, explicitly refutes any such neo-Platonic theory of emanation.[71] Neo-Platonic cosmology invokes *hule* as that stuff of prime matter out of which everything automatically evolves or emanates. The rabbinic Sages object to such a thesis: "Those are the heretics who say that the universe is an *automaton*."[72] The theory of "cosmos as *automaton*" is itself an Epicurean teaching according to which the world moves automatically, uncared for by the gods. Maimonides himself explicitly criticizes all cosmogenic theo-

ries which involve the existence of *prima materia* (υλη).[73]

According to Cohen, critical medieval Jewish thinkers reject neo-Platonic cosmology based upon their radical objection to divine immanence. As such, their critique reaches far beyond the question of cosmology. Neo-Platonic cosmology in its theory of divine overflow reiterates the "automatic" transition between domains—divine and worldly—indicated by the hylic flow of the divine. Therefore Cohen must reject neo-Platonic theories of immanence on both theological and ethical grounds, even though Maimonides at times invokes that terminology: "Know that the true reality and quiddity of prophecy consists in its being an overflow overflowing from God."[74]

Shim'ioth and *Consensus Gentium:* Ibn Daud on Local and Universal Ways of Reasoning

The Torah is rooted in faith. According to ibn Daud, the Torah includes various kinds of commandments—commandments that are not of equal value. Ibn Daud stresses that "the basic principle and pillar of the Torah is faith."[75] Accordingly, the most important parts of the Torah are those explicating Israel's faith, followed by those that teach ethical virtues.[76] Ibn Daud's classification of commandments formally adopts the classical Aristotelian exposition of ethics, translating its definitions of supreme happiness, ethical virtues, economics, and politics into a traditional Jewish context.[77] By reference to ibn Daud's saying that "the parts of the Torah are not all of equal value," Cohen constructs an affinity between ibn Daud and Maimonides' ethical rationalism, dislocating ibn Daud from his Aristotelian context, and positioning him within a Platonic tradition. In this way Cohen presents ibn Daud as "the most important and most intimately related predecessor of Maimonides' ethical rationalism."

"*The commandments that are not rationally grounded are of a very inferior grade.*" Cohen's reading of those commandments that are "not rationally grounded" is guided by Weil's translation, contrasting *shim'ioth* with those commandments which are "rooted in faith." Weil's translation creates an antithesis between the nonrational, merely traditional, positivistic commandments, on the one hand, and the laws relating to the foundations of Jewish faith, on the other.[78] Such an antithesis, however, might not be the best reading of ibn Daud's text. According to one contemporary interpretation, ibn Daud seems to be interested in the integrity of the Torah as a whole when suggesting that even those laws referred to as *shim'ioth* actually strengthen the Jewish faith:

> That the reasons for them [for the commandments of sacrifices, for example] are feeble does not mean that they are unreasonable—on the contrary, Ibn Daud lists four reasons for them. [Rather, a feeble reason means] that the reasons [for these commandments] are psychologically less compelling and less self-evident to people outside of the faith community of Israel.[79]

The reasons for *shim'ioth* may seem feeble because their rationale is self-evident merely to the legacy of Israel. Cohen, however, is hard put to accept such a claim, as Israel represents to him the avant-garde of universal ethical reasoning. Cohen obviously sees no danger or temptation in a totality exercised by the demands of ethical reasoning. He can therefore sympathize with ibn Daud's linking ethics to those commandments whose rationale is obvious to all, even though such a reading presents ethics in a non-Platonic fashion—namely as *consensus gentium.*

Rational commandments are equivalent to the conventional ones. The medieval Jewish term for *consensus gentium* is *mefursamoth.*[80] Ibn Daud, in particular, defines the *consensus gentium* as those norms of conduct or commandments concerning which "all the nations agree."[81] Cohen's subsequent equation of the *consensus gentium* or *mefursamoth* with rational laws (*sikhlioth*) results from a conflation of two passages in *The Exalted Faith.*[82] In one place, ibn Daud reports that some religious rules are, in the language of the logicians, "generally acknowledged" (*mefursamoth*). On the other hand, the *Mutakallimun* (literally, masters of science) call those rules rational laws (*sikhlioth*), such as

> righteousness is good, injustice is evil, it is good to praise him who is good, and it is improper to liken oneself to one's protector.[83]

From here we learn that "that which is accepted by all" is "rational." In contrast, there are those directives that

> in the language of the logicians, are called "traditions" [*mekubaloth*], or, in the language of the *Mutakallimun,* "revealed" [*shim'ioth*]. Examples include the observance of Shabbat and the prohibition against eating pork.[84]

Since ibn Daud attributes a "feeble rationale" to these laws,[85] Cohen contrasts them with rational laws, those laws concerning which there is universal agreement.

An agreement by convention that is postulated in terms of universal ethics is, of course, a completely non-Platonic argument. *Consensus gentium* means an opinion generally held, a view expressing public opinion.[86] The Aristotelian term for an opinion generally held is endoxa (ενδοξα), hence dogma.[87] Aristotle himself contrasts opinionated knowledge with scientific or true knowledge. The latter represents the pursuit of human perfection, which both Plato and Aristotle refer to as *episteme* (επιστημη), hence epistemology.[88] Cohen's entire critique of the Aristotelian readings of Maimonides, of course, turns precisely on the point that ethical knowledge is not just an opinion generally held, a prudence based upon general consent, as Aristotle is wont to claim. Ethics, rather, is knowledge of the highest kind. In his *Ethik des reinen Willens,* Cohen subsequently criticizes any ethics based upon general consensus; such an ethics is as arbitrary as the caprice of nature itself. Natural law is unreliable and opportunistic; ethical knowledge is not found in our bones.[89] Cohen's reading of ibn Daud's terminological equation—"ethical, rational laws" are those of "universal agreement"—accounts, however, for Maimonides' explicit adoption of Aristotelian terminology when representing the majority of the Ten Commandments as conventional laws, or *mefursamoth.*[90]

---

44. In his distinction among the various commandments of the Torah, ibn Daud finally discusses the archetype of ritual laws, the precepts of sacrifice. [Ibn Daud 1986, 214b–15a, 263–64.] His evaluation of sacrifices invokes the authority of Jeremiah, who in combating sacrificial rites alleges God to proclaim (7:22): "When I delivered your ancestors from Egypt, I did not speak with them or command them concerning holocausts or sacrifice." [See the commentary of Kimchi 1878 on Jeremiah 7:22. Other biblical references have been cited to this effect, such as I Samuel 15:22; Psalms 50:8, 51:17–18; Isaiah 1:11–14; and Micah 6:6–8, all expressly relating God's distaste for sacrifices with His quest for ethics.] In sacrifice, ibn Daud recognizes and assesses the historical and intrinsic cause of all ritualism. [*RoR* 173; *RdV* 200–201; Heinemann 1993, 74. Maimonides points to the educational value of the sacrifices as deterrents against idolatry. *Guide* 3:32, 530, 3:46, 581–82.]

45. In ibn Daud we ought to recognize the most important and most intimately related predecessor of Maimonides. Their mutual aversion to neo-Platonic mysticism demonstrates their congeniality. [Twersky 1980b, 384n. 73, 388n. 80, points to the congeniality of these two thinkers' unbending rationalism.] Maimonides is moved, first and foremost, with the intellectual honesty and boldness with which ibn Daud proceeds against the prejudice of equivalence accorded to all parts of the Torah. It is perhaps for this reason that Maimonides does not quote him. To be sure, Maimonides never becomes articulate on this point. Yet undeniably it serves Maimonides as a propelling principle in all his life's work that one must discriminate axiologically among the various contents of Torah. [Twersky 1980b, 276.] He never enunciates this principle explicitly lest he jeopardize the acceptance of the nonphilosophical part of his extensive systematic contribution to Judaism. [Ha-Am 1905; Leo Strauss 1988.] It is not, as it were, that he lacks the sincerity or lucidity to assert this principle, but he finds a formula that allows him to take productive advantage of it, and yet to avoid the pitfalls of provocative exposition. It was his ambition to present in one uniform corpus the entire scope of the Jewish religion, its political, civil legislation, its institutional and communal regulations, as well as its doctrines on creed and duty. Beginning with the uniqueness and unity of God as his premise, [Maimonides 1984–1996, *Hilkhoth Yesodei haTorah* 1] he sets out to present the multiplicity of laws comprehensibly and plausibly in a rationally structured system. [Twersky 1980b, 254–76.] In light of such a project it would have proven untenable to enunciate the severe principle of nonparity regarding the various parts of the Torah. Yet it stands to reason that his bearing this principle in mind helped him to facilitate the enormous organizational effort of surveying perspicaciously the vast volume of traditional material for his *magnum opus.*

46. Most of all, this principle of rational evaluation concurs with his dogmatics. The rationale of the laws [טעמי המצוות] is his supreme objective. [Heinemann 1993, 79–97; Twersky 1980b, 374–80.] The laws of disciplinary obedience, which are also termed traditional [מקובלות], were slated now to be validated on rational grounds as well. Inasmuch as he posits a rationale for the commandments, he summons them before the tribunal of reason. Maimonides proves to be most intrepid in issuing these summonses. Thus he classifies the dogma of creation not among the rational, but among the traditional dogmas. [*Guide* 2:24, 326–27; 2:16, 293–94.] Maimonides attempts to provide every one of the 613 commandments with a rationale. [*Guide* 3:35–49, 535–613.] In the few cases in which his method fails he expressly assumes personal, subjective shortcomings for it. It is obvious that Maimonides' evaluation of Jewish law is based entirely upon teleological grounds; the purpose of Jewish law derives from reason.

47. Critical reasoning reigns supreme in Maimonides' entire discussion of both individual commandments and their classes; he scrutinizes his sources with methodical exactitude. Reason to Maimonides means not merely the opposite of tradition and revelation. The two or more souls within this gigantic personality unfold before us: he was not just a philosopher of religious enlightenment and of the rationality of ethics, nor only a dialectician and systematizer of talmudic discussions. He was at the same time a pure logician of scientific problems. Therefore he was exceedingly cautious in attributing to reason any claim to truth for which reason lacks the terminological and methodological apparatus. His penetrating mind as a logician and his pure interest in the strictly scientific pursuit of logic defy such attempts. By virtue of the internal coherence of all disciplines within any given system of philosophy, the ethical content of the religious problem reaps the benefit of logical precision.

3

The Good beyond Being

Ethico-Political Intricacies of a Medieval Debate

In this third chapter, Cohen addresses the problem of the Aristotelian terminology in which mainstream medieval Jewish philosophy admittedly couches its ethics. Cohen demonstrates how the mechanical assumptions of Aristotelian cosmology and metaphysics and Aristotle's utilitarian understanding of the good are irreconcilable with Maimonides' theory of knowing God. He thereby provides an "esoteric" reading of Maimonides, in which Aristotelian language is used to disguise the Platonic foundations of Maimonides' theological position. Toward the end of this section, Cohen arrives at the heart of his argument, providing the philosophical grounds for a new formulation of Maimonides' theory concerning God's actional attributes.

Cohen's Founding of a Platonic Jewish Family

48. We had to preface our discussion with these elaborate remarks, in order to establish the grounds for a critical investigation of the thesis which seems to be a guiding principle of Maimonidean ethics: the laws of ethics are not rational laws [שכליות], nor traditional laws, but are to be classified as those of convention, of general agreement (מפורסמות).

49. The generally assumed doctrine—that Maimonides has proven himself in this central point to be an epigone of Aristotle—fails to provide us with viable historical understanding. This assumption seems to have

(*See 49.*) *"The generally assumed doctrine."* Maimonides refers to Aristotle extensively throughout the *Guide.* He clearly adopts Aristotle's metaphysical and scientific terminology and has thus been widely and authoritatively interpreted as an Aristotelian thinker. There is an oblique but authoritative allusion to Aristotle in the introduction to the *Eight Chapters*, and we find a most distinguishing remark on Aristotle in one of Maimonides' letters—"Aristotle's philosophy is the supreme achievement of human thinking."[1] All these factors taken together account for the fact that

ignored how much it deprecates the religious idea and its inherent value for Maimonidean ethics. With due respect to the God of Aristotle, he is truly not the God of Israel. [Cohen alludes here to Judah ha-Levi's classical distinction between the God of the philosophers and the God of Abraham; see *Kuzari* 1964, 4:16, 223. In Pascal and Kierkegaard this distinction attains a radically different meaning; see Kodalle 1988, 309–10.] It is well known, and we will have to investigate this painstakingly, how intimately ethics is related in Maimonides to the doctrine of the unique God, who demands goodness. And ought this not to be sufficiently decisive for the basic question about the cognitive value of ethics? Should the mere mention of the name God, or gods, in Aristotle have been sufficient for Maimonides to have been driven blindly into the arms of this pagan philosopher? We would discredit the peculiar distinctiveness of the concept of God in Jewish monotheism if we were to attribute to it such insignificant influence regarding the fundamental problem of ethics as a science.

50. Let us clarify the respective rationales of both Aristotle and Maimonides for rejecting the strict rationality of ethics. We are already familiar with Aristotle's animosity toward the Platonic idea, toward the idea of the Good. [Aristotle 1945, *NE* 1096a–1097a, 17–25; 1981, *Eudemian Ethics* 1217b, 223–33.] To be sure, Aristotle really ought to have arrived at a different conclusion. We

Aristotelian readings of Maimonides' ethics do prevail in contemporary scholarship. Maimonides' ethics emerges therein as a masterful but philosophically rather uncreative attempt to integrate Aristotelian philosophy with the Jewish sources.[2]

Cohen's innovative interpretation of Maimonides' ethics, on the other hand, situates Maimonides' attitude toward history, Jewish law, the doctrine of creation, and eschatology, as well as social and political theory within a philosophical context committed to weaving the Platonic idea of the Good into the fabric of Jewish tradition. Cohen is the first of a family of modern Jewish thinkers who makes the Platonic concept of the Good beyond Being interact and correspond with the concept of the Jewish God who demands justice and the Good. Cohen's Platonic reading of Maimonides constitutes the beginning of a prominently ethical bent among modern and contemporary Jewish thinkers who continue to read Jew-ish tradition in the light of the Platonic Good and in opposition to any fundamental ontology. Such divergent thinkers as Franz Rosenzweig, Leo Strauss, Steven Schwarzschild, and Emmanuel Levinas develop their own interpretations of Jewish tradition along the very lines of a Platonic reading. The ethical implications of these interpretations, however, have nowhere been as forcefully explicated as in this original text, Cohen's interpretation of Maimonides.

might say that it was precisely his antagonistic argumentation against the Platonic idea that gave him away. If ideas as such possess no validity, then the idea of the Good must also be invalid. If, however, in spite of the invalidity of the idea, a cognition, a metaphysics in the ontological sense, is derived from rational principles, why then is it not possible to validate a metaphysics of ethics—just in order to shun the idea of the Good? Does this rejection not imply the admission that without the idea of the Good there cannot be any metaphysics of ethics?

Aristotle's Ethics—Mere Practical Wisdom

51. The idea of the Good warrants the teleological interrelation between nature and ethics. Due to his principal opposition to the fundamental doctrine of the Good as idea, Aristotle turns into an opponent of ethics as science. Therefore he champions the inferior status of ethics—ethics can only instruct us about what is true "in rough outline" (παχυλως και τυπω). (Aristotle [1945], *NE* 1094b, [1:3, 7].) He denies the cognitive value of ethics, since he rejects the paradigmatic nature of the unique concept of the Good. Moreover, he refuses to recognize the Good as both the uniform purpose of the entire human situation and as an unalterable guiding precept. Furthermore, as a historical empiricist, he admits to only a relative rating of the Good, with respect to the various social classes and professions. We shall come to realize how an apparent exception, which may be assumed for his eudaemonia, only confirms his principal opinion. Aristotle proclaims that ethics does not come to teach "what virtue is, but rather how we may become virtuous." (επει ουν η παρουσα πραγματεια ου θεωριας ενεκα εστιν ωσπερ αι

(*See 51.*) *Aristotle turns into an opponent of ethics as science.* Aristotle divides human knowledge into theoretical and practical wisdom, *episteme* and *phronesis*, a distinction he inherited from Plato. Metaphysics, according to Aristotle, is the highest theoretical science whereas ethics is mere practical wisdom.[3] It is this traditional opposition between theory and practice that is rejected in Cohen's anti-Aristotelian advancement of "ethics as first philosophy," giving way to an ethical epistemology grounded in the original vision of the Good. Levinas picks up this "epistemology of a vision" when he proclaims that "ethics is an optics."[4] Cohen renews and upholds the Platonic claim that ethics itself constitutes a sublime and original form of theoretical wisdom, or *episteme.*[5]

Aristotle admits only a relative rating of the Good. He denies that there is any transcendental function of the concept of the Good.[6] The Good is used as a predicate defining skills that are relative to the utility of an object, or to a person's social class and profession—a good knife, a good business deal, a good musician.[7] In the context of Aristotle's ethics, which is an ethics of practical wisdom concerned exclusively with the performance of practical virtues the significance of the Good consequently refers to questions of prudence and experience only, without leading to any cognition of a higher good.[8]

αλλαι (ου γαρ ιν ειδωμεν τι εστιν η αρετη σκεπτομεθα, αλλ ιν ἀγαθοι γενωμεθα [ἐπει ονδεν ἀν εν οφελος αντης]) αναγ́καιον εστι τα περι τας πραξεις πως πρακτεον αυτας. [Aristotle] (1945), *NE* 1103b, 2:2 [75.]) It would be superfluous to emphasize that this educational consideration should hopefully not come into conflict with Socrates and Plato. Our main concern here, however, is this Aristotelian proclamation: the cognition of the Good does not figure as an objective in ethics, nor does the Good even constitute a cognitive problem. Therefore, when he defines ethical truth as being evidential, which he does not even do consistently, he distinguishes this kind of evidential truth from cognition as such. Hence, he turns ethics into a matter of psychological description and historical development, a sort of knowledge, in which assumption and probability prevail, rather than certainty and demonstration. [Aristotle 1945, *NE* 1141a and *NE* 1094b, 343, 7: "But these conceptions (the virtues of political science) involve much difference of opinion and uncertainty, so that they are sometimes believed to be mere conventions (δοκειν νομω) to have no real existence in the nature of things."]

Against an Ethics of Mere Intentions: Aristotle vs. Kant

Aristotle's ethics teaches how *we may become virtuous.* "For we are not investigating the nature of virtue for the sake of knowing what it is, but in order that we may become good."[9] Character disposition, according to Aristotle, is predicated upon one's actions, which, in turn, are a result of habitual character training. Against Plato, Aristotle claims that "the nature of goodness demands actualization."[10] Aristotle's definition of goodness in terms of its concrete actualization was adopted by Philo, the neo-Platonists, and most mystical traditions, as well as by Patristic and Scholastic literature.[11] Transmitted in similar form by rabbinic tradition, medieval Jewish thinkers have adopted this principle by coining the expression "*michok ha tov lehativ*" (goodness ought to be defined as doing good)."[12]

Cohen, in this case, adopts Aristotle's position. The principle that goodness demands actualization figures prominently in Cohen's own critique of any ethics of pure intentions. In a critical turn against Kant and his claim that "a good will is not good because of what it effects . . . but only because of its volition," and thus against an ethics that values the purity of intentions above all, Cohen defines ethical will as the "translation of will into action."[13] Cohen explicitly credits Aristotle with having emphasized the need for actualizing the Good.[14] But he invokes Aristotle's own concept of goodness for the sake of an even more radical *Platonic* reading in which the Good beyond Being signifies the ideational grounds for human social action.[15] Cohen thus incorporates Aristotle's principle of actualizing the Good into his Platonic reading of Maimonides' epistemology and its emphasis on the emulation of actional, divine attributes.

Aristotle's Cosmogony and the Propagation of Evil

52. Would it behoove Maimonides to accept unreservedly the formulations of Aristotle? Were this the case, the significance of Maimonides' rationalism, which manifests itself in his pursuit of a rationale for the respective commandments, would then be only of historical and anthropological interest. To be sure, Maimonides at times employs such an approach, but this does not represent his main focus. Rather, his basic aspiration, that theology should culminate in ethics, attests to his rationalism; likewise every stage of Maimonides' dogmatics tends toward ethics. [*RoR* 310–11; *RdV* 361.] Maimonides' acceptance of the Aristotelian approach toward ethics would thus undermine his rationalism. Such an ethics would then mainly consist of historical or anthropological clarifications, such as in the case of Maimonides' exposition of the Sabians. [*Guide* 3:29, 514–22, esp. 518.] The difference between the Aristotelian and Maimonidean approach lies consistently, and in every respect, in the significance of Maimonides' concept of God for his theology and also, as must be assumed, for his ethics.

(*See 52.*) *Would it behoove Maimonides?* Whereas Maimonides seems to follow Aristotle unreservedly in all matters of the natural sciences, his understanding of divine wisdom employs a transcendental Platonic method. This is true not only with respect to the doctrine of creation but in particular concerning Maimonides' ethical and educational rationalization of Jewish law. "Everything that Aristotle has said about all that exists in the sublunar, physical world is indubitably correct," Maimonides writes. However, "what [Aristotle] says about . . . some of the opinions regarding the divine . . . contain[s] grave incongruities and perversities that . . . propagate evil, and that he cannot demonstrate."[16] Although the context of the quoted passage refers specifically to the question of creation, Maimonides formulates his reservations toward Aristotle's cosmogony on *ethical* grounds. He claims that any theoretical speculation about the origin of the world, which ignores the question of the world's *purpose*, amounts to "propagating evil."[17]

On Historical Method: Pagan Practices and the Pedagogy of Torah

Maimonides, as in the case of the Sabians, sometimes employs a historico-anthropological approach toward Jewish law. Maimonides takes the Sabian practices of idolatry as his historical point of departure for mapping out a universal rationalization of all of the commandments:

> The meaning of many of the laws became clear to me . . . through my study of the doctrines, . . . practices, and cult of the Sabians. . . . The knowledge of these opinions and practices is a very important chapter in the exposition of the reasons for the commandments.[18]

Maimonides claims to have studied every literary work available on astrology and other pagan worship, and that these historical studies have in fact helped him to gain a clearer understanding of the commandments and their causes.[19] According to Cohen, Maimonides adopts this historical method merely in order to demonstrate the *pedagogical* rationale of his own reading of Torah, which is in direct opposition to pagan practices.

> The Torah may be viewed historically as a pedagogic-therapeutic instrument which uses a shaded spectrum of devices to uproot all vested or vestigial pagan beliefs and practices. The Torah consciously and energetically confronted Sabianism and with wisdom and cunning eradicated it.[20]

For Cohen, pagan practice signifies the very epitome of evil, exemplified by the sacrifice of children to Moloch, the local Ammonite god (Leviticus 18:21). The eradication of idolatrous practices, to Cohen, amounts to the eradication of evil:

> Idol-worship must be eradicated by all means . . . there ought to be no pity and no consideration when it comes to pagan practices. True worship of God uproots all quietism.[21]

An Unbridgeable Gap: Maimonides and Aristotle on Knowing God

The difference between the Aristotelian and Maimodean approaches. Maimonides' doctrine of *Imitatio Dei,* or Walking in God's Ways, figures centrally in Cohen's reading. Maimonides' concept of Knowing God, while idealizing a life of the intellect, demands active human emulation of God's actional attributes. Cohen stresses that such a concept clashes with Aristotelian metaphysics, according to which knowledge of God aspires to an emulation of the self-sufficiency of the

Active Intellect, predicated upon God's mere self-contemplation.[22] According to Cohen, Aristotle's ideal of Knowing God stands in conflict with Maimonides' demand that such a contemplative life ought to result in "ways of lovingkindness, justice, and true judgment."[23]

Ma'asseh Bereshith and *Ma'asseh Merkavah:* A Paradigm Shift in Matters of Creation

53. To be sure, it may be argued that Aristotle too teaches a concept of God in his Metaphysics—a concept of God that could then dispense with an ethics that is based on assumption and probability. Thus Maimonides terms metaphysics the "science of the divine" (חכמה אלוהית), meaning that God is the object of science. This analogy, however, is purely extraneous; yet it allows us to note the following true distinction: Maimonides' concept of God would have been identical with the God of Aristotle, had His inclusion in metaphysics been predicated on His exclusion from ethics.

(*See 53.*) *In Maimonides' terminology, metaphysics is called the "science of the divine."* Cohen attests to the fact that the terminology of Maimonides' metaphysics is clearly borrowed from Aristotle. In his definition of metaphysics, Maimonides adopts a distinctly Aristotelian formulation. Aristotle claims that there are three speculative sciences—mathematics, physics, and theology. Theology, the divine science, is the most perfect and most "honorable," since it deals with the most honorable Being—namely with "that which exists separately and is immovable."[24] Maimonides uses this definition almost verbatim in *Milloth ha-Higgayon:* theology or metaphysics (*hachokhma ha-elohit*) is that speculative science which concerns itself with the study of all that transcends matter—such as the deity, pure intellects, or the question of intelligences, as well as with questions concerning the ultimate causes of Being.[25]

Maimonides goes further and applies the Aristotelian distinction between physics or natural sciences, on the one hand, and divine science or metaphysics, on the other, to the traditional mishnaic and talmudic distinction of *ma'asseh bereshith* and *ma'asseh merkavah*.[26] *Ma'asseh bereshith* refers to the natural sciences, whereas *ma'asseh merkavah* relates to matters concerned with divine science. When dealing with divine matters in a strictly rabbinic context, Maimonides, however, avoids Aristotelian terminology[27]—a fact that may indicate a rejection of then-popular Aristotelian metaphysics. As such, Maimonides reiterates and emphasizes the talmudic admonition that *ma'asseh merkavah* ought not to be taught publicly, "not even to a single student." Further, a teacher may relate "hints and hidden allusions" concerning divine knowledge only to students who are already initiated and who understand by themselves.[28] Maimonides mentions fewer restrictions when discussing the public teaching of matters pertaining to *ma'asseh bereshith*.[29] Note, however, that Maimonides nowhere mentions the doctrine of creation in the context of *ma'asseh bereshith*—a fact that supports Cohen's transcendental reading of creation, elevating the doctrine of creation from the realm of natural sciences to that of ethics.

Cohen claims that precisely when Maimonides' terminology seems to merge with Aristotle's to the greatest degree—namely at the point where Maimonides defines the essence of divine wisdom—Maimonides' own thinking shifts toward the ethical and, hence, farthest from Aristotle. This shift of paradigm is most evident in Maimonides' much-cited Aristotelian definition of the "fourth wisdom," consisting "in the acquisition of the rational virtues . . . of true opinions concerning the divine things."[30] This teaching assumes a Platonic bent when examined in the context of Maimonides' doctrine of Knowing God's Goodness, and of emulating this goodness by Walking in God's Ways.

Messianic Projections of the Good: Futurity as Origin

54. In fact, the very opposite is true. Since for Maimonides no ethics is possible without the concept of God—we shall see how he formulates this interrelation as the foundation of his ethics—he can afford to employ the term *universally accepted,* or *conventional* not in the strict and exacting sense. He knows that as long as the interrelation between God and ethics is warranted, the interrelationship between ethics and reason is safeguarded as well. Besides, ibn Daud had already promoted the proximity of the two concepts to the mode of identity. [Ibn Daud 1986, 204.] When Maimonides first introduces the term *conventional* [מפורסמות] in his *Guide,* he conceives of Good and Evil

(*See 54.*) *Without the concept of God, no ethics is possible.* The conceptual relationship between God and ethics figures centrally in Cohen's *Ethik der reinen Willens* (Ethics of pure will). Ethical projections of the Good—in Maimonides' terms Knowing God or the ideal of human perfection, in Cohen's terms the messianic ideal of humanity—become incentives for human action. Inasmuch as these concepts are conceived of in futuric terms, human acts of goodness are anchored in the futurity of redemption. In other words, Knowing God—knowing what a redeemed world would look like and how the ways of lovingkindness and justice translate into human action—constitutes the origin of ethical will. In traditional terms, ethics originates with the divine promise of redemption, entrusting human beings with the task of paving the way for the messianic future.

(Good and Bad) as equivalent to Beautiful and Ugly [*Guide* 1:2, 25. By use of the terms *na'eh* and *meguneh,* Maimonides initially invokes an aesthetic judgment concerning all modes of social action in terms of their being "approved" or "disapproved."]: this usage demonstrates how little attention he pays in this instance to the specifically ethical significance of the Good. The same applies even to his discussion of this term in his *Terminology of Logic* (מילות ההגיון), wherein it is explained as one of the four classes of propositions that are self-evident. [Note that in terms of Maimonides 1987b, chap. 8, self-evident propositions that are based upon conventional agreement are distinct from those propositions representing *sikhlioth,* or rational truths.] Therefore the term *conventional* does not stand in polar opposition to rational truths, since like them it signifies a proposition that is self-evident.

Saadya's Dogmatism: More on *Sikhlioth* and *Shim'ioth*

55. However, we may better elucidate this issue by analyzing the author's general disposition rather than through such terminological considerations. Maimonides, in any case, did not borrow the term *conventional* directly from Aristotle, but had rather found it in the frisky polemics of ibn Daud. [1986, 214.] It was this parameter of *consensus gentium* that made possible the sharpest distinction between the two kinds of commandments in the Torah. Moreover, Saadya on his part had already divided the Torah into laws of reason and laws of tradition. [1976, 137–47] This differentiation was well meant; even ibn Daud maintained this good intention, as did Maimonides himself and all others before him and after him. Yet this good intention must have

(*See 55.*) *The dogmatism that "seemed to have been sanctioned . . . in such a seemingly harmless fashion."* Cohen claims that Saadya's differentiation between *sikhlioth* and *shim'ioth* sanctions dogmatism. Characterizing some laws as rational and subjecting others to the authority of mere tradition amounts to a dogmatic fixation. If not for this dogmatic distinction, the traditional laws (*shim'ioth*) would lend themselves to the same process of innovative, "rational" interpretation and commentary that characterizes all other parts of Jewish tradition. Furthermore, those commandments called rational (*sikhlioth*) are, of course, themselves part of tradition.[31] Maimonides, therefore, cautions against Saadya's distinction, proposing an integrated rationale for all commandments

irritated Maimonides on account of his scientific, methodological exactitude and conscientiousness; and this dogmatism, which seemed to have been sanctioned and nurtured in such a seemingly harmless fashion, must have scared his rationalism.

(*ta'ame ha-mitsvoth)* thereby advancing a unified purpose for the entire Halakhah.[32] Cohen's intuitive suggestion that Maimonides could not have endorsed a two-tiered rationale for the commandments ("it must have irritated, . . . must have scared" Maimonides) corresponds with Cohen's own interpretation of the Law as that way of reasoning which ethically integrates reality and ideality, the world with its human purpose: "*kol hatorah [kula] nitna la'asoth shalom ba'olam*" [the entire Torah was given for one purpose only: to create peace in the world], says Maimonides in the end of Hilkhoth Channukka. "Religion," Cohen says, "is the logic of purpose."[33]

Infinity and Totality

56. To be sure, the danger of dogmatism looms also for ethical laws in the civic domain. In jurisprudence and statecraft, people are only too ready to grant sovereignty to reason, to worship the prevalent reality as reasonable. But Maimonides, in turn, does not even recognize the dogma of Creation as a fundamental precept of faith. Would it have served him in good stead to ratify creation as a rational truth? On this topic he could conveniently invoke the authority of Aristotle which went unchallenged in his time, in the same way as he did, in fact, make use of Saadya's rationale for laws concerning incestuous relations which proved expedient in settling the question of whether these laws should be included among those universally accepted.

(*See 56.*) *To adore the present reality as reasonable.* This immanentism of reason was audaciously proposed by Hegel in his *Elements of the Philosophy of Right.*

> Everything real is reasonable, and everything reasonable is real.
>
> [Alles was wirklich ist, ist vernünftig, und alles was vernünftig ist, ist wirklich.][34]

We may say that Cohen's exposition of Judaism as ethical monotheism advances a philosophical, social, and political protest against the alleged equivalence of reason and reality. He charges that this linking of reason and reality leads to a reactionary sanctioning of the status quo and thus to political quietism. Based upon the idea that God is other to the world, Cohen appeals to Jewish traditionalists to remain "absolutely critical" of the social and political status quo. According to Steven Schwarzschild, most passionate Cohenian among the American neo-Kantians, Jewish critical reasoning is called upon to oppose itself to any teaching of immanence that proclaims what is real to be ideal.[35]

With Schwarzschild, we may read Cohen's reference to "the danger of dogmatism . . . in the civic domain" within the wider context of a fundamental critique of idolatry: a philosophy of identity which endows reality with the status of absolute being inevitably results in the worship of power.[36] The critique of idolatry when translated into the socio-political context constitutes a hermeneutical extension of Cohen's epistemological method of origin, invoking a meaning of infinity that deviates sharply from that of Hegel. While Hegel conceives of infinity as that totality which includes all dialectical movement within itself while being at rest as a whole, Cohen's conception of infinity conceives of the infinite as "alterity," as a limit-concept generating a radical critique of the totality of Being.[37] From Cohen's perspective, the Hegelian idea of the infinite as an all-inclusive totality which is itself at rest represents the prime philosophical example of idolatry.[38]

Ontology and Ethics: On *Creatio ex Nihilo*, an Esoteric Reading

Maimonides does not recognize the dogma of Creation as a fundamental precept of faith. Cohen reads Creation in the light of the prophetic promise of humanity; Creation means to bring about that promise. As in Rosenzweig's *Star of Redemption,* Creation is thus understood in the light of prophetic speech, and in the light of a future kingdom. The doctrine of Creation is thereby committed to an ethical reading, separating the idea of Creation from its ontological roots in cosmogony. The dogma of Creation—its claim that God created the world for a purpose—constitutes human responsibility toward the world, a responsibility that is itself predicated upon the idea of redemption as revealed by prophetic tradition. Scripture's proclamation of Creation amounts to the establishment of the purpose of Being. Cohen inverts the temporal order of Creation for the sake of an ethical order: it is messianism, the ideal of redemption—defined in terms of "lovingkindness, justice, and true judgment"—which constitutes the original grounds of Creation. Ethics, in Cohen's reading of traditional Jewish doctrine of Creation, is prior to ontology in that any knowledge of the world, or of Being, is predicated upon the knowledge of the Good (true Being), reminiscent of the much-cited commentary of Rashi on

Genesis 1:1: "The creation narrative does not come to teach us the chronological order of creation," but rather its [ethical] purpose.[39]

When emphasizing that Maimonides initially did *not* count the Creation dogma among the thirteen principles of faith,[40] Cohen inevitably refers to a mere cosmogenical, ontological concept of Creation. It is enlightening to note that when Maimonides finally did add the dogma of Creation to his Thirteen Principles of Faith, he did so in the context of the fourth principle, that "the Creator is the first and the last." Maimonides claims that *God's* Being is absolutely prior to all *ontic* being ("God's existence is prior to everything that exists") including the becoming of the world.[41] For Maimonides, as for any medieval religious thinker, this proposition counts among those truth-claims that are self-evident (*muskaloth*).[42]

Maimonides seems to question this self-evidence, however, when dealing with the scientific validity of any ontological or temporal account of the world's actual beginning. The traditional claim of Creation expresses itself in ethical terms, hinging upon the belief that the world lends itself to a process of *tikkun* or repair, independent of the various claims of science, astronomy, cosmogony, or astrophysics in the context of which the question of Creation is traditionally discussed. In this respect, Maimonides could "conveniently invoke the authority of Aristotle," since he agrees that, ontologically or scientifically speaking, *Creatio ex Nihilo* is disputable.[43] Cohen's "esoteric" reading of *Creatio ex Nihilo,* maintaining the priority of the ethical order of Creation over the ontological order of the cosmos, would remain viable even if we were to make room for Maimonides' unabashed endorsement of Aristotle's argument concerning the eternity of the world.

Consensus Gentium? Saadya's Sexual Psychology

Saadya's rationale for laws concerning incestuous relations. Maimonides draws on Saadya's psychology when designating halakic injunctions against promiscuous sexual relations as *consensus gentium* (matters universally accepted).[44] Both Saadya and Maimonides agree that some psychological barriers in social intercourse, such as not to entertain sexual relations with close blood relatives, are universally agreed upon. Saadya claims that laws concerning sexual relations ought therefore to be defined in terms of rational consensus. They are to assume the same status as injunctions against idolatry, bloodshed, and robbery—injunctions that the Sages call *mishpatim,* or laws that "if they would not have been legislated in the Torah we would have legislated them ourselves."[45] Maimonides agrees with Saadya that laws concerning forbidden sexual relations are matters of universal agreement (*mefursamoth*),[46] but he does not count these laws among the *mishpatim*—among the laws that are self-evident. He rather stresses that laws concerning sexual relations are to be treated as *chukkim*—laws whose very purpose is hidden from us.[47] He thus seems to say that matters of sexual relations do reflect a certain *consensus gentium,* although they are by no means matters that are self-evident or rational.

Nonetheless, Maimonides often gives psychological reasons for the laws of Torah (*ta'ame ha-mitzvoth*), such as in the case of Sukkoth, the celebration of the ingathering of the harvest. And the Feast of Tabernacles, Maimonides says, is done all for the sake of "rejoicing, gladness, and leisure." Here Maimonides expressly invokes the authority of Aristotle's *Ethics:* "Offerings are given because of the need for leisure after a laborious task. This is literally what Aristotle says."[48]

57. By now it has become obvious that there are general trends dominating Maimonides' way of thinking as a whole, which makes it plausible that Maimonides accepted Aristotelian terminology without much reservation, a kind of terminology that had been routinely adopted within Arabic philosophy. This routine adoption of Aristotelian terminology, however, does not even remotely indicate Maimonides' inner methodological dependence on Aristotle nor his agreement with Aristotelianism. If we had to assume such dependence and agreement, Maimonides' ethics would not rate as philosophical ethics based upon its own autonomous and unifying principle. Such an ethics would be self-contradictory even in its religious aspect; it would not fit the climactic conclusion of the *Guide,* [Maimonides' proposition of *chessed, tsedakah, umishpat* (lovingkindness, justice, and true judgment) as the parameters for a life devoted to the ultimate ideal of Knowing God. See *Guide* 3:54, 638; 3:53, 630–32.] not even as a homily; and even in his theological system, it would strike us as an unorganic and extraneous element.

58. We may relinquish once and for all this entire terminological confusion, which arises from the clichéd method of scrutinizing the similarities between or congruence of Maimonides' terminological usage and Aristotle's, thereby gauging Maimonides' comparative progress or stagnation. Aristotle himself assists in acquitting Maimonides of any extraneous agreement and dependence, in that Maimonides remains beholden to his teacher for one essential lesson: despite all that profoundly separates them, Aristotle serves him as master and model in his enthusiasm for pure theory, scientific cognition for its own sake, which is the ultimate and absolute purpose of human existence.

[Aristotle 1945, *NE* 1177a, 1178a, 613–19.] This deification of cognition raised the Stagirite to become a true Hellene. It is the compelling vigor of ancient Greek culture that cognition, and science insofar as it is cognition, represents an act of homage to the divine forces. Their mythology would not have matured into their philosophy had they not sensed that "all is divine and human is all."

Betselem Elohim: On Logos, Love, and Eudaemonia

59. The tenth book of the *Nicomachean Ethics* constitutes a torso by itself, the torso of a head, which is incompatible with the trunk of the preceding nine books. This concluding book bears close affinity to Book 12 of Aristotle's *Metaphysics,* insofar as the eudaemonian theory is truly applicable only to God, who may be emulated therein, however, by human beings. The significance and effect of this Aristotelian theory of God shall not be our concern at present. We only wish to note that striving for cognitive truth, and the deification of this objective and purpose of human existence, lends plausibility to the fact that Maimonides and other medieval Jewish philosophers found themselves able to follow Aristotle. The Jewish philosophers had no reason to suspect Aristotle's striving for cognitive truth, which he had raised to a dogma of the Absolute. Not that they actually looked up to him as the patron of this dogma. To be sure, he represented to them a Saintly One among the Gentile nations, [I found no explicit reference to Aristotle as *chassid umoth ha'olam.* See, however, Maimonides (1987; 1988, 553) in a

(*See 59.*) *Enthusiasm for pure theory.* The activity of the Aristotelian God consists of pure intellectual contemplation.[49] Subsequently, Aristotle defines the human intellect as that which is "divine in a human being,"[50] positing the engagement in pure contemplation as the ultimate human task of human existence.

That which is divine in a human being, human intellect, is termed by traditional Jewish sources *tselem,* or *betselem Elohim* (that which is in God's image).[51] Philo interprets *tselem* as Logos, signifying the intellectual and incorporeal part of a person, "the copy of the original seal."[52] Philo's reading reverberates more or less literally in the commentaries of Rashi, David Kimchi, Obadiah Sforno, and other medieval Jewish commentators on Genesis 1:27: "God created the human being in His image, in the image of God He created him." Prima facie, it is Maimonides who renders the most strikingly Aristotelian reading of this passage: "It is . . . because of the divine intellect conjoined with man, that it is said of the latter that he is *in the image of God and in His likeness.*"[53]

letter to Shmuel Tibbon; this is cited by Falaquera (1837, 107) in his commentary on *Guide* 2:22.] and more than this, a patron saint of strict, conscientious cognition, critically investigating the truth. Cognitive pursuit was indeed inscribed on the banner of this philosophical era. Since Jews are always wont to remain vindicators of their faith, concern with their religion drove them to champion cognitive approaches. Religion found itself in a state of deterioration. People often lament the disintegration of religion, and it is then that they summon philosophy in order to buttress their creeds. Against the suspicions of the obscurants and the scoffing of the skeptics, the defenders of religion claim that vindication is on the agenda and that only philosophy would be effective.

60. In his assessment of the validity of cognition, Maimonides sees himself as a disciple and follower of Aristotle. He emphasizes and develops chiefly the intellectual aspect of Aristotle's methodological dualism. [The dualism Aristotle has in mind is between empirical method as applied to both natural and social sciences (including ethics as a psychological discipline) and metaphysical speculation (as engaged in purely intellectual methods of contemplation and theoretical knowledge for its own sake).] Aristotle's sensualism, on the other hand, which forms, as it were, the psychological

In opposition to this tradition of a purely intellectual, metaphysical reading of "likeness," Cohen offers his own interpretation, transferring the discussion from the realm of mere intellect to that of love: *betselem Elohim* signifies a "correlation of God and human beings" that hinges upon the human ideal of lovingkindness and justice. Cohen invokes a classical discussion among the Sages:

> "You shall love your fellow-person as you love yourself": Rabbi Akiba says: "this is a great principle in the Torah." Ben Azzai says: "This is the story of mankind—this is a greater principle in the Torah: the day that God created man, He created him in the image of God—*betselem Elohim*.[54]

Cohen sides with the universal reading as expressed by Ben Azzai, tracing the demand of love beyond the limits of the self which are implied in an adverbial reading of Rabbi Akiba's "love your fellow-person as you love yourself."[55] Cohen introduces a transcendental (Platonic) twist into the discussion of what it means to emulate "that which is divine in a human being," transcending the ontological, Philonic—or neo-Platonic—"flow of divine intellect" by emphasizing the ethical claim implied in the expression *betselem Elohim.*

Aristotle terms the intellectual activity of "emulating God"

introduction to Aristotle's metaphysical system, had indeed been adopted and developed since Saadya by all predecessors of Maimonides. [Saadya 1976, 243–44.] Altogether, Arabic philosophy adopted this approach from Alexander of Aphrodisias. [Pines in *Guide* 1:lxiv–lxxv.] Thus even Maimonides does not fail to provide his ethics with an anthropological introduction. [Maimonides 1912, 37–46.] Yet this expresses merely the *Zeitgeist,* which does not indicate, however, any substantial linkage to Aristotle. According to Maimonides, the true Aristotle teaches that there are absolute principles of cognition, engendering cognitive science.

61. Maimonides therefore underestimated the danger implied in Aristotle's denigration of ethics. From his vantage point, it was easy to overlook this danger, since he knew the validity of ethics had been warranted by Jewish religion. Jewish religion only had to adjust to the basic claims of cognition, and then there would be no ill effect in Aristotle's exaggerated zeal for pure theory, which brings him to deny the cognitive validity of ethics. If only cognition as the spiritual ideal can be maintained as the raison d'être even for religion, then ethics per cognition is safeguarded within religion. Only when religion is in jeopardy would ethics also be on shaky ground.

eudaemonia; eudaemonia signifies "highest happiness," or "state of bliss."[56] A life engaged in the pursuit of pure intellectual activity is "a life of truest pleasure" (ἡδονη, *hedone,* pleasure).[57] According to Aristotle, true intellectual hedonism, unlike all other sensual pleasures, is not driven by some psycho-sociological motivation but rather constitutes an end in itself—which is why Cohen terms Book 10 of the *Ethics* a "torso" standing on its own.[58] However, the very concept of *hedone* itself, Cohen claims, represents the epitome of sensualism, as it is predicated upon the idea of pleasure in precise opposition to his own concept of the free ethical Self, or the task of facing the needs and suffering of others.[59]

The significance and effect of Imitatio Dei. The Aristotelian concept of *Imitatio Dei* points to a person's embracing a life of pure intellectual contemplation. In the Maimonidean context this concept takes on quite a different meaning—despite the fact that Maimonides, of course, endorses Aristotle's ideal of intellectual perfection:

> a person's ultimate perfection is to become rational *in actu,* . . . which would consist in knowing everything . . . that is within the capacity of man to know in accordance with his ultimate perfection.[60]

Consequently, Maimonides did not jeopardize his ethics by integrating it with religion, since he had established religion itself on cognitive principles. From this central vantage point, it seems evident that the question of the conventional as the main characteristic and principle of ethics, loses significance over against the cognitive significance of ethics, and therewith of religion.

However, Maimonides, unlike Aristotle, interprets the concept of *Imitatio Dei* in terms of God's actional attributes and their ideal function as paradigms for hu-man emulation.[61] The educational character of *Imitatio Dei* is the key, then, to Cohen's philosophical critique of any eudaemonian, Aristotelian reading of Maimonides' concept of Knowing God.

Wisdom and Volition

62. In his zeal for truth, pursuing cognition, Maimonides grounds his intellectualism. [In his commentary on the Mishna Chagigah 2:1, Maimonides (1992b, 1:240–43) states that whoever does not care for his intellectual and spiritual endowment (*betselem*) actually forfeits his human integrity and dignity.] Hence he cherishes the intellect, the ancient Greek *nous* above all, and makes it equivalent to volition. The autonomy of volition emerges as a problem only later with Crescas's doctrine of the *affect.* [Harvey 1988, 113–23; the Latin terms *affectus, affectio,* and *passio* all denote "accident" in the general sense, and can be traced to the Aristotelian term παθος. Wolfson 1958, 2:193–94.] In the absence of this doctrine, however, the autonomy of volition is not called into question, but rather remains safeguarded in its union with the intellect. (This may be taken as an addendum to Joël, "Don Chasdai Crescas' religionsphilosphische Lehren in ihrem geschichtlichen Einflusse," 1876, 2:71.)

(*See 62.*) *The ancient Greek nous is equivalent to volition.* In his argument against the *Mutakallimun,* Maimonides identifies divine wisdom (Hebrew *chokhmah,* Greek *nous*) with divine volition, claiming that both are inseparable from God's essence.[62] The identity of divine wisdom with divine will correlates with the demand for human knowledge to become identical with ethical volition: Maimonides defines the "highest human perfection" in terms of *chokhmah.*[63] The highest ideal of human knowledge (Knowing God's actional attributes), however, is itself formulated in terms of wisdom *and* volition. God's actional attributes—precisely in their being subject to human knowledge—become vectors for a person's ethical will.

Wisdom and Torah

63. Hence, according to Maimonides, cognition is the task and telos of religion, and consequently of ethics. Now the question arises: what is the object, the center toward which all this cognition converges? It is God. Maimonides, however, teaches us in the first part of the *Guide,* dedicated mainly to the problem of Knowing God, that cognition of divine attributes is impossible. How can we engage in substantive cognition of God without having access to the knowledge of His attributes?

(*See 63.*) *According to Maimonides, cognition is the task and telos of religion.* He emphasizes that all practical virtues, all practical aspects of the Jewish law, are merely preparatory means to achieve "the conception of . . . true opinions concerning the divine things."[64] In this vein, Maimonides makes a distinction between *chokhmah* and Torah, subordinating the latter to the former: "all the actions as prescribed by the Law . . . [are] not to be compared with this ultimate end, . . . being but preparations made for the sake of this end."[65] In the Parable of the Palace, practical observance of Torah is depicted as a preparatory step toward the knowledge of God, which alone constitutes "coming close to His presence."[66]

The prophetic claim toward the establishment of a panhuman community—a community inspired by the idea of humanity—can only be upheld when interpretation of the Torah is itself directed toward a higher plane of human wisdom. According to Cohen, a merely pragmatic understanding of Jewish law—what to do and what not to do—jeopardizes the Torah's embrace of the ideal of humanity, resulting in sectarian forms of religious hypocrisy. Cohen's violent response to Lazarus's *Ethik des Judentums* is to be understood precisely on the grounds of such a critique of merely moral or halakhic pragmatism.[67]

The Absence of the Absolute: Holiness and the Desacralization of the World

Cognition of divine attributes is impossible. It is of central concern to Maimonides' philosophical and religious agenda to demonstrate the inadmissibility of divine essential attributes: the concept of the "unique, incorporeal and incomparable God" does not allow for an "essential" definition of God, since any predicative description of God would imply composition, multiplicity, corporeality and therefore assume "likeness" between God and nature.[68] Throughout his own philosophical work, Cohen translates Maimonides' negative theology into an ethical, political, and hermeneutical agenda that objects to any ultimate manifestations of finitude and power in that it postulates the absence of the Absolute. This absence, this demand for a desacralized world, is a direct consequence of negating worldly manifestations of holiness for the sake of divine purity. Cohen's own philosophical work amounts to an advancement of the concept of purity; even his logic of origin works against the reduction of the inexhaustible grounds of thinking and interpretation to known first axioms of reason.[69] According to Cohen, Maimonides established within Jewish tradition a human commitment to a nonmanipulable God. Maimonides thus rejects as idolatry claims of a sacred entity, ideology, or theology fabricated in order to judge, force, dominate, or kill others in the name of God.[70]

Divine Attributes: The Intricacies of a Medieval Debate

64. This question challenges the terminology and the entire methodological apparatus of Maimonides, as well as that of his predecessors and successors. It even calls into question, at present as acutely as then, any idealist exposition of the God-concept. How do you intend to know God, and how can you comprehend God as the object of cognitive endeavor, if you denude this object of all attributes, by virtue of which alone we can attain the knowledge of any object? This whole medieval discussion of divine attributes, indeed, points, so it seems, to the question of the reality of the object, its essence and substantiality—or, in Christian terms, to the personality of God, since, without attributes, the trinity of the Godhead presents itself as a problem. How could Maimonides deny the cognition of

(*See 64.*) *The whole medieval discussion of devine attributes.* Medieval Jewish, Christian, and Muslim theology strove to reduce divine attributes to those "essential" attributes that resist further reduction—classically, life (or existence), omnipotence (or will), and omniscience (providence).[71] Saadya emphasizes that this multiplicity of attributes does not indicate a multiplicity in God's essence, but that such theological formulation is rather due to the inadequacy of our human language—"the Torah speaks in the language of men" [*dibbera Torah bilshon benei adam*].[72] Saadya, as well as his successors in this medieval discussion, including Maimonides, follow the tradition of the *Mutakallimun* who solved the problem of anthropomorphic images in the Koran by means of a

divine attributes on the one hand, and on the other hand proclaim knowledge of God as the main principle of his theology and his ethics?

theory of negative attributes from which they exempted only such essential and irreducible attributes: life, omnipotence, and omniscience.[73]

The reduction of these attributes to three seems to have its origin in Christian tradition and its attempt to correlate God's essential attributes with the elements of the trinity. It was Jacob Baradaeus, in particular, the sixth-century founder of the Syrian church, who suggested the correspondence of the essential attributes (Intellect, Word, Life) with the Godhead in its trinity (Father, Son, Holy Spirit).[74] Thus, the medieval Christian-Jewish disputations revolved around the question of how to resolve the tension between God's unity, on the one hand, and the multiplicity of His essential attributes, on the other. Christian dogmatic tradition resolved this tension by declaring multiplicity to be inherent in the Godhead (the one trinitarian God), whereas most medieval Muslim and Jewish philosophers sought to avoid any multiplicity of essential attributes, attempting to establish "holiness" and "uniqueness" in radical opposition to the ambiguities of the world. Maimonides went farthest in this development, claiming that even "life, omnipotence, and omniscience" are inadmissible as divine essential attributes.[75]

65. The solution to this problem will elucidate the Maimonidean concept of cognition. It is his doctrine of divine attributes that will disclose the solution.

Philosophy's Impotence: The Text That Is Prior to Reason

66. What are, indeed, the arguments marshaled for the negation of divine attributes? To be sure, such attributes cannot be denied in toto, since the revelation narrative itself posits such attributes. [Exodus 34:6–7.] It is precisely this point, however, that holds the solution to the puzzle that faces us here: there are no other divine attributes than those posited by revelation. It is philosophy's impotence that is exposed here. We shall see that Maimonides

(See 66.) *There are no divine attributes other than those specified in revelation.* It is philosophy's impotence that is exposed here, and Cohen sounds like an existentialist theologian. But his language is deceptive. In Cohen's reading of Maimonides, it seems that the reference to "revelation" does not refer to any irrational theological dictum, but rather to the translogical origin of ethical thinking as such. When asked to provide further

advanced forceful arguments that both took advantage of Aristotle and yet rejected him. Of what sort are the attributes articulated by revelation? The attributes revealed do not portray God according to the categories of space and time, or of substance and power, of number, magnitude, and infinity. [Aristotle 1983, *Categories* 17–19; Maimonides rejects all but one of the ten Aristotelian categories as unfit to represent divine attributes. The single exception is the category of "actional attributes," *Guide* 1:52, 114–19. "actional attributes," in turn, are expounded in terms of the thirteen attributes (Exodus 34:6–7): "compassionate and gracious" etc. *Guide* 1:54, 124.] Instead, revelation posits those attributes that reveal God solely and exclusively as an ethical being, as a being of ethics, according to the words of Scripture: compassionate and gracious, abounding in kindness and faithfulness (Exodus 34:6–7). This is the focus of Maimonides' doctrine of attributes: he pinpoints and limits the concept of a divine attribute to an ethical attribute, thus identifying the concept of God with the ethical concept of God.

proof for the validity of the Good, reason itself is powerless. Philosophy cannot provide further grounds for the Good. The original teaching itself, embodied in a narrative, the literary source, informs philosophy of its ultimate commitment to the Good. The biblical passage that Cohen specifies as his literary source and which, as he says, "holds the solution to the puzzle that faces us here," is the following:

> God, compassionate and gracious, slow to anger, abounding in kindness and faithfulness, . . . forgiving iniquity, transgression, and sin; yet He does not remit all punishment, but visits the iniquity of the fathers upon the sons.
>
> *[El rachum vechanun erekh apayim verav chessed veemeth, . . . notser chessed la'alafim, nosei avon valfesha vechata'a venakeh lo yenakeh.]* (Exodus 34:6–7)

Compassion and graciousness become constitutive points of reference for an ethical pursuit of Knowing God, in that they represent the goodness of God's ways—"I will pass all my goodness before thee" [*ani a-avir kol tuvi al panekha*].[76] We thus find that the ethical bent, which according to Cohen is mandatory for any Jewish interpretation of *Imitatio Dei,* is predicated upon that which transcends mere logical deduction—analogous to Plato's idea of the Good that is prior to logical hypothesis. "When asked to provide further grounds for the validity of the Good, reason itself is declared powerless," Cohen claims. He correlates the transcendence of the Platonic idea of the Good with the originality of the Jewish literary source. The literary source is prior to textual reasoning just as the Good is prior to thinking. Making this argument, Cohen closely follows Maimonides' interpretation in the *Guide,* where Maimonides defines the Thirteen Attributes—emerging from the literary source of Exodus 34:6–7—precisely in terms of God's goodness, proclaiming these scriptural attributes to be ethical attributes for emulation. Those attributes are significant only in the context of human interaction, just as the entire text of Scripture assumes significance only in the context of oral tradition.

Compassionate and Gracious: A Talmudic Dispute—the Opinion That Dwells Alone

Compassionate and gracious, abounding in kindness and faithfulness (Exodus 34:6–7). The thirteen attributes were originally recommended in Jewish tradition for recital in public penitential prayer services, as they seemed apt to effect atonement for the community. After all, the prayer of Moses—immediately following the revelation of these attributes to him—effected atonement for the community after Israel had worshiped the golden calf (Exodus 34). In the talmudic tractate Rosh HaShana, we find a dispute between Rabbi Yochanan, on the one hand, and Rav Yehuda, on the other, concerning the question of what precisely was the function of the public recital of Exodus 34:6–7.[77] Cohen's reading of Maimonides reflects an implicit agreement with Rav Yehuda who claims that the Thirteen Attributes allude to the covenant (*berith kerutah*) between God and man, rather than to the order of the Rosh HaShana liturgy.[78] Maimonides, indeed, sees in the communal recitation of God's attributes merely a religious custom, stressing that the main, halakhic significance of the Thirteen Attributes lies in their active application in performing the commandment "You shall walk in His ways" (Deuteronomy 11:22).[79] In this innovative reading, Maimonides stands, in fact, alone over against all earlier rabbinic authorities.[80]

Aristotle's God: No "Naught of Knowledge"

67. According to Aristotle, divine substance is identical with divine essence not only terminologically but due to his entire Aristotelian cognitive approach. This divine substance, however, is not the

(*See 67.*) *According to Aristotle, divine substance is identical with divine essence.* Aristotle defines God as the First Cause of the universe, subsequently specified as the prime, Unmoved Mover who is identical with eternal substance.[81] Cohen contrasts this static, self-referential definition of God (a God whose object of thought is God's own thinking, and whose essence is identical with divine substance) with Maimonides' claim that God's essence—a "naught of knowledge"[82]—is present in divine volition, in other words, in Creation. Creation, however, is a secret to be disclosed exclusively by reference to God's actional attributes, which in turn are paradigms for human emulation.

---

object of Knowing God according to Maimonides. Substance can only be recognized by its attributes, and divine attributes are inaccessible to man. The critique of positive attributes constitutes the most pivotal, fundamental, and prominent focus of Maimonides' teaching. Nonetheless, Maimonides asserts and demands the cognition of God—insofar as he can make this demand in light of this fundamental doctrine; indeed, he turns this cognitive demand into the cardinal principle and cornerstone of his theology and ethics. For him, the cognition of God means the cognition of the basic premise, as a paradigm, and regarding this paradigm, we may justifiably claim that it represents the idea of ethics.

God's Goodness: A Theory of Intersubjectivity

68. God's attributes are His ways [Exodus 33:13]; and His ways are the vectors of His actions. His attributes are therefore "attributes of action" (תארי מעשה). [Cohen uses the Hebrew term *te-are hama'aseh* in this context. However, ibn Tibbon and al-Charizi use *te-are hape'ulah,* which is closer to the original Arabic. Efros 1924, 121.] They are not essential attributes; they do not pertain to substance. Divine actions are only attributes insofar as they serve as paradigms for human conduct. [There are four main references in halakhic midrashim that discuss the idea of *Imitatio Dei: (a)* the Mekhilta on Exodus 15:2 (for Abba Shaul's ethical reading of ואנוהו/*ve'anvehu* in contradistinction to the aesthetical

(*See 68.*) *Gods attributes are His ways.* Maimonides identifies God's thirteen attributes with attributes of action, claiming that these attributes contain the answer to Moses' request (Exodus 33:13), "Show me now Thy ways, that I may know Thee." Moses' other request (Exodus 33:18), "Show me, I pray Thee, Thy glory," was denied to Moses (Exodus 33:20). Maimonides interprets this to mean that God's essence remains inaccessible to human knowledge—"No mortal can know [God] in essence,"[83] since (Exodus 33:20) "no person can see my face and live." God's answer to Moses' first request is contained in Exodus 33:19, "I will make all My goodness pass before

interpretation, see Mekhilta 1960, 127, and 1955, 78); *(b)* the Sifra on Leviticus 19:2 (Sifra 1959, 86); *(c)* the Sifre on Deuteronomy 11:22 (Sifre 1993, 114); and *(d)* TB Sotah 14a; also Soloveitchik 1983–1985, 2:170–73.] Hence, the cognition of God actually means the cognition of these paradigms, translated into rules, into legislation for human action, by virtue of which the action obtains the character of ethical conduct.

Thee." Maimonides subsequently relates God's goodness to the ways God governs the universe (nature) in general and in detail.[84] Maimonides specifies those ways, however, instantly in terms of compassion and graciousness, therewith establishing the priority of an ethical reading of Creation over an ontological one, defining God's goodness as the adumbration of "ethical human qualities" (*middoth ha-adam*).[85]

Maimonides' innovative conjunction of the mishnaic *middoth ha-adam* with the Thirteen Attributes becomes the key for Cohen's reading of Maimonides' theory of *Imitatio Dei*. The goodness of God—embodied in the Thirteen Attributes of action—is not meant as *genetivus subjectivus*—"the meaning here is not that He [God] possesses moral qualities," but the goodness of God rather assumes the form of an ideal whose significance lies exclusively in human emulation: "*He* [God] *performs* actions *resembling the actions* that *in us* proceed from moral qualities (emphasis added)."[86]

God's goodness thus becomes meaningful exclusively within the interpersonal context: "God is good" translates into "I [you] shall become good."[87] In opposition to the world of myth, Cohen argues, in his *Ethik*, that Judaism is not interested in whether God is good or just, but rather exclusively whether human beings act toward one another in ways of goodness and justice.[88] This ethical bent defines the meaning of Cohen's concept of the "correlation between God and man." It is in Cohen's reading of Maimonides where this concept of correlation emerges in the context of the classical Jewish literary sources.

"You Shall Become Holy": An Introduction to the Literary Sources

The divine actions are only attributes insofar as they serve as paradigms for human conduct. Maimonides does not formally cite the term *vehalakhta biderakhav* (you shall walk in God's ways) in his discussion of the Thirteen Attributes. Rather, he invokes the Sifra on Leviticus 19:2, as well as the Sifre on Deuteronomy 11:22—an innovative combination of the literary sources which, as we shall see, provides cogent support for Cohen's reading.[89]

Maimonides relies on two biblical passages and their attending halakhic midrashim in his interpretation of the Thirteen Actional Attributes in Exodus 34:6–7. First, he cites Leviticus 19:2, "You shall become holy" (*kedoshim tihyu*) together with the attendant Sifra in which Abba Sha' ul is reported to have introduced the idea of *Imitatio Dei* or *mechake lamelekh* (to imitate the King).[90] Second, Maimonides associates the demand of emulating the Thirteen Attributes with Deuteronomy 11:22: "If you then faithfully keep all this instruction that I command you, loving the Lord your God, walking in all His ways, and keeping close to Him." Maimonides also follows the interpretation of the attending Sifre of this passage: "Walking in His ways—these are the ways of God: compassionate and gracious, longsuffering."[91]

Maimonides' association of Abba Sha'ul's concept of *Imitatio Dei* with the concept of Walking in His Ways—defined in the Sifre on Deuteoronomy 11:22 in terms of the Thirteen Attributes—is unique among rabbinic interpretations. Maimonides therein establishes the very point of Cohen's own reading of Leviticus 19:2, "You shall become holy":

> For the utmost virtue of man is to become like unto Him . . . as far as he is able; which means that we should make our actions like unto His, as the Sages make clear when interpreting the verse "Ye shall become holy." They said: "He is gracious, so be you also gracious; He is merciful, so be also you merciful."[92]

Knowledge of God: On Autonomy and Revolution

69. The objection may be raised that an action obtains its ethical character merely by emulating a paradigm and by acting in accordance with rules. Conceived of as such, ethics would represent only copy and imitation, and not the genuine, free, autonomous act of reasoning and of rational volition. Such an objection, however, is merely polemic, not arising from any substantive criticism. In response, Maimonides himself—

(*See 69.*) *Imitatio Dei: the genuine, free, autonomous act of reason and rational volition.* Cohen stresses the autonomous character of Maimonides' concepts of Knowing God and of Walking in God's Ways, claiming that holiness is a task incumbent upon a person's ethical will, and therewith predicated upon the autonomy of human volition.[93] Cohen defines autonomy as "independence from any extrinsic, worldly

as we shall demonstrate further on—asserts the freedom of will. Against this position of Maimonides, one may not contend that it contradicts the aspect of emulation; for this contention will be refuted by Maimonides' own concept of cognition.

70. I cannot simply act as a mimetic follower of the divine paradigm: imitation is not cognition. The postulate of Knowing God is the *conditio sine qua non* for His ethical subsistence. Hence it can only be cognition in which and by which man, emulating God's actions, builds himself through his own conduct into an ethical person. Without cognition there is no ethics and no God.

71. Maimonides elucidated and ascertained through the doctrine of attributes that cognition constitutes the ethical foundation of theology. Accordingly, he could apply the term *conventional* to some ethical laws, and, if you wish, even to all of them, [*Guide* 2:33, 364] having made certain that the cognitive validity of ethics is established beyond doubt. For Maimonides, Knowing God warrants the cognitive validity of ethics.

72. For this theoretical insight, Maimonides was certainly historically and personally indebted to the fundamental approach of Greek culture, as represented by Aristotle. This debt holds true for

stimulus."[94] Cohen's concept of autonomy does not signify the self-sufficiency of reason, nor any other idealist solipsism, but rather an "activity desired for its own sake," an activity not dictated by external rewards. Likewise, Jewish tradition speaks of the desire to study Torah for its own sake, invoking a midrashic report about God who desires to play with Torah.[95] Most contemporary interpretations of Maimonides' concept of prophecy are hard put to accept such a reading, claiming, in turn, that there must be a radical difference between "autonomous" and "prophetic" knowledge.[96] Maimonides, indeed, makes a basic distinction between the intellect of Moses, the supreme prophet, and that of all other people, including other prophets.[97] However, the difference concerning the degree of prophecy leaves the autonomy of Moses' cognition unimpaired. Thus, when Moses went to Mount Sinai, "his imaginative faculty was annulled, together with all extrinsic sense perception."[98]

When discussing the intellectual and moral qualifications required for the attainment of prophetic knowledge, Maimonides emphasizes that the "detachment from any [egocentric interest in] sensual and physical reality" is a *conditio sine qua non.*[99] He thus stresses the autonomous nature of the moment of *yichud* (seclusion) between God and Moses. In contrast to the tradition made prominent by Judah

the entire ancient world beyond Hellas, as it remains for us and any subsequent culture. Wherever conscientious pursuit of truth is evoked and focused through the lens of an enthusiastic appreciation of science, there the lasting afterglow of Hellenism becomes manifest. The breadth and universal scope of Maimonides' scholarly life and work eminently attest to the epoch-making dimension of Hellas's contribution to the pursuit of science. Yet it seems adventitious and extraneous to argue that Maimonides' intellectualism in theology and ethics is simply derived from Aristotle. If this were so, we would have to recognize in Maimonides' concept of God the God of Aristotle. Since, however, God, the God of the prophets, represents for Maimonides an object of cognition, just like mathematics, logic, and metaphysics—and realizing that God is no longer identical with the Aristotelian divinity—it follows that the concept of Knowing God must be different from the metaphysical concept of Knowing God in Aristotle.

ha-Levi, Maimonides seems to maintain that the relationship between God and Moses on Mount Sinai becomes constitutive for Israel precisely by dint of its autonomy: Autonomy signifies receptivity with respect to an imperative that is "as old as the world."[100] The constitution of the Self, according to Cohen, is a task that originates with God's demanding the Good, just as freedom is constituted by an imperative that binds human volition from time immemorial. One rabbinic interpreter says, "Read not *charuth*—chiseled in stone—but rather *cheruth*—freedom" when referring to Moses' writing on the tablets.[101] In heeding this original demand, human volition must not be dictated by the utilities of external reality—lest the Self become enslaved to "things as they are"—but rather the self is called upon to *transform* reality. This task of transformation, as any revolutionary task, cannot begin with "what is" but rather must start out with a knowledge of what "will be." The scream of the pained creature demands that all things must become otherwise. This sort of eschatological knowledge pushes humanity beyond any quietist consent to the social and political status quo.

The deepest significance of the concept of purity lies in its [social, ethical, political] applicability.[102]

4

Religion as Idolatry

How (Not) to Know God

In this fourth chapter Cohen discusses the specificities of Maimonides' negative theology. Emphasizing the correspondence between Maimonides' theory of negative attributes and the docta ignorantia *of Nicolas of Cusa, and in a critical turn against Spinoza's philosophy of immanence, Cohen offers a detailed analysis of Maimonides' theory of attributes in relation to the Platonic Good as the non-foundational origin of human knowledge. Drawing upon the difference between negative and privative propositions as well as upon the proposition of infinite judgment, Cohen proposes a reading that corresponds with his own* Logik der reinen Erkenntnis: *The negation of privation inherent in Maimonides' theory of knowing God necessitates a reading of divine actional attributes as imperative grounds for human action.*

"Negative Attributes": (No Mere) Technicality

73. In the context of our discussion, the doctrine of so-called negative attributes demands a more elaborate analysis, in order to clarify the significance of Maimonides' God-concept for ethics, to the benefit of which it exclusively applies. It is only from the perspective of this doctrine that the entire Maimonidean philosophy emerges as a unified system; even the structure of the *Guide* appears coherent only as a result of such an analysis. His entire philosophy distinguishes itself from scholasticism whose technical argumentation is executed artificially for its own sake.

(*See 73.*) *The doctrine of negative attributes.* The medieval discussion of negative divine attributes throughout Muslim, Jewish, and Christian literature often took on an extremely technical character.[1] The original motive for this doctrine lay in the embarrassment caused by the many anthropomorphic images in the Koran, as well as in the Hebrew and Christian Scriptures. The purity and transcendence of God, to be sure, is itself not anchored in Scripture—to the contrary, Scripture abounds with anthropomorphic imagery.[2] Only in the wake of the Philonic doctrine of

Maimonides, on the contrary, always focuses his attention on the actual, vital meaning of the concepts, despite his scholarly competence in dialectics. The actuality of his concepts lies in ethics, and this intrinsic vitality lies at the root of the inexhaustible originality of his mind and of his work.

divine unity, incorporeality, and simplicity—as given in the biblical injunction "You shall not make for yourself a molten/sculptured image"—did anthropomorphic imagery become a problem for medieval religious thinkers.[3] Muslim theologians of the rationalist school of the Kalam were the first to address the issues partly by way of allegorical and metaphorical interpretation, partly by developing a theory of "negative attributes." The attempt to avoid multiplicity in God's essence while holding on to the three essential attributes of omniscience, omnipotence, and life resulted in the negation of divine attributes: "God is omniscient but not through knowledge as his attribute; God is omnipotent but not through power as his attribute, and so on."[4]

The majority of pre-Maimonidean Jewish medieval thinkers followed this technique—such as Saadya, Joseph ibn Tsaddik, Judah ha-Levi, Bahya ibn Pakuda, and ibn Daud.[5] Maimonides, however, proves the most radical in his denial of essential attributes.[6] Maimonides explicitly denies that life or existence should be counted among the positive divine attributes. But Cohen's point is rather that Maimonides explicitly subordinates the entire doctrine of divine attributes to the epistemological task of Knowing God in terms of divine actional attributes. And in this, Maimonides distinguishes himself as the ideal proponent for Cohen's ethical reading of the Jewish tradition.[7]

The Specter of the Late Cohen: Rosenzweig's Seminal Misreading

74. Since the discussion of the so-called negative attributes is concerned with the concept of God, we broach the entire problem of how religion relates to ethics. The doctrine of negative attributes as a locus classicus of Jewish philosophy is apt to clarify and resolve the problem of this relationship, if we were to succeed in demonstrating more incisively and plausibly the following: that Maimonides in

(*See 74.*) *Religion and Ethics.* Cohen later speaks of the "distinctive nature of religion," proposing a definition of religion in which the correlation of God and man is understood in radically subjective terms.[8] Guilt and atonement are central terms in Cohen's existentialist grounding of the correlation between God and man in terms of subjectivity.[9] Nonetheless, Cohen leaves unimpaired the ethical,

combating positive divine attributes was motivated not merely by scholastic subtlety, nor even theological concern for maintaining the conceptual purity of divine unity, but primarily by the pure rationalism of his ethics. Maimonides does not have a double standard of truth: whatever proves true for religion, must *eo ipso* apply to ethics. [*LrE* 605; *ErW* 439–66; *BdR* 50. Cohen provides a fundamental critique of the scholastic "double truth theory" in which "reason" and "revelation" constitute two independent sources of truth. Wolfson 1976b, 112–40.]

"messianic" purpose of that correlation. Even the distinctive nature of religion remains predicated upon the autonomy of a person's ethical resolutions.[10]

It is Cohen's definition of the distinctive nature of religion that prompted Rosenzweig's existentialist interpretation of the late Cohen in his celebrated introduction to Cohen's *Jüdische Schriften* of 1924.[11] Rosenzweig's reading—a seminal misreading—created the specter of Cohen as the seventy-year-old *baal teshuvah,* who discovers Judaism toward the end of his academic, philosophical career. The narrative of the "late Cohen" and his ascending path from the sterility of neo-Kantian abstraction to the fertile grounds of Jewish existence haunts the majority of Cohen's post-Rosenzweig readers, for whom critical philosophy and Jewish existentialism represent two diametrically opposed ways of thinking.[12] Cohen's ethical monotheism, his prophetic idea of humanity, his concept of correlation, of the priority of the Other, and his idea of messianism are thus being taken hostage by a polarized debate between idealists and existentialists—philosophers and Jewish religionists—whereby Cohen's genuine engagement of Jewish sources in a sustained line of ethical reasoning throughout his philosophical writings is overlooked.

European Cohen scholarship in the last thirty years—notably the work of Dieter Adelmann, Helmut Holzhey, Rivka Horwitz, Pierfrancesco Fiorato, Andrea Poma, and Hartwig Wiedebach[13]—has advanced a radically different reading, carefully demonstrating the continuity of Cohen's philosophical development. In my own commentary on Cohen's reading of Maimonides, I wish to demonstrate how Cohen's lifelong commitment to Jewish classical texts, Jewish hermeneutics, and ethical messianism expresses itself as critical thinking, and how intimately Cohen's reading of Jewish literature correlates with his main philosophical work, most notably his *Logic* and his *Ethics*.

Walls and Fences: Two Traditions of Legal Thinking

75. To be sure, as a dogmatist of rabbinic tradition, Maimonides had to erect an enormous hermeneutic wall [Mishna Avoth 1:1; Stein 1979, 301–29], in order to safeguard against the flood of exceptions, which develop within the confines of the law itself. Even in our own assessment of his unique epoch-making achievement, [Maimonides' *magnum opus,* his halakic code (*Mishneh Torah*), is revolutionary in its novel systematization and classification of *halakhoth.* See Twersky 1980b, 273] we must not be led astray by his involvement with the exceptions, insofar as we consider them relevant: rather, in this central point, we must gauge our historical understanding not so much by Maimonides' relationship to rabbinic tradition but rather by his relationship to the prophetic teaching. The monotheism of Israel originates with the God-concept of the prophets and not with that of the Talmud, although Maimonides felicitously aspires even with respect to this innermost core to invoke the authority of the haggadic part of the Talmud. In the Haggadah of the Talmud, it is ethics that features as the prominent problem of the law, and hence of the Torah. ["The interpreters of Haggadah say: if you want to know the One who 'spoke-and-the-world-came-into-being,' go and pursue the study

(*See 75.*) *"The wall around the law."* The metaphor of the "wall around the law" corresponds to the rabbinic dictum to "make a hedge for the Torah" (Mishna Avoth 1:1)—"to impose additional restrictions so as to keep at a safe distance from forbidden ground"—according to one opinion.[14] Travers Herford offers a more sympathetic reading: "The precautions taken to keep the divine revelation from harm, so that the sacred enclosure, so to speak, might always be . . . open for the human to contemplate the divine."[15] *The innundation of exceptions that develop within the wall itself.* Cohen's view of halakic reasoning is influenced by the legal tradition of Western Europe—based upon the Justinian Code and the Napoleonic Code—in which legal decisions are derived from statutory, apodictic rules in *application* to individual cases. Only in such a *deductive* system does it make sense to speak of exceptions to the rule.

Jewish law, on the other hand, based upon talmudic thinking, constitutes a casuistic system, not unlike the Anglo-Saxon common law, which is situational: if such and such happens, then it should be handled in such and such a manner. *Casus* refers to a unique situation that has occurred and demands legal judgment. A legal case is by definition "an unexpected disaster," and the process

of Haggadah, by dint of which you will come to know *the holy one,* blessed be He, and cleave unto His ways." Sifre 1993, 114–15.]

of legal decision making is thus a creative act that is by nature *inductive.* Even the "fence around the Torah" is part of this inductive process:

> [Maimonides realizes] that law has immanent uncertainties, and that the legist regularly and unavoidably faces unimagined contingencies and new hesitations. . . . Like the historical process or personal experience, law can never be purified of its mutations and individuality. A code is a rational construction which captures and freezes as much as possible of a fluid, unpredictable, sometimes recalcitrant reality, but there is always a fluctuating residuum which must be confronted openly and freshly.[16]

Esoteric and Exoteric Reasoning: Haggadah and Halakah

Maimonides' relationship to rabbinic tradition vs. his relationship to the prophetic message. Cohen diverts our attention from the halakhic aspect of Jewish tradition—to an appreciation of the meta-legal rationale in Maimonides' exposition of the Torah claiming that Maimonides subordinates legal reasoning to the prophetic ideal of Knowing God. According to the last chapter of the *Guide,* Maimonides proposes a relationship between Halakah (rabbinic tradition) and *chokhmah* (the ultimate wisdom) in which the legal thought takes on a subordinate role with respect to the achievement of a higher wisdom. Maimonides terms this prophetic knowledge, knowledge of God.[17]

"*The monotheism of Israel originates with the God-concept of the prophets and not with that of the Talmud.*" This statement, from the present paragraph, is wont to tempt the reader into the impression that Cohen's Jewish philosophy finds its groundings mainly in prophetic teachings and less so in the rabbinic tradition. Talmudic teachings—in as far as they are halakhic—are often exoteric in that they are orientated toward the practicability of everyday life. Both prophetic visions and haggadic narratives, on the other hand, are esoteric, enigmatic messages, especially since prophetic visions express an experience of God. Cohen claims that these esoteric prophetic and haggadic traditions serve Maimonides as stepping stones toward the development of his own doctrine concerning the ultimate human perfection.[18] Maimonides mentions that he, indeed, intended to write an exposition of all the haggadic material in the Talmud and in the prophets, focusing specifically on the question of how they relate to the ideal of Knowing God.[19]

In the Haggadah of the Talmud, ethics features as the prominent problem of the law. (Those who study Levinas's talmudic lectures on the haggadic parts of the Talmud will see in this sentence an almost programmatic agenda for Levinas's hermeneutical approach to talmudic literature.)[20] It says in the Sifre on "You shall walk in His ways":

> if you want to know the One who "spoke-and-the-world-came-into-being," go and pursue the study of Haggadah, by dint of which you will come to know the Holy One, blessed be He, and cleave unto His ways.[21]

This midrashic passage demonstrates the ethical focus of Cohen's reading. The one who "spoke-and-the-world-came-into-being" signifies the archetypal personification of the ethical that is grounded in speech. As such the study of Haggadah is endorsed as a foremost means to "walk in His ways." (Note that Cohen commits both Haggadah and Halakhah with equal rigor to his ethical interpretation, whereas some of Cohen's successors seem to have narrowed the scope of their reading: Levinas emphasizes Haggadah, whereas a neo-Kantian thinker like J. B. Soloveitchik stresses the priority of Halakhah.)

When looking more closely at the etymology of the term *haggadah,* we realize that this term is not merely restricted to denote those parts of the oral tradition that are of non-halakhic character. The contradistinction of Haggada and Halakhah itself constitutes a rather arbitrary distinction.[22] The etymological root of *aggada* expresses, in fact, precisely what is implied in Cohen's concepts of "living speech" and "correlation." The noun *haggadah* or *aggada* is derived from the causative of the three radical letters **ngd.* This denotes a positioning "over-against" in the sense of the Latin *objectus; haggadah* thus represents an object-lesson, a teaching conveyed by means of a living paradigm, including nonverbal, allusive means of communication, or otherwise demonstrative behavior. It is precisely in this sense in which this root is used in Micah 6:8, the prophetic passage which is fundamental to Cohen's entire interpretation of Judaism as ethical messianism:

> It has been demonstrated to you, o you human being, what is good [*higgid lekha adam ma tov*], and what the Lord requires of you: only to do justice, and to love kindness, and to walk unostentatiously with your God.[23]

Cohen could have invoked David Kimchi's commentary to this passage in Micah that expressly relates "walking humbly with your God" with the demand of Walking in His Ways.[24] Walking in His Ways thus advances beyond theological dogmatism in that it turns out to be a consequence of Haggadah: *higgid lekha adam ma tov.* This interpretation is offered by Maimonides' son Abraham who defines Haggadah—like Cohen—with direct reference to Micah 6:8.[25]

Religion Is Idolatry: Maimonides' Critique of Theology, and the Anti-Maimonidean *Polemos*

76. We cannot deny, however, that from the perspective of a person's absolute faith in God, the zeal for the doctrine of negative attributes spells something rather suspicious and oppressive. We are bidden to put our trust in the content of revelation, relying but upon its rational moorings, and yet we deprive rational cognition of its positive conceptuality: what foundation remains at our disposal for knowing God if we are left to operate merely with negative attributes? Would it not appear that a latent trait of aversion and of distrust against the very foundation of the God-concept, against its cognitive validity, prevailed throughout this entire Maimonidean argument? Maimonides was not bound to give himself a clear accounting of this, but this question makes the opposition of the unphilosophical community of believers more plausible and more palpable.

(*See 76.*) *The opposition of the unphilosophical community of believers.* The *pulmus* or *polemos* against Maimonides' rabbinic and philosophical writings—which eventually brought about the rejection of Maimonides' books—started in Maimonides' own lifetime. This *polemos* touches upon central political and theological questions concerning human perfection and the conditions of salvation, questions whose ramifications can be felt well into the present.[26] Philosophically speaking, the spiritual struggle of the pious against the philosophers is directed against the concept of purity—the Naught of knowledge that is God—which Maimonides advances as a fundamental concept of the Jewish faith. Maimonides (and the legacy he bequeathed) excludes from the body of authentic Jewish tradition any kind of religious fundamentalism that insists on the "positivity" of its theological images and makes use of the sacred for the sake of its political interests, forgetful of the ways in which one humbly approaches God.

Maimonides, indeed, accuses the "pious enemies of philosophy"—

simpletons, politicians, those who confuse their image of the sacred with God—of violating the injunction against idolatry. No positive definition of God is permissible, lest such people worship themselves when taking the products of their own imagination to be God. The consequences of such intellectual idol-worship are severe. All idolaters, according to Maimonides, are heretics who must be excluded from the community of Israel, forfeiting their "share" in the world-to-come.[27]

Abraham ben David of Posquieres opposed the harshness of Maimonides' rulings. In a trenchant critique of Maimonides, he exonerates such unphilosophical believers:

> Why has he called such a person an heretic? There are many people greater than and superior to him who adhere to such a belief on the basis of what they have seen in verses of Scripture.[28]

Maimonides, however, differs from their view:

> If, however, it should occur to you that one who believes in the corporeality of God should be excused because of his having been brought up in this doctrine or because of his ignorance and the shortcomings of his apprehension, you ought to hold a similar belief with regard to an *idolater.*[29]

Maimonides' rejection of any physical representation of the divine in terms of the sacred—even if only by pure imagination—represents the most radical position concerning the injunction against idolatry in Jewish tradition. His judgment, however, has talmudic support in a discussion of idolatrous worship in Talmud Bavli (Chagigah 16a), in which the Palestinian Sages object to the Babylonian practice of prostrating oneself at the sight of a rainbow. This practice developed in reminiscence of a passage in Ezekiel:

> Like the appearance of the bow which shines in the clouds on a day of rain, such was the appearance of the surrounding radiance [*hanoga saviv*]. That was the appearance of the semblance of the Presence of the Lord [*demuth kevod adonai*]. When I beheld it, I flung myself down on my face. (Ezekiel 1:28)

The Palestinian Sages oppose such prostration before natural phenomena:

> Against the Babylonian Sages we say that it is forbidden to prostrate oneself before the appearance of a rainbow—since this practice is suspected to be idolatrous.[30]

Many talmudic versions deleted this opposition to the practice of prostration before the rainbow from their editions,[31] and with this deletion they disposed of the entire question of the permissibility or impermissibility of worshiping divine manifestations in nature. They did so possibly in order not to offend idolatrous astrological practices deeply rooted in Babylonian culture. It stands to reason that the rejection of such a worship by the Palestinian Sages had caused an agitation among the guardians of popular folklore similar to the agitation that ensued upon Maimonides' rejection of popular theology.[32] Politically speaking, Maimonides' strictures against any kind of religious imagination involving divine corporeality were, in fact, directed against the widespread phenomena of fundamentalism in the thirteenth century.

Maimonides, Cusanus, and Modern Epistemology: The Construction of a Philosophical Tradition

77. On the other hand, we are now in a better position to appreciate the influence exerted by Maimonides not only upon scholasticism but even upon the period extending into the early Renaissance, and in particular upon the great Nicholas of Cusa. [1986, 60–61 and throughout. On the influence of Maimonides upon the Christian scholastic tradition, see the groundbreaking essay of Jacob Guttmann, which appeared in the same volume as Cohen's own essay on Maimonides (Guttmann 1971, 135–230). For a contemporary assessment of the relationship between Jewish and Christian scholasticism, see the study of Yossef Schwartz 2002.] However, the danger of rationalism proves itself here also to be a challenge to Judaism. Nicholas of Cusa could afford to play with the ambiguities of pantheism in a daring and meaningful fashion since he could use them to expound the mystery of the trinity. [*ErW* 447; but see *LrE* 31–32 where Cohen introduces Nicholas as the discoverer of the epistemological significance of infinity.] In contrast, Maimonides guards himself against the serpent

(*See 77.*) *Nicholas of Cusa, father of modern philosophy.* The philosophical significance of "negative theology" is so foundational to Cohen's own critical idealism that he, in fact, proclaims Nicholas of Cusa, rather than Descartes, to be the father of modern philosophy.[33] Cohen was followed herein by Cassirer, whose history of modern epistemology begins with a discussion of Cusanus.[34] We thereby meet with the construction of a philosophical tradition rooted in alterity and difference, one that spans from Maimonides and Nicholas of Cusa to Cohen and Cassirer. This tradition is challenged first by Spinoza and later prominently by Hegel and Heidegger.

of pantheism, although he is not disinclined toward the enchantment of neo-Platonism. [Kreisel 1994, 169–211, esp. 183–211.]

Spinoza's Annihilation of Alterity: The End of a Hermeneutical Tradition

78. Finally, this provides us with a keener and more substantive understanding of Maimonides' relationship to Spinoza. [*JS* 3:290–372; L. Strauss 1997, 147–92.] The more zealously Spinoza safeguards his concept of divine substance against all determinative restrictions, the more problematic the possibility of any positive, absolute knowledge of God becomes, and hence the more Maimonides' pan rises on the scale and seems to be outweighed. For Spinoza's concept of divine substance means neither exclusively nor even primarily the God of ethics, but merely the God of nature: *deus sive natura.* ["That eternal and infinite being we call God, or nature." Spinoza 1985, 544, 548, also 66. Cohen (*ErW* 45, 16) to the contrary, proclaims *Natura necnon Deus*: "If God and nature are identical . . . the difference between Being and Ought is suspended." Even in *LrE* (356–57), he contrasts religion as the logic of purpose to Spinoza's religion of immanence which "gives up on teleology and thus abandons the problem of ethics."]

79. Let us recall, however, how even Plato formulates his idea of the Good in seemingly negative

(*See 78.*) *Spinoza's concept of divine immanence.* Cohen refers to Spinoza's concept of divine immanence as the "serpent of pantheism." In contrast, Maimonides' epistemology is constituted as the task of ethical cognition rooted in the teaching of "the unique God."[35] According to Cohen, ethical cognition is the one and only way in which the relationship between God and human beings can be, or, in fact, ought to become, immanent. Spinoza, on the contrary, defines the concept of divine substance as an *ontological* immanence. In medieval terms, Spinoza negates all divine attributes, including attributes of action, as limitations of the divine substance, positing "infinite substance" instead.[36] Spinoza's "divine substance" cannot, according to Cohen, inspire human action, nor the kind of infinite hermeneutical creativity that so characterizes the Jewish oral tradition.[37]

Spinoza, on the other hand, criticizes the openness and associative nature of rabbinic hermeneutics in general and of Maimonides' philosophical writings in particular. Divorcing the question of truth from the reading of Scripture, Spinoza ends two thousand years of interpretive history.

terms as non-foundation. [Plato's conception of the Good as a non-foundation (*an-hypotheton*) expresses the notion that the idea of the Good is hypothetically excluded from the infinite process of scientific, conceptual deduction—see commentary for translation paragraphs 16 and 21 in chapter 1. The concept of the Good as non-hypothesis (*an-hypotheton*) thus constitutes the self-proclaimed ethical limit or end of reason. *LrE* 88. It is in this paragraph Cohen begins to explicitly correlate Plato's concept of non-foundation with Maimonides' theory of negative attributes.] The common translation renders this Platonic term [το ανυποθετον] incorrectly and inexactly as the Unconditioned Absolute. [See Cohen paragraphs 16 and 17.] I would venture to propose that in similar fashion, Maimonides by no means conceives of the negative attributes in a purely negative vein, but rather relates them to infinite judgment, which only apparently takes on the form of negation in that its formulation employs a negating particle. [*Guide* 1:58, 136.]

Over this time, Jews have entrusted their texts with the task of rendering ever new significance in their continuous search for truth. Spinoza, to the contrary, denies any transcendental grounds for the words of Scripture. He subsequently radically historicizes the text, rejecting any innovative reading that stipulates a "hidden" meaning as a dogmatic "textual distortion."[38]

Cohen, for whom the search of meaning beyond the letter is directly associated with a Jewish desire for transcendence, accuses Spinoza of willfully constructing a narrow-minded and primitive image of Judaism. He thereby lends support to the critique of Judaism as a religion that is centered around the letter of the law—an image which, according to Cohen, is but the reflection of Spinoza's own philosophy of immanence. Cohen sees it as a tragic irony of history that Spinoza's distortion of Judaism, his rejection of Maimonides and of his philosophical reading of the Jewish tradition, influenced and determined the views of many Enlightenment scholars. Spinoza's annihilation of Maimonides' critical thinking thus directly influenced the anti-Jewish prejudices of Kant, Lessing, and Herder, which in turn influenced Mendelssohn's *Jerusalem*. According to Cohen, it is Spinoza who precipitated the paradoxical view of classical Judaism that permeates post-Enlightenment Western philosophy and culture—whether Christian or Jewish.[39]

Nichts and *Ichts:* Cohen's Judgment of Origin and the "New Thinking"

80. In this context, Aristotle has rendered a disservice to the students of logic in his time, as well as to those of the Middle Ages and modern times, by failing to maintain the distinction between the two negating particles ου and μη. [Cohen claims (*LrE* 86) that Aristotle neglects the use of the relational negative particle μη. However, Aristotle preserves the distinction between privation and negation. Aristotle 1947, *Metaphysics* 1022b, 273–74; 1983a, *Categories* 12a–b, 85–89; also Wolfson 1973–1977, 2:215.] We find this distinction sharply outlined, and productively elucidated and developed by Plato. Although Maimonides had not read the Sophists and Parmenides, he probably knew *Timaeus.* [Pines's introduction to the *Moreh Nevukhim, Guide* lxxv–lxxvi, 283–84.] Even the latter presents the meaning of infinite judgment for that kind of negation which only appears to be a negation, in a forceful and lucid manner. Hence, Maimonides was able to find in Plato as well as in neo-Platonism the point of departure and support for developing his own fundamental doctrine of Knowing God: it is not through negation, but rather through a negation that is only apparent, that we attain a true and fast affirmation of God.

81. What may be argued against the preference for positive attributes in the first place is their formal connection with their negative counterparts.

(*See 80.*) *Two different kinds of negation.* In Democritus and Plato we find a distinction between the two negating particles, μη (*me*) and ου (*ou*). The first refers to a privation or relational negation whose logical and grammatical function is to lead the "non-existing to the truly existing, the Nothing to the Something."[40] Cohen translates Democritus's Greek description of this transition from nothing to something into an expression truly characteristic of the innovative idiosyncrasy of Cohen's language, playing with the terms *Nichts* and *Ichts*—with the terms of *naught* and *ought,* predicating the latter upon the former: *Nicht mehr ist das Ichts als das Nichts.*[41] One may say that the hermeneutical, or rather logical, structure of Rosenzweig's *Star of Redemption* is predicated upon what Cohen himself calls the "new thinking," a way of reasoning which originates in a nought—a nought which Cohen defines as the absence of a predetermined first body of knowledge, a "naught of knowledge."[42]

Cohen claims that absolute negations—expressed in Greek by the negating particle οὐ—are uncreative and uninstructive. On the other hand, privative predicative expressions—expressed by the particle μη—are interesting and creative. To refer to an example mentioned earlier, a proposition like "this man is inhuman" posits and

Wherever provision is made for positive attributes, there must logically be room also for negative attributes in every sense. Wherever references to perfection are predicated, even imperfections may not methodologically be excluded. The God-concept ought to be exempt from this general logical destiny of judgments. [*Guide* 1:52, 114–16; 1:55, 128–29; Wolfson 1973–1977, 2:195–97; also Altmann 1966.]

82. Maimonides opposes essential divine attributes because they imply the ambiguous duality of definition, which as such must be formulated in terms of genus and *differentia specifica.* [*Guide* 1:52, 115; also Wolfson 1973–1977, 2:161–94; Samuelson 1969.] Such differentiation predicated as it is upon the relation between genus and species is inadmissible in that it would establish a comparison between God and all nondivine beings. "Those who allow for essential attributes (תארים עצמיים) think that this position is compatible with the assumption that just as God's essence is not comparable to the essence of other beings, so His essential attributes are not comparable to those of other beings; they agree that one definition cannot at once contain divine and nondivine attributes (ולא יקצבם גדר אחד). However, they have failed to follow through their assumption rigorously: while maintaining the incomparability of divine and nondivine attributes, their very allowing for positive anticipates the nonexistent attribute, "humanity," in a way in which the absence of that attribute is felt as a privation. Cohen explains that the attribute "humanity" therewith enters into an infinitesimal equation with "this man" in such a way that the privation is felt as a judgment: "This man" is now judged by the attribute of "humanity" which he is specifically lacking.[43] Such an infinitesimal equation is termed by Cohen *judgment of origin.*

The privative judgment, resulting in an "opposition to inhumanity," according to Cohen, is by no means the same as a positive proposition that could advance humanity. The former task can be performed zealously without ever developing it into a dogmatic ideology. The latter demands a kind of knowledge that is not far from what religion calls "absolute knowledge," and which is looked at by Cohen with suspicion. It is Plato who fully develops Democritus's thesis that being originates in nonbeing (μηδεν εἰναι), or, in other words, that true Being (ὀντως ὀν) is not identical with existence.[44] Cohen's reading of Maimonides' theory of negative attributes systematically employs this Platonic distinction between true Being (essence) and being (existence), by proposing the subsequent aboriginal negation "true Being does not exist" as the *ethical* grounds of Jewish tradition. True being passes judgment on reality; it does not become identical with it.

attributes, indeed, amounts to the inclusion of divine and nondivine attributes within one definition." (*Guide* 1:55 [*sic*], Maimonides 1856–1861, 1:225.) [The passage is found in *Guide* 1:56, 131.] Since this incomparability precludes any definition as well as any essential attribute, the concept of divine being is incomparable to that of any natural being; this incomparability applies not only to essence, but equally to existence. [*Guide* 1:57, 132; Altmann 1988, 314–15; and Wolfson 1958, 1:121–25.] "God's existence is necessary. Accordingly, His existence is identical with His essence and His true reality, thus His essence is His existence" (*Guide* 1:57; Maimonides 1856–1861, 1:232. אמרנו עליו יתעלה שהוא מחויב המציאות תהיה מציאותו עצמו ואמיתתו ועצמו מציאותו.) [Pines in *Guide* 1:132.] Since existence may be transferred from man to God, and from God to man only as a homonym, [the attribute of existence when applied to God designates only a way of speaking: *dibbera Torah ki leshon bene adam* "the Torah speaks in the language of man." *Guide* 1:59, 140. God "exists, but not through 'existence' other than His essence. . . . He lives, but not through life, etc." *Guide* 1:57, 132] this term cancels itself out as an attribute of divine existence. [Maimonides anticipates Kant's critique of the ontological proof of God, denying that existence can be "superadded" to God's essence, therewith removing existence from those attributes upon which divine perfection is predicated. Plantinga 1965, 57–64.] It is in this context that the controversy about Maimonides' own opinion as to existence arose, namely in the context of the question whether existence may be considered a divine essential attribute, while constituting an accident when applied to natural beings (Maimonides 1856–1861, 1:232; and also Kaufmann 1877, 422ff).

Although Maimonides had not read the Timaeus, he probably knew of it. Maimonides, in fact, rejects the cosmogenic theory developed in Plato's *Timaeus,* based upon his critique of the Platonic concept of prime matter (ὕλη).[45] From Cohen's perspective, however, this critique is outweighed by Maimonides' indebtedness to the ethical groundings of Platonic methodology and of Plato's theory of creation.

83. Maimonides thus steadfastly insists upon attributes that are radically dissociated from essence. Even oneness is incompatible with essence. "Now to ascribe to Him the accident of oneness is just as absurd as to ascribe to Him the accident of multiplicity. I mean to say that oneness is not a notion that is added to His essence, but that He is one not through oneness." [*Guide* 1:57, 132.] (*Guide* 1:57, Munk, 234. כן הוא מן השקר עליו

מקרה האחדות ר"ל כי אין האחדות ענין נוסף על עצמו אבל הוא אחד לא באחדות., Maimonides 1856–1861, 1:234) [Ibn Ezra's *Sefer HaEchad* defines the number one as that which contains all multiplicity and division within itself. Ibn Ezra 1985, 399; according to medieval mathematics, one signifies immanence, constituting genus par excellence, since all other numbers turn out to be its species.] Hence positive attributes, even the most meaningful ones, become void of any meaning, since the meaning of the positive proposition as such has been invalidated.

84. Now, if Maimonides establishes Knowing God as the principle of and basis for his entire system, then its restriction to negative attributes signifies indubitably nothing but the following: that we may establish and maintain true knowledge of God preferably or even exclusively through negative attributes.

Getting Something from Nothing: Infinitesimal Equations—"The Wall That Does Not See"

85. Aristotelian logic, at least, offered Maimonides guidance in its differentiation between negation and privation (αποφασις and στερησις). There are two ways of positing absence. Accordingly, one may say, "The wall does not see," or more exactly, "The wall is non-seeing." Aristotle designates this non-being, that is, the wall's lack of sight, in terms of the negation particle ουκ ον, and not in terms of the privative particle μη ον. Or, he classifies it as indefinite (αοριστον ονομα). [Aristotle 1983a, 141; Boethius translates *nomen infinitum,* and therewith introduces the term *infinite judgment* into philosophical terminology. Boethius's Commentary on *De Interpretatione,* ad loc.; see Wolfson 1973–1977, 542–544.] Hence, positing absence in a radical way is restricted to those relations that present the lack not as

(*See 85.*) *Maimonides' distinction between negation and privation.* Aristotelian logic offered Maimonides its differentiation between negation (αποφασις) and privation (στερησις). Aristotle maintains that the privative judgment constitutes a proposition in which the predicate denotes a privation, for example, "This man is blind," whereas a negative judgment is a proposition in which the predicate constitutes a habit (εξις), such as, "That man is not seeing."

Cohen derives his terminology from ibn Tibbon's translation of the two Maimonidean Arabic terms אלעדם אלמכצוץ and אלעדם אלמטלק as *he'eder meyuchad* (relative privation)[46] and *he'eder gamur* (absolute privation). Al-Charizi translates the former as *ha-efes ha-mugbal* (infinitesimal zero), and the latter as *ha-efes*

deprivation, but that present the absence of the respective predicate as one that is expected . [As in case of the proposition "The wall is not seeing."] Thus the proposition conveys that something is lacking, but not wanting, rejecting the entire premise of the proposition, thereby confirming the absence of the predicate. [That is, the wall is not expected to see in the first place—how could one have possibly expected the wall to see?] Even the possibility of such a rejection, however, exposes the concept of God to the peril of relation. The more "relation" advances, the more questionable and ambiguous the profit of resorting to "absence" becomes.

86. But must we not attribute to God knowledge, hence reason, and therefore a soul—hence also life?—in order that He become compatible with living creatures, or at least with human beings, who possess a rational soul? By the same token, He may even exercise volition, and hence be subject to passion, or at least to *affects.* We notice how profitably "privation" recommends itself as an expedient to the naive: God must not be envious, irascible, spiteful, and vindictive; with reference to God, they hold that all affects must logically be considered privations. [Thus, the naive believers invest their God with positive attributes—they know that God is loving, caring, good, and merciful—and it is on the basis of this knowledge that they deny God *ha-gamur* or *ha-efes ha-muchlat* (absolute zero).[47] The concept of the "infinitesimal," a limit-concept by means of which eighteenth-century mathematicians and physicists began to measure movement and velocity,[48] figures centrally in Cohen's *Logik der reinen Erkenntnis.* There it signifies an epistemological method in which knowledge (something) is predicated upon a naught of knowledge (nothing). That naught, in which knowledge is generated, amounts to an infinitesimal origin, which Cohen also refers to as the Question:

> And thus we recognize the logical significance of the *question,* as the fulcrum of origin. . . . The question is the beginning of cognition [emphasis added].

And further:

> The *question,* however, is of such fundamental value only insofar as it leads towards an answer . . . but the way towards the answer must not be a straight one—since the origin of "something" cannot be sought in some other thing. The judgment therefore must not shy away from an adventurous detour. . . . It is *Nothingness* which constitutes this detour of thinking. It is by means of this detour nothingness that the judgment constitutes the origin of something [emphasis added].[49]

envy, spitefulness, and vindictiveness as privations that are not befitting the nature of God.] They reject them, but not as a combination of incomparables, as in the proposition of the unseeing wall. [This is what they should have done, since affects relate to God as seeing relates to the wall.] Logically speaking the rejection of divine affects must therefore not be one of privation but rather one of genuine negation; the positing of divine affects as such constitutes a contradiction. By contrast, polytheism, and no less pantheism, relates God to the whole gamut of modifications in human consciousness, no matter if in conflict or in concord. [The gods of the pantheon display human emotions, and are all too human in their dealings with one another and with the human world—love and hatred, anger, pride, jealousy. Rosenzweig 1990, 33–35; 1971, 36–38.]

This text leads us into the midst of the contemporary hermeneutical debate on deconstruction. Derrida writes:

> The impossible . . . has occurred: there is a history of the question, a pure memory of the pure question which in its possibility perhaps authorizes all inheritance and all pure memory in general. . . . [T]he question must be maintained. As a question . . . if this commandment has an ethical meaning, it is not in that it belongs to the *domain* of the ethical, but in that it ultimately authorizes every ethical law in general. . . . Thus the question is always enclosed; it never appears immediately as such, but only through the hermetism of a proposition in which the answer has already begun to determine the question. The purity of the question can only be indicated or recalled through the difference of a hermeneutical effort.[50]

Cohen's hermeneutical effort in this essay consists in working his method of origin through Maimonides' theory of actional attributes, trying to develop knowledge of God as an ethical position (something) predicated upon transcendence (nothing). "The wall does not see" is taken from Alexander of Aphrodisias's commentary on Aristotle's *Metaphysics*. It serves Maimonides as the paradigmatic proposition when demonstrating the nonrelativity of all divine attributes in their application to God.[51]

Alexander comments upon Aristotle's definition of privation in this way: whereas I can claim of both a man and a wall that they are "not seeing," it is only the proposition "this man is blind" that should be properly called a privation, and not the proposition "this wall is blind."[52] Commentators of the *Guide* elaborated much upon Alexander's example of the wall, making a distinction between total negations (*shelilah koleleth*) and specific negations (*shelilah meyuchedeth*) of divine attributes, the latter being reminiscent and logically analogous to Plato's negation particle μη ον.[53]

Citing Aristotle, Maimonides maintains, as we have seen, that "nothing can be described in privative terms unless the characteristic denied by the predicate constitutes a natural disposition of the subject."[54] When God assumes the role of the subject, it would seem, prima facie, that Maimonides' negation of all positive attributes would have to amount to an absolute negation in which subject and predicate are not related in any logical continuity—since no predicate would be expected naturally to pertain to God.[55] Cohen, however, reads the medieval discussion of privation from the hermeneutical perspective of his logic of origin. In this way—as the reader will realize—the most technical aspects of Maimonides' metaphysical terminology lend themselves to Cohen's innovative epistemology of "getting something from nothing"—an epistemology that figures centrally in Cohen's advancement of the ethical significance of Maimonides' theory of divine attributes.

Totalitarian Thinking: Aristotle, Hegel, and the Status Quo— A Note on Humankind

87. Thus Maimonides extends his avoidance of privation even to the point of rejecting life as a divine attribute. For Maimonides, God's life is identical with divine knowledge; (*Guide* 1:53; Maimonides 1856–1861, 1:213–14, (החכמה והחיים ענין אחד) divine knowledge, however, means God's knowing Himself, divine Self-awareness. (*Guide* 1:42; Maimonides 1856–1861, 1:150–51; see Kaufmann 1877, 400, with reference to the critique of Abravanel, (כל משיג עצמו חי וחכם בענין אחד.) Maimonides was able to avail himself here, formally speaking, of Aristotle's God-concept: God is the object of His own thought. [Aristotle 1977, 1072b, 149–51; *Guide* 1:68, 165–66; and Maimonides 1984–1996, Hilkhoth Yesodei haTorah 2:10.] Yet in thinking of Himself, the God of Maimonides

(*See 87.*) *Divine self-sufficiency.* Such self-sufficiency, which excludes humanity, characterizes the God of Aristotle. The God of Aristotle relates to the world ontologically, as its first cause, not ethically, as Aristotle's God is not postulated to represent the world's purpose.[56] The self-complacency of Aristotle's God, whose thinking represents an ontological totality, corresponds to and culminates in Hegel's notion of the "absolute spirit" and its dialectic manifestations in history, which, according to Cohen, represents an unabashed apology of the political and social status quo. In his *Ethik des reinen Willens,* Cohen criticizes Hegel's statement, "That which is rational is real," from *Elements of the Philosophy of Right:*

must not be the exclusive content of His thought. Such self-sufficiency, which excludes humanity, characterizes the God of Aristotle. This makes no sense, however, for the Jewish God. According to Judaism, when thinking of Himself, God must relate to mankind. The idea of man, however, must be the initiative of God, and must not be derived from human existence.

> Here the error of heteronomy is obvious. In no way does moral reason coincide with reality, and in no way does moral law coincide with the positive laws of historical reality or of any particular State. Here lies the enormous *difference between Hegel and Kant.* Kant would say: that which is rational is not real, but rather ought to become real [emphasis added].[57]

Confusingly enough, Maimonides' ethical bent and implicit critique of the Aristotelian doctrine of divine self-contemplation is itself framed throughout in classical Aristotelian terminology:

> His will and His wisdom . . . are not something other than His essence. Consequently He . . . is the ultimate end of everything and *the end of the universe is similarly a seeking to be like unto His perfection* as far as it is within its capacity. . . . Thus I have made it clear to you . . . that He is an efficient cause, a form, and an end. For this reason the philosophers designated Him as a cause and not only as a maker [emphasis added].[58]

The Aristotelian triumvirate of cause, form, and end is situated, within Maimonides, as an explication of the concept of *Imitatio Dei,* "a seeking to be like unto His perfection." This, in turn, is interpreted by Cohen Platonically as the actualization of love and justice, predicated upon the knowledge of the Good, upon the messianic perfection of humanity. Cohen refers to the term *mankind* not in its empirical, historical sense, but rather in its futuric, messianic sense: mankind does not yet exist; its actualization is incumbent upon the human will. True mankind has yet to be created—socially as well as politically.[59] "Messianism," as Cohen says, constitutes the "simple consequence of Jewish monotheism."[60]

More on Wisdom and Volition: More Critique of Ontology

88. From this perspective, it becomes plausible for Maimonides to equate divine volition with divine cognition. [*Guide* 2:13, 452; 3:25, 505–6; Diesendruck 1928, 508–10.] What

(See 88.) The inconsistencies of the medieval attempt to unify divine essence and divine will (*voluntas*) in an ontological equation led Spinoza to a denial of divine

does volition mean insofar as it is distinct from cognition? Obviously, that it initially generates its content and objective out of itself. This, however, creates a dichotomy of the mind's content. [*Guide* 2:18, 301; 2:21, 314–17; 3:20, 480–84.] Knowledge would then necessarily relate to things that did not yet become actual, whereas they should be already contained in God's self-awareness, which is unlimited in its actuality. Thus we would obtain not only a dichotomy in the content of divine cognition, but even in the concept of cognition itself, in terms of divine self-knowledge.

volition.[61] Cohen's reading of Maimonides, on the other hand, transcends the entire medieval discussion, claiming that will is not an ontological attribute of God—in the sense that God "has will"—but rather that divine will is an expression of ethical lawfulness (God's goodness and justice) in which *human*, ethical free will originates. Divine *voluntas* is postulated as a radical demand for the *human* pursuit of the messianic task.[62] Ethical will is therewith defined not in terms of potentiality, but precisely as the instantaneous *actualization* of the ideal Good.

Rashi on Genesis 1:1: A Non-ontological Concept of Creation

89. Hence, we also understand that the very concept of Creation must have been objectionable to Maimonides. The concept of Creation points to a relation of transcendence between God and man, whereas this relation has to be immanent. This immanence, grounded in cognition, is threatened by the concept of volition; the concept of Creation seems to carry out this threat. "Neither power nor will exists in, or belongs to, the Creator with respect to His own essence; for He does not exercise power over Himself, nor does He exercise volition over Himself. This would be unimaginable. Rather, these attributes can only be posited with reference to the mutual relationships between God, the Exalted, and His creatures." (Guide 1:53. וכן בלי ספק היכולת והרצון אין כל אחד

(*See 89.*) *The very concept of creation must have been objectionable to Maimonides.* Cohen's critique of medieval religious ontology results in a non-ontological, atemporal reading of creation, reminiscent of Rashi's commentary on Genesis 1:1:

> The biblical text of *bereshith bara* does not intend to teach us anything about the temporal order of creation—*velo ba hamikra lehoroth seder habria*—but rather the creation narrative instructs and ascertains that the world has a divine purpose: *bereshith* does not mean "in the beginning" but rather *for the sake of:* for the sake of *Torah* [for the sake of the perfection of the world] God has created it [emphasis added].[63]

נמצא לבורא בבחינת עצמו שהוא לא יוכל עצמו ולא יתואר ברצותו עצמו וזה מה שלא יציירהו אדם אבל אלו התארים אמנם יחשבום בבחינת יחסים מתחלפים בין השם יתעלה ובין ברואיו. Maimonides 1856–1861, 1:214, [*Guide* 1:53, 122.])

According to Cohen, it is not due to ontological considerations that Maimonides defends the doctrine of *Creatio ex Nihilo* against the various Greek cosmogenic traditions,[64] since any cosmogenic meaning of Creation will have to presume the immanence of divine essence. The ontological concept of Creation, as Cohen says above, "must have been objectionable" to Maimonides.[65]

God's Immanence: How to Anticipate the Kingdom

90. The concept of Creation as well as that of volition in general implies a distinction between potentiality and actuality. [Aristotle uses the terms *potential* and *actual intellect* in order to describe two states of the intellect: one before the act of thinking, when the intellect is in the state of a mere capacity; one contemporaneous with the act of thinking, when the intellect is an actuality. Aristotle 1975, 165; and Wolfson 1958, 1:404–5. Maimonides—like Aristotle—denies this form of potentiality when applied to divine cognition. Maimonides 1984–1996, Hilkhoth Yesodei ha-Torah 2:9–10; *Guide* 3:20, 483–84. Similarly, Maimonides rejects the association of a temporal sequence of events when referring to divine volition, emphasizing the fact that time itself is created. *Guide* 2:13, 281–83.] Potentiality, however, does not merely indicate contradiction-free thinkability; such thinkability is already implied in essence, in cognition. For potentiality, in contradistinction to thinkability, the concept of time comes into play: we understand potential to be that

(See 89.) Whereas the relationship between God and man has tobe immanent. Insofar as the very idea of Walking in God's Ways is predicated upon human cognition, the relationship between God and man is immanent—immanent for *thought.*[66] Such an immanence of God for thought (Cohen would say for ethical reasoning) constitutes what Cohen calls the correlation between God's Being and the world's Becoming.[67] The world will ever remain unfinished with its messianic task, because the ethical task transcends the ways of the world. Each individual person holds the key to the realization of this task. The individual, in fact, anticipates redemption when actualizing the Good in the face of another human being. Cohen calls such anticipation of redemption "ethical will." Ethical will—a transcendental moment in which redemption is immanent—points to the immanence of God's relationship with man. According to Cohen, the idea of transcendence excludes the immanence of man and God. But it includes the immanence of the *relationship* between God and man.

which is not yet actual. Thus privation and potentiality conjoin. This places a new burden on privation.

Relating to something potential must be excluded from God—hence even volition.

Docta Ignorantia

91. As a result of all these reflections, we may conclude that the negative attributes, of which Maimonides could avail himself, must inevitably take as their premise and prerequisite the privative attributes, in so far as we relate them to God. ["No doubt it is a primary notion that . . . with regard to Him all deficiencies must be denied." *Guide* 3:19, 477.] Instead of saying that Maimonides advocates the doctrine of negative attributes, we ought to say that he admits only those negative attributes that imply the negation of a privative attribute. Maimonides proposes by no means merely a *docta ignorantia.* [See paragraph 77, above.] He is not even ultimately concerned only with the unknowability of God's essence. Rather, by multiplying negations, Maimonides promotes the true, seminal, (ethical) cognition of God. [*Guide* 1:59, 138–39. Cohen associates this chapter with Maimonides' discourse on actional attributes in *Guide* 1:52, 118–19, and with the ethical reading of these attributes in *Guide* 1:54, 124.] The ordinary use of privation, as well as of affirmative superlatives, impedes and inhibits the true knowledge of God. This applies not only to those terms that are explicitly articulated as pantheistic expressions, but even to those

(*See 91.*) The term *docta ignorantia* coined by Nicholas of Cusa denotes a negation of any rational knowledge of God. To Cohen, the mere negation of the knowledge of God does not yet provide us with a helpful hermeneutical position, since such a negation functions logically like any other plainly affirmative dogma. (Cohen does not explore the possibility that the classical doctrine of *docta ignorantia* itself implies a *negatio negationis,* a critique of such simple negation of knowledge.) The negation of a privative proposition, on the other hand, such as "God is not unjust," constitutes a medieval technique of delimitation; this amounts to an affirmation of infinite ways in which the attribute whose privation is excluded—"justice"—ought to be established. Cohen points to the ethical bent of this medieval technique, claiming that its obsession with "exclusions of privations," in fact, reveals a deep concern for the establishment of those attributes that must remain beyond doubt—lovingkindness, justice, and true judgment. These actional attributes must remain, as they serve as arch-images (*Urbilder*) for human emulation.[68]

terms whose external appearance gives no indication of their latent negation: the concept of divine volition in itself creates such privative meaning. The analogy to consciousness, which is hardly inevitable, indicates the apparently almost insurmountable pitfall of privation. At this point, Maimonides sets out to revise the issue.

92. We are now in a position to appreciate how Maimonides' criticism of positive attributes distinguishes itself from that of his predecessors. Jewish philosophy prior to Maimonides had followed the path indicated by the neo-Platonists who had advocated the doctrine of negative attributes. (See Kaufmann 1877, 481.) Maimonides' criticism, however, expresses itself more pointedly and more radically. He puts forward his critique even at the risk of exposing himself to the suspicion of dispensing with the knowledge of God and of depriving it of all content. Why does he commit himself to this course and why did he feel impelled to do so? We know the focus of his thinking: it lies in ethics. Consequently he has to negate, concerning the content of Knowing God, anything based upon privation—implicit or formally explicit—in that it creates a link between God and something else by analogy or through any other relationship.

93. Let us recall that pantheism considers it to be the summit of cognition to impute nature to God, and thus to proclaim *deus sive natura.* In contradistinction, Maimonides relates God exclusively to ethics. Hence the only admissible divine attributes are attributes of action. These attributes, or characteristics [*middoth*], are the ways of God. ("It is clear that the ways the cognition of which Moses demanded of God, and which God proclaimed to him, are the actions proceeding from God. The Sages call them *middoth* and speak of thirteen *middoth.* This term, as they use it, is applied to moral qualities of man, such as nine [sic] *middoth* of those who visit the house of study, four *middoth* of those who give alms. This usage occurs frequently. The meaning here is not that God possesses moral qualities, but that He performs actions resembling the actions that in us proceed from moral qualities—I mean from the aptitude of the soul. . . . It is therefore clear that the ways and the characteristics are identical." הנה כבר התבאר כי הדרכים אשר ביקש ידיעתם והודיעו אותם הם הם הפעולות הבאות ממנו יתעלה והחכמים יקראום מדות ויאמרו שלוש עשרה מדות וזה השם נופל בשמושם על מדות האדם. ארבע מדות בהולכי לבית המדרש ארבע מדות בנותני צדקה וזה הרבה. והענין הנה אינו שהוא בעל מדות אבל פועל פעולות דומות לפעולות הבאות מאתנו ממדות ר"ל מתכונות הנה כבר התבאר לך כי הדרכים והמדות אחד. לא שהוא יתעלה בעל תכונות נפשיות הם. *Guide* 1:54; Maimonides 1856–1861, 1:218–19.) [The Hebrew word *middah* has been adopted from the Latin *modus,* which in turn is derived from the Greek μϵδοναι (measure, or limit), or in the transfigurative sense (a way of acting). See Bacher 1923, 69–70; for the usage in Jewish medieval philosophy in particular, Efros 1924, 67–68; Baneth 1985, 23; 1968, 2:146.]

Midrash and Ethical Judgment

94. If, however, this meaning of the *middoth* attributes that Maimonides articulates points to their character as a model for human emulation, then we must negate those privations that would create in human volition and conduct, a conflict with ethics, or even only a collision with them, as for instance in the case of emotions. It would be wrong to say that because emotion belongs to volition, God must be subject to emotion as well—indeed the opposite is true: since emotion depends on volition, we had better negate volition as applied to God, or sublate divine volition into cognition. Negation of privations—that is the true achievement of divine unity: the exclusion of all relativity from His essence. [Maimonides' rejection of God's relativity with reference to anything other than His essence extends even to a critique of God's syntactical involvement in grammatical constructive chains. For instance, one should say, "the living God," and not "the life of God"; see Maimonides 1984–1996, Hilkhoth Yesodei haTorah 2:10; also 1912, 100–101; and *Guide* 1:68, 161.]

(*See 94.*) *Divine Emotions.* Midrashic tradition, too, predicates the admissibility of divine attributes as paradigms for human emulation upon ethical judgment. Divine attributes such as vengeance, wrath, and anger are ruled out as paradigms for human conduct because they conflict with the pedagogy of Walking in His Ways.[69] Cohen points out that midrashic tradition passes ethical judgment on the biblical text when favoring some divine attributes over others, declaring some to be educationally more suitable for emulation than others. Cohen has no problem with such exercise of ethical judgment, since he sees in the oral tradition an expression of the very activity of critical, ethical reasoning itself. Even the midrashic concept of God, according to Cohen, does not escape the scrutiny of this critique when it fails to answer the human plea for providing an ultimate ground of goodness.[70]

95. We have at this point attained a more exact definition of negative attributes. Yet, are they now entirely free of the negative connotation that seemingly attaches itself to the term *negative attributes?* This question involves another weighty issue.

96. We have noted the ramifications of the ideas to which Maimonides had to resort in order to implement his thesis: he had to sublate divine volition into divine cognition. Hence one might be led into assuming a perspective from which the whole battle against privations seems a life-and-death struggle not only for religionists, but even for those who would identify religion with ethics. If we do identify God exclusively as the God of ethics, then the relation to mankind cannot in principle lie outside of the God concept. Thus negation of privations stands in need of modification, in the process of which its autonomous logical meaning shall be more clearly exposed.

Cohen's *Logik der reinen Erkenntnis* (Logic of Pure Cognition): An Eminently Jewish Book?

97. Here we have reached a point at which I pursue a basic idea of my own systematic logic. This pursuit means that the impartiality of discussion and the objectivity of historical elucidation is put to a difficult test. However, the reader as well as the author may rest their minds considering that the entire history of philosophy exposes itself to the risk of the autonomous interest of speculation and hence inescapably must be charged with the preference of certain problems; or rather, if one may say so, this ought to be the case. There exists only one means of safeguarding against such subjectivity: resort to painstaking research of the literary source material and the separation of hypothesis from fact.

(*See 97.*) *Here we have reached a point at which I pursue a basic idea of my own logic.* Cohen's hermeneutical approach in his reading of Maimonides is derived from Cohen's *Logik der reinen Erkenntnis*, in which he develops a logic of origin that is predicated upon the philosophical concept of purity. The concept of purity itself closely interrelates with Cohen's Jewish thinking: Cohen's advancement of the concept of pure thought and its plea for the infinite creativity of the human mind to interpret, change, and construct cultural facts owes itself to a cultural tradition whose hermeneutical creativity is predicated upon a God whose command to interpret, change, and construct human reality is rooted in His purity or Holiness. In other words, the concept of purity, which lies at the heart of Cohen's logic, is a concept that is rooted in the sensibilities of Jewish tradition.

On the other hand, Cohen's philosophical interpretation of purity becomes the yardstick for what is truly Jewish in Jewish tradition. Through it, the nonmanipulable God safeguards the inexhaustible grounds of creativity and of goodness (traditionally speaking, of holiness). The concept of purity thus generates a tradition within the tradition of which Maimonides is the most outspoken rabbinic representative. Cohen and Levinas are the most prominent modern heirs of this tradition.

Cohen's Logic correlates with the emphasis both on the oral and on the ethical character of the

Jewish tradition in that its very concept of origin establishes the priority of what is unknown over what is known, of the Other over the Self.[71] Rosenzweig's *Sprachdenken* and Levinas's "ethics as first philosophy" are ramifications of Cohen's Logic and his Ethics. We may therefore say that Cohen's *philosophical* work—and not his *Religion of Reason*—ultimately delineates the method of his *Jewish* thinking. Whereas tradition provides content and parameters for Cohen's Logic, especially the concepts of purity, origin, and infinity. Accordingly, Cohen terms *Jewish* a way of thinking infinitely occupied with the integration of limits as inspired by the concept of purity. Maimonides' theory of Knowing God represents such kind of thinking in that its ethical position is predicated upon a nought of knowledge in which goodness functions as a transcendental limit.

Cohen's rejection of Jewish mysticism as expressed in the tradition of Cabala and Chassiduth is grounded in prejudice: Cohen reads mysticism as an unveiling of divine knowledge.[72] Any unveiling or positing of divine knowledge, for Cohen, however, signifies a mythification—and myth, according to Cohen, Rosenzweig, and Levinas, sacralizes the world.[73] In order for the world to relate to the idea of humanity, however, it must first be radically desacralized.[74]

Philosophy and Oral Tradition: A Book May Be Closed, Lips and Mouths Continue to Speak

The risk of the autonomous interest of speculation. Cohen reassures himself and his traditional reader—both concerned with the limits of subjective interpretation—by recalling the fact that the interpretation of traditional Jewish texts at all times has been determined by "autonomous interests of speculation." Any hermeneutical activity continuously lends new meaning to the otherwise "silent letters" of tradition, and *must* be invested with such autonomous interests.[75]

It seems that Cohen consciously brings his own philosophical method in correlation with the traditional hermeneutics of Jewish oral tradition, and thus retrieves a premodern mode of discourse for his own critical philosophy. In the same way as ethical judgment is predicated upon the futurity of the messianic ideal, the significance of any text is predicated upon future interpretations. In this process, "the concept reigns supreme" (in the sense that there is no limit to this interpretative process), even though the fate of any interpretive tangent remains determined by the political structure of the community, and by its interaction with the specificity of the texts themselves.[76]

On Divine Attributes: A Theory of Relativity

98. If God is the God of ethics, the relationship to human beings must be inherent in Him. This is the meaning of essence, hence also of divine essence, that it constitutes the basis for relations. Therefore, while privations, which presume comparability between man and God, shall be negated, it in no way follows that the relationship between God and man is voided altogether through this negation of privative attributes; rather, on the contrary, in this way we create the prerequisite foundation for genuine (necessary) relatedness. Therein lies the preference for these attributes over against the positive ones. If I say, "God is wise," I can only intend to define His essence. The target of Knowing God, however, must not be cognition of His essence, but rather of His significance as the ethical paragon. On the other hand, if I say "God is not ignorant," or more accurately, "not not wise," the proposition aims at its grounding, at the origin of this attribute, and thus I attribute to God self-awareness and governance. Therewith, I relate to divine knowledge the world with all that it contains. [Cohen seems to suggest that the double privation "not not-x" (say, "God is not not-active") hermeneutically excels over both the simple position "x" and the simple negation "not-x," since it amounts to an affirmative proposition excluding "all forms of inactivity from God's essence in a way that activity must remain." Also Diesendruck 1935, 147; and Spero 1972, 73.]

(*See 98.*) *The relationship to human beings must be inherent in God.* Cohen's rigorous application of his principle of origin in this paragraph introduces a theory of relativity into Maimonides' theory of negative attributes. This prepares for an epistemological position in which divine actional attributes are interpreted as vectors for human action. As stated earlier, Cohen thereby converts the conventional reading of Maimonides' theory of attributes as negative theology into a philosophical formulation of Maimonides' ethical position.

99. Hence, these attributes are more positive, more germane, than positive attributes. If I say, "God is not powerless," this signifies that "His existence suffices for the bringing into existence of things other than He." [*Guide* 1:58, 136.] Thus the attribute "not powerless" constitutes the origin of other beings besides God, whereas the attribute of "omnipotence" is entirely incapable of attaining such a meaning.

100. Moreover, if I say "God is not inattentive or negligent," I mean "that all beings follow a certain order and governance; that they are not neglected and not given over to chance." (ואמרנו בו מפני אלו העניינים
שהוא יכול וחכם ורוצה. והכוונה באלו התארים

שאין לו אח . . . שמציאותו יש בה די להמצאת דברים אחרים זולתו. ועניין אמרנו ולא סבל שהוא משיג כלומר חי, כי כל משיג חי ועניין אמרנו לא נבהל ולא עוזב, כי כל אלה הנמצאות הולכות על סדר והנהגה, לא נעזבות והוות כאשר יקרה. *Guide* 1:58; Maimonides 1856–1861, 1:244) [*Guide* 1:58, 136.] The apparently negative attribute, that only seems to forfend a frivolity, implies governance and providence, whereas "will" does not imply such a transitive relationship.

101. Therefore, Maimonides defines the identity of essence and existence in such a way that "it by no means suffices for Him to exist solely for Himself, but myriad existences emanate from Him. And this emanation is unlike that of heat from fire and unlike the proceeding of light from the sun. Rather, this emanation constitutes the grounds of existence, its duration and order by means of wisely contrived governance." (שזה הנמצא אין מציאותו אשר הוא עצמו מספקת לו שהיה נמצא בלבד אבל שופעת מאתו מציאות רבות . . . אבל השפע ימשיך להם תמיד עמידה וקיום וסדיור בהנהגה מתוקנת. Guide 1:58; Maimonides 1856–1861, 1:243) [*Guide* 1:58, 136.] The essence of God consequently signifies not merely His own being [*Wesen*]—and insofar as God's essence is equated with existence, it relates not merely to divine existence—but extends even to the emanation of other beings, and to the governance of them.

102. Hence this is also the meaning of God's uniqueness: that He has no peer, which ultimately means that there is but One ethical grounding and origin for the ethical world.

103. By differentiating between emanation and irradiation, the concept of existence obtains the moment of action, and thus the attribute of divine existence becomes an attribute of action. Maimonides himself combines the two terms *negation* and *privation.* He calls our attention to the usage of attributes in the books of the prophets, "that they are attributes of action or that they indicate the negation of their privations in God." (אמנם שאר מה שבא בספרי הנביאים יקרא בעבור עליו אבל יאמינו בו מה שכבר בארנו שהם תארי פעולותיו או להורות על שלילת העדרים. *Guide* 1:59; Maimonides 1856–1861, 1:258.) Here, both pertinent moments are explicitly stated: the designation of the negative as negation of its privative has the sense of an infinite judgment as the proposition of origin; [As in the case of the infinite proposition "God is not-ignorant," in which the negation of privation indicates an infinite affirmation of God's knowledge: "God is the origin of cognition." The advancement of this epistemological position is predicated upon Cohen's concept of origin, which assumes an infinitesimal integrative function in interpreting cultural facts, as it is critical of all fundamental, dogmatic assumptions that are supposed to lie beyond the reach of the activity and creativity of interpretation/thinking itself.] at the same time, Maimonides equates the attributes thus defined with actional attributes.

The Priority of Ethics over Religion

104. Now we are in a position to appreciate Maimonides' innovative contribution to the doctrine of attributes in its historical perspective vis-à-vis his predecessors. In fact, he shares with all of them the tendency to fend off all corporeality and all anthropomorphism on behalf of pure Jewish monotheism. This relates to his basic tendency to ground the entire religion of Israel in ethics, and, insofar as it can be carried out, to dissolve religion into ethics.

(*See 104.*) *To ground the entire religion of Israel in ethics.* A clarification in terms of Cohen's notion of "religion" is useful here. Cohen's later modification of "religion" in terms of its peculiarity or specificity, in which he emphasizes the individual's existential relationship to God,[77] leaves the paramount importance of the ethical ideal in Judaism unimpaired. Throughout his later writings, Cohen continues to maintain the universality of the messianic objective in Judaism. He does so by emphasizing its redemptive promise for all people, thus continuously establishing the priority of ethics over religion.[78]

105. Even the methodological force of his philosophical speculation exceeds that of all his predecessors. Maimonides' combat is directed against materialism in all its consequences and rudiments. His victory is therefore the triumph of idealism. [Note that Cohen speaks here of *critical* idealism in sharp contradistinction to the idealism of Hegel which became the target of the existentialist critique.] Hence, his methodology alone does not permit us to conceive of him as an Aristotelian.

106. Moreover, in his capacity as an author Maimonides demonstrates his originality. His predecessors turn out to be more or less eclectics; hence in their discussions, even the thesis of negative attributes remains on the level of formalism. Only with Maimonides does the doctrine of negative attributes assume the vital seriousness that commands our attention: the far-reaching ramifications of his doctrine reveal themselves. Therefore only Maimonides provokes vehement polemics against this doctrine on the part of immature believers. Maimonides' oeuvre emerges from this situation as a true classic characterized by shunning eclecticism, enlivening the mere technicalities of argument, and lending vitality to their real consequences. Thus, he brings the problem of divine attributes toward a solution and its treatment to full maturity.

5

The "Unity of the Heart"

On Love and Longing (Where Ethical Method Fails)

Contemplating main topics of Maimonidean theology, such as the relationship of cognition and love, love and fear of God, and questions of eschatology, Cohen in this fifth chapter explores the consequences of his Platonic reading of Maimonides' theory of divine attributes for a Jewish theology that is grounded in but not exhausted by its rational foundations. In discussing the aesthetic dimension of love, Cohen here as well as elsewhere in his Jewish writings focuses upon the medieval thinker Bahya ibn Pakuda. The critique of the Aristotelian eudaemonian ethics continues to be the issue against which Cohen turns his critical argument.

Divine Omniscience and Human Volition

107. In keeping with his doctrine of attributes, Maimonides rejects the distinction between intellect and volition. Volition constitutes that force (יכולת) in which impulse merges with reason. Impulse has not yet reached the stage of affect and does not yet claim the status of an autonomous potency vis-à-vis reason. Hence Maimonides is able to teach freedom of will, but not merely in the psychological or anthropological sense, according to which Aristotle admits that even children and animals possess freedom—which freedom, however, lacks all ethical implication. [Aristotle 1945, *NE* 1111b, 129.] Maimonides insists

(*See 107.*) *No contradiction between the freedom of the human being and divine omnipotence.* According to Maimonides, the omniscience of God expresses itself as the rational order of the universe, and therefore divine omniscience does not contradict but rather endorses the faculty of human reasoning. Human reasoning, in turn, is predicated upon the freedom of will without which there would be no accountability for one's actions. Maimonides' concepts of divine and human will, Cohen claims, converge, or correlate in the ethical task of human perfection—Knowing God and Walking in His Ways.[1]

that intentionality is intrinsic to freedom, a demand that Aristotle dismisses. Maimonides does not brook any contradiction between the freedom of the human being and the omnipotence or omniscience of God. Otherwise we would have to admit a conflict between reason human and divine; it is precisely this conflict, however, that is resolved through the very definition of reason. Perhaps we may then say that ultimately the concept of reason in Maimonides means none other than the establishment of a basic ethical relationship between God and the human being. There can be but one reason upon which knowing God is necessarily predicated. Maimonides adopts the interpretation of ibn Ezra that we may read as a corollary to Hear O Israel: "The mediator between God and the human beings is reason." המלאך בין האדם ובין אלהיו הוא שכלו (See *Guide* 3:52 אשר בינינו ובין השי' השכל . . . הוא הדבוק) [also ibn Ezra 1985, 142; and ibn Ezra's commentary on Mishlei 22:21 in ibn Ezra 1884, 31].

Mediation and Kingship: Reading ibn Ezra

"*The Mediator between God and the human beings is reason*" [hamal'akh ben ha-adam uven elohav hu sikhlo], says ibn Ezra in his preface to his commentary on the Torah, emphasizing that the hermeneutical principles of biblical commentary and of the oral tradition reflect a *rational* practice of interpreting Torah. It is not by chance that Cohen discusses this statement in the context of Shema Yisrael, as he thereby alludes to a playful alliterative association of *malakh* and *melekh,* of "mediator" and "king," positing God's oneness as the mediating ground for the obligation traditionally expressed as "*kabbalath 'ol malkhuth shamayim*" [taking the yoke of God's kingship upon oneself].[2]

Cohen reads the Shema as the classical Jewish expression of the correlation between God's oneness and the messianic unity of mankind.[3] This reading renders incongruent any mythical imagery concerning the intellect mediating between God and the human being. Maimonides' use of the neo-Platonic image of divine overflow, "likening God to an overflowing spring of water,"[4] represents to Cohen a mere conventional way of speaking, as the implications of divine overflow seem to suggest a mediation of God and world in ontological ways. On the other hand, the concepts of holiness and purity, upon which Cohen's reading of Maimonides is predicated, demand that any such mediation between God and humankind be *volitional.*

Knowledge and Love

108. The unity of knowledge and will leads Maimonides to establish the fundamental identity of knowledge and love. [Maimonides 1971, 59, directive 3; Maimonides 1984–1996, Hilkhoth Teshuvah 10:6; Hilkhoth Yesodei haTorah 2:2, 4:12; *Guide* 1:39, 89; 3:28, 512–13; 3:51, 621.] He is not the first to propose this idea, nor even the first to develop it. We find this idea among all Jewish philosophers; [Haberman 1973, 190–92; the identity of knowledge and love originates with the biblical text. Genesis 4:1 and the Hebrew root **yd^*; also Rashi on Genesis 18:19.] Bahya, in particular, is of lasting significance due to his deeply significant correlation of this idea with his tenet of unity ["unifying the heart" in the Hebrew of ibn Tibbon: *yichud halev*]. The whole of rabbinic literature is suffused with this idea of love. Even in Scripture, this idea of love represents the distinctive mark of the monotheistic concept of God. [*JS* 3:48–52. Uncharacteristically, Cohen makes use of a classical *gematria*—substituting numerical values for the Hebrew letters—to emphasize the equation of love and oneness, both of which Hebrew terms—*ahavah* and *echad*—amount to the numerical value of thirteen. *JS* 3:49.]

(*See 108.*) *The fundamental identity of knowledge and love.* Against a purely rationalist reading of Maimonides' theory of Knowing God, Cohen argues that "if God were only an object of knowledge, then God would not be 'Unique,' for knowledge has other objects and other problems."[5] Striving to know God implies a commitment of love. Love of God results in an act of ethical volition: "If ethics had not discovered the principle of volition, it would have had to evolve from the [monotheistic] religion."[6] Love of God is, then, inextricably linked to a *cognitive* process—it is *episteme* in the truest sense of the word, since it refers to a process in which thought gives an account of itself.

Consequently, Cohen, when asked the question what it means to love God, emphatically declares: "How is it possible to love anything but an idea? . . . Only the ideal can I love. . . . The ideal is the archetype of ethics."[7] Scorned by the existentialist critics of rationalism as the "philosopher's love of God,"[8] Cohen's assertion that love of God is a *cognitive* commitment corresponds, in fact, with the traditional commentaries on Shema Yisrael and the pertaining Sifre:

> And what is called true love of God? The answer is "and these words shall be upon your heart"—by keeping "these words" close to your heart you will come to *know* God and will thus be able to cleave to His ways. [9]

Bahya ibn Pakuda and the "Unity of the Heart": Beyond Philology

Unifying the Heart. Cohen cites Bahya as follows:

> The unification of the heart has two aspects: firstly, the unity of the heart that is grounded in the unity of God; and secondly, the unity of the heart when it is directed towards God, when one performs an act directed towards the world-to-come, obligatory or voluntary.[10]

Throughout his reading of Bahya, Cohen argues that the unity of the heart and the unity of one's actions are both predicated upon the Jewish concept of the unity of God.[11] In other words, there is a correlation between the individual's innermost being (*lev*) with the one God which results in the unity of one's action (*yichud ha-ma'aseh*), an expression that we find in the Arabic original.[12] The unity or purity of the heart thus represents to Cohen the very culmination of the spirit of Judaism.[13]

Philologically there has been disagreement with Cohen's Tibbonite reading of Bahya's notion of "unity of the heart." Both Cohen's contemporary, the Arabist Wilhelm Bacher, as well as a contemporary Arabist, Yosef Kafih, point to the fact that there is no such notion as the "unity of heart," or *yichud ha-lev,* in Bahya's original Arabic text.[14] The philologists say that Cohen's entire commentary on Bahya's "unity of the heart" is the result of a philosophically germane mistranslation, namely that of Yehuda ibn Tibbon in his rendition of the Hebrew term *yichud ha-lev* for the Arabic original.

Cohen's answer to Bacher is poignant: adherence to philology is, indeed, necessary for any significant commentary, but adherence to mere philology may prove deficient when addressing a philosophical question.[15] First, we may say that even the literal translation of the Arabic *achlaz,* as *tohar ha-matspun*, does strengthen Cohen's reading, as *tohar ha-matspun* should itself be rendered as the purity of one's innermost being (*Innerlichkeit*).[16] Secondly, and more important, the Judeo-Arabic tradition itself coined the term *yichud ha-lev* in its classical rendition of the Arabic term *achlaz,* as Saadya himself associates that Arabic term with the biblical *yached levavi* (Psalms 86:11) in his translation of Psalms into Arabic.[17] Thirdly, the very connotation of the Hebrew term *lev* is one of a spiritual, cognitive, and volitional function, since the opposition of heart and mind does not exist for the Hebrew term *lev.*[18]

Where Ethical Method Fails: The Innermost Part of the Soul (*Innerlichkeit*)

109. The question of how the concept of love is to be combined with the God-concept is very difficult. The Greek gods are venerated, yet *love* is not a technical term of Greek worship; as we know, in fact, the elimination of all erotic elements from worship must have been the primary concern of the prophets. [Levinas shares Cohen's position: "Such Love [of God is] without Eros." See Levinas 1996, 140. For a critic of Levinas on this issue, see Bruckstein 2001, 128–35. Eroticism in Jewish worship has become a major issue among contemporary Kabbala scholars who dispute Scholem's claim that there is no *unio mystica* in Jewish tradition. See Scholem 1995, 123, and his critics: Idel 1988a, 24, 52; E. Wolfson 1995.] For them, from a merely linguistic perspective, the word love implies knowledge. [Genesis 4:1, 4:17, 4:25, 24:16; 1 Samuel 1:19.] Even if knowledge takes on sensual significance, sensuality cannot be considered its dominant meaning, but rather the sensual connotation has a concomitant metaphorical ring to it. [*RoR* 269; *RdV* 314, invoking Hosea 2:21; see also Jeremiah 2:2 and the gamut of metaphorical interpretations of Song of Songs.] On the other hand, love attains through this association a more spiritual and ethical character. Thus the love of human beings is generated by the

(See 108.) Cohen's focus on *Innerlichkeit,* or on the "unity of the heart," implies a critique of the ethical method and its universalism—a critique that hinges upon the person's uniqueness and particularity. Cohen develops this critique fully in his *Religion of Reason: Out of the Sources of Judaism.* Cohen's reading of Bahya's concept of the soul or heart as the "innermost part of one's being"—proposed first in this essay on Maimonides and later in his essay on Bahya—brings into focus a uniquely personal relationship with God. This relationship, by dint of its very specificity, must escape the structure of ethics: the *one* God does correlate with *one mankind,* but the correlation between the *unique* God and the *single* human soul escapes the universal method of ethics:

> Ethics, so to speak, is no respecter of persons. . . . Each one represents to ethics merely the self-same symbol of mankind.[19]

Cohen's concept of radical subjectivity is borne out by the relationship between the unique God and the single soul. Traditional Jewish concepts such as *devekuth* (cleaving to God), *ahavath hashem* (love of God), and *ahavath hareah* (love of one's neighbor) point

love of God: love of one's fellow, the stranger, hence of mankind. The love of mankind reflects the love of God, since God is the paragon for man. To love God means to cultivate ethics which, in turn, constitute the essence of God. [*RoR* 144–64; *RdV* 167–91; *ErW* 403.]

to relationships whose roots lie beyond the grasp of ethical method. In other words, the soul's passionate love of God, manifest in her compassionate response toward the suffering of her neighbor, testifies to an *aesthesis,* an emotional commitment. Such a commitment "penetrates body and soul,"[20] escaping all universal definitions of ethics and humanity, while remaining faithful to fulfilling precisely what ethics would demand.

Cohen's reading of Bahya points to the longing of the human soul. This longing is directed toward the fulfillment of that which is ethical, notwithstanding the fact that the ethical, due to its universal structure, cannot relate to the uniqueness of the soul, her particular existence. Ethical demands turn out to be precisely that—duties of the heart—and as such these demands of ethics themselves know no legal measure. They are predicated upon the passions of the soul ("love of one's fellow, love and fear of God, Walking in His Ways"), says a thirteenth-century compendium of Jewish law, and have no *shi'urim*—no quantified legal measure.[21]

Cohen's distinction between God's oneness and God's uniqueness, between ethical will and the human soul, teaches a knowledge of ethics that is itself anchored in the "innermost part of the soul."[22] The soul "tastes" God in a way that escapes both the ethicist and the theologian.[23] Cohen's *Ästhetik des reinen Gefühls* (Aesthetics of pure feeling)—a book that has not been studied enough and whose content is yet of profound influence for twentieth-century Jewish thought[24]—defines *aesthesis* as "feeling, taste, sensory knowledge." This emotional quality of *aesthesis* lies at the roots of one's commitments to others, and as such ethical commitments, in particular, are anchored in the very singularity of the individual, in the very singularity of the other person whose suffering touches one's own soul.[25]

Cohen's discussion of Bahya's concept of the "unity of the heart" in this essay is of much significance as it provides a new insight into the distinction between ethics and religion in his later work. Cohen's reading of Bahya's *yichud ha-lev* as the "innermost part of one's being" both transcends and undergirds the demands of ethics. Bahya himself says in his *Book of Direction to the Duties of the Heart:*

> [The obligations of the law] are of no avail to us unless our hearts choose to do them and our souls desire their per-

> formance. . . . These obligations are upon us constantly, everywhere and at all times, accompanying every hour, every minute, every situation, as long as our minds and souls are yet with us.[26]

Which obligations? Bahya exemplifies the "duties of the heart" by citing from Leviticus:

> Thou shalt not take vengeance, not bear any grudge. . . . Thou shalt love thy neighbor as thyself . . . depart from evil and do good; seek peace, and pursue it.[27]

Cohen's emphasis upon Bahya's concept of *yichud ha-lev* in this essay—alternately to be rendered as "the unity of the heart" and "the uniqueness of the human soul"—reaches far deeper than the philologist's critique: While ethics may not know the human soul, Bahya's "unity of the heart" does. The human soul—*die Seele*—and the human heart—*das Menschenherz*—are Cohen's terms for a person's innermost self in her relationship to the unique God. The soul is longing: "My soul longs for You, O God; my soul thirsts for the living God."[28]

Cohen quotes this Psalm often in order to express an emotional longing that transcends the confines of all theoretical structure while strictly heeding the ethical demands of the God who charges "to do justice and walk humbly before your God."[29] The concluding paragraph of Bahya's *Book of Direction to the Duties of the Heart* stresses the ethical ramifications that ensue from *yichud ha-lev,* from the relationship between a person's innermost being and God. We are exhorted

> to control your tongue, to rule over your senses, to master your desires, to restrain your members, to scrutinize your thoughts, to make your deeds the equal of your knowledge.[30]

"All My Goodness": A Critique of Cosmic Love

110. This conclusion, this equivalence, Maimonides achieves with great precision, with intense devotion, with classical perspicuity, and he applies it creatively to his entire theology and ethics. Knowing God is loving God, and love of God is knowledge of God; these are the two vectors of one and the same fundamental idea which promoted Maimonides to the status of Israel's

(*See 110.*) *Ethics is the recognizable attribute of God.* God's answer to Moses' request to know the ways of God is, "I will make all My goodness pass before Thee."[31] According to Maimonides, the knowledge of the goodness of God is not only predicated upon an understanding of the natural order (Cohen comments that goodness can never be demonstrated by

teacher *par excellence* for all time. Both love of God and knowledge of God, however, are equivalent to love and knowledge of ethics; for ethics is the recognizable attribute of God. There is no love of God that is not by definition knowledge of God, or knowledge of ethics. By knowledge of God, Maimonides does not mean some adjunct to metaphysics, such as knowing the Prime Mover of the spheres, [Aristotle 1977, *Metaphysics* 1072a–b, 147–49.] nor any ontological knowledge of the divine metaphysical substance, but rather he refers exclusively to the cognition of the divine ethical character, hence to knowledge as love. Thus it seems obvious that Maimonides reveals a more profound kinship with Plato than with Aristotle, although he may have only been familiar with *Timaeus*. [Pines's introduction to Moreh ha-Nebukhim, *Guide* lxxv. It was Diesendruck who first explored Cohen's Platonic reading of Maimonides. Diesendruck 1928, 415–535, esp. 416; also Cohen paragraph 32 in chapter 2 of this book.]

reference to natural order), but the goodness of God rather signifies an ethical order whose content has been *revealed* to Moses in terms of human ethical characteristics, the Thirteen Attributes.[32] Acting upon the *knowledge* of these attributes represents the love for God about which Cohen speaks. Aristotle's concept of the Prime Mover offers its own teleological explanation of "cosmic love": "the Good . . . is the end of some action which causes motion as being an object of love."[33] This explanation is reflected verbatim in Maimonides' cosmological claim that the motion of the stars is the result of "a desire for that which . . . is the beloved object: namely, the deity, may His name be exalted."[34]

Cohen, of course, reads this Aristotelian teleology of cosmic love within the context of mythical ontology. Whereas myth is interested in the ontological origins of things (such as the origin of motion, the origin of matter), Jewish monotheism focuses instead upon the origins of this world's *purpose*—arriving at God's word as the grounds of goodness, of justice, and of love of one another. Jewish thinking—or better, Cohen's own critical philosophy—takes up the task of opposing any ontology of origins. Aristotelian cosmology is associated with the panpsychic love of heavenly bodies while Cohen's reading of messianism correlates with the concreteness of love of one's neighbor.[35] According to both Cohen and Maimonides, cosmology and physics are subordinate to theology and ethics. This is why Maimonides' own physics, which is decidedly Aristotelian, does not stand in the way of Cohen's distinctly ethical and Platonic reading of Maimonides' metaphysical theory of Knowing God.[36]

Jeremiah's Wisdom: Saadya on Textual Reasoning

111. The *Guide* concludes characteristically with an urgent appeal to commit oneself to the pursuit of knowledge. Maimonides grounds himself in the authority of Jeremiah (9:22–23), that knowing God should motivate man's sole aspired dignity; and this knowing is characterized as wisdom (חכמה). Even adherence to the Law is reduced to "preciousness," and does not attain the rank of Knowing God. (Rosin 1876, 103, emphasizes the difference between knowledge of God and faith in God.) [Also Kafih's commentary on Sefer ha-Mitsvoth in Maimonides 1971, 58n. 1. See Maimonides' reading of Midrash Bereshit Rabba (1996, 333) in *Guide* 3:54, 636–37. The term *chefets* (desire) is used there in three different contexts: (*a*) *Chafatsekha* (Proverbs 3:15), "things you canst desire," which refers to worldly precious goods; (*b*) *chafatsim* (Proverbs 8:11), "things desirable," which refers to the commandments and good deeds that are precious and desirable to God; and, the most inspiring meaning, (*c*) *chafatsti* (Jeremiah 9:22), "that which God desires," which refers to lovingkindness, justice, and true judgment, "that you understandeth and knoweth Me." *Guide* 3:54, 636–37.] Maimonides makes the fundamental distinction between Torah and Wisdom (חכמה). [*Guide* 3:54, 634, 636: "the term wisdom (*chokhmah*), used in an unrestricted sense and regarded as the end,

(*See 111.*) *The authority of Jeremiah.* It is useful to quote Jeremiah (9:22–23) in full:

> Let not the wise man glory in his wisdom [חכמה]; let not the strong man glory in his strength; let not the rich man glory in his riches. But only in this should one glory: in his earnest devotion to Me. For I the Lord act with kindness, justice, and equity in the world. For in these I delight—declares the Lord.[37]

The context in which Maimonides discusses Jeremiah 9:22–23 in the *Guide* enhances Cohen's reading. *Chokhmah* (wisdom), as indicated by Jeremiah, refers to that kind of knowledge which establishes our existence in the world-to-come, and constitutes the highest human perfection.[38] Knowledge of God, however, is no intellectual achievement alone ("let not the wise man glory in his wisdom") but it rather hinges upon the actualization of "kindness, justice, and equity." Scripture goes on to say, "For I, God, act with kindness, justice, and equity in the world. For in these I delight."

Maimonides follows the rationalist tradition of Saadya's hermeneutics. Accordingly, oral tradition (any authoritative interpretation of Hebrew Scripture) must be attentive to the principles of correct speculation. Saadya advises that

means in every place the apprehension of Him; that all the actions prescribed by the Law [are] not to be compared with this ultimate end . . . being but preparations made for the sake of this end." Maimonides advances a functional concept of Torah in that "actions prescribed by the Law" lead to the higher end of Knowing God—a knowledge culminating in the active recognition of "lovingkindness, justice, and true judgment."] In this distinction he might well base himself upon a significant Haggadic passage: "When a person appears before the heavenly court they first ask: 'During your lifetime, have you fixed a schedule for studying Torah; have you devoted yourself to the pursuit of wisdom; have you drawn inferences from that which you were taught?'" [in TB Shabbat 31b; *RoR* 91; *RdV* 106.] Maimonides concludes: "It thus has become clear to you that, according to the Sages, knowledge of Torah is of one kind, and wisdom is of another kind, and that it is wisdom which must verify the teachings of the Torah through true speculation" (והוא לאמת דעות התורה בעיון האמיתי) (*Guide* 3:54). [*Guide* 634.]

"if Scripture does contradict reason [a convincing way of reasoning], the text in question should be interpreted accordingly."[39] Cohen proposes that it is just this corrective and creative attitude toward traditional texts which constitutes the distinct hermeneutical rationale of Jewish oral tradition. Creative interpretation, which Cohen refers to as the activity of "the concept," provides the grounds for a "construction" of the sources of Judaism.[40] Tradition itself teaches that the written text, the literal authority of Scripture, in fact, hinges upon and results from oral tradition. In other words, oral tradition does not provide the community with interpretation—where the written text serves as the passive basis for such interpretation—but rather the text itself is already a *poesis*, a poetic rendition of meaning, the result of a prior hermeneutical effort to make sense of the teaching.[41]

Moses taught the Torah for forty years before it was committed to writing, and once there was a lapidary written text, it could not be studied without commentaries.[42] Interpretative activity is prior to the text: oral tradition inseminates and thus generates what only literalists (fundamentalists) will consider to be "prior" to interpretation—namely the written text itself.[43] Cohen follows the authority of Saadya and Maimonides in their rational bent of this teaching, claiming that the rational investigation of the Writ—the hermeneutical quest for meaning—constructs the authority of the Jewish source.

Love, Awe, Fear

112. This identity of knowledge and love led to the important distinction between love and fear [*Furcht.*] [Bamberger 1929; Urbach 1987, 400–419. Sifre on Deuteronomy 6:5 (Sifre 1993, 54); Isaac ben Joseph of Corbeil 1937, 3–5, together with the gloss of Rabbenu Perets therein; Bahya 1973, 435–36; Judah ha-Levi 1964, 113–15, 143–50; Maimonides 1984–1996, Hilkhoth Teshuvah 10.] Just as love is, so also is fear a basic term in worshiping God. The concept of fear clearly links monotheism with polytheism. However, even the latter does not resign itself to fear, but rather develops it into shy reverence (αιδως). [*ErW* 490, *αιδως.] The biblical concept of awe does not connote terror-stricken dread, but rather grateful devotion, as demonstrated in the context of the verse: "You shall revere the Eternal, your God, to Him attach yourself." (תירא [. . .] ובו תדבק) [Deuteronomy 10:20.] To revere God means to attach oneself—whereas the natural effect of fear should be daunting, recoil and restraint. Thus we find that the Jewish philosophers, drawing on Talmudical sources, have linked awe and love as "awe-filled love" (יראה של אהבה). Here again Bahya precedes Maimonides with his deep sensitivity; yet the Maimonidean presentation of this linkage surpasses him. [Maimonides 1984–1996,

(*See 112.*) *Love and awe.* The term *awe* (*Ehrfurcht*) connotes an emotion of mingled reverence, dread, and wonder, inspired by something majestic or sublime. Fear (*Furcht* or *Angst*) on the other hand, refers to an "apprehension caused by the expectation of danger, pain, disaster, or the like."[44] Cohen associates serving God out of fear with an extrinsic (heteronomous) relationship whose motivation is dominated by material factors, reminiscent of the very nature of idol-worship. "The concept of fear clearly links monotheism with polytheism," he writes. Maimonides, too, claims,

> Let not a man say, "I will observe the precepts of the Torah and occupy myself with its wisdom, in order that I may obtain all the blessings written in the Torah, or to attain life in the world to come; I will abstain from transgressions against which the Torah warns, so that I may be saved from the curses written in the Torah, or that I may be cut off from life in the world to come."[45]

whereas awe or reverence correlates with "knowledge and love."[46]

Hilkhoth Yesodei haTorah 2:1–2: "God commands us to love Him and to be in awe of Him. . . . When a person contemplates God's works . . . she will immediately love, and praise, and . . . will be seized by a keen longing passion to know the Great Name. . . . When this person now deliberates upon all these things . . . she will be . . . conscious that she is but an insignificant, low and obscure creature, standing light-minded and ignorant before the Perfect Mind. . . . In accordance with these matters, I shall explain great principles of the work wrought by the Master of the cosmos, so that they may serve as a gateway for the cogitator to love God." (translation by author)]

113. We have highlighted Abraham ibn Daud's achievement of distinguishing categories among the laws of the Torah. [Paragraph numbers 41 through 45 in chapter 2 of this book.] Although Maimonides does not introduce such qualitative distinctions into the classifications of the commandments, he does devise a differentiation of trenchant character and thus surpasses him: performance of the commandments educates man toward the awe of God, whereas knowing God and his oneness leads man to the love of God. [*Guide* 3:52, 629–30; also Nachmanides on Exodus 20:8, relating "directive" commandments to love of God, and "injunctive" commandments to fear—or hold in awe—God: "And the former are greater than the latter, as love is higher than fear." Nachmanides 1971–1976, 2:309–10; also Rashi (1982, 529) on Deuteronomy 6:5 (Sifre 1993, 54).] Hence the ceremonial laws are relegated to a preparatory stage of worship, which expresses itself as fear. This stage is preliminary to and distinct from genuine worship, which is serving God through knowledge and love. Worshiping God by performing the commandments is equivalent to entering the antechambers of the sanctuary dedicated to the one God.

Becoming Like God—Righteous, Holy, and Wise: Plato's *Theaetetus*

114. The identity of knowledge and love led Maimonides to adopt and articulate an idea which is inherent theoretically and practically in all religions, namely "drawing close" to God (התקרבות). Greek culture employs the terminology "attaining likeness unto God" (ομοιωσις θεω); [Plato 1952, *Theaetetus* 176b, (*See 114.*) *"Attaining likeness unto God."* Plato writes that attaining likeness unto God is to "become like God, so far as this is possible; and to become like God is to become righteous, holy and wise."[48] The Greek ομοιωσις θεω (to become like God) in this passage is meant as a *nomen actionis*,

> 128–29; see *ErW* 111] and "deification" (θεοποιησις) represents an important concept not only for Christian folk belief, but also for the speculative beginnings of Christianity. [Cohen refers here to the church father Irenius.[47]] This belief constitutes the point of departure for asceticism, as well as for all mysticism. Nothing is more offensive and repulsive to Judaism than this allusion to the suspension of the difference between God and man. At its origin, this contraposition may vanish; since man is the product of divine creation, and reason correlates creator and creature. For the development of mankind, however, considering its end and purpose, any obliteration of this distinction must be considered crass blasphemy.

which indicates the process of "coming close to God" rather than the state of "being close to God." This is the reason why *Theaetetus* 176b became a central reference for those interpreters of Maimonides who—explicitly or implicitly—follow Cohen's Platonic reading.[49]

The passage of *Theaetetus*, however, is often elliptically quoted. The full passage reads

> But it is impossible that evils should be done away with, Theodorus, for there must always be something opposed to the good; and they [evils] cannot have their place among the gods but must inevitably hover about mortal nature and this earth. Therefore we ought to try to escape from earth to the dwelling of the gods as quickly as we can; and to escape is to become like God, so far as this is possible; and to become like God is to become righteous and holy, and wise.

Cohen sympathizes with Plato's conclusion "to become like God is to become righteous and holy, and wise." He finds himself in fundamental disagreement, however, with Plato's fatalist assumptions concerning evil: "Even the most penetrating of all profound thinkers, Plato, exposes the objectionable shallowness, that evil must persist as a contrast to the Good."[50] Neither does Cohen share Plato's escapist conclusion; "Therefore we ought to try to escape from earth . . . as quickly as we can."

Suffering in history, to the contrary, obliges humankind to labor at the repair (*tikkun*) of our social world. This is the contribution of Jewish messianism to human culture:

> Messianism, however, means the dominion of the good on earth . . . that injustice will cease. This view—which even Plato did not have—is the new teaching that the Unique

> God brings to messianic humanity . . . [that] ethics will become established in the human world . . . and the distinction between ideal and actuality will be buried by the Messiah.[51]

Cohen claims that the prophets, through their projection of a messianic future that pertains to all, introduced the concept of world history into human consciousness, breaking the lock of history's confinement to an eternal human suffering. The prophetic promise of messianic futurity in a history full of suffering, according to Cohen, constitutes the "miracle of monotheism."[52]

Sufist Trends: Love and Longing

115. Maimonides' principal aversion not only to asceticism but to mysticism altogether is characteristic of his ethics. His rationalism animates his intellectualism, so that it never ossifies into pietist spiritualism, nor is it seized by the wings of pantheism. Several prominent passages in his writings reveal his appreciation of the poetic vein in the mystical love of God, a fact that, due to the profundity of his universal mind, we would never have called into question; however, his intellectualism safeguards him against the looming danger of pantheism. Hence he deals exhaustively with the concept of approximation, of "drawing nigh" unto God. [See *Guide* 1:18, 44, in which Maimonides interprets Psalms 73:28—"the nearness of God is my good"—as "union in knowledge and drawing near through apprehension, [and] not in space." *Guide* 1:18, 44; also *RoR* 163–64; *RdV* 189–91.] Had he drawn on Aristotle in the more profound sense, it would have to become evident at this point; it

(*See 115*). *Maimonides' aversion to mysticism.* Sufist tendencies were strongly present in Maimonides' family, and greatly influenced Maimonides' own ascetic and ecstatic doctrines.[53] Cohen's argument—often said to be characterized by the *Kabbala-Angst* of nineteenth-century German liberalism[54]—is directed mainly against the irrationality of pietism and pantheism, which both conflict with Maimonides' supreme effort to ground the Jewish tradition in a rational concept of God's transcendence. Such philosophical grounding, however, by no means stands in conflict with Maimonides' ecstatic and impassioned plea for a way of life that is governed by the love of God and by a longing for "keeping close to God":

> to love the Eternal with a great and exceeding love, so strong that one's soul shall be knit up with the love of God, and one should be continually enraptured by it, like a lovesick individual whose mind is at no time free from

would then have been the most felicitous and most sympathetic idealizing exposition of "eudaemonia," if he would have replaced this term with "drawing close to God." Even his predecessors did not conceive of the concept of "drawing close to God" as referring to a substantive union with God. Bahya contends that the ideas of "immortality" and "resurrection" are sufficiently explained by the expression "proximity to God," or approximation. [Bahya 1973. Bahya does not cite Psalms 73:28 in this context. But see Cohen, *JS* 1:297, and read this passage in light of *RoR* 313–15 and *RdV* 363–65, where Cohen interprets the world-to-come not as a mythological, spiritual future state but rather as the ever present task of "drawing closer" by pursuing the archetypal attributes of lovingkindness and justice.] Like others before him, he refers to the word of the Psalmist [73:28]: "As for me, nearness to God is good." In the same spirit, Maimonides combats all sensuality and corporeality within God Himself, hence also in the relationship of man to God. To him, "drawing close to God" can only mean ethical emulation, ethical training according to the model, which model represents the elementary law of ethics. Thus emulation restricts the proximity to God to that which the love of God may aspire. This motion of drawing closer to God makes manifest the soaring of the loving soul as well as the blossoming of cognition.

> his passion for a particular woman. . . . Even more intense should be the love of God in the hearts of those who love Him.[55]

Maimonides' poetic Hebrew motto concluding the very last chapter of the *Guide* expresses the accessibility of such spiritual pursuit for all searchers:

> God is very near to everyone who calls—He is found by every seeker who searches for Him, if he draws towards Him and goes not astray.[56]

The climax of this universal expression we find in the much-cited passage of Hilkhoth Shmittah ve-Yovel where Maimonides discusses the privileged status of the tribe of Levy:

> Not only the tribe of Levy but every single individual from among the world's inhabitants, whose spirit moved him and whose intelligence gave him the understanding to withdraw from the world in order to stand before God to serve and minister to Him, and to know God, and who walked upright in the manner in which God made him, shaking off from his neck the yoke of the manifold contrivances which men seek—behold, this person has been totally consecrated, and God will be his portion and inheritance forever and ever.[57]

Drawing near to God constitutes both substantially and formally the conclusion of Maimonides' theory of Knowing God.[58]

"As for Me, Nearness Is Good"

Cohen himself reads the passage from Psalms as "*Die Nähe Gottes ist mein Gut.*" His translation is close to that of Mendelssohn who takes *tov* to be a noun: "*An Gott mich halten, ist mir hoechstes Gut.*" Buber translates *li tov* in the verbal sense, "*Ich aber, Gott nahn ist mir das Gute.*" The Septuagint translation is similar: εμοι δε το προσκολλασθαι (passive infinitive) τω θεω αγαθον εστιν.[59] Pines renders *li tov* in the *Guide* in a similar manner to Cohen: "The nearness of God is my good."[60] Maimonides interprets this expression as "drawing near through knowledge and love of God"—which is, of course, precisely Cohen's point.[61]

The Psalmist's words "the nearness of God is my good" are cited by Cohen as the highest expression of the ethical and aesthetic nature of Judaism. It serves as a central motif for Cohen's reading of Jewish philosophy,[62] whereby Cohen consistently emphasizes the aesthetic aspect of the longing of the human heart. It is Cohen's emphasis upon this longing for the nearness of God that distinguishes his passion from *unio mystica:*

> Only nearness to God, not union with God, can be the object of my longing.[63]

Nearness and Material Reward: On Zionism and Eudaemonia

"Immortality of the soul" and "resurrection" as espressions of "Proximity to God." Cohen emphasizes that many literary sources in Jewish philosophy explain "immortality" in the sense of "coming close to God," thereby rejecting religious notions that project an afterlife of spiritual and material well-being. Significant is Cohen's reference to Judah ha-Levi:

> Therefore we do not find in the Bible: "If you keep this law, I will bring you after death into beautiful gardens and great pleasures." To the contrary it is said: "You shall be my chosen people, and I will be a God unto you, who will guide you. Whoever of you comes close to me, and ascends to heaven, is as those who, themselves, dwell among the angels. . . . You shall remain in the country which forms a stepping-stone to this degree, namely the Holy Land of Israel [*erets hakedosha*]. Its fertility or barrenness, its happiness or misfortune, depend upon the

> divine influence which your conduct will merit. . . . All these promises have one basis, that is the anticipation of being near to God.[64]

Cohen agrees with Judah ha-Levi's concept of "anticipating the nearness to God." Characteristically, however, Cohen skips ha-Levi's references to *erets hakedosha,* the Holy Land. Cohen rejects ha-Levi's promise of Israel's dwelling in the Holy Land as a "reward for the righteous" as being a mythological interpolation which renders the entire process of drawing close to God impure by imputing an external, materialistic reward for it. Attachment to the land or to any otherworldly thing forfeits the pursuit of the highest good. Zionism, even in Judah ha- Levi's conception, is eudaemonia: "*Die Kerle wollen glücklich sein*" [Those chaps want to be happy].[65] Judah ha-Levi's concept of eudaemonian Zionism as divine reward for Israel's righteous conduct clashes with Cohen's reading of Maimonides' world-to-come as an ethical concept, whose transcendental status proves to be a corrective of materialist expectations.

Eudaemonia: On Intellectual Hedonism

116. Now, if the concept of drawing near to God allows and justifies only this clearly ethical connotation, are we then not entitled to ask how Maimonides could have resisted the temptation to translate "nearness" as "eudaemonia," and to recognize such nearness to God as personal bliss. Eudaemonia is the telos of Aristotelian ethics. [Aristotle 1945, *NE* 1177a–78a, 613–19.] One may argue that without eudaemonia Aristotle's ethics would never have gained its outstanding prestige. It contains the only speculative method featured in the entire book. Without this speculative element the book would merely be of interest and value to anthropologists, psychologists, behavioral scientists, and political scientists;

(*See 116.*) *Eudaemonia, the bliss of pure contemplation, constitutes the height of Aristotelian thinking.* Cohen claims that this "highest bliss of human intellectual activity" links Aristotelian ethics—otherwise of a pure pragmatic character—with Aristotelian metaphysics, which is otherwise considered pure theory.[66] Cohen launches an assault on the very principle of eudaemonia, claiming that it remains enslaved to the principle of material well-being, even if couched in intellectual or contemplative terms.[67] "I do not oppose the feeling of happiness but rather the idea of its absoluteness," says Cohen. And further, "where idealism ends, the dualism between materialism and spiritualism is unavoidable."[68]

however, this loquacious book would not offer any philosophical insight even into the Aristotelian system proper. Eudaemonia is the faint wisp of a connection between ethics and the core of his metaphysics. Although Plato contended with this type of eudaemonia, it was Socrates who initiated it. Thus, even if Aristotle's ethics is structured and developed in a sensory and empirical vein, it is eudaemonia that lends to it the renown of philosophical speculation. Aristotelian ethics is nothing but his eudaemonia.

117. This eudaemonia consists of pure theory, but actually only the Deity is perfectly capable of such cognitive purity. It is incumbent upon man, however, to emulate divine cogitation in order to partake, within the limits of the human condition, of divine bliss. This bliss consists of pure thinking—for human beings as for God; not of material fortune, of the boons of birth, of status, of power, and governance, but solely of the euphoria of engaging in theory, in vision, in cognition. As ever so often, so also in this case, Aristotle seems to have taken advantage of the contested Plato: he has rejected the Platonic vision of the idea, yet in a different etymological radix (θεωρια), he retained the self-same concept of vision as the end and purpose of ethics for God and man. [Aristotle retains the Platonic idea of emulating God in his ideal of pure *theory* and contemplation. Aristotle 1945, *NE* 1177a, 613; also 1947, *Metaphysics* 982b–83a, 15.]

Aristotelian metaphysics conceives of God as the ontological first cause, and not as the messenger of a teaching, or as the commander of justice. Accordingly, Aristotelian ethics does not proclaim the human pursuit of the Good as its highest aspiration. Whereas for Socrates the discovery of virtue was a revolutionary step that led toward the Platonic idea of the Good as the highest aspiration for human cognition, the post-Platonic bifurcation of practical virtue and intellectual virtue backslides into hedonistic sophism and materialism of which Aristotle's principle of eudaemonia is the epitomal expression.[69]

118. But does not the principle of drawing close correspond to the Aristotelian bliss of Deity and man? To all outward appearances, this correspondence suggests an essential similitude. All the more urgently, we face the question: how could Maimonides miss this opportunity to draw an analogy, and therewith fail to take advantage of the pretext, which he must have been looking for, to transfer into his system the esteemed and celebrated fundamental concept of eudaemonia. Or, let us put the question differently: how could he dare to oppose openly the doctrine of eudaemonia, while it is in particular this point of contest with Aristotle that could have aroused the suspicion that Maimonides restricts himself to a mere religious rationale for advancing his ethics. In other words, how could he begrudge and deprive ethics of its speculative principle, which principle was acknowledged to be none other than eudaemonia, and therewith remove ethics from any philosophical rationale?

119. With regard to this issue it seems important to pay attention to Maimonides' attitude toward Aristotle from the literary point of view. Maimonides attacks and criticizes him much more often and much more deeply than is obvious upon a superficial reading; his polemic, however, is unmistakable. He even employs irony in his argumentation against him, a sign of his independence and self-assurance vis-à-vis the great master. In general, he rather prefers to give and maintain the impression of tacit agreement with him. Not only because he felt truly indebted to the rational guidance of Aristotle and his basic idea of intellectualism, but also out of literary considerations in order to keep all sorts of critics and opponents at bay. [L. Strauss 1988.] In the eyes of the greatest intellects of those days, any criticism of Aristotle was tantamount to an attack upon or even a betrayal of philosophy itself. Regarding the entire question of the relationship between Maimonides and Aristotle, it is therefore of utmost importance to note: Maimonides opposes, contends with, and replaces the doctrine of eudaemonia. He does not replace it with the concept of approximation, "drawing near to God," as he could have done, but substitutes a different concept, one that contains within itself the force of a principle and which as a replacement for eudaemonia proves itself a far more effective principle. Before we advance to the discussion of this most profound principle, however, we shall first have to engage in a discussion of Virtue [αρετη (goodness, virtue, excellence)] and the virtues.

6

Practice and Performance

How (Not) to Walk in Middle Ways

In this sixth chapter Cohen discusses the concept of human perfection in critical relation to the Aristotelian theory of virtues, according to which virtues are mere practical human skills rather than ideal vectors for human action. Cohen therefore rejects the traditional understanding of the "golden mean" or the "middle way" as a "medium between two vices," trying to recontextualize the ideality of this teaching halakically and philosophically within the framework of Maimonides' great rabbinic code, Mishneh Torah.

Socrates and Plato: On Virtues and "The Good"

120. The concept of virtue originates in folk morality or mores; through the concept of virtue, folk morality expresses its standards of ethics. The distinction between ethics on the one hand, and good fortune and chance, force and power, nature and heredity, on the other, is articulated by the term *virtue.* [αρετη, Latin *virtus> *vir* suggests "manliness, manhood, strength, vigor, bravery, courage," and also "worth, excellence, virtue." See also *RoR* 402; *RdV* 466.] Even the distinction between ethics and piety, in which piety is

(*See 121.*) *Socrates defines the Good as a virtue.* The Socratic ideal of moral perfection is thus prescribed within the relativist framework of a moral theory in which a hierarchy of virtues determines which of the many virtues embodies the highest virtue of all. This virtue therefore will play a privileged role in the practitioner's pursuit of the highest happiness. "Thus it becomes understandable that the Socratic doctrine of the 'good' was unable to liberate itself from the ambiguities of utilitarianism and eudaemonia,"[1] Cohen

the conventional expression of civic religion, is thus defined. Nonetheless, there remains a naturalistic residue in the meaning of virtue, which is not surprising, considering the folkloristic origin of the term. Hellenic opinion distinguishes between virtue and cleverness (δεινοτης); [Aristotle 1945, *NE* 1144b, 371; 1144a, 367–69, 1152a, 427.] however, even in this Hellenic opinion virtue has not yet lost its ambiguous connotation of prowess. After all, virtue originally denoted manliness (αρετη).

121. Socrates already conceives of virtue in all of its ethical precision and stringency; yet the concept of the Good remains at the side of any virtue, and thus connotes the superior term. In Plato the virtues recede to a preparatory stage of the idea of the Good. The idea of the

says in his *Religion of Reason: Out of the Sources of Judaism.*

Plato, however, raises the Good above the realm of practical virtues in that he proclaims the Good to be foundational for human cognition as such. Plato thus subordinates the many virtues to the one idea of the Good in light of which ethics as theoretical knowledge first arises. From this perspective, from the perspective of an ethics predicated upon the cognition of the Good, the concept of virtue takes on a negative connotation, denoting mere practical skill. Aristotle, when removing the Platonic idea of the Good from the agenda of theoretical knowledge, holds precisely this against Plato: ethics has no share in the theoretical sciences, and virtue is therefore to be considered precisely that—mere skill or εξις.[2]

Good sublimates the virtues, and they shed all of their naturalist accreditation, idealized as irradiations of the Good. Aristotle, however, rejecting the idea of the Good, must again equate the Good with virtue. [Aristotle 1945, *NE* 1106a, 89–91.] Since he does not acknowledge the one Good, he must assume a multiplicity of virtues. [*ErW* 488.] Aristotle's ethics is not derived from principles, but represents a typology and classification based upon empirical, psychological, and historical data; thus his concept of virtue must also correspond to this psychologicoethical method.

Virtue—Skills and Goodness

122. The primary concern aroused by Aristotle's definition of virtue relates to the concept of skill (εξις). [Aristotle 1945, *NE* 1098b, 39; Aristotle 1970, 169–73.] Aristotle must emphasize this concept,

(*See 122.*) *Aristotle's concept of skill.* Aristotle defines virtue as any kind of practical skill. The medieval and modern Hebrew term *toviut* corresponding to the Greek αρετη (virtue), in contrast, is predicated etymologically upon the Hebrew root *tov* (good).[3] Cohen himself could have availed himself of this etymological development as a linguistic indication of the Platonic bent of Hebrew culture. Most of the medieval references use the term *toviut* when referring to God's goodness as a paradigm for human emulation.[4]

since his ethics does not deal with cognition, but rather with control of conduct. Hence it is skill that constitutes the objective of this ethical method. From the perspective of the idea of the Good, however, a person never achieves the skill of perfection [Ethics is conceived of by Cohen as an infinite approximation with which we are never done. In contrast, Cohen renders the Aristotelian concept of εξις in a German pun as *Fertigkeit,* suggesting precisely that: "to be done with it."] and may never dispense with the ever-new effort of cognition, when examining action to be taken with regard to its ethical value. Yet it is undeniable that the ideal of moral tact and of correct and balanced behavior is certainly within its limits desirable and indispensable, so that even social skills are not altogether suspect or objectionable.

Gradus ad Parnassum

123. Jewish philosophy uses two terms for virtue: *excellence* (מעלה) and *perfection* (שלמות). [Note the literal combination of *shlemuth* with *toviut* in Albalada 1583, 35a–36b, especially 35b.] Judging by its root, *excellence* may also be rendered as "rung, step, grade." [*עלה is "to ascend."] It would be a desideratum to investigate whether and to what extent this term may denote not only the state of excellence, but also a step in the ascending process of attaining it (עלה). [*RoR* 406–9; *RdV* 471–74.]

(*See 123.*) *"Excellence" and the process of "perfection."* Cohen remarks that, strictly speaking, the word *ma'ala* denotes a *nomen acti*—such as "rung, step, grade." A *nomen acti* is a noun that describes the result of an action, and not a *nomen actionis,* a noun which describes the *process* of an action. In support of his progressive, actional reading of the term *ma'ala* or *excellence,* Cohen therefore cites the Baraitha of Pinchas Ben Ya'ir, which deals with a person's spiritual ascent toward perfection on a rising ladder of successive "grades" (*ma'aloth*) of spiritual achievement:

> Zeal leads towards cleanliness, and cleanliness leads towards purity, and purity leads

124. Similarly, we may interpret the second term, *perfection.* This term as well seems in conflict with the fundamental demand of ethics: perfection is merely an end to be pursued, and hence virtue,

towards separation, and separation leads towards holiness, and holiness leads towards humility, and humility leads towards the avoidance of sin, and the avoidance of sin leads towards lovingkindness, and lovingkindness leads towards the spirit of holiness, and the spirit of holiness leads towards resurrection.[5]

We find a similar understanding of *ma'alah* in the agenda of various medieval and modern Jewish ethical works, whose chapter headings indicate "ascending steps" in the individual's pursuit of spiritual perfection.[6]

as perfection, can only present an end for pursuit, but does not denote a skill that one is able to acquire. [See *ErW* 424.] We shall see that these considerations do not remain alien to Maimonides, and that by rejecting the concept of eudaemonia, he vouchsafes to his alternative idea even the concept of virtue vis-à-vis these reservations.

125. Skill and perfection define the Aristotelian concept of virtue from the aspect of the soul's disposition and functions; [Aristotle 1945, 1098a, 33.] Aristotle even defines the substance and value of virtue: it is the mean (μεσον) between two moments or extremes. [Aristotle 1945, *NE* 1104a, 77; also 2:vi–vii, ff.] Maimonides himself adopts this definition, [Maimonides 1912, 58; Maimonides 1984–1996, Hilkhoth Deoth 1:2–4, 1:7, 2:2; Fox 1988, 93–96.] lending support to the impression that in his philosophical thinking, formulation, and systematization he is entirely and intimately dependent upon Aristotle. Yet to the contrary, it bespeaks Maimonides' philosophical originality that he displays no ostentation about his profound deviation from Aristotle on this point. Rather he leaves the impression that he has no objection to adopting this trite teaching, or that he would even acknowledge it as a decisive factor. We shall see that Maimonides, in a focal point of his discussion, actually throws this Middle Way doctrine overboard; just as even Aristotle himself had to admit exceptions to this panacea. [Aristotle 1945, *NE* 1107a, 97.] In any case, Maimonides had every reason not to categorically dismiss the "Middle Way," since the term *mean* (דרך אמצעי) is also talmudic usage. [Tosefta 1955–1988, Tosefta Chagigah 2:5, Tosefta Baba Kama 2:12. See Maimonides 1984–1996, Hilkhoth Deoth 1:4, 1:5, 1:7, 2:2; also in Falaquera 1970; Malter 1911, 160n. 15. It is Falaquera who explicitly associates the doctrine of the Middle Way with a talmudic source, Mo'ed Katan 5a; see Falaquera 1970, 5. In the Mishna, the term *benonit* is used in the sense of a modified position between two extremes, Mishna Avoth 5:13. See Herford 1974, 134, and Mishna Terumoth 4:3–4 on the distinction between *emtsai* and *benonit* in talmudic usage; Kohut 1955, 1:125b, 2:56a, 125b.]

126. The principle of mediocrity follows from Aristotle's basic stance against all ideal views and visions of mankind. Aristotle wants to keep ethics within the narrow boundaries of anthropological and historical empiricism; whatever passes beyond these confines he considers to be a phantasma overshooting the limits of the human condition and to be overbearing—hence to be false and evil.

127. On the other hand we should not deny that this thought of limiting ethics to what is humanly possible bears within it a profound, good, and true element. Indeed, all human virtue contains a moment of selfishness. The most sublime achievements of the mind are encumbered with earthliness. The light of the spirit and of virtue remains immured in matter. Thus even the highest level of virtue is still, under scrutiny, merely a median stage. In brief, one may argue that what has been granted and acknowledged of this principle is not merely a triviality. Yet it bears the marks of the basic fallacy in Aristotelian ethics.

128. The mean is not merely posited between two extremes, each of which partakes of this particular virtue to an equal or differing extent in such fashion that perfection would lie at the center; but rather it represents a mean state between two vices (μεσοτης δυο κακιων). Aristotle 1945, *NE* 1107a, (2:vi), [95.] Herein lies the basic fallacy: that two vices should produce virtue. To him, virtue means the avoidance of two deficiencies or vices; it is the lesser evil or the median one. Basically Aristotle thinks that a human being is unavoidably exposed to the malice of his nature and to the risks of historical seduction; thus he at least seeks to accommodate himself along the road of the golden mean. [Horace 1947, 130–31.] It is merely a prescribed path to virtue, as it were, arranged as the moral career for humanity.

129. Now Aristotle himself cannot help making an exception for the virtue of justice—little realizing that this exception invalidates his whole doctrine. [Aristotle 1945, *NE* 1107a, 2:vi, 97.] Justice for him is not an avoidance of two extremes; consider the avoidance of both rashness and cowardice, resulting in a prudent rationale for weakness—should the glory and power of courage then really be nothing but a maneuver of avoidance? The concept of the mean can only originate with an outlook in which nature and history reign supreme. In contradistinction, the idea of the Good prevails over all expedient considerations. Wherever a more profound demand of the interrelation between nature and ethics enters into ethical deliberations, a demand which defies all prudence, the principle of median ethics can no longer remain in control. A genuine principle will have to replace it.

Laws Concerning Character Dispositions: Know Who You Are

130. Turning now to Maimonidean ethics, we should expect that the concept of God, of knowing and loving God, would replace the Aristotelian doctrine of the mean. As has been demonstrated, however, the concept of Knowing God in Maimonides represents in substance exclusively the cognition of ethics. This is the reason why he could not conceive of the principle and problem of God apart from the principle and problem of man; for ethics constitutes the relationship between oneself and God, and as such the relationship between oneself and others as well as one's relationship to oneself. [*Guide* 3:35, 538.] It is remarkable how the doctrine of the mean demonstrates the fundamental difference between Aristotle and Maimonides—and we mean this not only with respect to the roster of exceptions.

(*See 130.*) *Halakhic implications of knowing oneself.* Maimonides, in his halakhic treatise "Laws concerning Character Dispositions and Ethical Conduct" (Hilkhoth Deoth), seems to suggest that the ultimate human task of Knowing God and Walking in His Ways is inextricably linked to a critical assessment of one's own character disposition, claiming that any pursuit of self-perfection is predicated upon a process of rigorous self-critique.[7] Hilkhoth Deoth is unique among Maimonides' writings in that it does not start out with normative legislative directives as do almost all other sections of his *Mishneh Torah* but rather with an assessment of one's own self, with an empirical survey concerning concrete character dispositions and temperaments of single individuals.

> Human beings are exceedingly different from one another, every single person has her own character dispositions, and as such no person equals another. One person is choleric, always irascible; another sedate, never getting angry . . . one man is haughty to excess, the other humble to the extreme. One is a sensualist whose lusts are never gratified, another is so pure in soul that he does not even desire the few things that our bodies need. . . . Furthermore, there are the sanguine and the melancholy, the stingy and the generous, the cruel and the merciful, the timid and those who like adventure, and so forth [translation modified by author].[8]

The halakhic implementations of this entire ethical treatise are predicated upon a critical assessment of the question "Who am I?" and upon subsequent pedagogical labor upon one's own ethical self. This is true whether we think of obligations that deal with the relationship between oneself and one's fellow (*ben adam lechavero*)—such as "You shall love your fellow person"—or whether we speak of those that address the relationship between oneself and God (*ben adam lamakom*)—such as "You shall walk in His ways." In a different context, Maimonides reiterates this point, claiming that all obligations between oneself and God are, in fact, only educational tools serving the task of improving one's self:

> Among the classes we have differentiated . . . [these] belong to the group devoted to the relationship between a man and his fellow man, while all the other classes deal with the relationship between man and God. For every commandment, whether it be a prescription or a prohibition, *whose purpose it is to bring about the achievement of a certain moral quality* or . . . the *rightness of actions which . . . concern the individual himself and his becoming more perfect* is called by the Sages a commandment dealing with the relationship *between man and God* [emphasis added].[9]

In Maimonides' treatise of Hilkhoth Deoth, ethical obligations *ben adam le'atsmo* (between a person and herself) for the first time gain halakhic status, as their primary objective is the empirical self-awareness of every individual:

> to imitate His ways, to cling to those who know Him, to love others, to love converts, not to hate one's fellow in your heart, to admonish someone who acts wrongly, not to put others to shame, not to oppress others, not to bear tales, not to take revenge, not to bear a grudge.[10]

All of these commandments require introspection and analysis with respect to one's self in relationship to others. Self-awareness thus constitutes the *methodological* starting point for self-perfection even though, logically speaking, Cohen would say that self-awareness is the very result of one's obligation toward another, in which thinking about one's self first originates.[11] Cohen, accordingly, reads Maimonides' adoption of the Aristotelian doctrine of the Middle Way as an empirical device, a psychological technique, that is quite distinct from the transcendental foundations of Maimonides' ethics, which lie in his epistemological theory of Knowing God.

The Middle Way: Normativity or Mediocrity?

The roster of exceptions. Maimonides formulates an explicit halakhic injunction against acting according to the Middle Way when it comes to anger and pride. In the cases of anger and pride one ought to incline toward the opposite extreme of completely subduing one's anger and of utmost humility.[12] The Law (Halakhah) in these cases is not according to the Middle Way, but rather demands that *middath chassiduth* (the standard of the Saintly One) becomes mandatory for all.[13]

Maimonides' reference to the Aristotelian doctrine of the Middle Way is ambiguous. At times he employs it in the Aristotelian psychological, technical sense, and at times he does so in a strictly normative and non-Aristotelian sense, for example when associating the Middle Way with God's ways, with the perfection of God's creation, or even with the Law as a whole.[14] Maimonides follows Aristotle when advocating the method of the Middle Way as a generally useful, empirical psychological device for dealing with all sorts of character traits.[15] When concerned with the pursuit of saintliness, however, Maimonides formulates an explicit halakhic injunction *against* the Middle Way, such as in cases of anger and pride—character traits that are detrimental to the pursuit of the Good, and in which cases any measure of "mediocrity" must be avoided.[16]

The fundamental difference between Maimonides and Aristotle in their employment of the Middle Way, according to Cohen, lies in their differing positions on the question of ethics as theoretical knowledge. Wherever virtue is defined in merely practical terms, a mere technical device is sufficient to improve a person's "skills" of virtue. Wherever ethics is defined as a highest form of cognition, however, the ideal of mediocrity proves inadequate to the ethical task.

Chassid and *Chakham:* Acting beyond Mediocrity

131. Maimonides, in introducing the doctrine of the mean into his theological magnum opus, [Maimonides, halakhic code, *Mishneh Torah*] immediately stipulates a fundamental reservation: the saintly men of yore departed from the Middle Road in their attitude and character (דעות) and adopted the

(*See 131.*) *The saintly men of yore.* In Cohen's reading, Maimonides favors the *chassid,* the saintly one who is "particularly scrupulous and deviates somewhat from the exact mean," over the *chakham,* the prudent one, who follows the Middle Way, and whose "character traits are intermediate and

principle of "voluntarily narrowing the boundaries of the law" (לפנים משורת הדין)(Hilkhot Deoth 1:1 [correctly 1:5]). [Maimonides 1984–1996, Hilkhoth Yesodei ha-Torah 5:11; Maimonides 1912, 4.] This principle is derived from the Talmud. [This halakic principle might best be rendered as "going beyond the boundaries of the law." Herzog 1980, 1:384–85; also TB Baba Metsia 83a; TY Baba Metsia 6:6; Bialik 1992, 741–42; Lichtenstein 1978, 102–23; Silberg 1984, 110; S. H. Cohen 1970.] This principle is equity, and may be considered a corrective that tempers the principle of justice. [Aristotle 1945, *NE* 1137a–38a, 313–17; *ErW* 618–21.]

equally balanced."[17] It is the former, the *chassid,* who represents pure, radical ethics which—according to Cohen—is the only ethics there is. The distinction between "prudence" and "saintliness" is reiterated forcefully by Steven Schwarzschild, identifying "saintliness" with ethics, and denigrating "median" ethics to Aristotelian mediocrity, mere "practical prudence."[18]

Maimonides, however, does not always keep the concepts *chassid* and *chakham* clearly distinct. He actually uses the term *chakham* also with reference to someone who goes "beyond the strict boundaries of the law."[19] Keeping Cohen's claim that there can be no mediocrity in ethics, but that ethics must rather be radically good (rooted in goodness), we may venture to say that both the *chakham* and the *chassid* represent ideal types of ethical conduct.[20] The *chassid,* for his part, does not so much represent any superogatory category of ethics, as rather a mandatory example of action demonstrated by certain people in certain situations: public figures, such as teachers or community leaders, for example, should always act beyond the strict boundaries of the law.[21] And the *chakham,* just the same, should go beyond the strict boundaries of the law, whenever he finds himself in a public situation where his personal conduct is wont to serve in setting an example for others.[22]

The Idea of Equity: Going beyond the Letter of the Law

132. Equity, pervading the entire legal system of the Talmud, challenges the subjectivity inherent in all human virtue by becoming itself the ultimate principle, the corrective and counterbalance of justice. Equity therewith attains

(*See 132.*) *Equity.* In his *Ethik des reinen Willens,* Cohen argues that it is, in fact, the very ideal of humanity that constitutes the normative content of the principle of equity (*Billigkeit*). Equity, representing the ideal of humanity, sets out to correct

the status of an autonomous legal principle, not subordinated to justice. [As in the case of Aristotle, for whom equity applies in those subjective instances in which the legal systems fail. Aristotle 1945, *NE* 1137a–38a, 313–17.] In this principle the Talmud acknowledges the Stoic principle of natural law [*lex naturalis*] which has always maintained the linkage between law and morals, jurisprudence and ethics. [*ErW* 618; also Wolfson 1947, 2:165–200; and Husik 1925.] The Talmudic appreciation of this principle of equity may be demonstrated by the homiletic lesson that attributes the destruction of the Second Temple to the violation of equity. [TB Baba Metsia 30b.] What benefit can be derived from scouting out the limit of the median line if true ethics rather demands conduct beyond this line? In any case, median ethics itself can no longer serve to delimit lawful conduct.

the legal claims of justice, balancing the letter of the law, complementing the very generality of its formulations: the body of the law, the stricture of its letter, is called upon to adjust itself when facing the specificity of a singular case to which no law readily applies. The talmudic principle *lifnim mishurath ha-din* (going beyond the boundaries of the law) allows the facticity of a particular case to become a corrective of a specific Halakhah in that this talmudic principle demands action "beyond the letter of the law."

This principle does so, however, without undermining the authority of the rabbinic legal system, since *lifnim mishurath ha-din* itself is a principle of halakic law. In this way the principle "to go beyond the strict letter of the law" asserts the universality of the ethical norm whenever it is in danger of being betrayed "in the name of the Law." Equity counterbalances lawfulness. But Cohen insists that the very principle of equity itself must be made part of positive law, lest it will be left to the whims of natural law:

> It is a calamitous illusion to think that equity belongs to Natural Law, whereas it is, in fact, an integral part of the positive Law.[23]

Equity—or correspondingly the talmudic principle of "going beyond the strict letter of the law"—therefore constitutes *Sollen* (Ought) in a strictly normative sense. It integrates the idea of lawfulness with the ideal of humanity, or, in traditional terms, rabbinic legal stricture with the messianic ideal of goodness and justice.

Cohen's reading has been emphatically reiterated by Aharon Lichtenstein's much-cited article "Does Jewish Tradition Recognize an Ethic Independent of Halakha?" In this article, the author claims that specific formulations of various halakhic obligations apply to an individual inasmuch as his or her case may be subordinated to a particular halakhic ruling. General, exhortative formulations of halakhic directives, on the other hand, like "going beyond the strict letter of the law," or "doing the right and the good in the eyes of God" (Deuteronomy 6:18) are expressions of equity that were integrated into halakhic reasoning and that are binding for the individual at all times and in all situations.[24] This article shows Lichtenstein's neo-Kantian lineage, remaining true to the features of the work of his teacher, J. B. Soloveitchik, who wrote a dissertation on Cohen's epistemology, and whose readings of classical rabbinic texts preserve a commitment to Cohen's ethical hermeneutics.[25]

The Select Few

133. Maimonides places this talmudic principle of equity in its proper systematic perspective. By placing equity in juxtaposition to the principle of the mean, he actually invalidates the latter as a norm. [Maimonides 1984–1996, Hilkhoth Deoth 1:5; and Maimonides 1992b, 1:286–87.] Maimonides seems to retain the doctrine of the mean merely as an educational, technical means, while dismissing it as a fundamental principle. Thus he undermines the entire basis of Aristotelian ethics, which is only concerned with human mediocrity, but not with the chosen who are summoned by the idea of the Good. Maimonides, however, advances the guideline of the "sage and the saintly." [See paragraph 131 in this chapter.] Thus, he drives the vector of his religion toward ethics.

(*See 133.*) *The elite to whom the ideal of the good applies.* The ethical gist of Cohen's reading demands that the ideal of the radical Good—the ideal of the so-called elite—must in principle relate to all humankind, since this radical Good constitutes the grounds for all human ethical action. Maimonides does not seem to fundamentally disagree with such a reading. He suggests, however, that most people will get distracted from the ultimate cognitive pursuit of God for various practical reasons—such as "lengthy preliminary studies," "limitations of their intellectual capacity," or "sickness and death"—which is why "only very few would arrive at that knowledge in their own lifetime" if there were no reliable and authoritative tradition of the "true teaching." It is the task of the "select few" to keep this tradition alive.[26] For mere empirical and practical reasons, "these matters of divine knowledge are only for a few solitary individuals of a very special sort, not for the multitude."[27]

Maimonides associates the *chassid* with the ideal of holiness (*kedusha*), which in turn is identified with the idea of human perfection, of Walking in His Ways and of *Imitatio Dei.*[28] All these ideals are expressions of what Cohen calls "radical, cognitive ethics." Maimonides' concept of *kedusha* suggests, at times, an ascetic bent, advising self-restraint and seclusion from society, prima facie implying political and social quietism.[29] But Cohen reads these passages as a rejection of eudaemonian materialism rather than as political quietism; he distinguishes between social affairs sought for the sake of pleasure, and social or political engagements resulting from one's commitment to doing good and pursuing justice.

Masquerades of Pride: "You Shall Have No Foreign Gods"

134. It is noteworthy that among others the main exception to which the method of the mean does not apply is the virtue of humility (ענוה), a fact that Maimonides points out with great emphasis. [Maimonides 1984–1996, Hilkhoth Deoth 2:3; also Maimonides 1992b, Avoth 4:4; and Rawidowicz 1969–1971, 1:436–39, especially nn. 132 and 135 in which Rawidowicz refers to Cohen's present essay on Maimonides.] He is not the first to accord humility a central position among the virtues. [*Demut* < *deomut;* that is, "the lowliness of a knight."] Abraham ibn Daud precedes him in this, although he links it with equity. [Ibn Daud 1986, 262; Bahya 1973, 304–27; also Kafih 1989; and Soloveitchik 1978.] Maimonides is perhaps nowhere as moving as when characterizing this virtue. (See especially [Maimonides 1992b]; Mishna Avoth 4; and 1984–1996, Hilkhoth Deoth 2:3. For example, "Therefore it is said of Moses: he was exceedingly humble.") This man, a scholar of world renown and man of the world pursuing his medical

(*See 134.*) *National Pride.* Humility, according to Cohen, is the ultimate expression of messianism, as it describes a relationship with others that is not self-centered.[30] True humility demands one's orientation and attention not only toward the other but also toward *the others,* transcending and invalidating all national borders. National pride, to be sure, tends to masquerade as humility. We see such rhetoric as, "The individual is nothing, security of the nation is everything." Yet even national pride, according to Cohen, is nothing but hatred of others in disguise:

> Hatred and gruesomeness may adorn itself with the highest motives: after all, in the name of religion people were burnt at the stake, and it is nationalism which declares hatred of others a duty.[31]

And further:

> We know the difference between state and ethnicity. The

profession: how great must have been his inner joy when focusing with such intense energy on this virtue, as if humility might stand for all—illustrating this through moving examples. Certainly the Jewish religion would not prove itself as the religion of martyrdom attesting to its truth in the face of all sorts of worldly pressure, were it not the religion of humility. A Jew says thrice daily after his main prayer: "Be my soul silent unto those who reproach me, be my soul lowly unto all as the dust." [See also *RoR* 427–28; *RdV* 496. Cohen alludes to the Shemoneh Esreh—the Eighteen Benedictions. The passage cited belongs to the private devotion of the individual that is recited immediately after the Shemoneh Esreh. TB Berakhot 17a. "Be my soul silent to those who reproach me" was a personal prayer of Mar, the son of Ravina. Elbogen 1993, 53–54.] Hence, Maimonides would not admit any calculations and search for the mean in this case; he demands self-effacement (שפל רוח) [Proverbs 16:19; 29:23; Isaiah 57:15; see also Abraham bar Chiya 1971 on Isaiah 57:15.] unconditionally and without exception. Pride is considered "equivalent to idolatry." It lies at the root of all vices and of all corruption in any social and national life. Genuine national pride might even appeal to humility as its living fountain, or, in more human terms, to modesty. Whoever does not categorically protect himself from the appeal of natural element of ethnicity may result in staining patriotism with the poison of nationalist vanity deteriorating into hostility and hatred. This natural facticity that today is termed nationalism actually represents the greatest enemy of all social and spiritual forces upon which the sincerity and dynamics of political advancement depends.[32]

Religion of humility, religion of martyrdom. Jewish messianism compromises its very essence when it encourages hatred of others in the guise of nationalism—especially when such nationalism is advocated in the name of Judaism itself.[33] Whether Cohen would have maintained this position were he to have seen the Shoah and the foundation of the State of Israel is a moot question. Steven Schwarzschild sharply reiterated Cohen's critique of Jewish nationalism even after the Shoah and after the foundation of the state of Israel. Guided by Cohen's critique of eudaemonia, Schwarzschild claims that Jewish nationalism is *Heilsgeschichte* (holy history), and that *Heilsgeschichte* is idolatrous.[34] Humility, Cohen insists, demands the renunciation of individual as well as national pride, and precisely in this capacity, Cohen emphasizes that humility figures prominently among Jewish virtues.[35]

Aristotle, on his part, treats modesty as an exaggerated parameter.[36]

such pride is lost to the cause of pure ethics. You will always find a well-reasoned argument to varnish any vice as a virtue. Hatred may thus masquerade as love. [*ErW* 628.] The same applies to one's personal life. By not making any allowance for average conduct in the case of humility, Maimonides surpasses the philosopher par excellence in human understanding and in worldly knowledge. [Aristotle does not grant humility the status of virtue, but rather sees in it a bashful feeling that is befitting for the young, but not for the "grown-up man." Aristotle 1945, *NE* 1128b, 249–50; 1108a–b, 105.]

135. One could argue, however, that this appreciation of humility, which is shared by both Christian and Jewish consciousness, expresses a typically medieval virtue prescribed by the church or by religion as the guiding principle for human conduct. In medieval times, one surrendered one's individuality to the religious community, and—in consonance or in conflict with this surrender—one relinquished control to the state community. What sort of dignity is accorded to the individual, if the church or the state to which he belongs obtains and affirms its own dignity at the individual's expense? Hence, one could view humility in an ambiguous light, and could interpret its exceptional status with reference to the doc-

The virtuous path, according to Aristotle, leads one to walk between bashfulness and humility, neither of which is, in fact, a virtue. Maimonides, to the contrary, presents humility as a *radical* demand—there exists no Middle Way when walking humbly before one's God. Jewish virtues are modeled upon God's actional attributes—"as He is gracious so you shall become gracious." So, too, is the virtue of humility. Both God and Moses, God's prophet, are depicted in rabbinic sources as "exceedingly humble."[37] Jewish tradition demands "blood testimony." Profaning God's name—violating justice—has to be resisted even at the cost of one's life.[38]

In *Religion of Reason,* Cohen associates the virtue of humility with the idea of "Israel's vicarious suffering for mankind," testifying to the "ethical truth of monotheism."[39] Cohen does see Israel in the role of Isaiah's "suffering servant,"[40] and his Christian interpreters have taken ample note of this. But Cohen's reading of the suffering servant does not advocate any masochism,[41] nor does it imply the justification of history. To the contrary, by having Israel assume the role of Isaiah's suffering servant, Cohen expresses a most radical opposition to human suffering: in defiance of all the pain in history, Jewish tradition proclaims the knowledge of a better world. According to Cohen, Israel's willingness to suffer for this defiance is her humility. It is only on account of her messianic knowledge that

trine of the mean as a threat to the ethical individual. These misgivings would then undermine Maimonides' entire ethics as he might not have restricted himself to this one point. Since we come to realize that what is called into question here is nothing less than the concept of the individual, the bearer of ethical self-awareness, [*ErW* 203–6, 356–57; Schmid 1995, 62.] it behooves us to scrutinize the connotation of humility in this respect.

Israel can be made accountable for the suffering of others. (Cohen claims that Israel forfeits this particular accountability once its national pride causes it to "become like all the nations.") This then is the significance—hypocrisy—of Jewish particularity according to Cohen, that it seems to imply "all are responsible, but I am more responsible than all."

Pride is considered idolatry. Maimonides contrasts both anger and pride with humility, but only of anger does he say "whoever gets angry is considered as if he worships idols." This links the mishnaic injunction "not to be quick to anger" to the passage in Psalms (81:10), "You shall have no foreign God."[42] The precise wording of Maimonides' statement: "anger is equivalent to idolatry" [*kol hako'es ke-ilu oved avodah zara*] is not found explicitly in talmudic literature.[43] Yet Maimonides is consistent in his citation of this statement.[44] Inasmuch as pride is considered "equal to idolatry," "humility" is associated with true knowledge of God.

Exceedingly Humble

136. In prescribing the practice of prayer, the Talmud cites the exegesis of a haggadic gnome, which points to the linkage between God's humility and His greatness, grounding God's greatness in His humility. [*RoR* 266, 425–26; *RdV* 311, 494; and TB Megillah 31a: "wherever you find God's mightiness (*gevurato; gedulato*) mentioned in Scriptures, there you find His humility." Most of the talmudic versions of this dictum have *gevurato* (mightiness), and not *gedulato* (greatness). Rabinovicz 1976 on Megillah 31a. Cohen obviously

(*See 136.*) *Humility and greatness.* There is a plethora of midrashic and other traditional material emphasizing humility—both in the social as well as in the spiritual sense. Classical examples are the commentaries on Isaiah 57:15 ("I dwell on high, in holiness; yet with the contrite and the lowly in spirit."[45]) or the midrashim on Psalms 68:5–11 ("Exult in His presence—the father of orphans, the champion of widows, God in His holy habitation.") In fact, much that came to be of prominence in Jewish

cites his text from the siddur—see the passage concluding the *catenae* of auspicious biblical verses initiating the workday week: "Rabbi Yochanan said: In every passage where you find the greatness [*gedulato*] of God mentioned, there you find also his humility"; also Judah ha-Levi 1977, 41; and the dispute between Yechezkel Segal Landau and Samuel Edels in Landau 1960, 2:1; also Moshe ben Jacob 1993, 1:102, injunctive 64.] It is in itself conspicuous that this virtue is attributed to God despite the traditional reluctance to innovate divine attributes. [TB Berakhot 33b; also Maimonides 1984–1996, Hilkhoth Tefillah 9:7, and *Guide* 1:59, 140 object to the recitation of a great many divine attributes—in order not to "exhaust" God's greatness. Also Nachman of Bratislava 1991, 101–8.] And how strange is this new attribute! The salvational purpose of humility divine, as it is known in Christology, has no place in Judaism. Like all other attributes, "humility" can only signify an ethical ideal. In concord with the above-mentioned haggadic gnome, Maimonides places humility at the center of his entire system of virtues: it follows not only that Maimonides confirms this divine attribute as the grounds of God's greatness, as the foundation of the idea of God, but rather that in so doing he affirms the even more important idea that the divine attribute as such can only be understood as an ethical paradigm. For what literal meaning could lie in ascribing humility to God? Only because it is incumbent upon man to reflect upon humility and to realize it, is God "humbled," as it were, by this attribute. The case of humility proves beyond doubt that the divine attribute as such does not refer to divine substance, but rather to a correlational concept of ethics.

tradition is described by the Midrash in terms of its humility: God humbly consulted with His angels before creating the world.[46] Mount Sinai was the most humble among the mountains; and the burning bush, which was not devoured when God revealed Himself there to Moses, was physically a most humble site.[47] Moses, God's prophet, was the "most humble among men."[48]

According to one midrashic tradition, it is only due to Moses' humility that God can speak face to face with him. Humility is a passivity that, according to tradition, expresses itself as receptivity vis-à-vis the presence of the divine. "What brought him [Moses] this distinction? His meekness . . . since whoever is meek will cause the *shekhinah* to dwell with [him] on earth, as it is said . . . 'I dwell in the high and holy place, with him that is of a contrite and humble spirit.'"[49] Cohen calls this passivity "humility." And Levinas, who terms it *election,* holds that it "is not a simple *effect* of the Good . . . it is in this passivity [in this humility] that the Good *is.*"[50]

Agnus Dei: Carrying Something on One's Neck

The salvational multipurpose of humility divine. The Christian image of the *Agnus Dei*—of Christ as the sacrificial lamb of God—is modeled upon the virtue of humility and readiness for sacrifice. "Blessed are the poor in spirit, for theirs is the kingdom of heaven," says Jesus in Matthew 5:3, and further (11:29), "Take My yoke upon you, and learn from Me, for I am gentle and humble in heart; and you shall find rest for your souls." The "poor in spirit" (πτωχοι) is a translation from the Hebrew עני (*ani* or "poor"), a word that is close to the Hebrew term ענו (*anaw* or "humble").[51] Cohen himself comments upon this etymological connection, repeatedly emphasizing the identity of the poor with the humble, associating both with those who are without blame, the innocent, the pious ones.[52] The poor are pious because their suffering is undeserved. Cohen writes,

> It is not true that poverty is caused by sin. Those inflicted by suffering are innocent and righteous. The God of the righteous must be the God of the poor.[53]

Cohen's adamant insistence that poverty is undeserved opposes the mythical contention that suffering is meted out as a punishment of the gods. Only when suffering is undeserved does the messianic imperative to abolish suffering make sense. Humanity is entrusted with the task of this abolishment. While humanity at large is so entrusted, the task falls particularly to those who carry the burden of a law that promises justice, those who take upon themselves the "yoke of the kingdom of Heaven."

According to Christian dogma, Jesus "takes upon himself the yoke of the kingdom," thereby setting the example for all of humankind. So it is said in Matthew 11:29, "Take My yoke upon you." Christian dogma traditionally associates the yoke with the cross borne by Jesus, which ever since symbolizes Christian humility. *Imitatio Dei* in Christian tradition is thus intrinsically related to the directive, "take up the cross and follow me."[54]

Cohen claims that it is the *salvational* aspect of divine humility—the fact that, dogmatically speaking, Christ's suffering and death vicariously *atones* for the transgressions of all—which is foreign to Jewish teaching. The image of the yoke, however, is deeply rooted in Jewish tradition. One takes upon oneself *ol malkhuth shamayim* (the yoke of the kingdom of heaven), or *ol hamitsvoth* (the yoke of commandments), both traditionally associated with Shema Israel.[55] Similarly, *ol Torah* (the yoke of Torah) is called *ol chokhma* (the yoke of wisdom).[56]

The literal meaning of *ol* refers to a bar that one carries on one's neck. Jewish tradition employs this expression metaphorically when relating it specifically to a person's commitment to the one God, whereby reciting Shema Israel—"Hear, o Israel, the Lord our God, the Lord is One"—becomes a concrete act of submission to God's will. Christian tradition, prima facie, translates *ol* back into physical terms when portraying the Son of God, Christ, in the bodily image as one who "takes up the yoke of the cross" in submitting to the will of God.

Transubstantiation: A Polemic against Institutionalized Salvation

137. The ethical wholesomeness of the more open-minded constitution of the Jewish religion proves itself in that its God cannot transubstantiate in his church for the sake of institutionalized salvation. Just as we have no cognitive access to His essence, so God cannot be substantiated or vicariously represented in "divine" institutions. Only by relating to God directly can we and may we establish ethics. However, someone unable to enter this relationship—what is she then, what will become of her? Can we achieve building a Self without relating to God?

(*See 137.*) *The Jewish God cannot transubstantiate in his church for the sake of institutionalized salvation.* Cohen's polemic against Christianity culminates in the claim that the Christian concept of *Imitatio Dei* impairs the autonomy or radicality of human freedom upon which Jewish teaching of the sole human responsibility for the pursuit of messianism is predicated.[57] Christ's death and atonement signifies to Cohen a regression to mythical religiosity in that Christianity institutionalizes salvation, sanctifying the Church as *holy space* in which salvation takes place. In his *Religion of Reason,* Cohen polemically contrasts this conception with the "institution" of Yom Kippur, where *sacred time* allows for the atonement of sins. Even in the ancient Jewish tradition according to which the high priest's vicarious performance of penitential acts in the Jerusalem temple on Yom Kippur were to effect atonement for transgressions between a person and God, such "vicarious performances" never included any transgressions toward one's fellows, for violations of the ethical pursuit of lovingkindness and justice. According to Cohen, there can be no vicarious fulfillment of the messianic task.

7

"He Is (Not) Like You"

How Suffering Commands Self or Soul

Having discussed the ideal of human perfection first halakhically and morally, Cohen in this seventh chapter sets out to ground the human pursuit of the ideal in the individual's responsibility. The concept of individual responsibility, which Cohen models after the teaching of the prophet Ezekiel, is of central importance to Cohen's theory of the Self as an infinite task *rather than a given entity. The* Self *emerges in the relationship to another—a* thou*—rather than in the lonely pursuit of the philosopher trying to achieve the bliss of theoretical knowledge as promised by Aristotelian eudaemonian ethics. Self-perfection, according to Cohen, means the pursuit of justice, a pursuit in which ethical self-awareness makes itself felt as an autonomous power of the human will.*

Self or Soul

138. In the language of religion we would search in vain for a term connoting the Self. The Self originates in self-awareness, and hence belongs to philosophical terminology. It is to the credit of prophetic religion that it discovered the concept of the person in the concept of the soul. The person as an individual emerges in relation to ancestors, kinfolk, and nation; and these social bonds cannot be severed. Thus we can speak of the individual only in the generic sense as son of man, as one of the children of man. [The term *ben adam* (son of man) applies in biblical sources in

(*See 138.*) *The Self.* There is no Hebrew term for Self in the Cartesian sense of *cogito ergo sum.* Maimonides employs the term *nefesh* (soul) for what one could read as an indication of the thinking Self.[1] However, the Hebrew term *nefesh,* although taken by medieval thinkers at times in the Aristotelian sense of intellect or rational soul, usually carries the implications of the Greek *psyche* and the Latin *anima.* Whereas the concept of Self in the modern philosophical sense always points to self-awareness (*Selbstbewusstsein*),

particular to the prophet Ezekiel himself who represents to Cohen the very responsibility of the single individual. *RoR* 211; *RdV* 246. In other instances, the term *ben adam* simply indicates the generic term *descendant of Adam* (a human being). The application of the term *son of man* to the founder of Christianity originates in Jewish apocalyptical, apocryphal writings close to the Essene movement. Flusser 1997, 124–33.] Even the individual cannot be conceived of in his or her own right except within this generic relationship. [Cohen's concept of the individual, pointing beyond the universal and generic domains of ethics (*BdR* 61–62; *RoR* 167–68; *RdV* 195–96), is strictly bound to the ethical pursuit of the ideal of humanity. *BdR* 58–59; *RoR* 167–68; *RdV* 195–96.]

medieval usage of the Hebrew *nefesh* often refers to pure physical vitality in explicit opposition to the intellect. Also the postbiblical Hebrew term *sekhel* for mind does not denote the Self but rather the rational faculty (νους, *intellectus*; *Vernunft*; reason) with no indication of any subjective self-awareness.

Ezekiel's Concept of the Individual and Individual Responsibility: The Meta-Ethical Self—*Teshuvah*

The prophets who discovered the concept of individual soul. Cohen refers to his favorite passage in Ezekiel (18:4, 20), *"hanefesh hachoteth hi tamuth"* [the soul that sinneth, it shall die]. Cohen credits his namesake, the prophet Ezekiel, with the discovery of the original human commitment toward the Good and, subsequently, with the discovery of ethical responsibility, by proclaiming that it is the individual alone who can be made accountable for her own transgressions: "The soul that sinneth, it shall die; the son shall not bear the iniquity of the father with him, neither shall the father bear the iniquity of the son with him."[2] It is Ezekiel who abrogates the concept of hereditary sin and of collective responsibility, which, according to Cohen, constitutes a main feature of mythical thought: "We must eradicate the archevil of myth, namely its claim that human nature is tainted with hereditary sin."[3]

The idea of free will and of individual responsibility results in the personal accountability of human action, giving rise to the concept of the individual Self. According to Cohen, the prophet Ezekiel discovers the concept of the "single individual" (*das Individuum als Ich*) and contributes it to the consciousness of human culture.[4] *Das Individuum als Ich* points to the unique Self, the meta-ethical Self that lies beyond the range of ethics:

> The problem of the single individual [*Ich*] can neither be

> exhausted through [ethical] propositions of universality, nor through any reference to social context, i.e., social plurality.[5]

Nonetheless, Cohen burdens his meta-ethical Self with an eminently ethical task that originates with the original obligation of the Self toward others. Cohen calls this task *teshuvah* (return or repentance). *Teshuvah* indicates a return to the original commitment, a mending of its betrayal.

Cohen claims that the Self is originally constituted in the process of *teshuvah*. There is no Self, Cohen says, that exists outside ethics, outside this process of return. Following Maimonides' exposition of the Laws of Repentance (Hilkhoth Teshuvah), Cohen claims that the ethical Self, in this process of return, mends its past by appealing to the futurity of its betterment. This process constitutes no less than the very creation of the Self: "The one engaged in the process of repentance . . . might want to change his name [to indicate that his identity has changed] as if to say: 'I am changed into another person, and have nothing in common with the one who has committed those deeds.'"[6] Cohen further says, "This possibility of self-transformation [*teshuvah*] turns the individual into a free I."[7]

Maimonides' reading of *teshuvah* as the very creation of the Self recalls another passage of his *Code*, a passage that deals with prophecy, with the question of what happens to a prophet when being addressed by God: "And when God's spirit addresses the prophet . . . he will be changed into another person, and will realize that he is not the same as he had been."[8]

The process of return, in fact, truly reflects the hermeneutics of prophecy in that it denotes self-transformation in the face of God who summons the individual Self toward its messianic task. This task is an eminently ethical one, Cohen claims, that is reiterated in any encounter with a suffering person whose face summons one to become another (better) person to become more humane than one has been. The ritual expression of this process is the day of atonement, Yom Kippur.[9] The existential significance of Yom Kippur, according to Cohen, lies in the enactment of Ezekiel's idea of individual responsibility.[10] Cohen invokes the Talmud in order to corroborate his reading of Ezekiel on individual responsibility as a privileged text:

> Rabbi Jose bar Chanina says: "Moses, our teacher, promulgated four decrees for Israel. Along came four prophets and abrogated them. . . . Moses said: 'He visits the iniquity of parents upon children' (Exodus 34:7); along came Ezekiel and superseded him by stating: 'The soul that sinneth, it shall die'" (Ezekiel 16:4).[11]

There is a Midrash that supports Cohen's reading as well, presenting a gradational line of interpretations on the subject of repentance. The Midrash rates lowest the scriptural idea of the unforgivable nature of an evil deed: "Evil shall always pursue the sinners" (Proverbs 13:21). It then progresses, unlike Cohen, to a *mythical* reading of the above-quoted passage from Ezekiel that the Midrash interprets as the expiation of sin through death: "The soul that sinneth, it shall die." The Midrash then touches upon the halakhic idea of compensating an evil deed through action: "Let him bring a guilt offering" (Leviticus 5:6) and finally culminates in the idea of individual repentance and atonement before God: "And the Holy One Himself replied: in penitence let him mend his ways and his sin shall be forgiven him."[12]

Menschensohn—ben adam. Cohen uses the biblical term *ben adam* in order to point to a correlation between the single individual and the ideal of humanity (*ben adam*). Individual repentance, the demand to "cast away from you all your transgressions, wherein you have transgressed, and make yourself a new heart and a new spirit,"[13] finds response by a God who is forgiving and long-suffering, *el rachum vechanun* (Exodus 34:6–7). According to Cohen, the correlation between the ethical responsibility of the individual and the forgiving God undergoes a fundamental change when Christian dogma adopts the term *son of God* to denote the son's vicarious suffering for the atonement of hereditary sins:

> It is a tragedy of monotheism that precisely the attribute of God's goodness, the forgiveness of sin, has endangered pure monotheism through the [Christian] concept of the Son of Man.[14]

139. The Self therefore is not just an expression of the empirical individual but rather represents an ideal concept in ethics, defining a task assigned to man—a task to which man has to commit himself inasmuch as he strives for self-perfection in his effort to become an ethical person. ["Incessantly the Self must remain the task which contains in itself the task of the moral law." *BdR* 59; also *ErW* 259. Thus the Self is for Cohen no empirical concept, but rather an ideal task, whose realization finds expression in the messianic ideal of humanity, which, in turn, is postulated by the idea of the one God. *RoR* 420–21; *RdV* 488; *BdR* 51–53; *ErW* 404–5.] This ethical labor, however, is linked to the idea of God, as it is directed toward God; thus the formation of the ethical Self is inconceivable without relating to God. The concept of humility is central to that relation, and thus it follows that humility relates to the human Self. The virtue of humility is meant to teach and educate a person who in trying to find herself, should not look for empirical or historical individuality, but solely for the pursuit of ethical self-perfection; namely, for self-perfection toward God. [Humility, according to Cohen, is the epitome of messianism. *RoR* 266–88; *RdV* 310–23; also see paragraph number 134 in chapter 6 of this book.] A person can and ought to recognize ethical self-perfection merely as an infinite task. She must never yield to the proud-hearted feeling of power and achievement, of greatness, [Deuteronomy 8:17.] of her integrity or her complacency. She should advance the concept of Self only as an ever-challenging task. Humility is a divine attribute in order to ensure that it may ever remain a human virtue; humility is *the rod and the staff* [Psalms 23:4] with which a person works toward the ethical ideal. The Self finds its model in God. Knowledge of God, as well as love of God, are meaningful exclusively in terms of human ethics, in terms of interpersonal relations, and of a person's relationship to herself.

140. Do we also find this meaning in the god of Aristotle? In a brief discussion of this question, we shall return to the problem of eudaemonia.

Knowledge, Knower, Known: A Critical Note on J. B. Soloveitchik

141. In Aristotle, thought and action are opposites. [Aristotle 1977, *Metaphysics* 12:9; 1945, *NE* 1177b, 337–53. The Aristotelian distinction between intellectual virtue (αρεται ηθικαι) and practical virtues (αρεται διανοηθικαι) testifies to the dissolution of ethics as science and therewith to the loss of the idea of the Good as a regulative ideal for human action. *RoR* 403 and *RdV* 467 on Aristotle 1945 *NE* 1103a, 67; *NE* 1178b, 623.] The life committed to the eudaemonia of thinking is therefore a life of leisure. [The Greek word σχολη (*scholei*), from which the English terms *scholar, scholarship,* and *school* derive, literally means "inactivity" or "leisure."] This leisure is identical with contemplation for which it provides

(*See 141.*) *Knowledge, knower, and known.* Maimonides adopts this metaphysical *terminus technicus* from Aristotle, and most commentators suggest a plain Aristotelian reading of this doctrine.[15] Cohen, of course, maintains that the ethical and political implications of Maimonides' doctrine of Walking in His Ways suggest a radical *critique* of the Aristotelian principle of mere divine contemplation.[16] We find a perceptive interpretation of Maimonides' theory of actional attributes in J. B. Soloveitchik's essay "And Thence They Request," whose ethical gist and anti-Aristotelian bent are clearly indebted to Cohen's reading.[17] Soloveitchik's interpretation, however, reverts to a plain reading of Aristotelian metaphysics when

the *conditio sine qua non.* A life of contemplative leisure is thus, in fact, a life of reason. Hence, this eudaemonia of thinking and of reason constitute divine excellence, or, if you wish, the characteristic of God. God as the Prime Mover means nothing but that; the automotive faculty is tantamount to a thinking whose object of thought consists exclusively of itself. For Aristotle, the automotive faculty is the principle of motion; hence a mind that thinks of itself (self-reflective thinking) is the principle of thinking. Therefore the thinking of the Aristotelian God means "thinking of thinking" (νοησις νοησεως). [Aristotle 1977, *Metaphysics* 1074b, 165.] What else can He, what else needs He, think? He thinks thinking (that is, He thinks Himself); for He is thinking, the very principle of thinking. And just as all motion emerges from the principle of motion, so all thinking emerges out of the principle of thinking. In thinking the thinking, or in thinking Himself, the universe, anything in motion becomes the object of this thinking; for the cosmos finds its origin and principle in this divine thinking. This then produces the equation of "knowledge, knower, and known" (שכל משכיל מושכל). [Maimonides 1984–1996, Hilkhoth Yesodei haTorah 2:10; *Guide* 1:68, 163–66; 3:21, 484–85; Maimonides 1912, chap. 8.] This equation proves meaningful not only with reference to God: pantheism applies it to human reasoning.

it comes to Maimonides' citation of the classical doctrine of God contemplating himself.[18]

142. Does this God, who finds His self-sufficiency in thinking of Himself, bear any resemblance to or kinship with the God of Maimonides? If so, one would have to assume that for Maimonides the essence of God is primarily defined in terms of Creation; it is precisely this definition, however, which Maimonides, in fact, rejects. What effect does this "thinking of thought" exert on ethics? Should ethics perhaps be grounded in the notion of God's celebrating His eternal bliss by thinking Himself? To which of the actional attributes, however, should we refer this divine bliss? Of God, we only know attributes of action. But in Aristotle, thinking and action are diametrically opposed. The pantheon is far removed from any action. Should the gods perhaps be executing deeds of virtue, or of justice? "Will it not seem ridiculous?" (Aristotle 10:8, *NE* 1178b, 11.) ["The gods, as we conceive them, enjoy supreme felicity and happiness. But what sort of actions can we attribute to them? . . . Will it not seem ridiculous (γελοιος) to think of them as making contracts, restoring deposits, and the like? . . . If we go through the list we shall find that all forms of virtuous conduct seem trifling and unworthy of the gods. Yet, nevertheless, they have always been conceived as . . . living actively. . . . But for a living being, *if we eliminate action, and a forteriori creative action,* what remains save contemplation? It follows that the activity of God . . . is the activity of contemplation; and therefore among human activities, that which is most akin to the divine activity of contemplation, will be the greatest source of happiness (emphasis added)." [(Aristotle 1945, *NE* 1178, 623.)] Here, Aristotle thinks merely in terms of trading amongst the gods themselves, ignoring, however, any relationship of the gods to mortals. Gods are exempt from acting and producing, hence they cannot serve as paradigms for human action, nor can their eudaemonia express itself as one of action. Thus we find eudaemonia of leisure diametrically opposed to eudaemonia of action. How can we imagine ethics without action? The gods are removed from virtuous conduct, hence they are divorced from virtue as such. It follows that they are excluded from any relationship to ethics. Since, according to Aristotle, however, the essence of God is characterized in terms of eudaemonia, Maimonides must needs reject the most fundamental principle of Aristotelian ethics (that is, eudaemonia) as he is bound to reject the God of a eudaemonia deprived of ethics.

143. What, then, is the meaning of eudaemonia as it relates to human ethics? Only vaguely can man aspire to an ethics expressed in eudaemonistic terms. The human mind shares in divine reason; hence one learns to master thinking. Human thinking is creative, like that of God. Human reason is not only receptive, but active (νους ποιητικος). [*Guide* 1:68, 164–65.] To be sure, the satisfaction of one who has achieved wisdom is greater than that of one who is searching for it. And yet, one does not necessarily have to renounce this bliss. If man only cultivates the thinking of wisdom, thereby displacing practical conduct, as Aristotle's ethics requires, he can advance himself by means of the intellectual engagement of the philosopher toward pure thinking, and in so doing arrive at God's essence consisting of eudaemonia. [*RoR* 403 and *RdV* 467 on Aristotle 1977, *Metaphysics* 1072b, 149; Aristotle 1945, *NE* 1175a, 597.] Eudaemonia is produced by virtuous thinking only, which exclusively applies to the "dianoetic virtues." Virtuous conduct may be impeded by many factors, being subject to financial circumstance, physical strength, and freedom of choice. Scientific activity, however, is not at all or is hardly affected by these.

144. Thus, according to Aristotle, the purpose of ethics consists in refraining from ethics; ethics aims at abstention from all virtuous human conduct. This characterizes the eudaemonia of Aristotelian ethics, which ensures that mortals become equal or similar to the gods. In practicing eudaemonia, not to say, in celebrating it, man gratifies the striving to assimilate to God. Both for man and for God, this eudaemonia actually raises a wall of separation blocking the way to ethics.

145. Such eudaemonia Maimonides was bound to reject, and with it any kind of eudaemonia—if systematic coherence of thought is to serve as a criterion at all. (Joël did not recognize even this decisive difference between Maimonides and Aristotle, consisting of the basic question of eudaemonia, due to his failure to recognize the ethical value of thinking defined by the cognition of God. See his essay on Maimonides 1876b, 1:49. For the correct insight, here as well as elsewhere, see S. Scheyer in his commentary to his translation of part 3 of the *Guide*, esp. 447.) Maimonides not only decisively and emphatically rejects the doctrine of eudaemonia, with broad and profound conclusions deriving from this opposition, as we shall further elaborate, but at the same time, he undertakes to introduce a substitute for this basic eudaemonian concept, as we have pointed out previously. The substitution must be found along the same path from which eudaemonia went astray. That is the path upon which self-improvement will move.

I and Thou: Asymmetrical Relationships and the Priority of the Other

146. It is an irresistible delusion that the lone thinker in his eudaemonian bliss will mature most safely into Selfhood. On the other hand, we know that this solitary Self of thinking cannot be identical with the ethical Self, because the latter Self demands action. For the ethical Self cannot exist as an I without a You. The Other is termed *Re'a* in Hebrew—he is like You; [Leviticus 19:18; and *JS* 1:145–95; as well as 3:43–97, esp. 52–65.] *Re'a* is the You who correlates with the I. The Self results from the eternal relationship between I and Thou; that is, it is the infinite ideal of this ever-continuing relationship. The ideal always remains ideal; the task remains a task. Yet the ideal is defined by its demand for zealous emulation, hence it opens up the

(*See 146.*) *I and thou.* Cohen formulates the dialogical principle that the Self is engendered by the Other, that "I originate with You," or, in typically Cohenian terms, "that the I correlates with the Thou."[19] In contributing the theme of I and Thou to twentieth-century Jewish philosophy of intersubjectivity, Cohen inspires dialogical thinking and the political and theological traditions of dialogue that ensued.[20] Cohen, in contrast to Buber, conceives of the relationship between I and Thou as an asymmetrical one, as he predicates the very concept of Self upon the priority of the Other whose suffering commands love and justice. The Thou imposes a claim on the Self, a commandment "to do good" that is prior even to ethical reasoning:

possibility of coming closer; just as the task is a task only insofar as it is incumbent upon me, insofar as it is my personal concern. Working at this task, I am working on myself, on my Self; this Self integrates the I and the Thou. In striving toward this aim, in which the Self is manifest, I am practicing that virtue which might best be termed *the virtue of the Self.* We have already met this virtue: it is humility. Maimonides, opposing the Aristotelian principle of eudaemonia, replaces this principle, and reformulates it in such a way that the Self is prominently exposed; he substitutes self-perfection for eudaemonia. [*RoR* 313, 315; *RdV* 364, 366–67; and *Guide* 3:35, 538.]

> Ethical method fails when facing this new problem of attaining the concept of *Thou*. . . . There arises the question whether it is not precisely in paying heed to the suffering of another in which this other appears no longer as him or her but rather as *Thou*.[21]

It is the suffering of the *Mitmensch*, the fellowperson, and her call for compassion that establishes, in Cohen's language, the priority of you over myself. The other person demands goodness of me in precisely the same way as God does, and as is stated in Micah 6:8: "He has told you, *adam*, what is good: . . . only to do justice, and to love goodness, and to walk humbly with God." The imperious cry of the creature demands the fulfillment of the commandment to do "the right and the good in the eyes of God."[22] The suffering of another reminds the Self of its original responsibility, a responsibility that is prior to reason. The other person provides the grounds for the messianic ideality of the Self.[23]

Re'a Fellow: Shepherding Others

The Other is termed re'a *in Hebrew.* Cohen gives the term *re'a* (fellow) a universalist bent, relating the term to the "fellow-Jew" as well as to the "foreigner."[24] The Hebrew text reads *"ve-ahavta le-re'akha kamokha"* (Leviticus 19:18). The term *re'a* (רע) is etymologically related to the root *רעה or "shepherding," suggesting that the word *re'a* implies a personal attitude of care or shepherding toward others.[25] This attitude of care, this *Befindlichkeit der Sorge*, unlike that of Heidegger, is not one that is concerned primarily with its own *Dasein*.[26] It rather constitutes, according to Cohen, a response to a commandment that is prior to one's own Being. Maimonides himself restricts the meaning of *re'akha* in Leviticus 19:18 to "your brother who is committed to the Torah and to the pursuit of the Commandments."[27] Here

Cohen disagrees, and we could argue that Maimonides' very restriction of *re'akha* to "your brother" seems sensible only if we grant the fundamental validity of Cohen's universalist interpretation.

Creation of the Ethical Self

He is like you. Cohen's translation of *kamokha* as "He is like you" stands in opposition to the adverbial interpretation which is usually given to the sentence, namely "Love your fellow as you love yourself." Cohen advances an adnominal reading instead: "Love your fellow, since he is one like you are."[28] Rosenzweig's translation leaves the meaning open, thus fully preserving the ambiguity of the text: "*Halte lieb deinen Genossen, dir gleich.*"[29] Buber on his part emphasizes the peculiar dative construction of the passage, featuring the indirect object, *ve-ahavta le-re'akha.* We do not read "Love your fellow" in the accusative sense, in the sense of a direct object, but rather "Act lovingly towards your fellow," suggesting a relational, existential commitment toward the other, which is grounded in the classical biblical commentaries on Leviticus 19:18.[30]

Cohen proposes the concept of Self as the integral limit for the ethical will in its pursuit of the ideal of humanity. He thus models his concept of intersubjectivity upon his principle of origin, in which the concept of limit (you are [not] like me) assumes an originative, creative function with respect to the very process of human cognition.[31] The ideal Self which constitutes itself as an "ought of self-awareness" [*das Sollen des Selbstbewusstseins*][32] when facing the needs of another, is not simply "given" within us, but rather has to be *created.* The very grounds of the creation of the Self, however, lie in the concrete needs and in the tangible sufferings of the other person. The facing of such need, Cohen says, brings about the creation of the ethical Self.

The Principle of Grace and the Principle of Justice

147. Maimonides defines the concept of self-perfection by subsuming it under the most important concept in Judaism, originally denoting justice, subsequently as well love, hence piety and ethics in general—*tsedaka* (צדקה). Yet since Maimonides offers this ulti-

(*See 147.*) *Justice and love.* Maimonides discusses the term *justice* (*tsedaka*) in conjunction with two other concepts, namely lovingkindness (*chesed*), and true judgment (*mishpath*).[33] The concepts lovingkindness, justice, and true judgment assume a pivotal

mate religious and ethical value as the substitute for eudaemonia, it is now equivalent to self-perfection. *Tsedaka* means self-perfection (השתלמות), for perfecting the Self is not merely a task for man in his relationship to himself but at the same time implies a relationship with God. On the other hand, human aspiration to perfection does not aim at the isolated self-sufficiency of the divine essence, but rather refers to the advancement toward the ideal Self, which represents the highest good. There is no other good, since only through this advancement does the ultimate purpose of man (תכלית אחרון) manifest itself, crowning human ethics and man's relationship to God. [*Guide* 3:54, 635. For the Hebrew translation see Maimonides 1987b, 597. Ibn Tibbon refers to the fourth highest perfection in Maimonides' concluding chapter of the *Guide* also as *shelemuth acheron[a],* indicating an ultimate perfection which is beyond natural disposition. Cf. ibn Tibbon's appendix of philosophical terminology in Maimonides 1987b, appendix 85. For the translation of Kafih, see Maimonides 1972, 692.] There is no purpose in human existence that remains unlinked to the purpose of ethics. Hence, the purpose of man cannot relate to a divine essence unconcerned with man. On the contrary, it is in directing itself toward human action that the divine being posits the ultimate purpose of human existence. Therefore self-perfection presents a position for Maimonides as he advances them as ideal expressions of a life lived in emulation of divine actional attributes. According to Cohen's reading, Maimonides' concept of *tsedaka* indicates justice in the fullest sense, including the concept of equity. Thus the term *tsedaka,* indicating more than "mere legality," assumes a central role in Cohen's definition of the content of humanity as ethical ideal.[34]

Maimonides defines the term *chesed*, on the other hand, as "beneficence toward one who has no right at all to claim this from you."[35] In other words *chesed* is analogous to what in Christian tradition is referred to as grace (χαρις). In his essay "*Liebe und Gerechtigkeit in den Begriffen Gott und Mensch,*"[36] Cohen emphasizes that lovingkindness, "assuming a gracious attitude towards others," is the first among all Jewish virtues. As such, it is the first of the divine actional attributes to emulate. Grace, inasmuch as it is defined as an undeserved gift of beneficence, however, cannot serve as a principle for ethical self-perfection. Such a principle, according to Cohen, would constitute an infringement upon the sovereignty of ethical will, and, as such, an infringement upon the very principle of individual responsibility.[37] Cohen therefore claims that "Maimonides defines *tsedaka* as the virtue of [ethical] self-perfection."[38] Maimonides' formulation of *tsedaka* quite literally endorses

perfect substitute for eudaemonia. Eudemonia provides an aim, a finish, a real end. A human being ought not to settle for such an end and terminal objective; the ultimate end is but continuous work; it is no idle work, however, but rather advancement in goodness, by dint of striving toward the Good.

148. The term *self-perfection* [literally, process of perfecting] is significant, since it distinguishes itself from the state of perfection (שלמות). Previously (See paragraph 123 in chapter 6.) we have tried to clarify the different terminological usages in Hebrew of virtue, and we pointed to the term מעלה in its connotation "grade," a process of development [*gradus ad parnassum*] than just the state of excellence. [See paragraph numbers 122 and 123 in chapter 6.] Perfection is suspect in its kinship with that sort of skill (ἕξις) which we had to reject. As a matter of fact, we should assume that the Hebrew term for perfection originated with Aristotle's term *entelechy,* by which he defines the soul. [Aristotle 1975a, *On the Soul,* 412a, 69. Aristotle's concept of entelechy indicates an immanent teleology, as it denotes a natural process that contains its telos or perfection within itself.] Entelechy means substance as reality brought to perfection; reality's telos (τελος) is inherent. In designating virtue as perfection, perfection is defined as the virtue of the soul, and therewith declared to be the substance of the soul, as the soul itself is not defined in terms of the perfection of entelechy. Whereas the process of *self-perfection* (τελειωσις) has never obtained any particular significance in Aristotelian ethics, [Aristotle 1947, Metaphysics 1021b, 266, where perfection (from τελειωσις) indicates an immanent teleology with no particular reference to any ethical telos.] this very term plays a significant role in Jewish ethics, most prominently in Maimonides. Thus we may be led to assume that the term perfection (שלמות) may have given rise to the later semantic development of the Hebrew term *self-perfection* (השתלמות). [*Hishtalmuth* is a modern term. Ben-Yehuda 1980, 1214a.] The perfection of the soul is projected into the process of perfecting the Self. Now we may dispense with the concept of eudaemonia, which, in any case, itself bodes ill.

149. It is to the credit of Maimonides, having achieved a great breakthrough in Jewish ethics, that he did away with the ambiguous concept of eudaemonia, replacing it with that concept through which rational ethics has always discussed the problem of free will, namely autonomous ethical self-awareness.

Cohen's claim that *tsedaka* "applies to every good action performed by you because of a moral virtue [ethical attribute] with which you perfect your soul."[39]

[*ErW* 258–84, 285–323.] It is this doctrine of the autonomous ethical Self which now mediates the generic concept of virtue: the process of perfecting (השתלמות) instead of perfection (שלמות).

To Inherit the Good—Studying Torah for Its Own Sake

150. This breakthrough is all the more meritorious as it is obtained in the face of that most intricate issue admittedly most amenable to seduction; that is, the eudaemonia of thinking. Even the luxury of contemplation is renounced, once the danger of the false principle has been recognized. Indeed, when facing the issue of eudaemonia, no less than the very grounds of ethics is at stake. No ethicist was ever so cruel as to deny the ethical person her claim to true happiness. ["I do not oppose the feeling of happiness, but only the idea of its absoluteness." *ErW* xii, 293–96.] She attains this happiness in the pursuit of self-perfection, whereas she must fail to achieve it under the false slogan of eudaemonia. The false principle will lead to false conclusions. How much Maimonides himself attributes his overcoming Aristotle to Jewish tradition he himself attests by stating his aversion to eudaemonia more explicitly in his halakic code (*Yad ha-Chazakah [Mishneh Torah]*) than in the *Guide*. "The one who serves God out of love is engaged in the pursuit of Torah and its laws, and follows the paths of wisdom, not for the sake of some mundane or earthly interest, nor for the sake of avoiding pain or suffering, and in

(*See 150.*) *To inherit the good.* In most versions of the traditional text of *kedusha desidra* especially among the Ashkenazi traditions, the expression "to inherit the good" (*lirosh hatov*) refers to the messianic days, counted among the promised rewards for performance of the commandments ("*ve-nirash tova . . . leshnei yemoth hamashiach*").[40] Cohen, of course, rejects such extrinsic reward for "doing the right and the good." We may point out, however, that Maimonides' Sephardi version of this text, in fact, did not make any mention of messianic days as a historically immanent, this-worldly reward for serving God, pointing instead to the world-to-come as the ultimate good.[41] In this way, the Sephardi tradition lends support to Maimonides' own explicit rejection of any ulterior, extrinsic, heteronomous motive for serving God. Maimonides, as we shall see, strictly distinguishes between the messianic days and the world-to-come. He labels the former "this-worldly" and "historically immanent," in contrast to the latter whose function is "transcendental" and whose reward, although contingent upon a person's pursuit of justice, lies "beyond human calculations."[42]

order to gain any hedonistic good (לא לירש הטובה) [Siddur 1943–1945, 1:204; TB Niddah 52a.] but rather one is engaged in the pursuit of truth for truth's sake . . . and this level is a very high one, and not every wise person attains it (ואין כל חכם זוכה לה)." And he continues: "This is the level of our forefather Abraham . . . the level that God has required of us through Moses." [See Maimonides 1984–1996 (*Hilkhoth Teshuvah* 10:2), also 10:4–5.] It seems beyond doubt that the phrase "not every sage" alludes to Aristotle and is derived from Maimonides' devotion to his own tradition rather than from the irony of any criticism in point; Maimonides refers here not only to Moses but also to Abraham vis-à-vis Aristotle, as if to say: my deviation from Aristotle is not to my credit, but is rooted in the basic attitude of Judaism.

The ideal of studying the Torah for its own sake, which Maimonides associates with the ideal of serving God out of love, is traditionally related to the rejection of any extrinsic, eudaemonian motive for studying Torah.[43] Historically speaking, the idea of "studying Torah for its own sake" (*Torah lismah*) found its most prominent expression in the Lithuanian movement of Talmud study initiated by R. Chayim of Volozhin in the early nineteenth century and by other disciples of the Vilna Gaon who related the idea of *Torah lismah* exclusively to the pursuit of studying and learning talmudic texts.[44] Maimonides, however, does not develop the idea of pursuing Torah for its own sake within the context of Hilkhoth Talmud Torah (as one would expect). Rather, he does so within the existentially and ethically broader context of Hilkhoth Teshuvah. *Torah lismah* becomes an expression for "serving God out of love."[45] As such, it is itself directed toward an emulation of God's ways, ways of lovingkindness and ways of justice.

The God of Abraham, Not the God of the Philosophers: Abraham and Moses

Maimonides portrays both Moses and Abraham as epitomes of human perfection, both distinguished in their knowledge and love of God. Abraham discovers God, the creator of the heavens and the earth, through "autonomous speculation," in a process of independent thinking which Maimonides denotes with the verb שוטט (*shotet*), indicating a meandering of one's thoughts.[46] Maimonides ascribes to Abraham not only the speculative discovery of God's uniqueness, but also the discovery of those ethical attributes that developed into the traditional characteristics of Abraham's faith: Walking in His Ways and love of God predicated upon "the way of lovingkindness," and the practice of "justice and righteousness."[47]

Maimonides emphasizes, however, that Abraham, in his independent, rational discovery of God, could never claim that "God has sent me to you" (thus Abraham was perpetually tempted by doubt), whereas Moses was tutored face-to-face by God.[48] Moses thus prima facie represents the higher stage of prophetic knowledge, personifying and embodying the ultimate knowledge of God in its intellectual, ethical, and political dimensions. But even this kind of perfection does not originate extrinsically: Maimonides stresses the nonsensual, pure character of Moses' knowledge of God when emphasizing the unbound, unlimited origin of Moses' closeness and intimacy with God.[49] Cohen reads this intimacy with a revolutionary bent, claiming that it frees Moses from the dictates of any given reality and its status quo.

Maimonides portrays both Abraham and Moses in contrast to a purely intellectual, contemplative pursuit idealized by the Aristotelian tradition. "This is the level of our forefather Abraham . . . the level that God has required of us through Moses."[50] This is the formulation of a traditional Halakah in which it is Abraham, in particular, who represents the ways of God (lovingkindness and justice), with Moses serving merely as the mediator of that ideal. The contrast between the God of Abraham and the God of Aristotle, or the God of the philosophers, a characteristic trope in Jewish medieval literature,[51] found its classical formulation in Judah ha-Levi's *Kuzari:*

> Now I understand the difference between *Elohim* and *Adonai*, and I see how far the God of Abraham is different from that of Aristotle. Man yearns for *Adonai* as a matter of love, taste, and conviction; whereas attachment to *Elohim* is the result of speculation. A feeling of the former kind prepares the adherents of the Jewish faith to sacrifice their life for His sake, and to prefer death to His absence. Speculation, however, makes veneration plausible only as long as it entails no harm to the believers, but nobody would bear pain for the sake of such rational faith.[52]

8

On Eudaemonian Eschatology and Holy History

Zionism as Betrayal of the Ideal

In his final three chapters Cohen discusses the ideal of human self-perfection within the context of prophetic messianism. The relationship between eschatology and ideal society, the immortality of the soul, repentance and resurrection in classical Jewish theology, and a socialist concept of messianism are the subjects of discussion in this short eighth chapter.

"Eudaemonian Eschatology" and Ideal Society

151. Indeed, one may ask, what are the circumstances and subordinate motifs to which the principle of eudaemonia owes its universal reception and indestructible appeal; for both its naturalistic ethics and its ambiguity must at all times have called its value and validity into question. For Plato, concupiscence is the very epitome of wickedness; [Plato 1982, *Phaedo* 68c–69c, 237–41; also Plato 1952a, *Philebus* 66–67, 393–99; *ErW* 145–46; *RoR* 403; *RdV* 467.] it demanded quite some audacity on the part of Aristotle to revive his

(*See 152.*) *Arabic Philosophers.* In some Islamic sources we find a prominent exposition of this kind of eudaemonian eschatology.[1] But not only in Islamic sources: Abraham ben David of Posquières defends what Cohen would call the mythical elements of Jewish eschatology, exonerating such ideas as the physical resurrection of the dead and the material well-being of the Jews in an other-worldly future.[2] The traditional depiction of messianic times does not focus only upon the eudaemonian aspects of spiritual happiness and

eudaemonia in the face of such an assemblage and such an ambience. What mockery and what satire of the wretched lot of humanity, in which but the theoretician, and only a philosopher, may relish such bliss! Could such eudaemonia provide comfort to humankind?

152. Eudaemonia gained other powerful allies. The universal tendency to promote the general welfare thwarts the exclusivity of an aristocratic pursuit of science. Even Plato could not resist the charms of a literary genre concerned with the social good. [See Plato 1942, *Timaeus* 25a–d, 41–43; Plato 1942, *Critias* 113b–121c, 279–306; and Cohen 1924, 1, 326.] Arabic philosophers have also developed this borderline domain of ethics and poetry. (S. Munk 1988, 438) [See also Maimonides' critique of the Islamic eschatological tradition. Maimonides 1984–1996, Hilkhoth Teshuvah 8:6.] Stoicism, in an era of slavery, but actually precipitating its disintegration, promoted the popularity of the ideas and ideals of socialism in their development of natural law and of the law of nations. [*ErW* 68–70. Inasmuch as the idea of social progress is linked throughout history to the ideal of a shared material common good, the pursuit of justice and of human rights remains attached to eudaemonian principles. Even modern socialism, according to Cohen, is essentially a question of material well-being, but often emphasizes instead the "birthpangs of the Messiahs," and the catastrophic, apocalyptic events announcing messianic times.[3]

Maimonides himself portrays messianic times in terms of improved material and social conditions. His portrayal of the messianic, ideal society does imply a political utopia,[4] but, according to Cohen, it should not be mistaken for being merely eudaemonia. Messianic socialist materialism is rather tied to the pursuit of justice and peace for its own sake, embodied in Israel's occupation with Torah and universal pursuit of knowledge of God:

> and then the entire world
> be occupied solely with the
> knowledge of God, and
> the people of Israel will
> be exceedingly wise, they
> will be initiated in matters
> that are now hidden, and
> they will achieve knowledge
> of their Creator according
> to everyone's capacity as it
> says in Isaiah [11:9]: "For
> the land shall be filled
> with knowledge of God
> as water covers the
> sea."[5]

The messianic future actualizes the ultimate Good, and the futurity of this Good transcends all political interests. "Therefore Israel . . . longs for the days of the messiah, so that they will be released from all politics," according to Maimonides.[6]

sustenance "heeding the demands of the stomach." *ErW* 295–96; *RoR* 240; *RdV* 281; also Schwarzschild 1956.] Indeed, the revolutionary ethical impetus of the earliest Christian communities found its reverberation here, inasmuch as that revolutionary impetus itself emanated from this socialist force. In Judaism, the original humanistic meaning of prophetic messianism had never become effete, even though the Jewish people drew their inspiration for this ethical vision from the hope for ultimate relief from temporal straits. Cosmopolitanism vis-à-vis the vandalism of migration, and socialism vis-à-vis the misery of the masses, provided the ferment which always revitalized the pursuit of eudaemonia. [The messianic ideal of the prophets, although providing the ferment for the socialist pursuit of a greater social and material good, preserves the idea of transcendence even in the midst of its most ambitious demands concerning the actual political implementations of this ideal in any societal context. An "irreconcilable contrast to what is called 'world politics' in historical terms lies within the ideal of prophetic messianism." *ErW* 407.]

153. Perhaps no less important for the survival of eudaemonia has been the eschatological element in the mythology of all cultures. [According to Cohen, fear of death—the human dread of facing the ephemerality of our own existence—lies at the bottom of all classical myths of the immortality of the soul, which extend the bliss of individual existence into an eternal future. *RoR* 247; *RdV* 288–89; also Rosenzweig 1971, 3; 1990, 3.] Out of apprehension concerning the human fate after death, the concept of the soul originally emerged, with all the attendant ambiguity, however, inherent in this origin. To the extent that such an image of the departed soul as haunting spook and specter loses its grip, and to the extent that this image becomes sublimated psychologically in focusing on consciousness and its unity, to that extent this image dematerializes and ceases to be relevant for solving the riddle of ethics. Leaving the provenance of mythology and religion, the concept of the immortality of the soul has become the subject of philosophical ethics. [Cohen reads Maimonides' concept of immortality—the world-to-come

In opposition to a long history of traditional Jewish messianism, Cohen claims that messianism precludes all Jewish nationalism. The weakness of Zionism, according to Cohen, lies in its attempt to create a political reality in which the messianic ideal merges with national existence. The political materialization of the messianic ideal, inasmuch as it is bound up with manifestations of national power, sacrifices the purity of the messianic ideal, which, in turn, provides the grounds for a radical critique of political reality.

(*olam ha-ba*)—as a concept of universal ethical significance, representing the fruit of one's knowledge of God irrespective of the question of one's national or religious identity. *RoR* 329–30; *RdV* 383; and Wiedebach 2000, 431–57.]

154. Consequently, in this point also Aristotle parted ways with Plato. Only the one who engages his soul in theoretical speculation, only the *Nous,* the creative faculty of thinking, is immortal according to Aristotle, and not the human soul as such. [Also Aristotle 1975b, *On the Soul,* 430a, 171; Maimonides 1912, 1:43; Maimonides 1984–1996, Hilkhoth Teshuvah 8:3; and *Guide* 1:68, 163–66; 3:27, 510–12.] Yet there exists something in a human being that shares in the life of the immortals. This admission, then, that Aristotle—from his point of view—presents to the general philosophical creed lends support to his eudaemonian theory.

155. Approaches toward the idea of immortality in the literature of Jewish tradition have at all times met with mental reservation; and prejudice prevailed among the generally well-educated that the inferior status of the Jewish religion is attested by its lack of any tenet of immortality. [Liebeschuetz 1967, 32.] Whoever is acquainted with the Hebrew Scriptures will have difficulties in comprehending the distortion presented by this opinion. Such prejudice becomes plausible, however, if we understand the demands that those educated in religion unceasingly make upon the doctrine of immortality—overtly or covertly. [Da Costa 1993, 47, might serve as an example in point, as after a long, existential search he outright negated that there can be any certainty in matters of immortality and salvation in Jewish (and Christian) tradition.] The same applies perhaps even more to the irreligious who are no less superstitious in matters of life after death. Scripture maintains immortality strictly within the ethical context, as circumscribed by the correlation between God and human beings.

Cohen vs. Scholem: On the Historicity of Jewish Tradition

156. It is the proximity of God (קרבת אלהים) that in Psalms 73:28 is termed a person's "goodly portion." [Cohen invokes the German noun *Gut* not in the adjectival sense of "good" but rather in the adnominal sense of "a portion of goods," alluding to Maimonides' reading of Sanhedrin 10:1: a

(*See 156.*) *The Hereafter rarely presents a distinct theme of religious imagination in Judaism.* The critical tradition within Judaism rejects all mythical perceptions of the Hereafter as inauthentic, claiming that they represent a betrayal of the integrity of the individual and of individual responsi-

"share/portion in the world to come." See also Cohen 1924, 1:297, and his reference to Judah ha-Levi there.] This is an idea almost unanimously limited by Jewish philosophers to the meaning and valence of immortality. [*RoR* 313–15; *RdV* 364–67.] The sufferings as well as bliss in the Hereafter were rarely allowed to present a distinct theme of religious imagination in Judaism. Resurrection is already portrayed in Ezekiel as a parable, [Ezekiel 37:1–14; and TB Sanhedrin 92b.] signifying none other than immortality, which, in the end, is merely an expression for ethical recompense. At times, even this recompense finds itself described and determined according to the prevailing *Zeitgeist;* yet even such deviations from the main stream of Jewish thinking are balanced through the irrepressible correction induced by the basic concept of repentance (תשובה)—a concept within which religious imagination and ethics become reconciled in Judaism. All fanaticism of retribution is deprived by one single moment of repentance of its infernal claim; repentance cheats Satan out of his blacklisting. [R. Abahu says: "The position that *ba'alei teshuvah* attain, the perfectly righteous cannot attain." Mishnah Avoth 4:17; TB Berakhoth 34b; TB Avodah Zara 17b; and Maimonides 1984–1996, Hilkhoth Teshuvah 7:4; also Maimonides 1912, vi.]

bility. About messianic times, Maimonides says:

> all these details about what will happen in messianic times is beyond the capacity of human cognition . . . those Sages who nonetheless talk about those matters, do this without the authority of our Torah. . . . Nobody shall therefore waste his time studying any of those apocalyptic legends about the coming of the Messiah . . . they have no deeper religious meaning, since they neither bring about the fear of God, nor do they teach the love of God.[7]

The predominant part of Jewish tradition, of course, runs counter to both Maimonides' rationalism and Cohen's reading of it, portraying a colorful picture of both apocalyptic and blissful images in Jewish traditions dealing with the imagined life in the Hereafter. Gershom Scholem criticizes the "great Jewish scholarship of the nineteenth and early twentieth centuries, who to a great extent determined the image of Judaism. In view of their concept of a purified and rational Judaism, they could only applaud the attempt to eliminate or liquidate apocalypticism from the realm of Judaism."[8] However, Cohen's hermeneutical agenda is different from that of Scholem and other scholars of history. For

Scholem, the ideal of historical and philological accuracy serves as a measuring stick for scholarship. Cohen's entire hermeneutical approach to Jewish literary sources is critical in that all textual and historical phenomena in Jewish tradition are themselves subjected to a critique grounded in a *hermeneutical agenda* in which the ethical reigns supreme.

Cohen knows that critically reading a specific tradition means not only to analyze its texts in philological objectivity but also to subjugate a given body of literature to a cultural agenda for which the interpreter bears responsibility. Reading a tradition critically implies that one becomes answerable for one's own approach to the text, opening oneself to the self-critical process of "giving an account" of one's own readings. One reflects upon the ethical and cultural implications of one's hermeneutical activity. It seems ironic that—while Scholem criticizes Cohen for his old-fashioned, nineteenth-century rationalism—Cohen's critical hermeneutics, in fact, provides conceptual tools for the contemporary, postmodern agenda of reappropriating Jewish sources, proceeding from decidedly ethical grounds.

Cohen's definition of Judaism proceeds methodologically in the form of a critical construction of "facts." Judaism as a "cultural fact" is itself not given, but is subject to the task of conceptual construction, as are all other facts of culture. According to Cohen, history is itself constructed, and as such history—rather than being accurate or inaccurate—stands trial before the critique extended by those who question it.

Ezekiel the Thirty-sixth

In the dispute on how to interpret Ezekiel's prophetic vision concerning the "quickening of dry bones," Maimonides and Rashi side with the opinion of the tannaitic master, Rabbi Yehuda, who reads this vision as a metaphor rather than a literal description of future events.[9] In joining this dispute, Cohen creates his own exegetical chain—the prophet Ezekiel, Rabbi Yehuda, Rashi, Maimonides, and himself, "Ezekiel, the thirty-sixth."[10] Cohen finds support for this reading in Maimonides' introduction to the *Guide*, where Maimonides claims that all visions of prophecy ought to be interpreted metaphorically: "[I am reading] the prophetic books and the dicta of the Sages in a way as if I translated words from one language into another, or as if I appropriated the meaning of the external sense of the speech."[11] According to Cohen, Ezekiel's narrative of resurrection is the external, literal sense by means of which the prophet speaks of closeness to God and of the longing for spiritual and ethical perfection.

Drastic elaborations of the soul's sufferings in hellfire (*gehinnom*) became popular especially within the kabbalistic pietist traditions during the early middle ages.[12] Traditions about the soul's mortification even report about the soul's future fate in the grave. This particular kind of apocalyptic imagination became so widely accepted that it eventually gained impact upon halakhic considerations as well.[13]

Fanaticism of Retribution vs. One Moment of *Teshuvah*

According to one opinion in the Talmud, the spiritual position attained by *ba'ale teshuvah* (masters of repentance) cannot be attained even by the perfectly righteous.[14] What Cohen calls "fanaticism of retribution," however, pervades even the concept of repentance itself. There are traditions that prescribe repentance and penance according to precise measure, opening up a balance sheet of one's personal account of transgressions and rewards.[15] Some halakhic thinkers, for example, took sexual promiscuity to represent the epitome of human transgressions, weighing the punishment in these cases in strict measure against the seriousness of the deed.[16]

Maimonides' treatment of repentance in such cases seems radically different. He defines *teshuvah* as an autonomous resolution of will through which a person overcomes her passion for a forbidden pleasure without being in need of any physical retribution. For Maimonides, it is, indeed, "one single moment of *teshuvah*," in which all need for retribution is abolished. This is the moment in which a person anticipates her better Self—a moment in which integrity creates a break with the past, so that a new Self emerges.[17] Cohen himself, as we have seen, terms such anticipation of the future a process in which redemption is anticipated.[18]

9

To Create Messianic Time

A Jewish Critique of Political Utopia on Prophecy

In this chapter Cohen provides a politically important distinction between messianic times and the world-to-come, two often conflated eschatological concepts in Maimonides' thought. In contradistinction to the historicity of messianic times, the futurity of the world-to-come represents a metahistorical dimension. Cohen correlates the metahistorical futurity of the world-to-come with the purity of the ethical ideal. His rejection of all totalitarian political movements is anchored in this separation of messianism as a political utopia from the messianism of the prophets, grounded in the futurity of the ideal as represented by Maimonides' concept of the world-to-come. Maimonides' introduction to the tenth chapter of the Mishna tractate Sanhedrin provides the textual basis for Cohen's discussion in this section.

Psychology of Prophecy: "Face to Face"

157. Maimonides' universal intellectual independence, with which he counters all dogmas through his emphasis on ethics, is perhaps nowhere as distinctly and cogently demonstrated as by the inferences drawn from his denial of eudaemonia. He replaces eudaemonia with self-perfection; and self-perfection he equates with "drawing close to God" (התקרבות). Thus he presents us with the most sublime reading of immortality. Now it only remains for him to expose the sham argument of social advantages promised by eudaemonia. Here Maimonides was able to take

(*See 157.*) *Maimonides' dialogical interpretation of the prophet.* Maimonides suggests reading prophetic messages as metaphorical images that demand interpretation and translation.[1] Especially in instances where prophetic visions invoke bodily images of God, these images are to be translated into an epistemology of Knowing God, and into social and political engagement. The prophets, according to Cohen, become the founders of Jewish messianism, in proclaiming the *relationship* between God and human beings to be foundational

advantage of his conception of prophecy, and in particular of his psychological interpretation of the prophet. [*Guide*, introduction and 2:46, 581–82.] Thus he arrives at a fundamental distinction invalidating the two main motives of eudaemonia. [Namely the bliss of pure contemplation, on the one hand, and of the pursuit of material well-being, on the other.] He distinguishes between Life Eternal (עולם הבא) [hereafter referred to as *olam ha-ba*] and the messianic era (עתיד לבוא). [*RoR* 310–11; *RdV* 361; and Maimonides 1984–1996, Hilkhoth Teshuvah 9:2.]

for God's very own Being. This stands in contrast to the ontological tradition inspired by Aristotle in which the self-sufficiency of the divine is proposed.

From the perspective of this reading, a theory of intersubjectivity that is distinctly dialogical emerges. God's speaking face-to-face with Moses provides Jewish tradition with the pedagogical and ethical mode of human discourse in which openness, receptivity, and listening creates a way of thinking different from mere self-sufficient rationality. Thus writes Alphonso Lingis:

> The locus where this imperative is articulated is the other who faces—the face of the other. Facing . . . is the move by which alterity breaks into the sphere of phenomena . . . responsibility is the response to the imperative addressed in the concrete act of facing.[2]

Jewish oral tradition embodies the reenactment of an original pedagogical moment. It is through Cohen's messianic epistemology and through Rosenzweig's concept of *Sprachdenken*—a way of thinking in which time figures centrally in taking "its cues from others"—that the pedagogy of Torah translates into the philosophical language of the West. In keeping alive the economy of an absolute passivity of thought with respect to that which precedes thought in the free gift of speech, contemporary philosophy and hermeneutics, in fact, do reenact an ancient gesture.

A Radical Critique of Political Utopia

Maimonides uses the terms *the future to come* (*atid lavo*) and *messianic days* (*yemoth ha-mashiach*) interchangeably when referring to the messianic era to be expected in the course of history.[3] It seems that neither the Talmud nor Midrash, nor Maimonides himself, are consistent in their terminological usage of the expression *atid lavo*.[4] Yet, Maimonides clearly distinguishes between *atid lavo* and *yemoth ha-mashiach*.[5]

The messianic era has been interpreted by Steven Schwarzschild as a future that is always in the coming, always to come—a future that is never to be fully realized.[6] Schwarzschild thereby intends to preserve the transcendental function of messianism in its radical opposition to and critique of the world's suffering and injustice. Both Maimonides and Cohen—to be sure—have expressed their expectation of messianic times in the near future.[7] Cohen reportedly exclaimed, "Please, let it be fifty years!"[8] However, when reading Maimonides' description of messianic futurity—a description that, according to Cohen's reading, is adamantly socialist[9]—the transcendental character of Maimonides' concept of messianic futurity is evident:

> There will be no poverty in messianic times . . . all fighting and wars will cease. . . . [We] do not hope for messianic days for the sake of worldly riches . . . but rather because there will be a dominion of goodness and of wisdom.[10]

Messianism, according to Cohen, is not identical with any political utopia. To the contrary, he writes that in messianic days, "Israel will be released from all matters of politics."[11] The concept of messianic times, of a radical futurity, provides Cohen with the conceptual grounds for a fundamental critique of all social reality. Realpolitik cannot divorce itself from war and from the perpetration of hatred and aggression: political prudence will always remain "the art of foreseeing war and of winning it by every means."[12]

It is the inherent historicity of Maimonides' concept of messianism that lends itself to the temptation of utopian politics, run by the "tyrants of heaven."[13] Cohen emphasizes, however, that Maimonides' concept of the world-to-come balances that danger. The world-to-come refers to a spiritual reality that coexists with this world in that it reflects one's own pursuit of the Good, representing, in fact, the very fruit of one's ethical labor. The world-to-come extends beyond the powers of human imagination—"No eye has seen it, o God, but you alone"[14]—transcending any worldly form. The world-to-come does not lend itself to messianic politics, but rather provides the grounds for a transcendental critique of political reality.

From this perspective, Maimonides' discussion of messianic days and the world-to-come in the context of Hilkhoth Teshuvah (The Laws of Repentance)[15] provides us with a more critical reading of messianism than the restorative description of political utopia in Hilkhoth Melakhim (The Laws of Kings):

> The Messiah will appear as the king of Israel who reinstates the former kingdom of David and reinvests it with its original sovereignty. He will reestablish the Holy of Holies in Jerusalem and bring about the ingathering of the Jews scattered amongst the peoples. All the laws which governed the former kingdom of David, including those concerning the Temple in Jerusalem, will be valid once again.[16]

Cohen, of course, advises to study this political utopia in light of Maimonides' own more radical messianic demand for the establishment of a humanity fully initiated in the ways of lovingkindness and justice and peace. What sounds like a nationalist restoration of the past, in fact, translates into a revolutionary social theory: "In messianic times there will be neither famine nor war, neither jealousy nor competitiveness, but rather goodness itself will rule."[17]

To Create Messianic Time: A Jewish Task (A Polemic That Overshoots Its Mark)

158. The genealogy of these ideas is obvious. Life Eternal belongs to mythical belief; [*RoR* 299–304; *RdV* 348–53.] the messianic era is the historiosophical idea of prophetic ethics. As these two ideas touch human fate in an innermost way, they conceptually intertwine. Early on, they originally tended to interrelate and intersect with each other in Jewish tradition and consciousness. Yet, in talmudic literature, we may trace the tendency to distinguish between these two concepts, and separate these two modes of time. [Throughout the Talmud, especially in the Talmud Yerushalmi, the term *atid lavo* signifies both messianic times and an eschatological world-to-come; we find a clear distinction between messianic times and the world-to-come, however, in TB Berakhoth 34b;

(*See 158.*) *On the Christian messiah.* Cohen's polemics against Christian eschatology focuses on the idea of Jesus the redeemer as guarantor of the world-to-come, as stated in John 14:6: "I am the way, the truth, and the life: no one cometh to the Father but through me." Cohen repeats his conviction that Christian dogma provides a purely extrinsic concept of salvation that is attained at the expense of Israel's personal and collective responsibility for the creation of messianic times in this world. In the *Religion of Reason: Out of the Sources of Judaism,* Cohen claims that the Christian doctrine of salvation replaces the sociopolitical, ethical imperative implied in the concept of messianism. This occurs through a passive, eschatological expectation of the advent of God's kingdom, which, according to John

and, of course, in Maimonides 1984–1996, Hilkhoth Teshuvah 9:2.] This distinction had to be articulated most pointedly vis-à-vis Christianity. Christianity announced itself as messianism; its messiah, however, was predicated upon the creed of Life Eternal; he, and he exclusively, wanted to be its guarantor. Thus Christianity presented a challenge to Jewish thinking, provoking clarification and self-examination with regard to the radically different meaning inherent in the messianic idea from its inception. The messiah does not represent the redeemer of human beings in the other world, but the redeemer of human beings in this world.

159. In his commentary on the Mishna, Maimonides establishes this fundamental ethical significance of the distinction between the world-to-come and messianic days vis-à-vis all the inaccuracies, lack of definition, obscurities, and confusions concerning the eschatological terms in Jewish tradition. [Maimonides provides a comparative analysis of the concepts "garden of Eden" (*gan eden*), hell (*gehinnom*), resurrection of the dead (*techiath ha-methim*), messianic days (*yemoth ha-mashiach*), and the world-to-come (*olam ha-ba*) in his introduction to Sanhedrin, 1992b, 137–40.] To what extent this conceptual separation is due to Maimonides' rejection of eudaemonia, we find demonstrated by his definition and distinction of

18:36, is "not of this world."[18] Cohen defends the Jewish immanence of this imperative in contrast to the Christian exteriority of the future kingdom:

> In my personal worship of God, the kingdom of God ought not be relegated to the future, but it rather must be ever present. This idea is expressed by the Jewish traditional concept of "taking upon oneself the yoke of the kingdom of God." . . . Therefore I must not simply wait and pray for the kingdom of God to appear, but rather through my own firm intention, my own volition, I precipitate its realization.[19]

The polemic, of course, is itself one that is constructed. Jewish sources, too, stress the extrinsic character of the "coming of the kingdom,"[20] and Christian tradition, certainly teaches ethical responsibility in the context of God's second coming. Cohen's polemic against Christian doctrines of hereditary sin and what he calls institutionalized salvation tries, principally, to advance a critical reading, in which redemption signifies the universal task of anticipating the Good and assisting in the creation of the messianic kingdom. What Cohen calls the ethical task of Judaism is the prophetic demand to create messianic time, to bring futurity into

the two ideas, the Hereafter and the this-worldliness of the messianic age, predicated upon the ethical principle of self-perfection. [*RoR* 312–15; *RdV* 362–67.]

the present, to anticipate redemption. It is this task, according to Cohen, that is incumbent upon every human being, and it is in this task that Israel represents humanity.

The World-to-Come: Ephemeral Moments of Redemption

160. Myth conceives of Life Eternal in a worldly style, as in the Isles of the Blessed. [*ErW* 401; *RoR* 247; *RdV* 289. The utopian idea of the Isles of the Blessed originates with Greek myth as an imaginary island at the Western edge of the world on which the souls of the blessed enjoy a blissful existence after death. Hesiod 1920, 98–99.] Even if we leave the realm of myth, however, there is no dearth of images in which Life Eternal is presented as the realm of the future, as it is believed that it will occur at the Parousia of Jesus, at his eschatological return. [Matthew 24:1–31; Mark 13; Luke 21.] In Jewish eschatology, the Hereafter and the messianic future become confusingly entangled; even with regard to the surviving souls, belief has it that their domain will come into existence only in the future within or outside of the context of the messianic era. [Nachmanides 1983. Nachmanides gives a detailed account of the rewards and punishments of the individual souls in the Hereafter. Note, however, that Nachmanides also quotes Maimonides' interpretation of the world-to-come as "one that has already come, or that is presently coming," drawing upon midrashic and kabbalistic traditions, as in

(*See 160.*) *The world-to-come* (olam ha-ba). The meaning of the Hebrew term *ha-ba* is actually ambiguous, as it may refer in Hebrew either to the perfect or to the present tense. In the perfect tense, the expression *olam ha-ba* reads as "the world that has already come." In the present (future) tense it means "the world that is about to come." Cohen claims that most interpreters have mistakenly understood *olam ha-ba* in the futuric sense, confusing *olam ha-ba* with a utopia of materialist reward to be enjoyed by the righteous in the future.

Maimonides, to the contrary, reads *olam ha-ba* as a spiritual existence whose very *presence* resides in our effort to know and serve God.[21] The world-to-come represents an effort of ethical and spiritual self-perfection, which in the light of Maimonides' discussion of divine actional attributes and God's ways of lovingkindness and justice, gains social and political dimensions. For Maimonides then, the world-to-come does not depict a utopian future, but rather embodies the fruits of our very labor at an ethical existence in this world. "The world-to-come presently exists and is

Scholem 1980, 114, and references there; Bahir 1912, 30. Nachmanides equates the world-to-come with the original light of creation, which according to Rashi was hidden as a reward for the souls of the righteous in the world-to-come, and which Nachmanides—much in the spirit of Maimonides—identifies with *chokhmah.* Nachmanides 1983, 117–20.] It might have been of primary concern to disrupt the materialism implied in the images of Life Eternal as a future world; the Hebrew idiom *olam ha-ba* (the coming world) favors such a materialistic interpretation. Maimonides obliterates this materialistic image. [*RoR* 310–11; *RdV* 361.]

161. Maimonides succeeds in accomplishing this annihilation by dint of his principle of self-perfection. "When the Sages refer to the world-to-come, they do not mean that the world-to-come does not presently exist—that this world would have to perish before that world could be established. That is not the case. Rather the world-to-come is already present . . . for the individual, however, life in the world-to-come becomes accessible only after his life in this world has expired." (Hilkhoth Teshuvah 8:8.) Life Eternal constitutes an organic accrual of the human individual for the sake of and in the cause of her maturing toward an ethical personality. The term *Life Eternal* does not imply that anything is to be expected in the future, nor is it predicated upon

firmly established,"[22] says Maimonides in his *Mishneh Torah.* The human pursuit of God's ways constitutes the *anticipation* of the world-to-come within a single moment. All acts of goodness are but ephemeral moments of redemption—moments in which history is judged by what Cohen calls prophetic messianism:

> It is incredible that messianism defies all political pragmatism, denigrates reality, treats it with contempt, and annihilates it without mercy, substituting this sensible presence with a new kind of [presence] . . . which is futurity. . . . The great contribution of messianism is its creation of the future, representing, in effect, the true political reality.[23]

Levinas terms Cohen's messianism "the presence of the eschaton." He reaffirms the significance of Cohen's theory of infinity (and the infinitesimal) for a contemporary theory of messianism. Levinas writes that "it is not the last judgment that is decisive, but the judgment of all the instants in time, when the living are judged."[24] Maimonides' definition of *olam ha-ba* as the presence of the future kingdom has rootings in midrashic and kabbalistic sources.[25] As such—in conjunction with the pertinent passages in *Sefer ha-Bahir*—it was reiterated throughout medieval Jewish literature.[26]

any future event; Life Eternal exists in its own right. It exists insofar as it is due; since Life Eternal is the acquisition of individual ethical pursuit, it must come.

162. According to the innermost train of thought, Life Eternal constitutes an ethical mode of Being; it is conceived of as an ethical idea. It is the idea of ethical individuality, predicated upon its eternity, which is termed *the world-to-come.* The prospective world of spiritual existence has turned into the ethical world of the eternal individual. [*RoR* 329–30; *RdV* 383–84.]

163. In the same context, Maimonides also refers to the problem of resurrection. [Maimonides 1992b, 138; also Maimonides 1997–1998, 1:339–74. Scholars are divided about the authenticity of this letter; for an argument against its authenticity, see Goldfeld 1986. Even those who take the letter to be authentic, however, point out that Maimonides wrote it under external pressure exerted by rabbinical authorities disturbed by his radical rationalism. Kellner 1986, 55.] About Gehenna, he remarks that the Talmud does not elaborate on this punishment. [Maimonides 1992a, 137–38 maintains that the talmudic references leave the matter unresolved; see TB Avodah Zara 3b and TB Sanhedrin 108a.] Even eternal bliss is interpreted in a purely spiritualized mode. He also spiritualizes resurrection; it is a fundamental rational principle (יסוד) but not a fiducial tenet (דת), nor related to such a tenet. [See Wiedebach 2000, 440–41; *RoR* 82, 91–92; *RdV* 96, 107; but see also Kellner 1986, 20–21; and Maimonides 1992b, 138.] Such terminological distinctions that permeate the entire literature are eloquent symptoms of the tendency to restrict the power of dogma. However, the efficacy and lucidity of Maimonides' rational principles make this tendency most prominent.

Internalizations

164. Describing the bliss in the world-to-come, [Maimonides 1984–1996, Hilkhoth Teshuvah 8:2.] Maimonides is led by the talmudic dictum that "in that life the righteous shall enjoy the splendor of the *shekhinah*" [TB Berakhoth 17a; and Maimonides 1984–1996, Hilkhoth Teshuvah 8:2. Midrash Exodus Rabba 1887, 3a; ascribes this spiritual state of "enjoying the

(*See 164*) *On reward and punishment.* Cohen alludes here again to Maimonides' introduction to *Perek Chelek:* "And if you heed all these commandments, I shall assist you in their performing . . . even if you fulfill only parts of the commandments motivated by love and true endeavor, I shall help you to succeed with all of them."[27] The ethical significance of Mai-

splendor of the *shekhinah*" to Moses at the "forty days of revelation," during which time he was in no need of any material sustenance. Deuteronomy 9:9; and Maimonides 1992a, 142–43.] to further spiritualize this blissful delight by claiming it to consist of cogitation, cogitation meaning continuous knowledge of God. One might thus gain the not-groundless impression, considering certain passages in Maimonides' writings, that Life Eternal even for him is vouchsafed purely for the theoretician. However, his principle of self-perfection is of such central importance that it must have systematically transformed Aristotelianism even in this controversial issue. Thus Maimonides attains to the ethical interpretation claiming that even retribution, reward, and punishment are only expressions for the divine "promotion" of human ethical endeavor (אסייע לך).

165. Interpreting the idea of perfection in the Hereafter as the paradigm for the amelioration of human nature, Maimonides presents us with the crowning achievement of spiritualization, of ethical advancement—that a person aspires to perfect herself, that human nature be

monides' definition of reward, according to Cohen, lies in Maimonides' emphasis on its internalization. The reward of keeping a commandment is that it leads to keeping another commandment, and the punishment for committing a transgression is that it leads to another transgression.[28] "And in the Talmud it says: 'whoever aspires to purity shall find support,'[29] [and] 'for the path which a person chooses to pursue, [s]he will find support.'"[30]

perfected, that nature should not obstruct the existence of the soul and its cognitive pursuit: this is the meaning of Life Eternal. "When a person pursues the Good and avoids evil, she improves her humanity (ישלם בו ענין האנושי) and distinguishes herself from the beast, and a person shall perfect herself, as human nature is to be perfected, that no obstruction will disturb the rational sustenance of the soul, and this is 'life eternal.'" (Mishna, Commentary on *Perek Cheklek,* 128a) [Maimonides 1992b, 139.] Thus it is the idea of perfecting nature that is postulated by the principle of self-perfection. This idea is bound up with Life Eternal, precisely in the sense of the "rational sustenance of the soul" [—which is Knowing God.]

10
The Human Face
Anticipating a Future That Is Prior to the Past

Cohen's essay on Maimonides' ethics culminates in the exaltation of Jewish messianism and its sublimity, stressing the social and humane dimensions of Maimonides' concept of messianic times. Toward the end of this work, Cohen grounds his Platonic reading once again in the traditional sources of Maimonides' rabbinic code and his commentary on the Mishna. Cohen thereby evokes the universality of human cognition and the eternal validity of the equality and unity of mankind. Jewish messianism—by holding on to the purity of these ideals in the midst of a history full of corruption, violence, and human pain—burdens its adherents with the task of bearing witness to the unending struggle for the reign of human justice in the world.

This World and the World to Come: The Powers of Messianism

166. The removal of sensualism from the World Beyond corresponds to the idealization of the temporal world in the messianic era. The distinction between these two corresponding states, the denial of their being identical, establishes the ethical correlation between the two. The yearning for the messianic redeemer has not lost its universal human significance, despite all political terrorization and persecutions of Israel; however, skepticism or mysticism has turned the idea of the messianic future into utopianism. [*RoR* 247–48, 310–11; *RdV* 289, 361.] Maimonides discerns the same old eudaemonia in the utopianism of Arabic political theories;

(*See 166.*) *The temporal world—and the world to come.* Maimonides' distinction between this world and the world-to-come is crucial to Jewish critical thinking, since any identification of the status quo with some ideality, according to Cohen, must lead to political quietism, violating the revolutionary character of prophetic messianism. However, the very concept of messianic times lends itself to the temptations of proclaiming the messianic reality before it has been attained. A strictly transcendental concept is needed. Cohen proposes the ethical concept of the world-to-come as a counterbalance to the temptations of messianism.

[Maimonides 1984–1996, Hilkhoth Teshuvah 8:6; and note paragraph number 151 in chapter 8 of this book.] actually, Sir Thomas More was also a stoic eudaemonist. [*ErW* 584; *ArG* 1:301; 2:114. "Utopia"—literally, ου-τοπια, "no-place"—is the name given by Sir Thomas More to the imaginary island in his political fiction of the same name (1516), whose perfect laws and politics are contrasted with the evils of the social and political *status quo.*] Maimonides could take advantage of an ethicized Beyond, defined in terms of the ideal state of self-perfection, as a model for the messianic era, by presenting the messianic era as the preparatory stage for that Beyond. To aspire to one's qualification for and ascertainment of self-perfection is tantamount to recognizing the messianic idea.

167. We would like to pursue yet another direction concerning the principle of self-perfection, stressing the messianic era and its own substantive significance vis-à-vis the World Beyond. Although the Beyond, too, is ultimately geared toward the sublimation of human nature, self-perfection relates to humanity, as the human condition presents it. This historical dimension of the human condition is particularly represented in the messianic idea; the human individual can only mature by being involved in the ethical development of every part of mankind. State and legislation should provide guidance for the

Maimonides' description of messianic times, however, stresses the perfection of the human condition, attainment of universal justice, and the ceasing of war, poverty, and of all political struggle. Maimonides' idea of the messianic future—although to be realized in this world—thus transcends the various states of empirical reality of past and present:

> The sages and prophets did not long for the days of the Messiah that Israel might exercise domination over the world, or rule over the heathens, or be exalted by the nations, or that it might eat and drink and rejoice . . . but rather they longed for the days of the Messiah so that Israel be worthy of life in the world to come.
>
> In that time there will be neither famine nor war, neither jealousy nor strife. Blessings will be abundant, comforts within the reach of all. The one preoccupation of the whole world will be to know the Lord. "For the earth will be full of the knowledge of God as the waters cover the sea."[1]

Messianism implies that the past and the present must be measured by, and, in fact, be predicated upon the future. Predicating the past upon the future means to actively anticipate that future. In his *Logik des reinen Erkenntnis* (Logic of

human endeavor of self-perfection; however, in their respective historical actualizations they can only signify approximations toward this objective. Just as messianism must be purged of all eudaemonistic elements, it must also beware of indifference toward the injustices of history, an indifference for which the problem of theodicy is merely of aesthetic interest. Eudaemonia favors egotism and the opportunistic stance of nations and potentates. Historical realism proves to be materialism as evidenced by its attendant social injustice. Social utopianism, however, places itself in jeopardy from the opposite direction by employing a fallacious principle, inasmuch as its alternative valuation of life seems to be primarily concerned with material welfare.

pure cognition), Cohen develops his concept of futurity in a way that expressly captures the critical perspective of messianism:

> Anticipation is the fundamental activity of time . . . the past is predicated upon the future that is anticipated. It is not the past that is prior to one's [critical] thinking, but rather the future.[2]

The ethical and religious implications of this logical principle of anticipation are apparent from the following passage, in which Cohen distinguishes mythical and prophetic visions of redemption:

> Myth knows no vision of the future; it relegates its images about a peaceful time among man and nature to the past, to a "Golden Age." The prophet, however, projects his ethics onto the future. The concept of futurity distinguishes the Jewish religion from all myth. . . . It is the concept of futurity which has torn the one God from the limitations of a mere national divinity, and which proclaims Him as the unique God, the God of all peoples, the one God of mankind.[3]

And in his *Religion of Reason: Out of the Sources of Judaism*, Cohen elaborates:

> The concept of futurity constitutes the grounds for a new ethics. . . . The "end of days" is conceived of as that point in the future toward which all politics must strive, and toward which all reality must direct itself. Neither the present, nor the past shall direct us—however glorious it may be and however many sacred narratives it may hold.
>
> Time is grounded in futurity and only in futurity. Past and present vanish in the face of this temporal mode of futurity.[4]

Jews, Christians, and Moslems: Pave the Way for King Messiah!

168. The incisiveness and lucidity of Maimonides' ethical thinking cannot be admired enough precisely at the point of demarcation between theory and practice, particularly since so many have failed in this distinction. [*ErW* 27.] "And therefore all Israel, their prophets and their sages, long for the days of the Messiah, that they will be released from the burden of politics, in order to become worthy of eternal life; for in those days of the Messiah there will be an increase in cognition and wisdom and truth." [Maimonides 1984–1996, Hilkhoth Teshuvah 9:2.] Cognition constitutes the fundamental premise for the messianic conversion of the social world order; cognition as knowledge, not merely as religious behaviorism, establishes the truth. [Maimonides 1984–1996, Hilkhoth Melakhim 12:4–5 and Hilkhoth Teshuvah 9:1–2; *Guide* 3:54, 636.] The intention envisioned for the messianic age is not merely the intensive and extensive augmentation of the body of knowledge, but rather everyone's personal share in this cognitive pursuit. [Maimonides 1984–1996, Hilkhoth Shmittah veYovel 13:13.]

169. The converting of the historical nature of human beings is predicated upon the universal spreading of knowledge—upon the broadening of the shared human faculty of cognitive pursuit. "But in those days it will be very easy for the children of

(*See 168.*) *Cognition constitutes the premise for messianic conversion.* It is cognition, and not merely religious or political behaviorism, upon which the messianic conversion of the social world order is fundamentally predicated. Acting upon the messianic vision of lovingkindness, justice, and peace, means to anticipate redemption, and as such, the concept of redemption is prior to the action that it arouses. Cohen finds support for his decidedly universalist reading of the messianic vision of peace in Maimonides' concluding Halakah on the laws of the Jubilee year:[5]

> Not only the tribe of Levi, but every single person from among the world's inhabitants whose thinking motivated her and whose intelligence gave her the understanding . . . and who walked upright in the manner in which God made her . . . behold every such person [will be] completely consecrated [to God's ways of holiness].[6]

In Mishna Avoth we find an expression of messianism that found its way into traditional prayer: "That the temple should be speedily rebuilt in our days, and *grant us our share* in the pursuit of your Torah [emphasis added]."[7] Cohen's reading, unlike that of other classical commenta-

man to earn their livelihood; with minimal effort one will achieve maximal results . . . and wisdom will increase . . . and war and strife will cease . . . and great perfection will come about among humankind . . . one ought not to consider it far-fetched that the thousand-year reign will sustain itself. However, we long and hope for the days of the Messiah not because of abundant bounty and riches . . . but rather because there will be a predominance of the pious, and Good and wisdom will rule (הנהגת הטובה והחכמה)" [Maimonides 1992b, 138–39]—the Good of wisdom, or ethical wisdom. Wisdom, cognition alone, is the Good to be pursued; all social and cosmopolitan ramifications of messianism are predicated upon such wisdom.

tors on this Mishna,[8] predicates all messianic aspirations of building the temple speedily in our days upon *our* (everyone's) share in the prophetic vision of peace: *ten chelkenu betoratekha* ("and afford us our share in thy Torah"). All study of Torah must be directed toward this messianic cognition, as "the entire Torah was given for one purpose only—namely to make peace in the world."[9]

According to Maimonides, Jews and Christians and Muslims share this prophetic task, all pursuing it in their own ways. Indebted to the teachings of Jesus and Muhammad, Christians and Muslims pave the way toward redemption precisely through their commitment to Christianity or Islam:

> All these matters relating to Jesus of Nazareth, and to the Ishmaelite [Muhammad] who came after him, only served to pave the way for King Messiah, to prepare the whole world to worship God with one accord, as it is written: *For then will I return the peoples to a pure language, that they may all call upon the name of the Lord, to serve Him with one consent.* [emphasis added][10]

Isaiah's Vision Versus al-Razi's Pessimism: Capturing a Messianic Gesture

170. In contradistinction to al-Razi's pessimism, [Abu Bakr Muhammad ibn Zakariyya al-Razi (850–932) was a Muslim physician and philosopher who Maimonides reads as a pessimist, cf. *Guide* 3:12, 441–42; see Pines's introduction in *Guide* cxxxi–xxxii.] Maimonides

(*See 170.*) *The vision of Isaiah.* Maimonides cites Isaiah's vision of peace as a metaphor for messianic social conditions:

> Let no one think that in the days of the Messiah any of the laws of nature will be set aside, or any innovation be

adduces the parable in the vision of Isaiah portraying the peaceful coexistence of the wolf and the lamb, [Isaiah 11:6; Maimonides 1984–1996, Hilkhoth Melakhim 12:1; and *Guide* 3:12, 441.] and thereby claims the cosmos, and not the empirical individual, as the criterion for the universal Good. He argues in favor of an anthropological theory proclaiming the equality of humankind. This original human equality has to be developed, formulated, and acted upon. There can be no doubt that this equality manifests itself in reason, and that this egalitarian assumption is predicated upon the equality of human reason despite all empirical differences.

171. This argument reinforces the central function of cognition. "Wisdom will increase"—that is cognition in which the unity of reason is attested. Maimonides expressly differentiates between wisdom and Torah. [*Guide* 3:54, 634, 636.] Only wisdom (knowledge) provides us with rational demonstration, even with respect to the interpretation of Torah, which is verified through such demonstration, correct reasoning (עיון האמיתי; see paragraph 111 in chapter 5). ["According to them (the Sages), the science of the Torah is one species and wisdom is a different species, being the verification of the opinions of the Torah through correct speculation." *Guide* 3:54, 634.] True perfection, the fourth perfection in which gen-

> introduced into the order of creation. The world will follow its normal course. The words of Isaiah: "And the wolf shall dwell with the lamb, and the leopard shall lie down with the kid" (Isaiah 11:9) are to be understood figuratively, meaning that Israel will live securely among the evil nations.[11]

In the *Guide,* Isaiah's metaphor becomes a crucial reference in the context of which the very question of good and evil is discussed. Much in support of Cohen's reading, Maimonides draws from the vision of Isaiah the very criterion for truth:

> For through cognition of the truth, enmity and hatred are removed and the inflicting of harm by people on one another is abolished. It holds out this promise, saying: *And the wolf shall dwell with the lamb, and the leopard shall lie down with the kid, and so on* [emphasis added].[12]

In characteristically Platonic fashion, Maimonides maintains that absence of knowledge is the root of evil, whereas the cognition of truth is identical to the presence of the universal Good. Cohen comments:

> The concept of the messianic God developed in distinct op-

uine human perfection is attained, and in which the ultimate telos is realized, this is the perfection of intellectual virtues (מעלות שכליות). [*Guide* 3:54, 635; Maimonides 1984–1996, Hilkhoth Teshuvah 9:2 and Hilkhoth Melakhim 12:5; Altmann 1987, 60–129. Altmann's article presents a critique of Pines's more agnostic stand on the problem of speculative knowledge in Maimonides. Pines 1988, 91–122; also Fox 1990, 26–46.]

position to the dualistic principle of Parsism. Evil in itself does not exist. Evil is a concept which is deduced from the concept of freedom. The power of evil exists in myth only.[13]

Religion diverts its interest from the question of the origin of evil, and rather directs it towards the origin of the good.[14]

Cohen rejects the idea that the individual's grade of happiness may ever turn into a criterion for measuring the universal Good. To measure the universal Good by the greatest amount of individual happiness—as utilitarian ethics, in fact, suggests—is to agree with al-Razi's pessimistic dictum that "there is [always] more evil than good in what exists."[15]

> The reason for this whole mistake [of al-Razi's pessimism] lies in the fact that this ignoramus . . . considers only that which exists with reference to a human individual. Every ignoramus imagines that all that exists exists with a view to his individual sake.[16]

Maimonides takes issue here with Saadya's anthropocentric teleology, which proclaims that humankind represents the "crown" or "end" of creation: "It is not [true] that man is an end," says a Maimonides scholar of Platonic bent, "but that man is given an end."[17] Subsequently, Maimonides defends a cosmocentric teleology in which it is the particular task of human beings to actualize the ultimate Good:

> the true way of considering this is that all the existent individuals . . . are . . . of no value at all in comparison with the whole that exists and endures. . . . Man is merely the most noble among the things that are subject to generation.[18]

In other words, "The Lord hath made everything *le-ma'anehu*"—both "for *His* own sake" and "for *its* own sake."[19] God's goodness signifies the creation of goodness in the world.

Maimonides' anti-utilitarian teleology provides an answer to the question of theodicy. The concept of messianism demands an active opposition to human suffering. Suffering commands goodness. The only significance that suffering can have is that it ought to be abolished. Thus, Cohen writes, "The very concept of the God who demands the Good beyond Being contains in itself the answer to theodicy."[20] The task of opposing human suffering, according to Cohen, is the foremost task in human existence; al-Razi's pessimism betrays the prophetic commitment to "only do justice and love goodness." As such, Cohen claims, pessimism indicates a betrayal of the other.[21] But lovingkindness, according to Cohen's reading of Maimonides, captures a messianic gesture. "And God will wipe away the tears from every single face" (Isaiah 25:8). It is precisely when this gesture becomes human that we speak of the anticipation of the Kingdom. Levinas underscores this point: "God is perhaps none other but this permanent oppositzion to a history which would come to terms with our private tears."[22]

The World Will Follow Its Normal Course: Messianism as the Fulfillment of Prophecy

172. In his evaluation of these intellectual virtues (αρεται διανοητικαι), Maimonides admittedly has reference to Aristotle; [*RoR* 403; *RdV* 467] this is no accidental reference, but rather derives from historical context. The sovereignty of reason, a Hellenistic principle, expresses itself in the dianoetic virtues, with all the ambiguities of intellectualism inherent in them. Maimonides, however, absolves himself of these ambiguities; indeed, he remains independent even in this point. Thinking for him is not leisurely contemplation, and hence it is not the philosophical engagement of the elect few in their typical social milieu. Maimonides' proclamation "The world will follow its normal course" (עולם כמנהגו נוהג) is not intended to assert any reac-

(*See 172.*) *The world will follow its usual course.* Maimonides rejects the traditional materialist, eschatological images pervading medieval thinking on messianic days and the world-to-come. Maimonides adopts the phrase *"olam ke-minhago noheg"* [this world will follow its normal course] from the talmudic Sages who use it in order to designate the strict adherence of "this world" to the laws of nature.[23] He trusts that the supreme validity of natural laws and their normative function within the cosmos is unbreakable, even when facing the question of miracles. Miracles, according to Maimonides, are the fulfillment of a prophesied event. Miracles thus were inscribed into the order of creation, and as such, they do not signify any disruption or suspension of the natural order.[24]

tionary complacency in the face of the desirable progress of political development, but is meant rather to oppose any expectation of miraculous transformation. Maimonides does not grant legitimacy to the preservation of any routine, not even to a routine concerning the logical questions of natural science (Maimonides 1856–1861, 1:403; S. Munk 1988, 321, 378.) [*Guide* 1:73, 206–9. Cohen reads this proposition as a critique of the assumption that habit plays a significant role in the phenomena of nature.]

By anchoring the concept of miracle in the very concept of creation, Maimonides opposes the theories of the Islamic *Mutakallimun* who claim an instantaneous creation of the world at every moment.[25] According to both Cohen and Rosenzweig, such a concept of creation, presupposing a capricious God, makes knowledge of God, or, in fact, any act of faith, entirely impossible.[26] Inasmuch as the concept of messianism is meant to guarantee the knowledge of God, Maimonides safeguards the concept of messianic times from the capriciousness of the Kalam's atomistic theories of creation: "The idea of God demands that nature's laws be consistently valid—in order that we can be assured of the eternal validity of ethics."[27]

None Is Exempt from the Messianic Task: On the Strict Measure of Judgment

173. Maimonides argues against the *Mutakallimun,* whose orthodox theology defends the skeptical principle that natural phenomena are only perceived as proceeding in an orderly fashion on account of our habituated impressions; they defend this skeptical principle against the energetic principle of causality. Within ethics, however, even Maimonides does not recognize any so-called natural law, which would hamper the ideal of continuous human progress. ["The philosophical bias, allegedly metaphysical, that we should conceive of the foundation of ethics as a law of nature—as 'bred in our bones'—

(*See 173.*) *The educational task of guiding the masses.* It is commonly understood that Maimonides uses the expression *hamon* (the multitude) in a derogatory way, opposing them to the intellectual elite initiated into the secrets of the divine science.[28] The multitude, according to Maimonides or, as he also says, the "vulgar among the people," live in ignorance and darkness, and "the truth is entirely hidden from them."[29] As such, Maimonides explicitly bars common people from studying metaphysics, following the opinion of the talmudic Sages.[30]

implies the danger of scientific dogmatism." *ErW* 98–99. In other words, the pursuit of justice cannot be generated by any empirical, natural, even habituated, process, but rather depends upon the transcendence of the ethical ideal in proclaimed opposition to both natural and historical forces—which are both to be considered as reactionary when proclaimed as philosophical principle.] All people are called upon to attain knowledge of God; this knowledge, however, is predicated upon cognition as such. Hence all people without exception must gain unhampered access to cognitive advancement. This constitutes the compelling vigor of the messianic idea: no optimal social conditions without the universalism of cognition. Truly, the messianic idea implies the universal cognition of God. [Maimonides 1984–1996, Hilkhoth Melakhim 12:5; Maimonides 1992a, 138–39; and *RoR* 242–43; *RdV* 283–85.] There ought to be no worship of God without he endeavor to know God. This endeavor of Knowing God, however, implies the difficult educational task for every person, even the masses (המון) to gain insights into what is implied within the idea of God—that God is incorporeal and that there is nothing physical about Him; and that His knowable attributes are but those that relate to ethical action. [*Guide* 2:54, 124.] Would this not suggest to those capable of appreciating it that the popular understanding of God (that of the

Cognition of God, however, to Maimonides, is a universal prerequisite for human perfection. Such cognition, however, cannot be compromised because the multitude may be physically or mentally unsuited for abstract speculation, or because the average mind easily falls back upon configurations of anthropomorphic images. Due to its imperative nature, the highest wisdom imposes itself as a task upon humankind, notwithstanding the insufficiencies of human nature and its difficulties in adequately grasping the divine science. Due to this imperative nature, true knowledge of God is demanded of all, even of the multitude, whose imaginations about a god of flesh and blood, according to Maimonides, halakhically speaking, never constitutes anything but a form of idolatry. In other words, the multitude is held accountable for its opinions in matters of divine science in just the same way as the intellectual elite:

> If, however, it should occur to you that one who believes in the corporeality of God should be excused because of his having been brought up in this doctrine or because of his ignorance and the shortcomings of his apprehension . . . [you should know that] there is no excuse for one who does not accept the authority of the people who inquire into the truth and are engaged in spec-

ulation if he himself is incapable of engaging in such speculation.[31]

entire people and of all of humankind) ought solely to be based upon ethics? This alone elevates the philosophy of knowledge to a general requirement for humanistic education. This kind of intellectualism is not Aristotelian, but is genuinely, truly, and perennially Platonic. [It should be noted that Cohen revised his socialist reading of Plato in a critical turn in favor of the prophets in his later writings (see *JS* 1:317–22; and Wiedebach 2002, 314–23).] Averroës translated Plato's *Republic.* (See Munk 1988, 314.) Did Maimonides read it? We might at least assume that their concord is based on their congeniality regarding the messianic idea. Hence, Maimonides arrives at his conclusion, supported by the Sifra: "You shall sanctify yourself, and you will become holy" (Leviticus 11:44), which by no means applies to external sanctification at all (אינם ענין טומאה וטהרה כלל). In the same vein, Maimonides recognizes only the one "who pursues truth for it own sake" (המאמין באמת לעצם האמת) as the one who "serves God out of love." ([Perek] Chelek f. 127b) [Maimonides 1992a, 131.]

Sanctify Yourself: The Friendliness of the Face

Sanctify yourself and become holy. Maimonides maintains that

> "Sanctify yourselves therefore, and be ye holy, for I am holy" . . . does not apply at all to uncleanness and cleanness. [The] *Siphra* states literally: This concerns sanctification by the commandments; they [the Sages] also say of His dictum Ye shall be holy that this concerns sanctification by the commandments.[32]

Maimonides' exclusive association of holiness with the "sanctification by the commandments" toys with the literal affinity of the two biblical passages, "Ye shall be holy, for I am holy" and "Sanctify yourselves therefore, and be ye holy, for I am holy."[33]

Cohen's point, of course, is that the concept of "holiness" *(kedusha)* is the very opposite of the concept of the sacred,[34] in that holiness is not predicated upon any inherent, mythical quality, as it is the case with any sacred object, or taboo. *Holiness,* to Cohen, is rather a correlative term, associated with a person's self-sanctification in her fulfillment of the command "do the good and the right in the eyes of God" when facing the need of another.[35]

What is then the true expression of a person's self-sanctification and humanity? Cohen says that it is friendliness that radiates toward a person's face *(sever panim yafoth)*:

> Friendliness is not just goodness, since it is free of any hypocrisy. Neither is friendliness the same as love, as it remains free of the ambiguity of love. Friendliness is not even the same as friendship, since friendship is generated by preference and sympathy, even though it is grounded in faithfulness. Friendliness does not know any of those fearful choices between one person and another. Respect and love converge in friendliness. And it is the face of the person [*das Menschenanlitz*] which radiates friendliness. It is the face in which friendliness can be spied even when the face is clouded by an attempt of its denial. And it is the friendliness of human feelings which radiates from the innermost light of a person; the feeling of friendliness can be darkened and scared, but it nonetheless constitutes the original light of a person—a light that only expires with a person's last breath. Friendliness is the light of humanity.[36]

Maimonides claims that among the foremost ways of defiling holiness are the cardinal transgressions of idolatry, adultery, and the shedding of blood.[37] Whereas one who goes beyond the letter of the law (*ve-ya'asseh lifnim mishurath hadin*) and who turns toward others with friendliness (*umekabbelam be'sever panim yafoth*) indeed sanctifies God's name (*harei ze kiddesh et haShem*).[38] Cohen's association of friendliness with the "innermost light of a person" (*dem Urlicht des Menschen*) reverberates with the priestly blessing:

> Bless us, . . . with the light of Thy countenance; for by the light of Thy countenance thou hast granted us the Teaching of life, and lovingkindness and justice, blessing, compassion, life and peace. May it be good in Thy eyes to always bestow blessing upon your people Israel, and to promote peace in the world.[39]

Walking in God's Ways, sanctifying God's name, means to turn to and reflect "the light of Thy countenance." "*Die Freundlichkeit ist die Leuchte der Menschlichkeit*" [Friendliness is the light of all that is humane].[40]

174. Without such knowledge of God we cannot attain true love of God, and hence cannot attain ethical cognition. Ultimate perfection is not founded upon rules of conduct, nor upon conventions and traditions, but rather solely upon one's critical awareness: cognition lays and ensures the grounds for conventions and for moral conduct. Hence, Maimonides carries through his intellectualism in his presentation of messianism. It seems undeniable that ethical volition is maintained within the intellect.

175. Just at that point where Maimonides seems most closely allied terminologically with Aristotle, he actually distances himself farthest from him. According to Aristotle, only the elect may engage in intellectual virtues, since the economic and political system affords leisure only to them. In the world of antiquity, the individual is subject to absorption by the State; for Maimonides, however, the principle of self-perfection is decisive. It expresses itself in autonomous activity of the individual Self devoted to the development of her own ethical Self; at the same time, self-perfection means the aspiration to an ever higher level of Self which is the task and telos of ethical perfection. It is not without a polemic tenor against this ancient and Aristotelian notion that Maimonides cites against the abandonment of the Self: "Do not abandon your own dignity to others," and "it was my own vineyard which I did not guard." [Proverbs 5:9 and Song of Songs 1:6 are both quoted by Maimonides in the context of his definition of the "true, ultimate human perfection." This perfection gives the individual "permanent endurance," and consists in the autonomous acquisition of "rational virtues . . . a perfection belonging to him alone." It is through this perfection that the humanity of a person is established: "through it a human being is a human being." All quotes from *Guide* 3:54, 635.] The messianic ideal can only be the ideal of mankind by virtue of developing and crystallizing the principle of self-perfection. The Self requires humanity, and humanity claims the Self. The ideal of humanity represents the perfected individual; it leads each person toward the telos of self-perfection.

176. The world-to-come of the individual and this world of human civilization are two aspects of the single unfolding principle of self-perfection. Even the doctrine of immortality does not consider the mere external, so-called personal traits of the individual, but rather a person's ethical character. Hence, Maimonides could afford to follow Aristotle with respect to the idea of pure cognition, without risking entanglement in Aristotle's one-sided intellectualism. Maimonides defines the individual (the Self) as human spirit which is not identical with any native faculty of the soul. ["Know that it behooved us to compare the relation obtaining between God . . . and the world to that . . . between the acquired intellect and man; this intellect is not a faculty in the body but is truly separate from the organic body and overflows toward it." *Guide* 1:72, 193. A neo-Platonic reading of Maimonides' theory of Knowing God and of *Imitatio Dei*—triggered by Maimonides' use of the term *overflow*—is suggested by Kreisel 1994 in contradiction to the transcendental ethos of Cohen's reading.] This spirit, however, actualizes itself exclusively upon the exertion of thinking (כל הנקנה).

177. Since such spirit guarantees the unity of knowledge, Maimonides may legitimately infer the impending unification of all thinking individuals. To recognize this inner connection we need not to resort to mysticism, neither in this world nor in the Beyond, but rather need focus upon messianism, which postulates and proclaims the unity of all thinking individuals in the united messianic community. [Maimonides 1984–1996, Hilkhoth Melakhim 12:5. Also Sifre 1993 and Rashi 1982 on Deuteronomy 6:4 and their citation of Zephaniah 3:9, supporting the idea of a messianic community unified through the messianic lucidity of language. Cited in Maimonides 1984–1996, Hilkhoth Melakhim 11:4.] Maimonides raises the ethical vigor, wholesomeness, and sublimity of messianic cognition above any dogmatic or mystical pursuits. Messianic cognition purges and permeates his ethical cognition.

178. In advancing the messianic idea, prophecy reaches its very climax. At the same time, the messianic idea serves as the fulcrum for the idea of God. The messianic idea is the energizing spirit of Judaism and of its historical endurance. It is of profound significance for the integral nature of Maimonides' thinking that he succeeds in integrating all tributaries of Greek and Arabic knowledge and thought into the One life-stream of the Jewish spirit, namely into his messianic ethics; that his prophetic cognition of God, to wit: love of God and love of one's fellow, unifies all multiplicity and diversity of thought; that the prophetic cognition of God signifies love of God—as reflected through the love of one's fellow.

179. It is the ultimate and most articulate meaning of Maimonides' theory of attributes that God is not the God of metaphysics, nor the God of cosmic substance, but the God of ethics, that is the God of humankind. God as the paradigm and ideal for human emulation and for the human Self: solely as this human ethical ideal does God relate to the world and to humanity.

180. Even the doctrine of creation recedes as a metaphysical problem in Maimonides' ethics. It is truly amazing how he violates the dogmatic medieval agenda on this issue, with which agenda he is generally in agreement. This boldness, however, is only the result of the ethical principle guiding his theology.

Maimonides' ethics signifies messianic cognition of God, repelling all one-dimensional intellectualism by dint of universal love of humanity, integrating cognition and volition, ethicizing knowledge of God as loving God, reinforcing the ethical character of human love by loving God, and establishing the oneness of humanity through the love of the ideal messianic Self.

Abbreviations

ArG	*Ästhetik des reinen Gefühls* by Hermann Cohen
BdR	*Der Begriff der Religion im System der Philosophie* by Hermann Cohen
CEM	"Charakteristik der Ethik Maimunis," in *Moses ben Maimon,* by Hermann Cohen
ErW	*Ethik des reinen Willens* by Hermann Cohen
Guide	*The Guide of the Perplexed* by Moses Maimonides
JS	*Hermann Cohens Jüdische Schriften* by Hermann Cohen
LrE	*Logik der reinen Erkenntnis* by Hermann Cohen
MGWJ	*Monatsschrift für die Geschichte und Wissenschaft des Judentums*
NE	*Nicomachean Ethics* by Aristotle
RdV	*Religion der Vernunft aus den Quellen des Judentums* by Hermann Cohen
RoR	*Religion of Reason: Out of the Sources of Judaism* by Hermann Cohen
SPhZ	*Hermann Cohens Schriften zur Philosophie und Zeitgeschichte* by Hermann Cohen
TB	Talmud Bavli
TY	Talmud Yerushalmi

Notes

Preface

1. Cohen 1977, *"Ofiah shel torath-hamiddoth leha-rambam,"* 17–59. The Hebrew translation of the "Charakteristik" due to the difficulty of the text and the lack of commentary left little impact upon contemporary debate. See, however, Navon 1991, 29–43; and Steinberg 1985, 148–201.

Introduction

1. For a comprehensive introduction to Cohen's intellectual biography in English, see Zank 2000.
2. Cohen [1908] 1971, 63–134, reprinted in Cohen 1924, 3:221–89 (hereafter cited as *JS*). Maimonides 1971, 63–134.
3. See Holzhey 1986.
4. Even in contemporary literature, Cohen's *Jewish Writings* are sometimes referred to as "edited by Franz Rosenzweig," an imprecision that is symptomatic not only of the impact of Rosenzweig's introduction, but also of the extent to which Cohen's Jewish writings and Rosenzweig's own thought appear to be interwoven into one dynamic strand of tradition, especially for Jewish scholars of the European philosophical tradition. See Schweid 1999, 21n. 2.
5. Bruno Strauss, on the other hand, tells of the late Cohen's wish to "collect his small, Jewish writings"; Strauss 1924, v.
6. Albert Görland and Ernst Cassirer were students of Cohen at Marburg, and were among the most prominent representatives of the Marburg school after Cohen died.
7. See Cohen 1928 (hereafter cited as *SPhZ*). This collection was edited by Cohen's students and colleagues Albert Görland and Ernst Cassirer.
8. Cf. Niewöhner 1991.
9. JS 3:290–372.

10. Maimonides 1963, 3:54, 636–38 (hereafter cited as *Guide*). Maimonides 1975, Hilkhoth Melakhim 12:5.
11. See also Schweid 1991, 51–52.
12. In Jerusalem, shortly before his death, I asked the Jewish philosopher Eliezer Berkovitz, himself an observant Jew, about his own experiences as a visiting student at the Hochschule für die Wissenschaft des Judentums in Berlin, about the students' relationship to Hermann Cohen as a teacher, and whether they were ever critical of him. Berkovitz's response was emphatic: "God forbid, we would not question his authority. Hermann Cohen's word was to us like the word of God!"
13. According to Brenner 1996, 5 (emphasis added): German Jewry "was characterized neither by a radical break with the past nor by a return to it. Indeed, it used distinct forms of Jewish traditions, marking them as *authentic,* and presented them according to the demands of contemporary taste and modern cultural forms of expression."
14. See Adelmann 2000, 29–31.
15. Society for the Advancement of Jewish Studies, *MGWJ* 48(1904), 52–64.
16. Society for the Advancement of Jewish Studies, *MGWJ* 48(1904), 60–63.
17. Philippson and Lucas 1904, 752.
18. Bacher et al. 1908–1914, viii.
19. Philippson and Lucas 1904, 752–54.
20. The protocol mentions Israel Abrahams (Cambridge), Wilhelm Bacher (Budapest), Eduard Baneth (Berlin), Chaim Brody (Nachod), Ismar Elbogen (Berlin), Simon Eppenstein (Briesen), Jakob Guttmann (Breslau), Saul Horovitz (Breslau), Israel Levy (Paris), Adolf Posnansky (Warsaw), Arthur Zacharias Schwarz (Vienna), and David Simonsen (Copenhagen). Philippson and Lucas 1904, 754.
21. Philippson and Lucas 1904, 754.
22. Bruckstein 1997c, 1998.
23. Cohen 1972, 24 (hereafter cited as *RoR*); Cohen 1995, 28 (hereafter cited as *RdV*).
24. Levinas 1987.
25. See Cohen 1997, 1981, 1982, 1996 and *RoR*/*RdV*. Holzhey 1988, 202, speaks of Cohen's "narrating philosophy of origin."
26. Cohen in a December 1904 letter to the *Frankfurtloge,* as cited in Rosenzweig 1924, *JS* 1:323, my translation.
27. Adelmann 2000.
28. *Wissenschaft* itself, according to Cohen, means nothing else but to "render an account."
29. Based on Cohen. 1997, 84 (hereafter cited as *LrE*)
30. *RoR* 24–34; *RdV* 27–40.
31. *LrE* 36.
32. Parchon 1844, Chelek ha-Diqduq 11b. I quote the uncensored version, based upon an early manuscript at the Hebrew University, Jerusalem, the text of which I saw in the annotated copy of *Machberet ha'Arukh* belonging to my teacher, Z. Gotthold.

33. The term *Sprachdenken* was coined by Rosenzweig 1937, 387; see also Glatzer 1972, 199–200; *RoR* 28; *RdV* 32–33.
34. Talmud Yerushalmi (hereafter cited as TY) Peah 2:6.
35. Deuteronomy 5:18 with Targum Onkelos. For English Bible citations I am using the translation of the Jewish Publication Society 1985 throughout.
36. *RoR* 34 (paraphrase); *RdV* 39–40 (paraphrase).
37. Exodus 34:27.
38. Boyarin 1994b; 2 Corinthians 3:5; 5:12.
39. Bacher 1881, 173–75; Ibn Ezra 1985, 316, 319.
40. Ha-Levi 1964, 202. This point is made even clearer in the translation of this work by Kafih; see Ha-Levi 1997, 150.
41. *RoR* 28; *RdV* 33.
42. Deuteronomy 31:12–14.
43. *RoR* 28; *RdV* 33.
44. Talmud Bavli (hereafter cited as TB) Nedarim 38a.
45. TB Gittin 60b; also *Guide* 175–76.
46. Mishna Eduyot 1:5.
47. Culbertson 1995, 50–51, n. 55.
48. *JS* 3:245–56.
49. *JS* 3:226, 229.
50. *JS* 1:246. Citation refers to Exodus 34:6–7.
51. Cohen 1981, 54, 333–38 (hereafter cited as *ErW*).
52. Micah 6:8; *ErW* 54.
53. Bruckstein 1997b, 271–72.
54. *ErW* 54.
55. *RoR* 258; *RdV* 301.
56. Levinas 1997, 67.
57. *LrE* 154.
58. Wiedebach 1998.
59. Genesis 18:19; *RoR* 316–18; *RdV* 368–69.
60. Maimonides Hilkhoth Teshuvah 1984–1996, 8:8.
61. Levinas 1997, 68–69.
62. Culbertson 1995, 189, slightly modified.
63. Ricoeur 1998, 332.
64. See also Kepnes 1996, 2–4.
65. In oral communication with Professor Moshe Idel, Hebrew University. For a critical discussion of whether these two principles of translation, first suggested by Schleiermacher, can be kept distinct in Rosenzweig's theory of translation, see Askani 1997, 117–24.
66. Rosenzweig 1994, 40.
67. See Rosenzweig's epilogue to his translation of Judah ha-Levi's poems in Rosenzweig 1926, 154. See also Askani 1997, 121 on this. Author's translation.
68. Felstiner 1995, xvi.
69. Rosenzweig 1937, 202; cf. Askani 1997, 123.
70. Rosenzweig 1937, 134.

71. Here I borrow Robert Gibbs's term coined in his talk on Hermann Cohen's concept of messianism at the International Conference on Hermann Cohen's Religion of Reason in Zurich, September 1998. The main contribution to an understanding of Cohen's messianic epistemology in the German language was made by Fiorato 1993; 1994, 366–78.

1. Socrates and Plato

1. Diogenes Laertes 1942, 1:15, 19.
2. *ErW* 1.
3. Charron 1986.
4. Pope 1950.
5. *ErW* 530.
6. Plato 1982, 81–89; Stone 1988, 81–83, 253n. 14.
7. *LrE* 84; Fiorato 1993, 10–11; Wiedebach 1997a, 68–77.
8. *LrE* 84.
9. *ErW* 338–40, 350.
10. Lingis 1998, xxxvii. See also Schmid 1995, 261–63.
11. See *SPhZ*. See also Gibbs 1992, 17–23; and Lembeck 1994.
12. Holzhey 1997, 226–41; Poma 1997, 21–36, 177–84.
13. Gibbs 1992; R. Cohen 1994; Bruckstein 1997a, 16–21.
14. Lewis and Short 1980.
15. *SPhZ* 54–55.
16. *Guide* 7.
17. Jeremiah 1:11–12; Abravanel 1956, 306; *Guide*: 43, 392; Maimonides 1984–1996, Hilkhoth Yesodei haTorah 7:2–4; Carlebach 1982.
18. Deuteronomy 34 with commentaries; *SPhZ* 54; see also Adelmann 1997, 2.
19. Exodus 24:7.
20. *ErW* 190–94; Cohen 1982, 359–63 (paraphrase; hereafter cited as *ArG*).
21. *LrE* 257.
22. *LrE* 87–88.
23. Plato 1980, 6:110; see also Shorey 1980, xxxiii–xxxvi.
24. *LrE* 86–89.
25. Aristotle 1983, *On Interpretation* 19b, 141; *Categories* 12a–b, 85.
26. For a differentiation within Aristotle's privative judgments, see Wolfson 1973–1977, 2:544.
27. Cohen's combined reading of Aristotle's categories finds precedent in the commentary by Averroës on Aristotle's *On Interpretation* claiming that the infinite judgment, "A is not-seeing," and the privative judgment, "A is blind," are propositions which make sense only if the property denied by the predicate is expected to be by its nature present in the subject. Averroës, as quoted in Wolfson 1977 2:548n. 32; also Maimonides 1987a, 56.
28. *LrE* 85.
29. *LrE* 154; *RoR* 290–91; *RdV* 338–39.
30. Kant 1950, 113.
31. Bergman 1967, 124–27, 267–69; Bruckstein 1992, 36–37.

32. Rawls 1972 also exhibits a Platonic bent in that justice assumes the status of a foundational Good.
33. Aristotle 1945, *NE* 1177a–79b, 613–29.
34. Aristotle 1947, *Metaphysics* 993b, 87.
35. *ErW* 89; Wiedebach 1997a, 106–13.
36. See Blumenberg 1985, 49.
37. See Blumenberg 1985, 28–29.
38. Diogenes Laertius 1942, 1:27; *SPhZ* 1:7; *RoR* 40; *RdV* 47.
39. See paragraph number 66 in chapter 3 of this book.
40. *RoR* 72; *RdV* 84.
41. *ErW* 54.
42. *ErW* 190–94; *ArG* 359–64.
43. Hegel 1977, 84–88; Priest 1987, 2–17.
44. Wolfson 1947, 1:327–32.
45. Wolfson 1947, 2:94–138.
46. *RoR* 107; *RdV* 124.
47. References to Philo play no major role in a book like Lasker 1977.
48. Ibn Gabirol 1959, 257–85.
49. "Gabirol's *Fountain of Life* suffered a rather curious fate. Written in Arabic, the total work has been preserved only in a Latin translation . . . of the twelfth century. This translation was well known to Christian scholastics who variously called its author Avicebrol, Avicebron, or Avencebrol. Because of the total absence of all biblical and rabbinic quotations from the work, some scholastics considered its author a Muslim, while others . . . considered him a Christian Arab. Not until the middle of the nineteenth century, when Salomon Munk discovered and published a Hebrew florilegium by ShemTob Falakera (1225–1290), was it established that ibn Gabirol and Avicebrol are one and the same author." Hyman and Walsh 1991, 358. See also Guttmann 1973, 101–3; and, differently, Kaufmann 1899, 111.
50. *RoR* 107; *RdV* 124.
51. Bieler 1933, 57–58. Even if ibn Gabirol's doctrine of divine will could be interpreted to constitute the final cause of creation (Bieler 1933, 64–68), the doctrine still implies an ontological relationship between God and world.

2. Maimonides: A Radical Platonist

1. It is precisely this supposed practical Jewish concern with ethics that Cohen (*JS* 3:1–35) refutes in his biting critique of Lazarus.
2. *JS* 1:306–30. In this exploration, Cohen becomes increasingly critical of the Platonic tradition, finding ethics and true socialism later, primarily in the prophets. See "Das Soziale Ideal bei Plato und den Propheten."
3. Strauss 1995; Green 1993, 56, 168n. 3. Green pays little attention to the vital contribution of Cohen's essay "Charakteristik der Ethik Maimunis" on Strauss 1995, 151n. 11; but cf. also Green 1997, 72.
4. Berman 1961, 53–61; Kellner 1990; Twersky 1980b; Hartman 1976; Harvey 1990, 11–12.

5. TB Berakhoth 12a; also TY Berakhoth 1:4.
6. Saba 1879, 16b, on Exodus 11:9–10, reminiscent of Shelomoh al-Kabez's famous formulation in the hymn "Lekha Dodi."
7. *ErW* 99.
8. *RdV* 96–97; *RoR* 82–84; *ErW* 99.
9. Schwarzschild 1990, 29–59; see also Niewöhner 1988, 84–87.
10. Maimonides 1984–1996, Hilkhoth Melakhim 8:11; *ErW* 70, 599–600, 618–20.
11. N. Cohen 1995, 281–84; Urbach 1987, 290–92.
12. Romans 6; Galatians 3. Paul uses the term "yoke of the Law" (ζυγον) in Acts 15:10 and Galatians 5:1.
13. On "pharisaic self-justification versus divine grace," see Luther 1932, 6:447–62. For Lutheran commentaries, see Burton 1988, 142–77; Longenecker 1990, 110–25; and more radically, Martyn 1998, 324–28. On the other hand, see the critical discussion of Sanders 1991, esp. 1–12, against nineteenth-century German Lutheran, but also English Anglican scholarship, as being anti-Semitic. See also Betz 1979; Dunn 1988, lxiii–lxxii. I am grateful to John Reumann for his helpful suggestions in finding my way through the literature on the subject.
14. Boyarin 1994b, 2–12.
15. *RoR* 343–44; *RdV* 399–400.
16. *RoR* 343–44; *RdV* 399–400.
17. *RoR* 213; *RdV* 249.
18. Mishna Avoth 1:3; *Guide* 3:53, 631.
19. *RoR* 213; *RdV* 249.
20. *RoR* 345; *RdV* 401; also *JS* 1:284–305.
21. According to Rosenzweig 1924, 1:334.
22. Hegel 1977.
23. Jonas 1972, 141–43.
24. Schwarzschild 1990, 63.
25. *RoR* 33, 40–41; *RdV* 38, 47–48.
26. *BdR* 27, 32–84, esp. 45; *RoR* 11–23; *RdV* 12–27; *JS* 3:290–372; and L. Strauss 1924, 5–314.
27. Sifre 1993, 114.
28. *Guide* 3:54, 630–38.
29. TB Berakhoth 25b; TB Yoma 30a; TB Kiddushin 54a.
30. *RoR* 408; *RdV* 473–74.
31. Maimonides 1984–1996, Hilkhoth Teshuvah 5:4, my translation.
32. *JS* 3:40. On Job, see *RoR* 87, *RdV* 101.
33. See also on "correlation," Adelmann 1968, 209; *RoR* 86; *RdV* 100–101.
34. Cohen develops his concept of the "correlation between God and man in ethical reasoning" in *RoR* precisely in the same context as in this essay, namely in relationship to Job 32:8; *RoR* 87; *RdV* 101.
35. The phrase "Korrelation zwischen Gott und Mensch" was formally introduced by Cohen in *BdR* 45.
36. *RoR* 82–83; *RdV* 96.
37. *RoR* 86; *RdV* 100–101.

38. *RoR* 86; *RdV* 100–101; *ErW* 462–65.
39. *RoR* 98, 103–6; *RdV* 114, 119–20; Altmann 1987, 301–17.
40. *Guide* 2:45, 576; and Maimonides 1984–1996, Hilkhoth Yesodei haTorah, chaps. 7 and 8. Maimonides intended to write a separate essay on prophecy; see *Guide* 9.
41. Maimonides 1984–1996, Hilkhoth Melakhim 8:11; and Schwarzschild 1990, 29–59.
42. Maimonides 1987a, 46; and *Guide* 2:33, 364; where Maimonides refers to the third to tenth commandments as *mekkubaloth;* that is, as heteronomous acceptance of tradition.
43. Cohen terms the task of ethical self-awareness autonomous: a thinking that is not driven by, or simply the result of, external stimuli of natural necessities. *ErW* 324–26.
44. Maimonides seems to endorse this view in *Guide* 1:34, 72–79; and also Maimonides 1984–1996, Hilkhoth Yesodei haTorah 4:11.
45. *RoR* 109–12; *RdV* 127–30.
46. Klatzkin 1968, 106–8, 133–34; Ben Yehuda 1980, 7275b–76a, 7569a–71a.
47. Abraham bar Chiyya 1971, 146.
48. Rosenblatt (in Saadya 1976, 145) translates *shim'ioth* (Arabic **sm'y*) as "revealed precepts." Altmann (in Saadya 1965, 102) renders the term "revelational laws." Samuelson, too (in ibn Daud 1986, 214a, 263), translates the term as "revealed commandments." Husik (1966, 39) avoids the dichotomy between revelation and reason and felicitously speaks of traditional laws. Guttmann (1973, 79) uses "commandments of obedience." Similarly *Kafih* (in Saadya 1970, 122, and in Maimonides 1972, 553); Jakob Guttmann (1882, 135n. 2) refers to Saadya's commentary to Sefer Yetzirah 1:1 and Saadya's usage of *sikhlioth* and *shim'ioth* there—though the authorship of Saadya for this commentary is only attributed. Cohen himself, like Guttmann, stresses the character of obedience to tradition when discussing the term *shim'ioth,* applying the term "revelational" for the revelational character of human reasoning itself. *RoR* 351; *RdV* 409.
49. *Guide* 3:26, 507.
50. *Guide* 3:56, 507; also see Kafih in Maimonides 1972, 3:26, 552; I follow Kafih in rendering the Arabic (גאיה) as rationale, or purpose; also *Guide* 3:33.
51. Maimonides 1912, 77, also notes on 41–42; see also Maimonides 1992a, 302n. 5 and the additional note in the appendix.
52. *RoR* 25; *RdV* 29; *Guide* 3:26, 507, modified translation; see also Maimonides 1912, 77–78n. 3, in which Gorfinkle explicitly refers to Cohen's "Charakteristik der Ethik Maimunis."
53. Maimonides 1987a, chap. 8; *Guide* 1:2, 25; 2:33, 364.
54. Cf. the controversy between Maimonides and Nachmanides about the issue of whether or not Knowing God is to be considered part of Positive Law or whether it rather constitutes the very grounds for the law, as Nachmanides maintains; Nachmanides 1981, 141–42.
55. Introduction to *RoR*. Here Cohen seems to prefigure a thesis currently developed by Daniel Boyarin (2002) concerning the interdependence of canon-

ical homonoia in Christian tradition and increasing polysemic polynoia among the rabbinic authorities.

56. TB Eruvin 13b; *RoR* 28; *RdV* 32–33; also *ErW* 33–34.
57. Deuteronomy 5:19; TB Sanhedrin 17a; *Guide* 2:33.
58. Maimonides on Mishna Peah 1:1 in Maimondes 1992b, 1:54–55.
59. Maimonides 1992a, 144; also Maimonides 1984–1996, Hilkhoth Teshuvah 9:1.
60. Maimonides 1957–1961, 2:495–98; Maimonides 1997–1998, 2:610–11; Maimonides 1995a, 22n d; and Philo 1937, 1–95. Saadya, too, develops his traditional list of commandments on the basis of the Decalogue: Saadya 1941, 185–216; Nachmanides 1963–1964, 2:521; see note by Chavel there.
61. TY Berakhoth 1:5; Ginzberg 1971, 1:166.
62. *RoR* 359; *RdV* 418.
63. Jeremiah 31:30–33; *RoR* 81–82; *RdV* 94–95.
64. Liddell and Scott 1968, 394b; Sperber 1984, 84–86.
65. Bammel 1960, 313–19; also Roetzel 1970, 377–90; and Behm 1964, 133–34: "The task of Jesus . . . is to execute the new decree which God has published to settle the relation between Himself and man. . . . His bloody death, represented by the eucharistic cup, gives life to the new divine order." For a typical Jewish and Muslim medieval critique of the Christian abrogation of the Law, see ibn Daud 1986, 201–4.
66. *RoR* 342–44; *RdV* 399–400.
67. *RoR* 342; *RdV* 398; cf. Mishna Rosh haShana 3:4–5; also Charles 1964, 561; Maimonides 1984–1996, Hilkhoth Teshuvah 3:4; also Maimonides 1971, 128, directive 137, where Maimonides distinguishes between the concepts *signal* and *symbol.*
68. Heschel 1954, 122; also Kochan 1997, 53–75.
69. Mishna Pessachim 10.
70. Gerrish 1996.
71. Guttmann 1973, 165–66; ibn Daud 1919, 67; Saadya 1976, 55–56; also Sefer Yetzirah 1972, 105; and Saadya 1984, 219.
72. Midrash Tehillim 1947, 22; and Lieberman 1974, 223.
73. *Guide* 1:75, 223–24.
74. *Guide* 2:36, 369.
75. Ibn Daud 1986, 263.
76. Ibn Daud 1986, 257.
77. Aristotle 1945, *NE* 1179b–1181b, 629–43; ibn Daud 1986, 256–57.
78. Ibn Daud 1919, 131.
79. Ibn Daud 1986, 263–64.
80. Maimonides 1987a, chap. 8; and Samuelson in ibn Daud 1986, 212n. 2.
81. Ibn Daud 1986, 263.
82. Cohen reads ibn Daud 1986, 263 (section 214) in light of 204 (section 172a).
83. Ibn Daud 1986, 204; Maimonides 1987a, chap. 8, cites partly the same examples in his definition of *mefursamoth.*
84. Ibn Daud 1986, 204; Maimonides 1987a, chap. 8.
85. Ibn Daud 1986, 264.

86. Maimonides 1987a, chap. 8.
87. Aristotle 1945, *NE* 1145b, 377.
88. Aristotle 1945, *NE* 1139b, 333.
89. *ErW* 99.
90. Efros 1924, 77; *Guide* 1:2; 2:33, 364; and Kasher 1985.

3. The Good beyond Being

1. Maimonides 1912, 35–36; Maimonides 1997–1998, 2:553.
2. Sirat 1985, 4.
3. Aristotle 1945, *NE* 1140a–b, 337, 1179b, 629–43; Aristotle 1947, *Metaphysics* 983a, 15.
4. Levinas 1992, 23.
5. Plato 1980, *Republic* 508–9c, 6:100–107.
6. Aristotle 1945, *NE* 1096b, 23–24.
7. Aristotle 1945, *NE* 1097a, 25–26.
8. Aristotle 1945, *NE* 1040a, 337.
9. Aristotle 1945, *NE* 1103b, 75.
10. Aristotle 1945, *NE* 1098b–99a, 39.
11. Wolfson 1947, 1:202. For an example of the neo-Platonist viewpoint, see Luzzatto 1987, 22–26. In Patristic (Augustine, Dionysus Areopagita) and also in Scholastic literature (Thomas Aquinas), this principle—that the concept of the good implies actualization—is rendered as *bonum est diffusivium sui.* Thomas Aquinas 1952, 25–26.
12. Sefer ha-Chinukh 1977, 545; Nachmanides 1989, 125–26; Sforno 1980; see also Nachmanides and Sforno on Gen. 22:1.
13. Kant 1997, 50; and Cohen 1910, 216; *ErW* 182–89.
14. *ErW* 169.
15. Plato 1952b, *Theaetetus* 176b, 129.
16. *Guide* 2:22, 319–20.
17. Even Shmuel associates Maimonides' critique of Aristotle's cosmogony and metaphysics with Maimonides' rejection of mythology; see in Maimonides 1935–1960, 3:109–13.
18. *Guide* 3:29, 518, 521; also Twersky 1980b, 391.
19. Maimonides' epistle on astrology, Maimonides 1997–1998, 2:481; also Gotthold 1972, 75–85. Cohen's source on the Sabians was most likely Chwolson 1856, 1:689–97.
20. Twersky 1980b, 389–91; also Funkenstein 1970.
21. *RoR* 52; *RdV* 60.
22. Aristotle 1977, *Metaphysics* 1072b, 149.
23. *Guide* 3:54, 638.
24. Aristotle 1977, 87–89; *Metaphysics* 1064b; and 1947, 1026a, 297.
25. Maimonides 1987a, 107–8; Efros 1924, 49–50; also Wolfson 1973–1977, 1:493–545.
26. *Guide* Introduction, 6; 1:33, 72.
27. Such as Maimonides 1984–1996, Hilkhoth Yesodei haTorah 4:10–11, and his commentary on Mishna Chagigah 2:1 in Maimonides 1992b, 2:250.

28. Mishna Chagigah 2:1.
29. Maimonides 1984–1996, Hilkhoth Yesodei haTorah 4:10–11.
30. *Guide* 3:54, 635.
31. Maimonides 1992b; "completions and corrections" refers to p. 302n. 5. Situating this Maimonidean critique of Saadya's distinction between "reason" and "tradition" within the work of the contemporary philosopher Gadamer and his critique of a reason that imagines itself to be without the prejudice of tradition, will make a most interesting reading. See Gadamer 1975, 281–90.
32. Maimonides 1912, 77; *Guide* 3:33, 532–34.
33. *LrE* 43; also *ErW* 320–22.
34. Hegel 1996, 20.
35. Schwarzschild 1990, 61–81, esp. 65–67.
36. Schwarzschild n.d.
37. *LrE* 180.
38. Schwarzschild 1987.
39. Rashi 1982 on Genesis 1:1.
40. Kellner 1986, 53, see also 174n. 348; also Abravanel 1982, 70, 76.
41. Maimonides 1984–1996, Hilkhoth Yesodei haTorah 1:1–3. See Cohen's discussion of Being and Becoming in the context of Creation. *RoR* 59–70; *RdV* 68–81.
42. Maimonides 1987b, chap. 8.
43. *Guide* 1:2, 25.
44. Maimonides 1987a, 45; Saadya 1970, 119, 121–22; 1976, 141, 144; also Sefer ha-Chinukh 1977, 92.
45. Sifra on Leviticus 18:4 (1959, 850); Rashi 1982 on TB Yoma 67b; Guttmann 1882, 136, 139; Maimonides 1912, 77; 1972, 553n. 5. See also marginal note in TB Yoma 67b; for a different solution to the problem of Maimonides' deviation from the text in Yoma, see Maimonides 1992a, 303.
46. Maimonides 1987a, chap. 8.
47. Maimonides 1992b, 2:258–59; Maimonides 1912, 77; and marginal note in TB Yoma 67b by Pick-Berlin. For a different solution to the problem of Maimonides' deviation from the text in Yoma, see Maimonides 1992a, 303; and Kafih in Maimonides 1972, 553n. 5.
48. *Guide* 3:43, 572; also Maimonides 1984–1996, Hilkhoth Sukkah veLulav 8.
49. Aristotle 1977, *Metaphysics* 1072b, 149–51.
50. Aristotle 1945, *NE* 1177b, 617.
51. Genesis 1:27; 5:1–3.
52. Philo 1929, 3.
53. *Guide* 1:1, 23; also Saadya 1976, 114, on *betselem Elohim.* Emphasis in original.
54. *RoR* 85–93; *RdV* 99–108; Sifra on Leviticus 19:18 (Sifra 1959, 89); TY Nedarim 9:4, 26a; and Midrash Bereshit Rabba 1996, 236–37 and n. 12.
55. *RoR* 119; *RdV* 137–38.
56. Aristotle 1945, *NE* 1177a, 613.
57. Ibid.

58. Aristotle 1945, *NE* 1178a, 619; and Armstrong in Aristotle 1977, 429. On the relation of Aristotle's concept of eudaemonia to ethical virtues, see Wolfson 1947, 175–76.
59. *RoR* 17–19; *RdV* 19–22; Bruckstein 2000, 129–55.
60. *Guide* 3:27, 511; also *Guide* 3:54, 635; and Altmann 1981, 71.
61. *Guide* 1:54, 124.
62. *Guide* 1:69, 170; Rosenzweig (1971, 126–29; 1990, 114–16) emphatically reiterates this point.
63. *Guide* 2:54, 632–36.
64. *Guide* 3:54, 635.
65. *Guide* 3:54, 635.
66. *Guide* 3:51, 619; Kellner 1990, chap. 3.
67. See *JS* 3:1–35, for a critique of Lazarus.
68. *Guide* 1:52, 114–19; and Wolfson 1977, 2:195–230.
69. *LrE* 36–38.
70. *ErW* 628; Cassirer 1974, 277–96.
71. Saadya 1976, 101–2.
72. TB Berakhoth 31b; TB Yebamoth 71a; TB Baba Metsia 31b, 4; also Twersky 1979, 239.
73. Husik 1966, xxiii, xliv.
74. Husik 1966, 34.
75. *Guide* 1:53, 121–22.
76. Exodus 33:19.
77. TB Rosh HaShana 17b.
78. Exodus 34:10 and Rashi 1982 on this; *JS* 3:46–47.
79. Maimonides 1957–1961, 505–9; Maimonides 1997–1998, 2:604–6; Maimonides 1971, commandment 8, 62–63.
80. Hildesheimer 1987, 98–99n. 433.
81. Aristotle 1977, *Metaphysics* 1072a–73a, 149–53.
82. *LrE* 83–85; reiterated by Rosenzweig 1990, 22–26; 1971, 20–24.
83. *Guide* 1:54, 124.
84. *Guide* 1:54, 124.
85. See Maimonides' reference to Avoth 5:13 in *Guide* 1:54, 124.
86. *Guide* 1:54, 124.
87. *JS* 3:176–96; *ErW* 56; *RoR* 160; *RdV* 185–86. On Cohen's translation of Leviticus 19:2, "You shall become holy," see *RoR* 96, 426; *RdV* 111, 494–95.
88. *ErW* 55, 403.
89. *Guide* 1:54, 128.
90. Schechter 1969, 199–218.
91. The imperative "You shall walk in His ways" appears only once in the Pentateuch—in Deuteronomy 28:9. Maimonides, however, explains that the commandment in the infinitive verbal expression (Deuteronomy 8:6, 10:12, 11:22, 19:19, 26:17, 30:16) has the same binding force as the imperative. See Maimonides 1971, directive commandment 8, 62–63.
92. *Guide* 1:54, 128.

93. *JS* 3:183–96; also *RoR* 110–12; *RdV* 127–30.
94. *ErW* 326.
95. Psalms 119:77, 92, 143, 174; cf. also Proverbs 8:30–31 with attending midrashim.
96. Such as Shapiro 1957, 692.
97. Maimonides 1984–1996, Hilkhoth Yesodei haTorah 7:6; *Guide* 2:35, 367–69.
98. Maimonides 1992b, 142–43.
99. *Guide* 2:36, 369–73.
100. I borrow this term from Levinas's talmudic lecture "As Old as the World," 1994b, 70–88.
101. According to R. Yehoshua ben Levi; cf. Mishna Avoth 6:2.
102. *ErW* 391.

4. Religion as Idolatry

1. The classical exposition that served Cohen himself as a source is Kaufmann 1877.
2. Halbertal and Margalit 1992, 9–36.
3. Wolfson 1947, 2:94–101.
4. Wolfson 1947, 2:126–38; Husik 1966, xxii–xxiii.
5. Saadya 1976, 101–2; Josef ibn Tsaddik 1903, 56–59; Judah ha-Levi 1964, 84–85; Bahya 1973, 132–49; Ibn Daud 1986, 147, 153.
6. *Guide* 1:57, 132; Altmann 1988, 148–65, esp. 161–62; and Wolfson 1973–1977, 2:31.
7. *RoR* 161–62; *RdV* 187–88.
8. *BdR* 10, 61–64; *RoR* 15–16, 178–235; *RdV* 18, 208–75.
9. Zank 2000.
10. *BdR* 65.
11. Rosenzweig 1924, xiii–lxiv, esp. xlvii–l.
12. Buber 1988, esp. 52–62; Bergman 1991, 150–55; Fackenheim 1996, 21; more moderately, Mosès 1992, 45–49; Klein 1976, 132–48, esp. 135–43; with the notable exceptions of Guttmann 1973, 415–16; Altmann 1987, 301; and Schwarzschild 1970.
13. Adelmann 1968 stresses the "unity of consciousness" in Cohen's philosophy; Holzhey 1986, 1:67–79, carefully distinguishes the agenda of Cohen's philosophy from that of his colleague Paul Natorp and (1:343) invokes Cohen's statement that "our philosophy of culture is in complete harmony with our [Jewish] religion." We find an explicit critique of Rosenzweig's "late Cohen" in Poma 1997, 157–69.
14. Mishna Avoth 1877, 25.
15. Herford 1974, 21.
16. Twersky 1980b, 139; also Halbertal 1997.
17. *Guide* 3:54, 636–37. "The term wisdom [*chokhmah*] . . . means . . . the apprehension of Him . . . and that similarly all the actions prescribed by the Law . . . [are] not to be compared with this ultimate end and [do] not equal it, being but preparations made for the sake of this end." *Guide* 636. Note

the significant fact that the entire halakhic code, the *Mishneh Torah,* ends with the prophetic vision of Isaiah 11:9 in which the universal knowledge of God is made manifest. Prophecy—the knowledge of God—precedes faith in the Law. *Guide* 576.

18. *Guide* 5–14; Strauss 1988.
19. Maimonides 1992a, 140, 143, 184 (editor's comments); and *Guide* 9.
20. Levinas 1990.
21. Sifre 1993, 114–15.
22. *RoR* 28; *RdV* 32; also Bialik 1944, 9–28.
23. *ErW* 54, 403; *RoR* 33; *RdV* 39; also 2 Samuel 19:7 with Hirsch's commentary on Deuteronomy 26:3, Pentateuch 1989, 5:478.
24. Kimchi 1878, 114b.
25. Abraham ben Moses ben Maimon 1953, 81.
26. Halkin 1979.
27. Maimonides 1984–1996, Hilkhoth Teshuvah 3:6–7; *Guide* 1:36, 82–85.
28. Twersky 1980a, 282. Twersky cites Scholem and other scholars who associate the Rabad's critical attitude toward Maimonides with his kabbalistic, mystical leanings. See Abraham ben David of Posquières 1985, 56–57, on Hilkhoth Teshuvah 3:7. Naor cites the various editorial versions of that gloss, demonstrating the attempt to blunt the biting barb of Rabad's *ad hominem* critique.
29. *Guide* 84–85; also Abraham ben David of Posquières 1964, 127; and Rawidowicz 1969–1971, 1:171–233.
30. TB Chagigah 16b; also TB Berakhoth 59a; TB Kiddushin 40a; and in the uncensored version, ibn Chabib 1961, 3:74.
31. According to Rabinovicz 1976 this critical opinion has been deleted from most editions of *Ein Ya'akov.*
32. Rabinovicz 1976.
33. *LrE* 31–32, 215.
34. Cassirer 1994.
35. *JS* 3:371 (paraphrase).
36. Spinoza 1985, 1–8, 85–86; also Wolfson 1958, 71–78.
37. *RoR* 331; *RdV* 385–86.
38. Spinoza 1951, chap. 15; and Yovel 1989, 3–26.
39. *JS* 3:371; *RoR* 331; *RdV* 385–86; also L. Strauss 1924.
40. *LrE* 85; and *RoR* 62–63; *RdV* 71–72; also Hartmann 1965, 147.
41. *LrE* 85.
42. *LrE* 34; Rosenzweig 1999; Rosenzweig 1990, 26–27; 1971, 20–22; Wiehl 1988. For an entirely different reading, see Samuelson 1988.
43. *LrE* 90.
44. *LrE* 86.
45. Samuelson 1994, 100–101.
46. *Guide* 1:17, 42–43; Efros 1924, 37–38; note that Efros reads Maimonides' theory of privation in a purely Aristotelian, rather than Platonic, context. See also Maimonides 1856–1861, 1:245.
47. See the translation of al-Charizi in Maimonides 1904, 2:18 [*sic*], 164; and Wolfson 1973–1977, 2:195–230.

48. *LrE* 83–84.
49. *LrE* 83–84; Cohen's logic radicalizes the Platonic theory about wonder and astonishment (θαυμαζειν) as origin of all philosophical thinking. Plato 1952, *Theaetetus* 155d, 54–55.
50. Derrida 1995, 80.
51. *Guide* 1:58, 136.
52. Hayduck (ed.) *Alexander in Metaphysica,* according to Wolfson 1973–1977, 2:209.
53. Narboni 1852, 10; and Falaquera 1837, 87a; Wolfson 1973–1977, 2:210.
54. Maimonides 1987b, 78 (paraphrase).
55. *Guide* 1:58, 136–37.
56. Rosenzweig 1990, 53–54; 1971, 58.
57. *ErW* 331; Poma 1997, 78.
58. *Guide* 1:69, 170.
59. Schwarzschild 1956.
60. *RoR* 255; *RdV* 297.
61. Wolfson 1958, 1:406–7.
62. Also *JS* 3:38–42 and throughout *ErW*; also Schwarzschild 1990, 63–64.
63. Rashi 1982 on Genesis 1:1. Rashi takes his point of departure in deliberating upon the meaning of the first letter of the Torah—*bet*—which he reads as an instrumental rather than a temporal proposition. Also Zornberg 1996, 3–4.
64. *Guide* 2:13–24, 39–54.
65. Kellner 1986, 53–61.
66. *RoR* 59–70; *RdV* 68–81.
67. *RoR* 41–46; *RdV* 47–53.
68. *RoR* 110–11; *RdV* 128; also *ErW* 88.
69. Marmorstein 1950.
70. *ErW* 88–89; *RoR* 324; *RdV* 377.
71. *ErW* 212–13.
72. *RoR* 414; *RdV* 480.
73. See Bruckstein 2000, 29–55.
74. Levinas 1994a, 141.
75. *RoR* 28; *RdV* 32–33.
76. *RoR* 8–11; *RdV* 9–12; Boyarin 1994a, esp. 117–29; Halbertal 1997, 45–89.
77. *BdR* 10; *RoR* 15–16; *RdV* 18. See above paragraph number 74 in this chapter.
78. *RoR* 186–87; *RdV* 218–19.

5. The "Unity of the Heart"

1. *RoR* 99–115; *RdV* 85–99.
2. Mishna Berakhoth 2:2.
3. *RoR* 31–33; *RdV* 36–39; and Rosenzweig's comment, 1937, 297; also Rashi's commentary on Deuteronomy 6:4, based upon Sifre 1993, 54.
4. *Guide* 2:12, 279; 3:37, 374–75.
5. *RoR* 50; *RdV* 58.
6. *RoR* 50; *RdV* 58.

7. *RoR* 160–61; *RdV* 185–87; cf. the controversy between Buber and Cohen on this issue, Buber 1988.
8. Buber 1988, 104.
9. Sifre on Deuteronomy 6:6 (Sifre 1993, 59) as interpreted by Rashi (1982, emphasis added); also Mizrachi's supercommentary (1973, 5:9b) on Rashi discussing Deuteronomy 6:6; and Maimonides 1971, 59, directive 3.
10. Cohen cites Stern's edition: אחד מהם ליחד הלב ביחוד הבורא, והשני ליחד המעשה לשמו ולעבדו לכבודו בלבד; cf. also *JS* 3:218.
11. *JS* 3:218, 1:291. The Sifre on Deuteronomy 6:5 defines the division of the heart (*chilluk ha-lev*) as the opposite of *yichud ha-lev,* associating the division of the heart with the disturbing presence of the evil impulse. See Cohen's discussion of this Sifre in *JS* 3:215; and Sifre 1993, 55.
12. Bacher 1910a.
13. *JS* 3:220.
14. Cf. Bacher 1910a and 1910b. Kafih translates *tohar ha-matspun* instead of ibn Tibbon's *yichud ha-lev* (Bahya 1984, 244) just as Bacher translates *Läuterung der Gesinnung, oder des Inneren* instead of Cohen's *Einheit des Herzens.* Bacher 1910a, 349, and 1910b, 733–34.
15. *JS* 3:218–19.
16. Bahya 1984, 244; oral communication by Rav Josef Kafih.
17. Cf. Saadya's translation and commentary (1966, 200) on Tehillim.
18. Cf. *Guide* 1:39; and the commentary attributed to Saadya on Sefer Yetzirah 1:4, Sefer Yetzirah 1972, 65n. 83.
19. *RoR* 15–16; *RdV* 18; *BdR* 55–56.
20. *RoR* 162; *RdV* 190.
21. Sefer ha-Chinukh 1977, 41.
22. *JS* 3:214–17.
23. Judah ha-Levi 1964, 223, is reminiscent of Psalms 34:9.
24. Cf. Wiedebach 1997a, 162–94.
25. *RoR* 18–19; *RdV* 21–22.
26. Bahya 1973, 89, 91.
27. Leviticus 19:18; Bahya 1973, 105.
28. Psalms 42:2–3.
29. Micah 6:8.
30. Bahya 1973, 446.
31. *Guide* 1:54, 124.
32. Exodus 34:6–7.
33. Aristotle 1977, *Metaphysics* 1072b, 147.
34. *Guide* 2:4, 256.
35. *RoR* 120–21; *RdV* 139–40.
36. In his introduction to the *Guide*, when discussing the influences of Aristotle and Plato, Pines himself refers exclusively to questions of cosmogony, theories of creation, and physics. *Guide* lxi–lxiii, lxxv–lxxvi.
37. *Haskel veyadoa oti.* Kafih in his commentary on Sefer haMitsvoth 1:1 (Maimonides 1971) emphasizes the distinction between Knowing God and belief in God, claiming the latter to be a dogmatic and un-Maimonidean ren-

dition of the classical Arabic *sahada.* This same dogmatic reading of the Arabic *sahada* is reflected in the traditional rendition of the Thirteen Principles as *ani ma-amin* (I *believe* in the one God). The Thirteen Principles subsequently have come to assume a catholic function of catechism in Jewish tradition. See also Kellner 1986, 5–6. The prayer that begins, "For I the Lord," can be found in Jeremiah 9:23; *RoR* 256; *RdV* 299; also Mishna Avoth 4:1.

38. Maimonides 1984–1996, Hilkhoth Teshuvah 9:2; Maimonides 1992, 139; and Rawidowicz 1969–1971, 1:333–45; for an abridged English version, 1974, 317–23; see also the discussion of "the thing that survives" in Altmann 1987, 60–129. Altmann's article is a critique of Pines's more agnostic stand on the problem of speculative knowledge in Maimonides; see Pines 1988; also Fox 1990. See also *Guide* 3:54, 635; Altmann 1981, 71–74.
39. Saadya 1965, 157–58; also Maimonides' correspondence with the rabbis of southern France, 1997–1998, 2:478–79.
40. *RoR* 1–34; *RdV* 1–40.
41. Paraphrase from N. Z. Y. Berlin's introduction to his commentary on the Torah (1937, vols. 2 and 3); also Melammed 1975, 1:1–128; and Simon 1988; Fishbane 1986; Boyarin 1994a, 11–9; Handelman 1982, 40.
42. Meiri 1964, 17.
43. Culbertson 1995, 99n. 26 on the etymological root connection between "Torah" and the root **yrh,* "to shoot" or "to inseminate."
44. Cf. Otto 1943, 12–15.
45. Maimonides 1984–1996, Hilkhoth Teshuvah 10:1.
46. *RoR* 406–8; *RdV* 472–74; Maimonides 1984–1996, Hilkhoth Yesodei haTorah. 2:1; Bahya 1973, 436.
47. Cohen 2001, 464; also Cohen 1997, 133; *ErW* 306.
48. Plato 1952, *Theaetetus* 176a b, 126–29.
49. Shapiro 1975, 29; and Diesendruck 1928, 416, 523.
50. *ErW* 298.
51. *RoR* 21 and *RdV* 24–25, corresponding to Maimonides' reading of Jeremiah 9:23 in *Guide* 3:54, 637.
52. *RoR* 70; *RdV* 81.
53. Twersky 1980b, 463; also Maimonides' son, Abraham ben Moses 1973; and Margaliot 1953–1954. Maimonides shares Aristotle's aversion to the sense of touch and to sexual pleasure. *Guide* 3:8, 432–33 and throughout.
54. Scholem 1995, 1–3.
55. Maimonides Hilkhoth Teshuvah 10:3 in the translation of Twersky 1980b, 478.
56. *Guide* 3:54, 638.
57. Maimonides Hilkhoth Shmittah ve-Yovel 13:13 in the translation of Twersky 1980b, 441–42.
58. Literally speaking, Bahya, and not Maimonides, uses the Hebrew form *hitkarvuth* the way Cohen reads it (Bahya 1984, 156); also Menachem ben Zerach 1880, 40a and 42b, uses the term *hitkarvuth* precisely in Cohen's sense, pointing to the love of God.
59. Also Targum Onkelos: ואנא למקרב ביי לי טב.

60. *Guide* 1:18, 44.
61. *RoR* 162–64; *RdV* 188–91. The translator of *RoR* unfelicitously renders the term *Selbstannaehrung,* "approaching God" (literally, "bringing one's Self near"), as "self-nearing."
62. *JS* 1:251–52 and 1:21.
63. *RoR* 212; *RdV* 248; also *JS* 1:251–52; and Rosenzweig 1924, i, lvii. According to Nahum Glatzer, Nehemiah Nobel chose this verse from Psalms 73:28 for the inscription on Cohen's tombstone. Glatzer 1972, 256.
64. Judah ha-Levi 1964, 75–76.
65. *JS* 1:cx; see also *RoR* 360–63; *RdV* 419–22; Wiedebach 1998, 9.
66. Cohen rejects Aristotle's antithesis of "pragmatic" versus "intellectual" virtues, and therewith the very concept of an "isolated" intellectual perfection. Aristotle 1945, *NE* 1177a–78a, 613–19.
67. *RoR* 400–403; *RdV* 464–67.
68. *ErW* xii; and Poma 1997, 108; *RoR* 403; *RdV* 467.
69. *RoR* 403; *RdV* 467.

6. Practice and Performance

1. *RoR* 402; *RdV* 466.
2. Also Schmid 1995, 237–38.
3. Klatzkin 1968, 1:17; also Simon's Hebrew translation in Xenophanes 1960, 12n. 3. In talmudic literature we find "virtue" also rendered in Hebrew as *tivut.*
4. Consider the Christian sources on *unus est bonus—Deus.* Matthew 19:17, Mark 10:18, Luke 18:19. Also *The "New Zohar,"* cited in Blankstein 1964, 382.
5. *RoR* 406; *RdV* 471; cf. TB Sotah in Liss 1979, 2:368; whereas Cohen cites only one version of Pinchas Ben Yair's *Gradus ad Parnassum,* there are, in fact, many more. Liss 1979, 2:369.
6. Cf. "gates" of content in Bahya 1973; similarly Abraham ben Moses ben Maimon 1973, 189; and Luzzatto 1995, ix–x.
7. Maimonides 1984–1996, Hilkhoth Deoth 1:1.
8. Maimonides 1984–1996, Hilkhoth Deoth 1:1.
9. *Guide* 3:35, 538; also Maimonides 1984–1996, Hilkhoth Issure Mizbe ach 7:11; Maimonides 1992b, Menachoth 8:5.
10. See also Wolfson 1947, 2:312; Maimonides 1992b, Avoth 1:2; Peah 1:1; Maimonides 1984–1996, Hilkhoth Deoth table of contents.
11. *ErW* 339.
12. Maimonides 1984–1996, Hilkhoth Deoth 2:3.
13. Maimonides 1984–1996, Hilkhoth Deoth 1:5.
14. Maimonides 1984–1996, Hilkhoth Deoth 1:7; Maimonides 1984–1996, Hilkhoth Deoth 1:7; *Guide* 2:39, 380; Maimonides 1912, 64; also *Guide* 2:28, 335–36; Fox 1988, 109.
15. Maimonides 1984–1996, Hilkhoth Deoth 1:2–4.
16. Maimonides 1984–1996, Hilkhoth Deoth 2:3.
17. Twersky 1980b, 462; Maimonides 1984–1996, Hilkhoth Deoth 1:4.

18. Schwarzschild 1990, 137–60.
19. Rawidowicz 1969–1971, 1:430n. 118 and 431n. 119; also Rabinovitch, on Hilkhoth Deoth, in Maimonides 1990, 1:23–25.
20. For a Jewish adoption of Max Weber's concept of the "ideal type" as represented in Spranger's *Types of Men,* cf. Soloveitchik 1991, 1 and 139n. 1.
21. Herzog 1980, 1:385.
22. Maimonides 1984, Hilkhoth Yesodei haTorah 5:11; also Maimonides 1997–1998, 1:37.
23. *ErW* 618.
24. Lichtenstein 1978, 114–17.
25. Soloveitchik 1933; cf. R. Munk 1996.
26. *Guide* 2:39, 75.
27. *Guide* 1:34, 79.
28. Maimonides 1984–1996, Hilkhoth Tum'ath Okhalim 16:12; *Guide* 1:54, 128.
29. Maimonides 1984–1996, Hilkhoth Tum'ath Okhalim 16:12.
30. *RoR* 266–67, 426–27; *RdV* 310–11, 493–95; *ErW* 549; Schmid 1995, 261–63.
31. *ErW* 628.
32. *ErW* 629.
33. See the correspondence on Zionism between Cohen and Buber in 1916. *JS* 2:319–27; also Wiedebach 1997, 23–36, as well as Buber 1920.
34. Schwarzschild n.d.
35. *RoR* 426–28; *RdV* 494–96.
36. Aristotle 1945, *NE* 1128b, 249–50; 1108a–b, 105.
37. *RoR* 266; *RdV* 311; paragraph number 136 in this chapter.
38. Maimonides 1984–1996, Hilkhoth Yesodei haTorah 5; and H. Soloveitchik 1976, 281–319.
39. *RoR* 267–68; *RdV* 312–13.
40. Isaiah 53; also ibn Ezra (1964, 91) on Isaiah 53:2.
41. Schulte 1997, 219; also Bruckstein 2000, 129–55.
42. Maimonides 1984–1996, Hilkhoth Deoth 2:3; Maimonides 1992b, Avoth 2:13; Maimonides 1946, 67n. 5.
43. Cf. TB Shabbat 105b; and TB Nedarim 22a.
44. Maimonides 1957–1961, 2:728.
45. See the commentary by Abraham bar Chiya 1971, 62.
46. Ginzberg 1968, 2:51–52.
47. Ginzberg 1968, 3:83–84; Ginzberg 1968, 2:304; Bialik and Ravnitzky 1992, 707–12.
48. Numbers 12:3.
49. Mekhilta 1960, 238 on Exodus 20:18; Mekhilta 1949, 273.
50. Levinas 1987.
51. Matthew 5:3. The Greek allows for the same ambiguous reading as the Hebrew *ani/anaw,* Hatch and Redpath 1954, 2:1239b; cf. also Cohen 2002, 365–66, Wiedebach's commentary, note 4.
52. *RoR* 265; *RdV* 310; also Wiedebach 1997b, 243–44n. 4.

53. *JS* 1:242.
54. Matthew 16:24 and synoptic parallels: "If anyone wishes to come after Me, let him deny himself, and take up his cross."
55. Mishna Berakhoth 2:2.
56. This meaning is preserved in Ben Sira, Ecclesiastes 51:26.
57. Cf. Levinas 1997, 89–90, on TB Sanhedrin 98b.

7. "He Is (Not) Like You"

1. Maimonides 1984–1996, Hilkhoth Yesodei ha-Torah 4:8.
2. Ezekiel 18:20; also Jeremiah 31:28–29; Deuteronomy 24:16 and the classical commentaries thereon.
3. *JS* 1:245.
4. *RoR* 183; *RdV* 216.
5. *RoR* 187; *RdV* 218.
6. Maimonides 1984–1996, Hilkhoth Teshuvah 2:4.
7. *RoR* 193; *RdV* 225.
8. Maimonides 1984–1996, Hilkhoth Yesodei haTorah 7:1.
9. *RoR* 216–35; *RdV* 252–75.
10. Zank 2000.
11. TB Makkoth 24a; also *JS* 1:157–58.
12. Pesikta 1975, 369; also TY Makkoth 2:1.
13. Ezekiel 18:31; *RoR* 194; *RdV* 226.
14. *RoR* 211; *RdV* 246.
15. Aristotle 1977, *Metaphysics* 1075a, 167.
16. Also Schwarzschild 1990, 143–44.
17. Soloveitchik 1979, 115–235.
18. Soloveitchik 1979, 180–97, esp. 195–97.
19. *ErW* 208–12; *RoR* 14–15, 165; *RdV* 17, 192.
20. See R. Munk 2000, 275–86.
21. *RoR* 16–17; *RdV* 18–19, italics in the original.
22. Levinas 1994, 50; also Levinas 1992, 200.
23. *RoR* 16–19; *RdV* 19–21.
24. *JS* 1:186–91.
25. Naphtali Herz Tur-Sinai in his note to Ben-Yehuda's entry on רעה (shepherding). Ben-Yehuda 1980, 6642b.
26. Heidegger 1962, 235–44, esp. 237.
27. Maimonides 1984–1996, Hilkhoth Evvel 14:1.
28. Cohen sides with Hartwig Wessely (Naphtali Herz Wessely) against Mendelssohn in their controversy over the reading of Leviticus 19:18; cf. Mendelssohn 1972 on the Torah, Leviticus 19:18.
29. According to the Buber-Rosenzweig translation, Bible 1987–1994, Leviticus 19:18.
30. See Buber's preface to Cohen 1935. See Nachmanides' commentary of the Torah on Leviticus 19:18, 19:33–34, Nachmanides 1971–1976, 2:292–94.
31. *ErW* 208–12.

32. *ErW* 283.
33. Pines translates *mishpath* as "judgment," and *tsedaka* as "righteousness," *Guide* 630. My translation is guided by Cohen's own reading of *chessed vetsedaka* as *Liebe und Gerechtigkeit* or "*lovingkindness* and justice."
34. *ErW* 617–21.
35. *Guide* 3:53, 631.
36. *JS* 3:43–97.
37. *JS* 3:76.
38. *JS* 3:81.
39. *Guide* 3:53, 631; *JS* 3:81.
40. TB Niddah 64a.
41. Goldschmidt 1978, 205; see also the various traditional Sephardi prayer books.
42. Maimonides 1984–1996, Hilkhoth Teshuvah 8:7; and paragraph number 160 and following beginning in chapter 9 in this book.
43. Maimonides 1984–1996, *Hilkhoth Teshuvah* 10:5. Sifre 1993, 87; and the Mishna Avoth 1:3 on Antigonos of Socho.
44. Lamm 1989; Solomon 1993.
45. *Guide* 3:51, 620–21.
46. Maimonides 1984–1996, Hilkhoth Avoda Zara 1:3, 2:1; also Ginzberg 1968, 5:210n. 16. Bacher 1923, 336, points to Maimonides' terminological innovation of the term *shotet*. In the sense of "speculative reasoning," this was used, however, already by Judah ibn Tibbon (Bahya 1949, 17) in his translation of *Chovot ha-Levavot*.
47. Maimonides 1984–1996, Hilkhoth Evel 14:2. Genesis 18:19; Maimonides 1984–1996, Hilkhoth Matnot Aniyim 10:1.
48. *Guide* 2:39, 379; Bruckstein 1997a, 283–84.
49. Maimonides 1984–1996, Hilkhoth Yesodei haTorah 7:6; *Guide* 2:35, 367–69. See Maimonides 1992b, 142–43; Altmann 1987, 82–83.
50. Maimonides 1984–1996, Hilkhoth Teshuvah 10:2; also Tosefta 1955–1988, 167.
51. Judah ha-Levi 1964, 223; also Bahya 1973, 432–33.
52. Judah ha-Levi 1964, 223; modified translation.

8. On Eudaemonian Eschatology and Holy History

1. Niewöhner 1999.
2. TB Sanhedrin 92b.
3. Scholem 1995b, 8–9.
4. Idel 1998b, 53.
5. Maimonides 1992a, 138; Maimonides 1984–1996, Hilkhoth Teshuvah 8:2 and Hilkhoth Melakhim 11:4; TB Berakhoth 34b; cf. also Maimonides 1984–1996, Hilkhoth Shmittah ve-Yovel 13:13.
6. Maimonides 1984–1996, Hilkhoth Teshuvah 9:2.
7. Maimonides 1984–1996, Hilkhoth Melakhim 12:2.
8. Scholem 1995b, 8–9; also Idel 1998, 20; and for a demonstration of midrashic sources on Jewish eschatology and apocalypses, see Patai 1988.

9. TB Sanhedrin 92b with Rashi; see also Maimonides' letter to Josef ibn Aknin in Maimonides 1997–1998, 1:354.
10. Rosenzweig 1924, 1:lii.
11. *Guide* 3: Introduction, 416, slightly modified translation.
12. See the anonymous medieval treatises *Tractate of Gehenna* (Masekhet Gehennom) and *The Book on the Scourge in the Tomb* (Sefer Chibbut haKever) in Jellinek 1982, 1:147–52; and Higger 1970, 253–61, and the bibliographical list there, 93–94. Saadya (1970, 213n. 90) is the first medieval Jewish philosopher to refer to these apocalyptic traditions under the term *Chibbut ha-Kever.* For a kabbalistic adoption of this theme, cf. Hillel ben Semuel of Verona 1981, 199–200.
13. Caro 1993, 384; also the fourteenth-century halakhic code *Orchot Chayim* in Aharon ha-Cohen of Lunel 1959, 2:596.
14. TB Berakhoth 34b.
15. For example, Ele'azar ben Judah of Worms 1967, 25–26, on Hilkhoth Teshuvah and Teshuvat ha-Mishkal.
16. Cf. the glosses of Tzvi Hirsch Chayoth on TB Sotah 3a in the standard Vilnius-Form editions.
17. Maimonides 1984–1996, Hilkhoth Teshuvah 2:4.
18. Reminiscent of Rosenzweig's analysis of prayer in Rosenzweig 1971, 272–73, and 1990, 303–4.

9. To Create Messianic Time

1. *Guide* 2:46, 404.
2. Lingis 1998, xix.
3. Maimonides 1984–1996, Hilkhoth Bet ha-Bechirah 6:14, 16–17; and Hilkhoth Melakhim 12.
4. According to Maimonides' son, Abraham ben Moses ben Maimon 1953, 61, 66.
5. Maimonides 1984–1996, Hilkhoth Teshuvah 8:7.
6. Bruckstein forthcoming.
7. See Maimonides' letter to the Jew of Yemen in Maimonides 1997–1998, 1:152.
8. Rosenzweig 1926, 239.
9. *RoR* 311; *RdV* 361.
10. Maimonides 1992a, 138–39.
11. Maimonides 1984–1996, Hilkhoth Teshuvah 9:2.
12. Levinas 1992, 21, modified translation of Isaiah.
13. Rosenzweig 1971, 271–72; 1990, 302.
14. TB Berakhoth 34b; TB Sanhedrin 99a; Maimonides 1984–1996, Hilkhoth Teshuvah 8:7; and *RoR* 313; *RdV* 363.
15. Maimonides 1984–1996, Hilkhoth Teshuvah 9.
16. Maimonides 1984–1996, Hilkhoth Melakhim 12:1–5.
17. Maimonides 1984–1996, Hilkhoth Melakhim 12:1–5.
18. *RoR* 309; *RdV* 360.
19. *RoR* 310; *RdV* 360–61.

20. See TB Sanhedrin 98a on the coming of the Messiah at a time of moral and ethical corruption. Most of the texts which portray the future kingdom in a utopian sense, however, use the ambivalent term *atid lavo* which is often explicitly related to the world-to-come; for example, TB Ketuboth 111b.
21. Maimonides 1984–1996, Hilkhoth Teshuvah 8:8.
22. Maimonides 1984–1996, Hilkhoth Teshuvah 8:8.
23. *RoR* 291; *RdV* 338–39; also Bruckstein 2000, 129–55.
24. Levinas 1992, 23.
25. Scholem 1970, 114–15.
26. Nachmanides 1983, 117–18; Falaquera 1970, 24; Albo 1929–1930, 4:306–16; also Scholem 1970, 114.
27. Maimonides 1992a, 137.
28. Mishna Avoth 4b and Maimonides' commentary on this in Maimonides 1992b.
29. TB Shabbat 104b.
30. TB Makkoth 10b.

10. The Human Face

1. Maimonides 1984–1996, Hilkhoth Melakhim 12:4–5.
2. *LrE* 154; Fiorato 1993, 152–55; also Wiedebach 1997a, 68–73, although I do find myself in disagreement with Wiedebach's ontological reading of Cohen's concept of the national spirit of the Jewish people.
3. *ErW* 405–6.
4. *ErW* 405–6; *RoR* 249–50; *RdV* 291.
5. *ErW* 406.
6. Maimonides 1984–1996, Hilkhoth Shmittah veYovel 13:13, based on the translation by Twersky 1980b, 441–42.
7. Mishna Avoth 5:23. My translation is based upon Herford 1974, 143; see also the conclusion of the Amidah, the Eighteen Benedictions.
8. Mishna Avoth 5:18; Maimonides 1992b, 119. A reading that comes close to the one advanced by Cohen is that of Maimonides' grandson on Mishna Avoth 5:28, David ben Abraham Maimuni 1944, 119.
9. Maimonides 1984–1996, Hilkhoth Channuka 4:14.
10. See the uncensored version of Maimonides' Hilkhoth Melakhim 11:4 as quoted in Twersky 1980b, 452; the uncensored version of Hilkhoth Melakhim is found in Maimonides 1975, 693. Cf. also the edition of Kafih, Maimonides 1984–1996, 23:353nn. 8–10, based upon Yemenite manuscripts and cf. the textual versions listed by Frankel in Maimonides 1998, 626. On the quote of Zephamia 3:9 in this passage, see also Rashi 1982, 529; on Deuteronomy 6:4; and TB Avodah Zava 24a.
11. Maimonides 1984–1996, Hilkhoth Melakhim 12:1.
12. *Guide* 3:12, 441.
13. *ErW* 452.
14. *ErW* 362.
15. al-Razi as quoted by Maimonides in 3:12, 441.

16. *Guide* 3:12, 442.
17. Saadya 1976, 4:180–81; Diesendruck 1928, 456.
18. Diesendruck 1928, 456.
19. See Maimonides' reading of Proverbs 16:4 in 3:13, 452; also Diesendruck 1928, 448n. 76, 510.
20. *ErW* 451.
21. *ErW* 449–50; and *JS* 1:253–54.
22. Levinas 1994a, 20.
23. TB Avodah Zarah 54b, 4:7; and commentary on Avodah Zarah 6:7 in Tosefta 1937, 469–70.
24. See *Guide* 2:29, 345; also Maimonides' commentary on the Mishna Avoth 5:5 in Maimonides 1994, 101. It is Rosenzweig (1971 and 1990) who picks up this Maimonidean reading of miracles after Cohen.
25. See Maimonides' discussion of the *Mutakallimun* on the freedom of divine will in *Guide* 1:73, 199–200; also Pines's introduction in the *Guide*, lxxxiv, cxxiv–cxxxi; and Pines 1997, 32–40.
26. Rosenzweig 1971, 117–18, 130–31; and 1990, 122–24, 136–37.
27. *ErW* 446.
28. *Guide* 1:34, 79; and Maimonides' introduction in *Guide* 6–7, based on the discussion in TB Chagigah 13a.
29. *Guide* 8.
30. TB Chagigah 13a; *Guide* 1:17, 42–43; also *Guide* 1:34, 79.
31. *Guide* 1:36, 84–85; and Maimonides 1984–1996, Hilkhoth Teshuvah 3:6–7.
32. Sifra on 19:2 (Sifra 1959, 86); and Sifre on Numbers 15:41 (Sifre 1992, 127). For Maimonides' own elaboration of the midrashic sources there, see Maimonides 1971.
33. See Bruckstein 1997b, 271.
34. Levinas 1994a, 141.
5. *RoR* 16–20, 103; *RdV* 19–23, 120; also *JS* 3:177.
36. *ErW* 627.
37. *Guide* 3:47, 595, based upon the Sifra on Leviticus 16:16; also Schechter 1969, 205.
38. Maimonides 1984–1996, Hilkhoth Yesodei haTorah 5:11.
39. Recited in response to the priestly blessing of the *cohanim.* My translation includes Saadya's universalist clause "to promote peace in the world," cf. Saadya 1941, 19.
40. *ErW* 627.

Bibliography

Abraham bar Chiya. 1971. *Hegyon ha-Nefesh ha-Atzuvah*. Edited by Geoffrey Wigoder. Jerusalem: Mossad Bialik.

Abraham ben David of Posquières. 1964. *Ba'ale Nefesh*. Edited by Yosef Kafih. Jerusalem: Mossad ha-Rav Kook.

_______. 1985. *Hassagot ha-Rabad le-Mishneh Torah: Sefer ha-Mada ve-Sefer Ahavah*. Edited by Bezalel Naor. Jerusalem:Yeshiva and Eshel Avraham.

Abraham ben Moses ben Maimon. 1953. *Milchamot Adonai*. Edited by Reuven Margoliot. Jerusalem: Mossad ha-Rav Kook.

_______. 1973. *Ha-Maspik le-Ovde ha-Shem*. Second edition. Translated and edited by Joseph ben Tzalach Duri. Jerusalem: Keren Hotza-at Sifrei Rabbeinu Bavel.

Abravanel, Isaac. 1956. *Perush al Nevi'im Acharonim*. Jerusalem: Hotza-at Sefarim Torah ve-Da'at.

_______. 1982. *Principles of Faith* (*Rosh Amanah*). Translated by Menachem Kellner. London: Associated University Presses.

Adelmann, Dieter. 1968. Einheit des Bewusstseins als Grundproblem der Philosophie Hermann Cohens. Ph.D. dissertation, University of Heidelberg.

_______. 1997. H. Steinthal und Hermann Cohen. In *Hermann Cohen's Philosophy of Religion: International Conference in Jerusalem 1996*, edited by Stéphane Mosès and Hartwig Wiedebach. Hildesheim, Germany: Olms.

_______. 2000. Die "Religion der Vernunft" im "Grundriss der Gesamtwissenschaften des Judentums." In *"Religion der Vernunft aus den Quellen des Judentums": Tradition und Ursprungsdenken in Hermann Cohens Spätwerk*, edited by Helmut Holzhey, Gabriel Motzkin, and Hartwig Wiedebach. Hildesheim, Germany: Olms.

Aharon ha-Cohen of Lunel. [1902] 1959. *Orchoth Chajim*. Edited by M. Schlesinger. Volumes 1–3. Reprint, New York: Mekhon Menorah.

Albalada, Moses ben Jacob. 1583. *Reshit Da'at*. Venice.

Albo, Joseph. 1929–1930. *Sefer ha-Ikkarim* (*Book of Principles*).Translated and edited by Isaac Husic. Volumes 1–4. Philadelphia: Jewish Publication Society.

Altmann, Alexander. 1966. The Divine Attributes: A Historical Survey of the Jewish Discussion. *Judaism* 15:40–60.

———. 1981. Maimonides' Four Perfections. In *Essays in Jewish Intellectual History*. Hanover, N. H.: University Press of New England.

———. 1987. *Von der mittelalterlichen zur modernen Aufklärung: Studien zur jüdischen Geistesgeschichte*. Tübingen: J. C. B. Mohr, Paul Siebeck.

———. 1988. Essence and Existence in Maimonides. In *Maimonides: A Collection of Critical Essays*. South Bend, Ind.: University of Notre Dame Press.

Aristotle. [1926] 1945. *The Nicomachean Ethics*. Translated by H. Rackham. Volume 19 of *Aristotle in Twenty-three Volumes*. Reprint, Cambridge, Mass.: Harvard University Press, Loeb Classical Library.

———. [1933] 1947. *The Metaphysics: Books 1–9*. Translated by Hugh Tredennick. Volume 17 of *Aristotle in Twenty-three Volumes*. Reprint, Cambridge, Mass.: Harvard University Press, Loeb Classical Library.

———. [1926] 1970. *Problems: Book 1*. Translated by W. S. Hett. Volume 15 of *Aristotle in Twenty-three Volumes*. Reprint, Cambridge, Mass.: Harvard University Press, Loeb Classical Library.

———. [1926] 1975a. *The Art of Rhetoric*. Translated by John Henry Freese. Volume 7 of *Aristotle in Twenty-three Volumes*. Reprint, Cambridge, Mass.: Harvard University Press, Loeb Classical Library.

———. [1937] 1975b. *On the Soul/Parva Naturalia/On Breath*. Translated by W. S. Hett. Volume 8 of *Aristotle in Twenty-three Volumes*. Reprint, Cambridge, Mass.: Harvard University Press, Loeb Classical Library.

———. [1935] 1977. *Metaphysics: Books 10–14/Oeconomica/Magna Moralia*. Translated by Hugh Tredennick and G. Cyril Armstrong. Volume 18 of *Aristotle in Twenty-three Volumes*. Reprint, Cambridge, Mass.: Harvard University Press, Loeb Classical Library.

———. [1929] 1980. *The Physics: Book 1*. Translated by Philip H. Wicksteed. Volume 4 of *Aristotle in Twenty-three Volumes*. Reprint, Cambridge, Mass.: Harvard University Press, Loeb Classical Library.

———. [1935] 1981. *The Athenian Constitution/The Eudemian Ethics/On Virtues and Vices*. Translated by H. Rackham. Volume 20 of *Aristotle in Twenty-three Volumes*. Reprint, Cambridge, Mass.: Harvard University Press, Loeb Classical Library.

———. [1938] 1983a. *The Categories/On Interpretation/Prior Analytics*. Translated by Harold P. Cooke and Hugh Tredennick. Volume 1 of *Aristotle in Twenty-three Volumes*. Reprint, Cambridge, Mass.: Harvard University Press, Loeb Classical Library.

———. [1937] 1983b. *Problems: Book 2 / Rhetorica ad Alexandrum*. Translated by W. S. Hett and H. Rackham. Volume 16 of *Aristotle in Twenty-three Volumes*. Reprint, Cambridge, Mass.: Harvard University Press, Loeb Classical Library.

Askani, Hans-Christoph. 1997. *Das Problem der Übersetzung—dargestellt an Franz Rosenzweig: Die Methoden und Prinzipien der Rosenzweigschen und Buber-Rosenzweigschen Übersetzungen*. Tübingen: J. C. B. Mohr, Paul Siebeck.

Bacher, Wilhelm. 1881. Abraham ibn Esra als Grammatiker: Ein Beitrag zur hebräischen Sprachwissenschaft. In *Jahresbericht der Landes-Rabbinerschule in Budapest für das Schuljahr 1880–1881*. Budapest.

_______. 1910a. Die "Einheit des Herzens" und die "Einheit der Handlung." *Monatsschrift für die Geschichte und Wissenschaft des Judentums* 54:348–51.

_______. 1910b. Zu Bachja ibn Pakudas Herzenspflichten. *Monatsschrift für die Geschichte und Wissenschaft des Judentums* 54:730–46.

_______. [Binyamin Ze'ev]. 1923. *Erkhei Midrash*. Translated by A. S. Rabinovitz. Tel Aviv: n.p.

Bacher, Wilhelm, Marcus Brann, David Simonsen, and Jacob Guttmann, eds. 1908–1914. *Moses ben Maimon: Sein Leben, seine Werke und sein Einfluß*. Volumes 1–2. Leipzig: Buchhandlung Gustav Fock.

Bahir. 1912. *Sefer ha-Bahir. With the Commentaries Torah Or, Hagahot ha-Gra and Or ha-Ganuz*. Vilna, Lithuania: Romm.

Bahya ben Joseph ibn Pakuda. 1854. *Chovot ha-Levavot*. Translated by E. Baumgarten and edited by Salomo G. Stern. Vienna: Adalbert della Torre.

_______. 1949. *Chovot ha-Levavot*. Translated by Judah ibn Tibbon and edited by A. Zifroni. Tel Aviv: Hotza-at me-Chaverut la-Sifrut be-Siyua Mossad ha-Rav Kook.

_______. 1973. *The Book of Direction to the Duties of the Heart* (*from the original Arabic version Al-Hidaya ila Fara'id al-Qulub*). Translated by Menahem Mansoor. London: Routledge & Kegan Paul.

_______. 1984. *Torat Chovot ha-Levavot*. Translated by Yosef Kafih. Jerusalem: Feldheim.

Bamberger, Bernard Jacob. 1929. Fear and Love of God in the Old Testament. *Hebrew Union College Annual* 6:39–53.

Bammel, E. 1959–1960. Gottes διαθηκη und das Jüdische Rechtsdenken. *New Testament Studies* 6:313–19.

Baneth, David Zvi. 1985. On the Philosophic Terminology of Maimonides. *Studies in Maimonides* 5:10–40.

Bar-Shaul, Elimelech. 1972. *Mitzvah ve-Lev*. Volumes 1–2. Rechovot, Israel: n.p.

Behm, Johannes. 1964. διαθηκη, B–D. In *Theological Dictionary of the New Testament*, translated by Geoffrey W. Bromiley II and edited by Gerhard Kittel. Grand Rapids, Mich.: William B. Eerdmans Publishing Company.

Ben-Yehuda, Eliezer. [1908–1947] 1980. *Thesaurus Hebraitatis et Veteris et Recentioris*. Volumes 1–7. Reprint, Jerusalem: Makor.

Bergman, Samuel Hugo. 1967. *The Philosophy of Solomon Maimon*. Translated by Noah J. Jacobs. Jerusalem: Magnes Press.

_______. [1940] 1990. *Mavo le-Torat ha-Hakkarah* (Introduction to the Theory of Knowledge). Reprint, Jerusalem: Magnes Press.

_______. 1991. *Dialogical Philosophy from Kierkegaard to Buber*. Translated from the Hebrew by Arnold A. Gerstein. Albany: State University of New York Press.

Berlin, Naftali Zvi Judah. [1879] 1937. Ha'amek Davar. In *Chamisha Chumshe Torah im Targum Onkelos ve-Perushe Rashi ve Toldot Aharon ve im Perush ha-Nikra Ha'amek Davar*. Volumes 1–5. Reprint, Jerusalem: Bamberger et Wahrmann.

Berman, Lawrence V. 1961. The Political Interpretation of the Maxim: The Purpose of Philosophy Is the Imitation of God. *Studia Islamica* 15:53–61.

Betz, Hans-Dieter. 1979. *Galatians: A Commentary on Paul's Letter to the Churches in Galatia.* Philadelphia: Fortress Press.

Bialik, Hayim Nahman. 1944. *Halachah and Aggadah.* Translated from the Hebrew by Leon Simon. London: Education Department of the Zionist Federation of Great Britain and Ireland.

Bialik, Hayim Nahman, and Yehoshua Hana Ravnitzky, eds. 1992. *The Book of Legends. Sefer ha-Aggadah: Legends from the Talmud and Midrash.* Translated by William G. Braude. New York: Schocken.

Bible. 1985. *Tanakh: A New Translation of the Holy Scriptures according to the Traditional Hebrew Text.* Philadelphia: Jewish Publication Society.

________. [1954–1962] 1987–1994. *Die Schrift.* Volumes 1–4. Translated by Martin Buber and Franz Rosenzweig. Reprint, Heidelberg: Lambert Schneider.

Bieler, Majer. 1933. *Der göttliche Wille (Logosbegriff) bei Gabirol.* Breslau, Poland: D. Rothenberg.

Blankstein, Elazar. 1964. *Mishle Israel ve-Umot ha-Olam: Be-Hitpatchutam le-Nuscha-otehem ve-le-Leshonotehem Makbilim Ish el Achiv ve-Mesudarim be-Seder A-B.* Edited by Shemuel Ashkenazi. Jerusalem: Kiryat Sefer.

Blumenberg, Hans. 1985. *Work on Myth.* Translated by Robert M. Wallace. Cambridge, Mass.: MIT Press.

Boyarin, Daniel. [1990] 1994a. *Intertextuality and the Reading of Midrash.* Reprint, Bloomington: Indiana University Press.

________. 1994b. *A Radical Jew: Paul and the Politics of Identity.* Berkeley: University of California Press.

________. 2002. *Den Logos Zersplitten: Zur Genealogie der Nichtbestimmbarkeit des Textsinns im Midrasch.*" Schriftenreihe Ha'Atelier Collegium. Berlin: Philo.

Brenner, Michael. 1996. *The Renaissance of Jewish Culture in Weimar Germany.* New Haven, Conn.: Yale University Press.

Bruckstein, Almut Sh. 1992. *Hermann Cohen's "Charakteristik der Ethik Maimunis": A Reconstructive Reading of Maimonides' Ethics.* Ann Arbor, Mich.: University Microfilms International Dissertation Information Service.

________. 1997a. The Height of the Good: Correlations in Rosenzweig and Levinas. *Religious Studies Review* 23:16–21.

________. 1997b. How Can Ethics Be Taught? Socratic and Post-Socratic Methods in Maimonides' Theory of Emulation. *Jewish Studies Quarterly* 4:268–84.

________. 1997c. On Jewish Hermeneutics: Maimonides and Bachya as Vectors in Cohen's Philosophy of Origin. In *Hermann Cohen's Philosophy of Religion: International Conference in Jerusalem 1996,* edited by Stéphane Mosès und Hartmut Wiedebach. Hildesheim, Germany: Olms.

________. 1998. Joining the Narrators: A Philosophy of Talmudic Hermeneutics. In *Reasoning after Revelation: Dialogues in Postmodern Jewish Philosophy,* edited by Steven Kepnes, Peter Ochs, and Robert Gibbs. Boulder, Colo: Westview.

_______. 2000. "Lachen und Weinen: Eine jüdische Kritik am Mythos." In *Frankfurter Judaistische Beitiäge* 27.

Buber, Martin. 1920. Voelker, Staaten und Zion. In *Die jüdische Bewegung: Gesammelte Aufsätze und Ansprachen*. Berlin: Jüdischer Verlag.

_______. 1924. *Das verborgene Licht*. Frankfurt am Main.: Ruetten and Loenig.

_______. 1935. Foreword to *Der Nächste: Vier Abhandlungen über das Verhalten von Mensch zu Mensch nach der Lehre des Judentums,* by Hermann Cohen. Berlin: Schocken.

_______. [1952] 1988. The Love of God and the Idea of Deity: On Hermann Cohen. In *Eclipse of God: Studies in the Relation between Religion and Philosophy*. Reprint, Atlantic Highlands, N.J.: Humanities Press International.

_______. [1937] 1994. *I and Thou*. Translated by Ronald Gregor Smith. Reprint, Edinburgh: T. & T. Clark.

Buber, Martin, and Franz Rosenzweig. 1994. *Scripture and Translation*. Translated by Lawrence Rosenwald with Everett Fox. Bloomington: Indiana University Press.

Buijs, Joseph A., ed. 1988. *Maimonides: A Collection of Critical Essays*. South Bend, Ind.: University of Notre Dame Press.

Burrell, David B. 1988. Aquinas's Debt to Maimonides. In *A Straight Path: Studies in Medieval Philosophy and Culture: Essays in Honor of Arthur Hyman,* edited by Ruth Link-Salinger. Washington, D.C.: Catholic University of America Press.

Burton, Ernest de Witt. [1921] 1988. *A Critical and Exegetical Commentary to the Epistle to the Galatians*. Reprint, Edinburgh: T. & T. Clark.

Carlebach, Joseph. 1982. Stil und Persönlichkeit. In *Ausgewählte Schriften,* edited by Miriam Gillis-Carlebach. Hildesheim, Germany: Olms.

Caro, Joseph ben Ephraim. 1993. *Shulchan Arukh*. Edited by Tzvi H. Preissler and Shmuel Havlin. Jerusalem: Hotza-at Keturim.

Cassirer, Ernst. [1946] 1974. *The Myth of the State*. Reprint, New Haven, Conn.: Yale University Press.

_______. [1922] 1994. *Das Erkenntnisproblem in der Philosophie und Wissenschaft der neueren Zeit*. Volumes 1–3. Reprint, Darmstadt: Wissenschaftliche Buchgesellschaft.

Charles, Robert Henry, ed. [1913] 1964. *The Apocrypha and Pseudepigrapha of the Old Testament in English*. Reprint, Oxford: Clarendon.

Charron, Pierre. 1971. *Of Wisdom*. Amsterdam: Theatrum Orbis Terrarum.

_______. 1986. *De la Sagesse*. Text revised by Barbara de Negroni. Paris: Fayard.

Chwolson, Daniel. 1856. *Die Ssabier und der Ssabismus*. Volumes 1–2. St. Petersburg: Buchdruckerei der Kaiserlichen Akademie der Wissenschaften.

Cohen, Hermann. [1908] 1971. Charakteristik der Ethik Maimunis. In *Moses ben Maimon: Sein Leben, seine Werke, und sein Einfluß,* edited by Wilhelm Bacher, Marcus Brann, David Simonsen, and Jakob Guttmann. Reprint, Hildesheim, Germany: Olms.

_______. 1910. *Kants Begründung der Ethik nebst ihren Anwendungen auf Recht, Religion und Geschichte*. Berlin: Bruno Cassirer.

_______. 1924. *Hermann Cohens Jüdische Schriften*. Edited by Bruno Strauss. Volumes 1–3. Berlin: C. A. Schwetschke & Sohn.

_______. 1928. *Schriften zur Philosophie und Zeitgeschichte*. Edited by Albert Görland and Ernst Cassirer. Volumes 1–2. Berlin: Berlin: Academie Verlag.

_______. 1935. *Der Nächste: Vier Abhandlungen über das Verhalten von Mensch zu Mensch nach der Lehre des Judentums*. Berlin: Schocken.

_______. 1972. *Religion of Reason: Out of the Sources of Judaism*. Translated by Simon Kaplan. New York: Frederick Ungar.

_______. 1977. *Iyyunim be-Yahadut u-ve-Ba'ayot ha-Dor* (Selected Essays from *Jüdische Schriften*). Translated from the German by Tzvi Voyeslavsky. Jerusalem: Mossad Bialik.

_______. [1907] 1981. *Ethik des reinen Willens*. Volume 7 of *Werke*. Reprint of second edition. Hildesheim, Germany: Olms.

_______. [1912] 1982. *Ästhetik des reinen Gefühls*. Volumes 8–9 of *Werke*. Reprint, Hildesheim, Germany: Olms.

_______. [1928] 1995. *Religion der Vernunft aus den Quellen des Judentums*. Revised according to the manuscript of the author. Reprint, Wiesbaden, Germany: Fourier.

_______. [1915] 1996. *Der Begriff der Religion im System der Philosophie*. Volume 10 of *Werke*. Reprint, Hildesheim, Germany: Olms.

_______. [1914] 1997a. *Logik der reinen Erkenntnis*. Volume 6 of *Werke*. Reprint of second edition. Hildesheim, Germany: Olms.

_______. 1997b. *Kleinere Schriften* 5. Volume 16 of *Werke*. Hildesheim, Germany: Olms.

_______. [1910] 2001. *Kants Begründung der Ethik*. Volume 2 of *Werke*. Reprint of second edition. Hildesheim, Germany: Olms.

_______. 2002. *Kleinere Schriften* 6. Volume 17 of *Werke*. Hildesheim, Germany: Olms.

Cohen, Naomi G. 1995. *Philo Judaeus: His Universe of Discourse*. Frankfurt am Main: Peter Lang.

Cohen, Richard A. 1994. *Elevations: The Height of the Good in Rosenzweig and Levinas*. Chicago: University of Chicago Press.

Cohen, Shear Yashuv. 1970. *Lifnim mi-Shurat ha-Din*. In *Sefer Adam Noach: Sikkaron le-R. Adam Noach Dr. Braun,* edited by Chayim Lifshitz, Shear Yashuv Cohen, and Tzvi Kaplan. Jerusalem: Mekhon Harry Fischel.

Culbertson, Philip L. 1995. *A Word Fitly Spoken: Context, Transmission, and Adoption of the Parables of Jesus*. Albany: State University of New York Press.

Cusanus, Nicholas. [1954] 1986. *Of Learned Ignorance*. Translated by Germaine Heron. Reprint, Westport, Conn.: Hyperion Press.

Da Costa, Uriel. 1993. *Examination of Pharisaic Traditions*. Translated and edited by H. P. Salomon and I. S. D. Sassoon. Leiden: E. J. Brill.

David ben Abraham Maimuni. 1944. *Sefer Midrash David al Masechet Avot*. Translated by Ben Zion Kreihnfuss. Jerusalem: Hotza-at Ben Zion Kreihnfuss.

Davidson, Israel. 1957. *Thesaurus of Proverbs and Parables*. Jerusalem: Mossad ha-Rav Kook.

Derrida, Jaques. [1978] 1995. Violence and Metaphysics: An Essay on the Thought of Emmanuel Levinas. In *Writing and Difference,* translated by Alan Bass. Reprint, Chicago: University of Chicago Press.

Descartes, Rene. 1986. *Meditations on First Philosophy.* Translated by John Cottingham and with an introduction by Bernard Williams. Cambridge: Cambridge University Press.

Diesendruck, Zevi. 1928. Die Teleologie bei Maimonides. *Hebrew Union College Annual* 5:415–534.

_______. 1935. Maimonides' Theory of the Negation of Privation. *Proceedings of the American Academy for Jewish Research* 6:139–51.

Diogenes. [1925] 1942. *Lives of Eminent Philosophers.* Translated by R. D. Hicks. Volumes 1–2. Reprint, Cambridge, Mass.: Harvard University Press, Loeb Classical Library.

Dunn, James Douglas Grant. 1988. *Romans 1–8.* Word Bible Commentary 38A. Dallas: Word Books.

Efros, Israel. 1924. *Philosophical Terms in the Moreh Nebukim.* New York: Columbia University Press.

Elbogen, Ismar. 1993. *Jewish Liturgy: A Comprehensive History.* Translated by Raymond P. Scheindlin. Philadelphia: Jewish Publication Society.

El'azar ben Judah of Worms. 1967. *Sefer ha-Rokeach ha-Gadol.* Edited by Barukh Shimon Schneerson. Jerusalem: n. p.

Fackenheim, Emil. 1996. Hermann Cohen: After Fifty Years. In *Jewish Philosophers and Jewish Philosophy,* edited by Michael L. Morgan. Bloomington: Indiana University Press.

Falaquera, Shem Tov. 1837. *Moreh ha-Moreh.* Edited by Mordekhai Leib. Bratislava, Slovakia: Schmid.

_______. [1894] 1970. *Das Buch der Gerade von Schemtob B. Joseph ibn Falaquera.* Edited by Ludwig Venetianer. Reprint, Jerusalem: Hotza-at Makor.

Felstiner, John. 1995. *Paul Celan: Poet, Survivor, Jew.* New Haven, Conn.: Yale University Press.

Fiorato, Pierfrancesco. 1993. *Geschichtliche Ewigkeit: Ursprung und Zeitlichkeit in der Philosophie Hermann Cohens.* Würzburg, Germany: Königshausen & Neumann.

_______. 1994. "Die Gegenwart muss indessen zur Zukunft werden": Ueber die "logischen" Grundlagen des Cohenschen Messianismus. In *Neukantianismus: Perspektiven und Probleme,* edited by Ernst Wolfgang Orth and Helmut Holzhey. Würzburg, Germany: Königshausen & Neumann.

Fishbane, Michael. 1986. "Inner Biblical Exegesis: Types and Strategies of Interpretations in Ancient Israel." In *Midrash and Literature,* edited by Geoffrey H. Hartman and Samford Budick. New Haven, Conn.: Yale University Press.

Flusser, David. 1997. *Jesus.* Jerusalem: Magnes Press.

Fox, Marvin. 1988. The Doctrine of the Mean in Aristotle and Maimonides: A Comparative Study. In *Maimonides: A Collection of Critical Essays,* edited by Joseph A. Buijs. South Bend, Ind.: University of Notre Dame Press.

_______. 1990. The Range and Limits of Reason. In *Interpreting Maimonides: Studies in Methodology, Metaphysics, and Moral Philosophy.* Chicago: University of Chicago Press.

Frank, Erich. 1945. *Philosophical Understanding and Religious Truth.* London: Oxford University Press.

Funkenstein, Amos. 1970. Gesetz und Geschichte: Zur historisierenden Hermeneutik bei Moses Maimonides und Thomas von Aquin. *Viator* 1:147–78.

Gadamer, Hans-Georg. 1975. *Truth and Method.* Edited by Garret Barden and John Cumming. New York: Seabury Press.

Gerrish, B. A. 1996. Eucharist. In *The Oxford Encyclopedia of the Reformation,* edited by Hans J. Hillerbrand. Volume 2. New York: Oxford University Press.

Gesenius, Wilhelm. [1907] 1966. *A Hebrew and English Lexicon of the Old Testament.* Translated by Edward Robinson and edited by Francis Brown. Reprint, Oxford: Clarendon.

Gibbs, Robert. 1992. *Correlations in Rosenzweig and Levinas.* Princeton, N.J.: Princeton University Press.

Gilson, Etienne. 1955. *History of Christian Philosophy in the Middle Ages.* New York: Random House.

Ginzberg, Louis. [1909–1938] 1968. *The Legends of the Jews.* Volumes 1–7. Reprint, Philadelphia: Jewish Publication Society.

_______. [1941] 1971. *Perushim ve-Chiddushim be-Yerushalmi.* Volumes 1–3. Reprint, New York: Ktav.

Glatzer, Nahum N. [1961] 1972. *Franz Rosenzweig: His Life and Thought Presented by Nahum N. Glatzer.* Reprint, New York: Schocken.

Goldfeld, Lea Naomi. 1986. *Moses Maimonides' Treatise on Resurrection: An Inquiry into Its Authenticity.* New York: Ktav.

Goldschmidt, E. D. 1978. *On Jewish Liturgy: Essays on Prayer and Religious Poetry.* Jerusalem: Magnes Press.

Gotthold, Zev. 1972. Ha-Ma-avak al ha-Itztagninut bi-me ha-Rishonim. *Machanayyim* 125:48 86.

Green, Kenneth Hart. 1993. *Jew and Philosopher: The Return to Maimonides in the Jewish Thought of Leo Strauss.* Albany: State University of New York Press.

_______, ed. 1997. Editor's introduction to *Jewish Philosophy and the Crisis of Modernity: Essays and Lectures in Modern Jewish Thought.* Albany: State University of New York Press.

Guttmann, Jakob. 1879. *Die Religionsphilosophie des Abraham ibn Daud aus Toledo: Ein Beitrag zur Geschichte der jüdischen Religionsphilosophie und der Philosophie der Araber.* Göttingen, Germany: Vandenhoeck & Ruprecht.

_______. 1882. *Die Religionsphilosophie des Saadia.* Göttingen, Germany: Vandenhoeck & Ruprecht.

_______. [1908] 1971. "Der Einfluß der maimoinidischen Philosophie auf das christliche Abendland." In *Moses ben Maimon: Sein Leben, seine Werke, und sein Einfluß,* edited by Wilhelm Bacher, Marcus Brann, David Simonsen, and Jacob Guttmann. Reprint, Hildesheim, Germany: Olms.

Guttmann, Julius. [1964] 1973. *Philosophies of Judaism: The History of Jewish Philosophy from Biblical Times to Franz Rosenzweig.* Translated by David W. Silverman. Reprint, New York: Schocken.

Ha-Am, Achad. 1905. Shilton ha-Sechel: Le-Zekher ha-Rambam. *Ha-Shiloach* 15:291–319.

_______. 1922. The Supremacy of Reason: To the Memory of Maimonides. In *Ten Essays on Zionism and Judaism,* translated from the Hebrew by Leon Simon. London: Routledge.

Haberman, Abraham Meir. 1973. Iyyunim be-Shoresh "Yada." In *Ketav, Lashon ve-Sefer: Pirke Iyyun.* Jerusalem: R. Mass.

Halbertal, Moshe. 1997. *People of the Book: Canon, Meaning, and Authority.* Cambridge, Mass.: Harvard University Press.

Halbertal, Moshe, and Avishai Margalit. 1992. *Idolatry.* Translated by Naomi Goldblum. Cambridge, Mass.: Harvard University Press.

Halevi, A. A. 1977. *Aggadot ha-Amora'im: Ha-Aggadda ha-Biografit shel Amoraey Eretz Israel u-Babel le-Or Mekorot Yavaniim ve-Latiniim.* Tel Aviv: Hotza-at Dvir.

Halkin, Abraham S. 1979. *Be-Ikvot Rambam.* Jerusalem: Merkaz Zalman Shazar.

Handelman, Susan A. 1982. *The Slayers of Moses: The Emergence of Rabbinic Interpretation in Modern Literary Theory.* Albany, N.Y.: State University of New York Press.

Hartman, David. 1976. *Maimonides: Torah and Philosophic Quest.* Philadelphia: Jewish Publication Society.

Hartman, Geoffrey H., and Sanford Budick, eds. 1986. *Midrash and Literature.* New Haven, Conn.: Yale University Press.

Hartmann, Nicolai. 1965. *Platos Logik.* Berlin: de Gruyter.

Harvey, Warren Zev. 1988. Crescas versus Maimonides on Knowledge and Pleasure. In *A Straight Path: Studies in Medieval Philosophy and Culture: Essays in Honor of Arthur Hyman,* edited by Ruth Link-Salinger. Washington, D.C.: Catholic University of America Press.

_______. 1990. Maimonides on Human Perfection, Awe and Politics. In *The Thought of Moses Maimonides: Philosophical and Legal Studies,* edited by Ira Robinson, Lawrence Kaplan, and Julien Bauer. Lewiston, N.Y.: Edwin Mellen.

Hatch, Edwin, and Henry A. Redpath. [1897] 1954. *A Concordance to the Septuagint and the Other Greek Versions of the Old Testament (Including the Apocryphal Books).* Volumes 1–2. Reprint, Graz, Austria: Akademische Druck und Verlagsanstalt.

Hegel, Georg Wilhelm Friedrich. 1977. *Faith and Knowledge.* Translated by Walter Cerf and H. S. Harris. Albany: State University of New York Press.

_______. 1996. *Elements of the Philosophy of Right.* Translated by H. B. Nisbet and edited by Allen W. Wood. Cambridge: Cambridge University Press.

Heidegger, Martin. 1962. *Being and Time.* Translated by John Macquarrie and Edward Robinson. New York: Harper & Row.

Heinemann, Isaak. 1927. Die Lehre vom Ungeschriebenen Gesetz im Jüdischen Schrifttum. *Hebrew Union College Annual* 4:149–71.

_______. [1942–1957] 1993. *Ta'ame ha-Mitzvot be-Sifrut Yisrael.* Volumes 1–2. Reprint, Jerusalem: Hotza-at ha-Sefarim Choreb.

Herford, R. Travers, ed. [1925] 1974. *The Ethics of the Talmud: Sayings of the Fathers.* Translated by R. Travers Herford. Reprint, New York: Schocken.

Herzog, Isaac. [1936, 1939] 1980. *The Main Institutions of Jewish Law.* Volumes 1–2. Reprint, London: Soncino.

Heschel, Abraham J. 1937. Der Begriff des Seins in der Philosophie Gabirols. In *Festschrift Dr. Jakob Freimann zum 70. Geburtstag*. Berlin: n.p.

———. 1938. Der Begriff der Einheit in der Philosophie Gabirols. *Monatsschrift für die Geschichte und Wissenschaft des Judentums* 82:89–111.

———. 1954. *Man's Quest for God: Studies in Prayer and Symbolism*. New York: Scribner's Sons.

Hesiod. 1920. *Theogonia*. In *The Homeric Hymns and Homerica*. Translated by Hugh G. Evelyn-White. London: Heinemann.

Higger, Michael, ed. [1931] 1970. *Massekhet Semachot, Massekhet Semachot de-Rabbi Chiyya, Sefer Chibbut ha-Kever, ve-Hossafot al "Sheva Massekhtot Ketanot" ve-al "Massekhet Sofrim" II*. Reprint, Jerusalem: Hotza-at Makor.

Hildesheimer, Naftali Tzvi. [1888–1890] 1987. Hakdamat Halakhot Gedolot. In *Halakhot Gedolot,* edited by Esriel Hildesheimer. Volumes 1–3. Reprint, Jerusalem: Mekitze Nirdamim.

Hillel ben Semuel of Verona. 1981. *Sefer Tagmule ha-Nefesh* (Book of the Rewards of the Soul). Jerusalem: The Israel Academy of Sciences and Humanities.

Holzhey, Helmut. 1986. *Cohen und Natorp*. Volumes 1–2. Basel: Schwabe & Co.

———. 1988. Cassirers Kritik des mythischen Bewusstseins. In *Über Ernst Cassirers Philosophie der symbolischen Formen,* edited by Hans-Juergen Braun, Helmut Holzhey, and Wolfgang Orth. Frankfurt am Main: Suhrkamp.

———. 1997. Platon im Neukantianismus. In *Platon in der abendländischen Geistesgeschichte: Neue Forschungen zum Platonismus,* edited by Theo Kobusch and Burkhard Mojsisch. Darmstadt, Germany: Wissenschaftliche Buchgesellschaft.

Horace. 1947. *Horace: The Odes and Epodes*. Translated by C. E. Bennett. London: Heinemann.

Husik, Isaac. 1925. The Law of Nature, Hugo Grotius, and the Bible. *Hebrew Union College Annual* 2:381–417.

———. [1916] 1966. *A History of Medieval Jewish Philosophy*. Reprint, New York: Harper & Row.

Hyman, Arthur, and James J. Walsh, eds. 1991. *Philosophy in the Middle Ages: The Christian, Islamic, and Jewish Traditions*. Second edition. Indianapolis: Hackett.

Ibn Chabib, Jacob ben Solomon. 1961. *Ein Ya'akov*. Volumes 1–5. Jerusalem: Hotza-at Am Olam.

Ibn Daud, Abraham (Abraham ben David Halevi). [1852] 1919. *Das Buch Emunah Ramah; oder, Der erhabene Glaube* (Sefer ha-Emunah ha-Ramah). Translated into the German by Simon Weil. Reprint, Berlin: Louis Lamm.

———. 1967. *The Book of Tradition* (Sefer ha-Qabbalah). Translated by Gerson D. Cohen. Philadelphia: Jewish Publication Society.

———. 1986. *The Exalted Faith*. Translated by Norbert M. Samuelson and edited by Gershon Weiss. London: Associated University Presses.

———. 1987. *Emuna Rama*. Hebrew translation from the Arabic by Shelomo Lavi and Shemuel Motut. Edited by Yehuda Eisenberg. Jerusalem, Haskel.

Ibn Ezra, Abraham. 1884. *Birkat Abraham ve-Hu Perush Rava al Sefer Mishle.* Edited by Chaim M. Horowitz. Frankfurt am Main: Chaim M. Horowitz.

_______. [1873] 1964. *The Commentary of ibn Ezra on Isaiah.* Edited and translated by Michael Friedländer. Reprint, New York: Feldheim.

_______. 1985. *Yalkut Abraham ibn Ezra.* Edited by Israel Levin. New York: Hotza-at Keren Matz.

Ibn Gabirol, Solomon. [1954] 1959. Keter Malkhut. In *Ha-Shirah ha-Ivrit be-Sefarad uve-Provence: Mivchar Shirim ve-Sippurim mi-Menachem ibn Saruk ad Yehudah ibn Bal'am,* edited by Chayim Shirman. Volume 1. Reprint, Tel Aviv: Dvir.

Idel, Moshe. 1988. *Kabbalah: New Perspectives.* New Haven, Conn.: Yale University Press.

_______. 1998. *Messianic Mystics.* New Haven, Conn.: Yale University Press.

Isaac ben Joseph of Corbeil. 1937. *Amude Gola (Sefer Mitzvot Katan).* Satu Mare, Romania: Tipografia Hirsch.

Jellinek, Adolph, ed. [1853–1878] 1982. *Bet ha-Midrash.* Volumes 1–2. Reprint, Jerusalem: Wahrmann.

Joël, Manuel. 1866. *Don Chasdai Creskas' religionsphilosophische Lehren in ihrem geschichtlichen Einflusse dargestellt.* Breslau, Poland: Schletter'sche Buchhandlung.

_______. 1876a. *Beiträge zur Geschichte der Philosophie.* Volumes 1–2. Breslau, Poland: H. Skutsch.

_______. [1859] 1876b. *Die Religionsphilosophie des Mose ben Maimon.* Reprint, Breslau, Poland: H. Skutsch.

Jonas, Hans. [1963] 1972. *The Gnostic Religion: The Message of the Alien God and the Beginnings of Christianity.* Reprint, Boston: Beacon Press.

Josef ibn Tsaddik. 1903. *Der Mikrokosmos des Josef ibn Saddik.* Edited by S. Horovitz. Breslau, Poland: Schatzky.

Judah ha-Levi. [1905] 1964. *The Kuzari: An Argument for the Faith of Israel.* Translated from the Arabic by Hartwig Hirschfeld. Reprint, New York: Schocken.

_______. 1973. *Sefer ha-Kuzari le-Rabbi Yehudah ha-Levi.* Translated and edited by Judah Even Shemuel. Tel Aviv: Hotza-at Dvir.

_______. 1997. *Sefer ha-Kuzari.* Translated and edited by Yosef Kafih. Kiryat Ono, Israel: Mekhon Mishnat ha-Rambam.

Kafih, Yosef. 1989. Ha-Yesh Mitzvah min ha-Torah Lehiyot Anav? In *Ketavim,* edited by Yosef Tobi. Volume 1. Jerusalem: Ha-Wa'ad ha-Klali le-Kehilot ha-Teimanim b-Irushalaim.

Kant, Immanuel. [1929] 1950. *Critique of Pure Reason.* Translated by Norman Kemp Smith. Reprint, London: Macmillan.

_______. 1997. Groundwork of the Metaphysics of Morals. In *Practical Philosophy,* translated and edited by Mary J. Gregor. Cambridge: Cambridge University Press.

Kasher, Hannah. 1985. Maimonides' Philosophical Divison of the Laws. *Hebrew Union College Annual* 56:1–7.

Kaufmann, David. 1877. *Geschichte der Attributenlehre in der jüdischen Religionsphilosophie des Mittelalters von Saadja bis Maimuni.* Gotha, Germany: Friedrich Andreas Perthes.

———. 1899. Studien über Salomon ibn Gabirol. In *Jahresbericht der Landes-Rabbinerschule in Budapest für das Schuljahr 1898–1899*. Budapest: n.p.

Kellner, Menachem Marc. 1986. *Dogma in Medieval Jewish Thought from Maimonides to Abravanel*. London: Oxford University Press.

———. 1990. *Maimonides on Human Perfection*. Atlanta: Scholars Press.

Kepnes, Steven. 1996. *Interpreting Judaism in a Postmodern Age*, edited by Steven Kepnes. New York: New York University Press.

Kimchi, David. 1878. *Sefer Radak*. Lemberg: Pessel Balaban.

Klatzkin, Jacob. [1928–1935] 1968. *Thesaurus Philosophicus Linguae Hebraicae et Veteris et Recentioris*. Volumes 1–3. Reprint, New York: Philipp Feldheim.

Klein, Joseph. 1976. *Die Grundlegung der Ethik in der Philosophie Hermann Cohens und Paul Natorps: Eine Kritik des Marburger Neukantianismus*. Göttingen, Germany: Vandenhoeck & Ruprecht.

Kochan, Lionel. 1997. *Beyond the Graven Image: A Jewish View*. Hampshire, England: Macmillan.

Kodalle, Klaus M. 1988. *Die Eroberung des Nutzlosen: Kritik des Wunschdenkens und der Zweckrationalität im Anschluß an Kierkegaard*. Paderborn, Germany: Schöningh.

Kohut, Alexander, ed. [1878–1890] 1955. *Aruch Completum: Lexicon Targumicis, Talmudicis et Midraschicis*. Reprint, New York: Pardes Publishing House.

Kreisel, Howard. 1994. *Imitatio Dei* in Maimonides' *Guide of the Perplexed*. *Association for Jewish Studies Review* 19:169–211.

Lamm, Norman. 1965. Man's Position in the Universe: A Comparative Study of the Views of Saadia Gaon and Maimonides. *Jewish Quarterly Review* 55:208–34.

———. 1989. *Torah Lishmah: Torah for Torah's Sake in the Works of Rabbi Hayyim of Volozhin and his Contemporaries*. Hoboken, N.J.: Ktav.

Landau, Yecheskiel. 1960. *Noda Biyhudah: She-elot ve-Tshuvot be-Arba'a Chalake Shulchan Arukh*. Volumes 1–2. Jerusalem: Pardes Publishing House.

Lasker, Daniel J. 1977. *Jewish Philosophical Polemics against Christianity in the Middle Ages*. Hoboken, N.J.: Ktav.

Lazarus. 1904–1911. *Die Ethik des Judentums*. Volumes 1–2. Frankfurt, Germany: J. Kauffmann.

Lembeck, Karl-Heinz. 1994. *Platon in Marburg: Platonrezeption und Philosophiegeschichtsphilosophie bei Cohen und Natorp*. Würzburg, Germany: Koenigshausen & Neumann.

Levinas, Emmanuel. 1987. Humanism and Anarchy. In *Collected Philosophical Papers*, translated by Alphonso Lingis. Boston: Martinus Nijhoff Publishers.

———. [1969] 1992. *Totality and Infinity: An Essay on Exteriority*. Translated by Alphonso Lingis. Reprint, Pittsburgh: Duquesne University Press.

———. 1994a. *Nine Talmudic Readings*. Translated and with an introduction by Annette Aronowicz. Bloomington: Indiana University Press.

———. 1994b. Revelation in the Jewish Tradition. In *Beyond the Verse: Talmudic Readings and Lectures*, translated by Gary D. Mole. Bloomington: Indiana University Press.

———. 1996. God and Philosophy. In *Basic Philosophical Writings*, edited by Adriaan T. Peperzak, Simon Critchley, and Robert Bernasconi. Bloomington: Indiana University Press.

_______. [1990] 1997. Messianic Texts. In *Difficult Freedom: Essays on Judaism,* translated by Sean Hand. Reprint, Baltimore: Johns Hopkins University Press.

Lewis, Charlton D., and Charles Short. [1879] 1980. *A Latin Dictionary.* Reprint, Oxford: Clarendon.

Lichtenstein, Aharon. 1978. Does Jewish Tradition Recognize an Ethic Independent of Halakha? In *Contemporary Jewish Ethics,* edited by Menachem Kellner. New York: Sanhedrin Press.

Liddell, Henry George, and Robert Scott. [1940] 1968. *A Greek-English Lexicon.* Reprint of the ninth edition. Oxford: Clarendon.

Lieberman, Saul. 1955–1988. *Tosefta ki-Feshuta: A Comprehensive Commentary.* Volumes 1–8. New York: Jewish Theological Seminary of America.

_______. 1974. How Much Greek in Jewish Palestine? In *Texts and Studies.* Hoboken, N.J.: Ktav.

Liebeschuetz, Hans. 1967. *Das Judentum im deutschen Geschichtsbild von Hegel bis Max Weber.* Tübingen: J. C. B. Mohr, Paul Siebeck.

Lingis, Alphonso. [1974] 1998. Translator's introduction to *Otherwise than Being; or, Beyond Essence,* by Emmanuel Levinas. Reprint, Pittsburgh: Duquesne University Press.

Liss, Abraham, ed. 1979. *The Babylonian Talmud: Tractate Sotah.*Volumes 1–2. Jerusalem: Institute for the Complete Israeli Talmud.

Longenecker, Richard N. 1990. *Galatians.* Word Biblical Commentary 41. Dallas: Word Books.

Luther, Martin. 1932. Introduction to St. Paul's Epistle to the Romans. In *Works of Martin Luther with Introductions and Notes.* Volume 6. Philadelphia: Muehlenberg.

Luzzatto, Moshe Chayim. [1966] 1987. *Mesillat Yesharim: The Path of the Just.* Translated by Shraga Silverstein. Reprint, Jerusalem: Feldheim.

_______. [1936] 1995. *The Path of the Upright (Mesillat Yesharim).* Translated and edited by Mordecai M. Kaplan. Reprint, Northvale, N.J.: J. Aaronson.

Maimonides, Moses. 1856–1861. *Le Guide des Égarés: Traité de Théologie et de Philosophie par Moïses ben Maimoun dit Maïmonide.* Volumes 1–2. Translated from the Arabic by Salomon Munk. Paris: Franck.

_______. 1904. *Moreh Nevukhim.* Translated by Judah ben Solomon al-Charizi and edited by Arye Leib Schlossberg. Warsaw: Ha-Tzefirah.

_______. 1912. *The Eight Chapters of Maimonides on Ethics: A Psychological and Ethical Treatise.* Translated and edited by Joseph I. Gorfinkle. New York: Columbia University Press.

_______. 1935–1960. *Moreh ha-Nebukhim.* Translated by Shemuel ibn Tibbon and edited by Yehudah Even Shmuel. Volumes 1–3. Jerusalem: Mossad ha-Rav Kook.

_______. 1938. *Maimonides' Treatise on Logic.* Translated and edited by I. Efros. *Proceedings of the American Academy for Jewish Research* 8 (entire issue).

_______. 1946. *Sefer Ha-Mitzvot.* Second edition. Translated from the Arabic by Moshe ibn Tibbon. Jerusalem: Mossad ha-Rav Kook.

_______. 1949–1979. *Mishneh Torah: The Code of Maimonides.* Volumes 1–13. New Haven, Conn.: Yale University Press.

_______. 1957–1961. *Teshuvot ha-Rambam.* Translated and edited by Yehoshua Blau. Volumes 1–3. Jerusalem: Mekitze Nirdamim.

———. 1963. *The Guide of the Perplexed*. Translated with an introduction and notes by Shlomo Pines. Chicago: University of Chicago Press.

———. 1971. *Sefer ha-Mitzvot*. Translated from the Arabic by Yosef Kafih. Jerusalem: Mossad ha-Rav Kook.

———. 1972. *Moreh Nebukhim,* Translated from the Arabic by Yosef Kafih. Jerusalem: Mossad ha-Rav Kook.

———. 1975. *Mishneh Torah*. Facsimile of the 1480 Rome edition. Jerusalem: Mosad ha-Rav Kook.

———. 1981. Perek Chelek. In *Mishnah Commentary on Tractate Sanhedrin,* translated and edited by Fred Rosner. New York: Sefer Hermon.

———. 1982. *Moses Maimonide's Treatise on Resurrection*. Translated by Fred Rosner. Hoboken, N.J.: Ktav.

———. 1983a. *The Book of Knowledge: From the Mishneh Torah of Maimonides*. Translated by H. M. Russel and J. Weinberg. Hoboken, New Jersey: Ktav.

———. [1975] 1983b. *Eight Chapters*. In *Ethical Writings of Maimonides,* edited by Raymond L. Weiss and Charles E. Butterworth. Reprint, New York: Dover.

———. 1984–1996. *Mishneh Torah*. Edited by Yosef Kafih. Volumes 1–23. Jerusalem: Mekhon Mishnat ha-Rambam.

———. 1985. *Crisis and Leadership: Epistles of Maimonides*. Translated by Abraham Halkin. Philadelphia: Jewish Publication Society.

———. [1935] 1987a. *Milloth ha-Higgayon* (Introduction to Logic). Edited by Leon Roth and D. H. Baneth. Reprint, Jerusalem: Magnes Press.

———. [1959] 1987b. *Moreh ha-Nevukhim*. Translated by Shemuel ibn Tibbon and edited by Yehuda Even Shmuel. Reprint, Jerusalem: Mossad ha-Rav Kook.

———. 1990. *Mishneh Torah: Sefer ha-Mada*. Volumes 1–2. Jerusalem: Ma'aliyot.

———. 1992a. *Hakdamot ha-Rambam la-Mishna*. Edited by Yitzchak Shailat. Jerusalem: Ma'aliyot.

———. [1958–1963] 1992b. *Mishna im Perush Rabbenu Moshe ben Maimon*. Translated and edited by Yosef Kafih. Volumes 1–3. Reprint, Jerusalem: Mossad ha-Rav Kook.

———. 1994. *Perush ha-Rambam la-Avot*. Edited by Yitzchak Shailat. Jerusalem: Ma'aliyot.

———. [1947] 1995a. *Hilkhot ha-Yerushalmi*. Edited by Saul Lieberman. Reprint, New York: Jewish Theological Seminary of America.

———. 1995b. *Maimonides' Introduction to His Commentary on the Mishnah*. Translated by Fred Rosner. New York: J. Aronson.

———. 1997–1998. *Iggerot ha-Rambam*. Edited by Yitzchak Shailat. Volumes 1–2. Jerusalem: Ma'aliyot.

———. 1998. *Mishneh Torah: Book of Shofetim*. Edited by Shabse Frankel. New York: Congregation Bnei Yosef.

Malter, Henry. 1911. Shem Tob ben Joseph Palquera: A Thinker and Poet of the Thirteenth Century. *Jewish Quarterly Review* 1:151–81.

Margaliot, Reuven. 1953–1954. Ha-Rambam ve-ha-Zohar: He'arot al Sefer "Mishneh Torah" le-ha-Rambam be Hashva-ah im Shitot ha-Zohar. *Sinai* 32:263–74; 33:9–15, 128–35, 219–24, 349–54; 34:227–30, 386–95.

Marmorstein, Arthur. 1950. The Imitation of God (*Imitatio Dei*) in the Haggadah. In *Studies in Jewish Theology: The Arthur Marmorstein Memorial Volume,* edited by J. Rabbinowitz and M. S. Lew. London: Oxford University Press.

Martyn, J. Louis. 1998. *Galatians: A New Translation with Introduction and Commentary.* The Anchor Bible 33A. New York: Doubleday.

Meiri, Menachem ben Shlomo. 1964. *Bet ha-Bechira al Masechet Avot.* Edited by Binyamin Ze'ev Halevi Prag. Jerusalem: Mekhon Talmud ha-Israeli ha-Shalem.

Mekhilta. [1933] 1949. *Mekilta de-Rabbi Ishmael.* Translated and edited by Jacob Z. Lauterbach. Volumes 1–3. Reprint, Philadelphia: Jewish Publication Society.

________. 1955. *Mekhilta de Rabbi Shimon ben Yochai.* Edited by Jacob Nachum Epstein and Ezra Zion Melammed. Jerusalem: Mekitze Nirdamim.

________. [1931] 1960. *Mechilta d'Rabbi Ismael.* Edited by H. S. Horovitz and I. A. Rabin. Reprint, Jerusalem: Bamberger & Wahrmann.

Melammed, Ezra Zion. 1975. *Mefarshe ha-Mikra.* Volumes 1–2. Jerusalem: Magnes Press.

Menachem ben Zerach. 1880. *Sefer Tzeda la-Derekh.* Warsaw: Chaim Kelter.

Mendelssohn, Moses. [1938] 1972. *Hebräische Schriften.* Volume 1. Edited by Haim Borodianski. Reprint, Stuttgart, Germany: Friedrich Frommann.

Midrash Bereshit Rabba. 1996. *Midrash Bereshit Rabba.* Jerusalem: Shalem Books.

Midrash Exodus Rabba. 1887. *Midrash Rabbah al Chamisha Chumshe Torah ve-Chamesh Megillot.* Vilnius, Lithuania: Romm.

Midrash ha-Gadol. 1975. *Sefer va-Yikra.* Edited by Adin Steinsaltz. Volume 3 of *Midrash ha-Gadol.* Jerusalem: Mossad ha-Rav Kook.

Midrash Shemot Rabbah. 1984. *Midrash Shemot Rabbah: Perakim.* Edited by Avigdor Shinan. Volumes 1–4. Jerusalem: Devir.

Midrash Tankhuma. [1885] 1964. *Midrash Tankhuma.* Edited by Solomon Buber. Volumes 1–2. Reprint, Jerusalem: Chanokh ve-Geshel.

Midrash Tehillim. [1891] 1947. *Midrash Tehillim ha-Mekhuneh Socher Tov.* Edited by Solomon Buber. Reprint, New York: Om Publishing.

Midreshe Ge'ulah. 1954. *Midreshe Ge'ulah: Pirke ha-Apokalipsah ha-Yehudit me-Chatimat ha-Talmud ha-Bavli ve-ad Reshit ha-Elef ha-Shishi.* Edited by Yehuda Even Shemuel. Jerusalem: Mossad Bialik.

Mishnah Avoth. 1877. *Sayings of the Jewish Fathers.* Translated and edited by Charles Taylor. Cambridge: Cambridge University Press.

Mizrachi, Elijahu. [1862] 1973. Perush al Rashi. In *Otzar Mefarshe ha-Torah.* Volumes 1–2. Reprint, Jerusalem: n.p.

Mosès, Stéphane. 1992. *System and Revelation: The Philosophy of Franz Rosenzweig.* Translated by Catherine Tihanyi. Detroit: Wayne State University Press.

Mosès, Stéphane, and Hartwig Wiedebach, eds. 1997. *Hermann Cohen's Philosophy of Religion: International Conference in Jerusalem 1996.* Hildesheim, Germany: Olms.

Moshe ben Jacob of Coucy. 1993. *Sefer Mitzvot Gadol ha-Shalem.* Jerusalem: Mechon Yerushalayim.

Moshe Narboni. 1852. *The Commentary of Moshe Narboni on the Moreh Nebuchim of Maimonides.* Edited by J. Goldenthal. Vienna: K. K. Hof und Staatsdruckerei.

———. 1986. Commentary on the *Guide of the Perplexed*. In *Moshe Narboni,* edited by M. R. Hayoun. Tübingen, Germany: J. C. B. Mohr, Paul Siebeck.

Munk, Reinier. 1996. *The Rationale of Halakhic Man: Joseph B. Soloveitchik's Conception of Jewish Thought*. Amsterdam: J. C. Gieben.

———. 2000. Who Is the Other? Alternity in Cohen's "Religion der Vernunft." In "*Religion der Vernunft aus den Quellen des Judentums": Tradition und Ursprungsdenken in Hermann Cohens Spätwerk*, edited by Helmut Holzey, Gabriel Motzkin, and Hartwig Weiderbach. Heidescheim, Germany: Olms.

Munk, Salomon. [1857] 1988. *Melanges de Philosophie Juive et Arabe*. Reprint, Paris: Vrin.

Nachmanides, Moses. 1963–1964. *Kitve Ramban*. Edited by Chayyim Dov Chavel. Volumes 1–2. Jerusalem: Mossad ha-Rav Kook.

———. 1971–1976. *Moshe ben Nahman: Ramban (Nachmanides') Commentary on the Torah*. Translated by Charles B. Chavel. Volumes 1–5. New York: Shilo Publishing House.

———. 1981. *Sefer ha-Mitzvot le-ha-Rambam im Hassagot ha-Ramban*. Edited by Chaim Dov Chavel. Jerusalem: Mossad ha-Rav Kook.

———. 1983. *The Gate of Reward*. Translated by Charles B. Chavel. New York: Shilo Publishing House.

———. [1969] 1989. *Perush la-Torah le-Rabbenu Moshe ben Nachman*. Edited by Chayyim Dov Chavel. Volumes 1–2. Reprint, Jerusalem: Mossad ha-Rav Kook.

Nachman of Bratislava. 1991. *Sefer Sippure Ma'asiyot*. Jerusalem: Mechon Torat ha-Netzach.

Navon, Ephraim. 1991. Plato versus Aristotle. In *I Filosofi della Scuola di Marburgo,* edited by Brunella Antomarini. Naples: Edizione Scientifiche Italiane.

Newman, Louis I., ed. and trans. [1934] 1987. *The Hasidic Anthology: Tales and Teachings of the Hasidim*. Reprint, New York: Schocken Books.

New Testament. 1986. *Novum Testamentum Graece*. Edited by Kurt Aland. Stuttgart, Germany: Deutsche Bibelanstalt.

Niewöhner, Friedrich. 1988. *Veritas sive Varietas: Lessings Toleranzparabel und das Buch von den drei Betrügern*. Heidelberg, Germany: Lambert Schneider.

———. 1991. Anmerkungen zum Begriff eines jüdischen Humanismus. In *Archiv für Begriffsgeschichte*. Volume 34. Bonn, Germany: Akademie der Wissenschaften und der Literatur.

———. 1999. Jenseits und Zukunft: Über eine Differenz im 12. Jahrhundert. In *Unsterblichkeit,* edited by Friedrich Niewöhner and Richard Schaeffler. Wiesbaden: Harrassowitz.

Otto, Rudolf. 1943. *The Idea of the Holy: An Inquiry into the Nonrational Factor in the Idea of the Divine and Its Relation to the Rational*. Translated by John W. Harvey. London: Oxford University Press.

Parchon, Shlomo ben Abraham. 1844. *Machberet ha'Arukh*. Edited by Zalman ben Gottlieb Stern. Bratislava, Slovakia: Schmid.

Patai, Raphael. 1988. *The Messiah Texts*. Detroit: Wayne State University Press.

Pentateuch. [1956–1962] 1989. Translated by Samson Raphael Hirsch. Volumes 1–5. Reprint, London: Honig.

Pesikta. 1975. *Pesikta de Rab Kahana: R. Kahana's Compilation of Discourses for Sabbaths and Festal Days*. Translated by William G. Braude and Israel J. Kapstein. Philadelphia: Jewish Publication Society.

Philippson, Martin, and Leopold Lucas. 1904. Protokoll der Ausschuss-Sitzung der "Gesellschaft zur Förderung der Wissenschaft des Judentums." *Monatsschrift für die Geschichte und Wissenschaft des Judentums* 48:751–55.

Philo. 1929. *On the Account of the World's Creation Given by Moses/Allegorical Interpretation of Genesis 2*. Translated by F. H. Colson and G. H. Whitaker. Volume 1 of *Philo in Ten Volumes*. Cambridge, Mass.: Harvard University Press, Loeb Classical Library.

________. 1934. *On the Special Laws: Book 4/On the Virtues/On Rewards and Punishments*. Translated by F. H. Colson. Volume 8 of *Philo in Ten Volumes*. Cambridge, Mass.: Harvard University Press, Loeb Classical Library.

________. 1937. *On the Decalogue/On the Special Laws: Books 1–4*. Translated by F. H. Colson. Volume 7 of *Philo in Ten Volumes*. Cambridge, Mass.: Harvard University Press, Loeb Classical Library.

Pines, Shlomo. 1988. The Limitations of Human Knowledge according to al-Farabi, ibn Bajja, and Maimonides. In *Maimonides: A Collection of Critical Essays*, edited by Joseph A. Buijs. South Bend, Indiana: University of Notre Dame Press.

________. 1997. *Studies in Islamic Atomism*. Translated by Michael Schwarz and edited by Tzvi Langermann. Jerusalem: Magnes Press.

Plantinga, Alvin, ed. 1965. *The Ontological Argument: From St. Anselm to Contemporary Philosophers*. With an introduction by Richard Taylor. New York: Doubleday.

Plato. [1929] 1942. *Timaeus/Critias/Cleitophon/Menexenus/Epistles*. Translated by R. G. Bury. Volume 8 of *Plato in Twelve Volumes*. Reprint, Cambridge, Mass.: Harvard University Press, Loeb Classical Library.

________. [1925] 1952a. *The Statesman/Philebus/Ion*. Translated by Harold N. Fowler and W. R. M. Lamb. Volume 3 of *Plato in Twelve Volumes*. Reprint, Cambridge, Mass.: Harvard University Press, Loeb Classical Library.

________. [1921] 1952b. *Theaetetus/Sophist*. Translated by Harold N. Fowler. Volume 7 of *Plato in Twelve Volumes*. Reprint, Cambridge, Mass.: Harvard University Press, Loeb Classical Library.

________. [1935] 1980. *The Republic: Books 1–2*. Translated by Paul Shorey. Volumes 5–6 of *Plato in Twelve Volumes*. Reprint, Cambridge, Mass.: Harvard University Press, Loeb Classical Library.

________. [1914] 1982. *Eutyphro/Apology/Crito/Phaedo/Phaedrus*. Translated by Harold N. Fowler. Volume 1 of *Plato in Twelve Volumes*. Reprint, CambridgeMass.: Harvard University Press, Loeb Classical Library.

Poma, Andrea. 1997. *The Critical Philosophy of Hermann Cohen*. Translated from the Italian by John Denton. Albany: State University of New York Press.

Pope, Alexander. 1950. *An Essay on Man*. Edited by Maynard Mack. London: Methuen.

Priest, Stephen, ed. 1987. *Hegel's Critique of Kant*. Oxford: Clarendon.

Rabinovicz, Raphael Nathan Nata. [1867–1897] 1976. *Sefer Dikduke Soferim (Variae Lectiones in Mischnam et in Talmud Babylonicum)*. Volumes 1–16. Reprint, New York: M. P. Press.

Rashi. 1982. *Perush al ha-Torah.* Edited by Chayyim Dov Chavel. Jerusalem: Mossad ha-Rav Kook.

Rawidowicz, Simon. 1969–1971. *Iyyunim be-Machshevet Israel.* Edited by Benjamin C. I. Ravid. Volumes 1–2. Jerusalem: Rubin Mass.

________. 1974. On Maimonides' Sefer ha-Madda. In *Studies in Jewish Thought.* Philadelphia: Jewish Publication Society.

Rawls, John. 1972. *A Theory of Justice.* Oxford: Oxford University Press.

Ricoeur, Paul. 1998. *Thinking Biblically: Exegetical and Hermeneutical Studies,* translated by David Pellauer and edited by André LaCocque and Paul Ricoeur. Chicago: University of Chicago Press.

Robinson, Ira, Lawrence Kaplan, and Julien Bauer, eds. 1990. *The Thought of Moses Maimonides: Philosophical and Legal Studies.* Lewiston, N.Y.: Edwin Mellen.

Roetzel, Calvin. 1970. Διαθηκαι in Romans 9:4. *Biblica* 61:377–90.

Rosenzweig, Franz. 1924. Introduction to *Hermann Cohens Jüdische Schriften,* edited by Bruno Strauss. Berlin: C. A. Schwetschke & Sohn.

________. 1937. *Kleinere Schriften.* Berlin: Schocken Verlag / Jüdischer Buchverlag.

________. 1971. *The Star of Redemption.* Translated by William W. Hallo. South Bend, Ind.: University of Notre Dame Press.

________. [1988] 1990. *Der Stern der Erlösung.* Reprint, Frankfurt: Suhrkamp.

________. 1994. Scripture and Word: On the New Bible Translation. In *Scripture and Translation,* edited by Martin Buber and Franz Rosenzweig and translated by Lawrence Rosenwald with Everett Fox. Bloomington: Indiana University Press.

________. 1999. *Franz Rosenzweig's "The New Thinking."* Translated and edited by Alan Udoff and Barbara E. Galli. Syracuse, N.Y.: Syracuse University Press.

________. trans. 1926. *Jehuda Halevi: Zweiundneunzig Hymnen und Gedichte: Deutsch.* Berlin: Lambert Schneider.

Rosin, David. 1876. *Die Ethik des Maimonides.* Breslau, Poland: H. Skutsch Verlagsbuchhandlung.

Saadya (Saadya Gaon). 1845. *Saadja Fajjumi Emunot we-Deot, oder Glaubenslehre und Philosophie.* Translated by Julius Fürst. Leipzig: Otto Wigand.

________. 1941. *Siddur R. Saadja Gaon: Kitab Gami As-Salawat Wat-Tasabih.* Edited by I. Davidson, S. Assaf, and B. I. Joel. Jerusalem: Mekitze Nirdamim.

________. 1965. Saadya Gaon: Book of Doctrines and Beliefs. In *Three Jewish Philosophers.* New York: Harper & Row with Jewish Publication Society.

________. 1966. *Tehillim im Targum u-Ferush ha-Gaon Rabbenu Sa'adya ben Yosef Fayumi.* Translated and edited by Yosef Kafih. Israel.

________. 1970. *Sefer ha-Nivchar be-Emunot u-ve-Deot le-Rabbenu Sa'adya ben Yosef Fiumi.* Translated and edited by Yosef Kafih. Jerusalem: Ha-Machon le-Mechkar ve-le-Hotza'at Sefarim.

________. [1948] 1976. *The Book of Beliefs and Opinions.* Translated from the Arabic and the Hebrew by Samuel Rosenblatt. Reprint, New Haven, Conn.: Yale University Press.

_______. 1984. *Perushe Rav Sa'adya Gaon leBereshit* (Saadya's commentary on genesis). Translated and edited by Moshe Zucker. New York: Jewish Theological Seminary of America.

Saba, Abraham. 1879. *Sefer Shemot.* In *Tzeror ha-Mor.* Warsaw: Aharon Walden.

Samuelson, Norbert M. 1969. On Knowing God: Maimonides, Gersonides and the Philosophy of Religion. *Judaism* 18:64–77.

_______. 1988. The Concept of "Nichts" in Rosenzweig's *The Star of Redemption.* In *Der Philosoph Franz Rosenzweig, 1886–1929: Internationaler Kongress-Kassel 1986,* edited by Wolfdietrich Schmied-Kowarzik. Volume 2. Freiburg: Karl Alber.

_______. 1994. *Judaism and the Doctrine of Creation.* Cambridge: Cambridge University Press.

Sanders, E. P. [1977] 1991. *Paul and Palestinian Judaism: A Comparison of Patterns of Religion.* Reprint, Minneapolis: Fortress Press.

Schechter, Solomon. [1909] 1969. *Aspects of Rabbinic Theology: Major Concepts of the Talmud.* Reprint, New York: Schocken.

Scheler, Max. 1949. *Die Stellung des Menschen im Kosmos.* Munich: Lehnen.

Schmid, Peter A. 1995. *Ethik als Hermeneutik: Systematische Untersuchungen zu Hermann Cohens Rechts- und Tugendlehre.* Würzburg: Koenigshausen & Neumann.

Schmied-Kowarzik, Wolfdietrich, ed. 1988. *Der Philosoph Franz Rosenzweig, 1886–1929: Internationaler Kongress-Kassel 1986.* Volumes 1–2. Freiburg: Karl Alber.

Scholem, Gershom. [1941] 1995a. *Major Trends in Jewish Mysticism.* Reprint, New York: Schocken.

_______. [1971] 1995b. Toward an Understanding of the Messianic Idea in Judaism. In *The Messianic Idea in Judaism: And Other Essays on Jewish Spirituality.* Reprint, New York: Schocken.

Schulte, Christoph. 1997. Theodizee bei Kant und Cohen. In *Hermann Cohen's Philosophy of Religion: International Conference in Jerusalem 1996,* edited by Stéphane Mosès and Hartmut Wiedebach. Hildesheim, Germany: Olms.

Schwarzschild, Steven S. 1956. The Democratic Socialism of Hermann Cohen. *Hebrew Union College Annual* 27:417–38.

_______. 1970. F. Rosenzweig's Anecdotes about H. Cohen. In *Gegenwart im Rückblick,* edited by H. A. Strauss and K. Grossman. Heidelberg: n. p.

_______. 1987. The Religious Stake in Modern Philosophy of Infinity. *Bar Ilan* 22/23:63–83.

_______. 1988. Franz Rosenzweig and Martin Heidegger: The German and the Jewish Turn to Ethnicism. In *Der Philosoph Franz Rosenzweig, 1886–1929: Internationaler Kongress–Kassel 1986,* edited by Wolfdietrich Schmied-Kowarzik. Volume 2, 887–890. Freiburg: Karl Alber.

_______. 1990. *The Pursuit of the Ideal: Jewish Writings of Steven Schwarzschild.* Edited by Menachem Kellner. Albany: State University of New York Press.

_______. n.d. Franz Rosenzweig and Martin Heidegger. Unpublished manuscript, edited by Almut Sh. Bruckstein.

Schweid, Eliezer. 1991. *Chashivah me-Chadash: Pritzot Derekh be-Machshavah ha-Yehudit ha-Datit ve-ha-Leumit be-Meah ha-20.* Jerusalem: Akademon.

________. 1999. *Nevi'im le-Amam u-la-Enoshut: Nevuah ve-Nevi-im be-Hagut ha-Yehudit shel ha-Meah ha-Esrim.* Jerusalem: Magnes Press.

Sefer ha-Bahir. [1923] 1970. *Das Buch Bahir: Ein Schriftdenkmal aus der Frühzeit der Kabbala.* Edited by Gerhard Scholem. Reprint, Darmstadt, Germany: Wissenschaftliche Buchgesellschaft.

________. 1994. *Sefer ha-Bahir al Pi Kitve ha-Yad ha-Kedumim.* Edited by Daniel Abrams. Los Angeles: Cherub Press.

Sefer ha-Chinukh. 1977. *Sefer ha-Chinukh.* Edited by Chayyim Dov Chavel. Jerusalem: Mossad ha-Rav Kook.

Sefer Yetzirah. 1972. *Sefer Yetzirah.* Translated and edited by Yosef Kafih. Jerusalem: Ha-Va'ad le-Hotza-e Sifre Rasag.

Sforno, Obadiah ben Jacob. 1980. *Perush al ha-Torah.* Jerusalem: Mossad ha-Rav Kook.

Shapiro, David Shlomo. 1957. Ha-Shlemut ha-Elyonah be-Shitat ha-Rambam. *Ha-Doar* 36:692–95.

________. 1975. The Doctrine of the Image of God and *Imitatio Dei.* In *Studies in Jewish Thought.* New York: Yeshiva University Press.

Shorey, Paul. 1965. *What Plato Said.* Abridged edition. Chicago: University of Chicago Press.

________. [1935] 1980. Introduction to *The Republic,* translated by Paul Shorey. Reprint, Cambridge, Mass.: Harvard University Press.

Siddur. 1943–1945. *The Authorized Daily Prayer Book of the United Hebrew Congregations of the British Empire.* Edited by J. H. Hertz. London: National Council for Jewish Religious Education.

Sifra (Torat Cohanim). 1918. Edited by Israel Meir ha-Cohen of Radin. Volumes 1–2. Pietrikov: n.p.

________. [1862] 1959. *Sifra de-be-Rav: Hu Sefer Torat Kohanim.* Edited by Isaac Hirsch Weiss. Reprint, Jerusalem: Sifra.

________. [1956] 1970. *Assemani Codex Manuscript of the Sifra.* Edited by Louis Finkelstein. Reprint, New York: Jewish Theological Seminary of America.

________. 1983–1991. *Sifra on Leviticus.* Edited by Louis Finkelstein. Volumes 1–5. New York: Jewish Theological Seminary of America.

________. 1992. *Sifra de-be-Rav: Hu Sefer Torat Kohanim.* Edited by S. Koliditzky. Volumes 1–2. Jerusalem: Hotza-at Sefarim Torani-im.

Sifre (on Deuteronomy). [1939] 1993. *Sifre al Sefer Devarim.* Edited by Louis Finkelstein. Reprint, New York: Jewish Theological Seminary of America.

Sifre (on Numbers). [1917] 1992. *Siphre d'be Rab: Fasciculus Primus: Siphre ad Numeros Adjecto Siphre Zutta.* Edited by H. S. Horovitz. Reprint, Jerusalem: Wahrmann Books.

Silberg, M. [1961] 1984. *Kach Darko shel Talmud (Principia Talmudica).* Reprint, Jerusalem: Akademon.

Simon, Uriel. 1988. The Religious Significance of the "Peshat." *Tradition* 23:41–63.

Sirat, Colette. 1985. *A History of Jewish Philosophy in the Middle Ages.* Cambridge: Cambridge University Press.

Society for the Advancement of Jewish Studies. 1904. First annual report. *Monatsschrift für die Geschichte und Wissenschaft des Judentums* 48:52–64.

Solomon, Norman. 1993. *The Analytic Movement: Hayyim Soloveitchik and His Circle.* Atlanta: Scholars Press.
Soloveitchik, Haim. 1980. Maimonides' Iggeret ha-Shemad: Law and Rhetoric. In *Rabbi Joseph H. Lookstein Memorial Volume,* edited by Leo Landman. New York: Ktav.
Soloveitchik, Joseph B. [Solowiejczyk, Josef]. 1933. Das reine Denken und die Seinskonstituierung bei Hermann Cohen. Ph.D. dissertation, University of Berlin.
_______. 1978. Majesty and Humility. *Tradition* 7:25–37.
_______. 1979. *Ish ha-Halakhah—Galui ve-Nistar.* Jerusalem: ha-Histadrut ha-Zionit ha-Olamit.
_______. 1983–1985. *Shiurim le-Zecher Aba Mari Zal: Maran R. Moshe ha-Levi Soloveitchik.* Volumes 1–2. Jerusalem: Mekhon Yerushalaim.
_______. [1983] 1991. *Halakhic Man.* Translated from the Hebrew by Lawrence Kaplan. Reprint, Philadelphia: Jewish Publication Society.
Sperber, Daniel. 1984. *A Dictionary of Greek and Latin Legal Terms in Rabbinic Literature.* Ramat Gan, Israel: Bar Ilan University Press.
Spero, Shubert. 1972. Is the God of Maimonides Truly Unknowable? *Judaism* 12: 66–78.
Spinoza, Benedict de. 1951. *A Theologico-Political Treatise and a Political Treatise.* Translated by Robert Harvey Monroe Elwes. New York: Dover.
_______. 1985. *The Collected Works of Spinoza.* Edited and translated by Edwin Curley. Princeton, N. J.: Princeton University Press.
Stein, Siegfried. 1979. The Concept of the "Fence." In *Studies in Jewish Religious and Intellectual History: Presented to Alexander Altmann on the Occasion of His Seventieth Birthday,* edited by Siegfried Stein and Raphael Loewe. Tuscaloosa: University of Alabama Press.
Steinberg, Bernard. 1985. Nachman Krochmal, Hermann Cohen and the Influence of Maimonides on Their Thought. Ph.D. dissertation, Hebrew University.
Stone, I. F. 1988. *The Trial of Socrates.* Boston: Little, Brown and Company.
Strauss, Bruno. 1924. Foreword to *Hermann Cohens Jüdische Schriften,* edited by Bruno Strauss. Volume 1. Berlin: C. A. Schwetschke & Sohn.
Strauss, Leo. 1924. Cohens Analyse der Bibel-Wissenschaft Spinozas. *Der Jude* 8:294–314.
_______. [1952] 1988. *Persecution and the Art of Writing.* Reprint, Chicago: University of Chicago Press.
_______. 1995. *Philosophy and Law: Contributions to the Understanding of Maimonides and His Predecessors.* Translated by Eve Adler. Albany: State University of New York Press.
_______. [1965] 1997. *Spinoza's Critique of Religion.* Translated by E. M. Sinclair. Reprint, Chicago: University of Chicago Press.
Talmage, Frank. 1989. Apples of Gold: The Inner Meaning of Sacred Texts in Medieval Judaism. In *Jewish Spirituality from the Bible through the Middle Ages,* edited by Arthur Green. New York: Crossroad.
Talmud. 1520–1524. *Talmud Yerushalmi.* Venice: Bomberg.
Talmud. 1880–1886. *Talmud Bavli.* Vilnus, Lithuania: Romm.
Targum Onkelos. 1884. Edited by Abraham Berliner. Berlin: Hzkowski.

Thomas Aquinas. 1952. *The Summa Theologica of Saint Thomas Aquinas.* Translated by Fathers of the English Dominican Province and revised by Daniel J. Sullivan. Volume 1. Chicago: Encyclopaedia Britannica.

Tosefta. 1937. *Tosephta.* Based on the Erfurt and Vienna Codices. Jerusalem: Bamberger & Wahrmann.

Tosefta. 1955–1988. *The Tosefta.* Edited by Saul Lieberman. New York: Jewish Theological Seminary of America.

Twersky, Isadore. 1979. Joseph ibn Kaspi: Portrait of a Medieval Jewish Intellectual. In *Studies in Medieval Jewish History and Literature,* edited by Isadore Twersky. Cambridge, Mass.: Harvard University Press.

———. 1980a. *Introduction to the Code of Maimonides (Mishneh Torah).* New Haven, Conn.: Yale University Press.

———. 1980b. *Rabad of Posquières: A Twelfth-Century Talmudist.* Philadelphia: Jewish Publication Society.

Urbach, Ephraim E. [1975–1979] 1987. *The Sages: Their Concepts and Beliefs.* Translated from the Hebrew by Israel Abrahams. Volumes 1–2. Reprint, Jerusalem: Magnes Press.

Weinsheimer, Joel C. 1985. *Gadamer's Hermeneutics: A Reading of Truth and Method.* New Haven, Conn.: Yale University Press.

Wiedebach, Hartwig. 1997a. *Die Bedeutung der Nationalität für Hermann Cohen.* Hildesheim, Germany: Olms.

———. 1997b. Hermann Cohens Theorie des Mitleids. In *Hermann Cohen's Philosophy of Religion: International Conference in Jerusalem 1996,* edited by Stéphane Mosès and Hartwig Wiedebach. Hildesheim, Germany: Olms.

———. 2000. Unsterblichkeit und Auferstehung im Denken Hermann Cohens. In *"Religion der Vernunft aus den Quellen des Judentums": Tradition und Ursprungsdenken in Hermann Cohens Spätwerk,* edited by Helmut Holzhey, Gabriel Motzkin, and Hartwig Wiedebach. Hildesheim, Germany: Olms.

Wiehl, Reiner. 1988. Logik und Metalogik bei Cohen und Rosenzweig. In *Der Philosoph Franz Rosenzweig, 1886–1929: Internationaler Kongress-Kassel 1986,* edited by Wolfdietrich Schmied-Kowarzik. Volume 2. Freiburg, Germany: Karl Alber.

Wolfson, Elliot R. 1995. *Circle in the Square: Studies in the Use of Gender in Kabbalistic Symbolism.* Albany: State University of New York Press.

Wolfson, Harry Austryn. 1947. *Philo: Foundations of Religious Philosophy in Judaism, Christianity, and Islam.* Volumes 1–2. Cambridge, Mass.: Harvard University Press.

———. [1934] 1958. *The Philosophy of Spinoza.* Reprint, New York: Meridian.

———. 1973–1977. *Studies in the History of Philosophy and Religion.* Edited by Isadore Twersky and George H. Williams. Volumes 1–2. Cambridge, Mass.: Harvard University Press.

———. [1970] 1976a. *The Philosophy of the Church Fathers: Faith, Trinity, Incarnation.* Reprint, Cambridge, Mass.: Harvard University Press.

———. 1976b. *The Philosophy of the Kalam.* Cambridge, Mass.: Harvard University Press.

Wurzburger, Walter. 1982. The Maimonidean Matrix of Rabbi Joseph B. Soloveitchik's Two-Tiered Ethics. In *Through the Sound of Many Voices*. Edited by Jonathan V. Plaut. Toronto: Lester and Orphen Dennys.

Xenophanes. 1960. *Memorabilia*. Translated by Leon Simon. Jerusalem: Magnes Press.

Yovel, Yirmiyahu. [1989] 1992. *Spinoza and Other Heretics*. Volumes 1–2. Reprint, Princeton, New Jersey: Princeton University Press.

Zank, Michael. 2000. *The Idea of Atonement in the Philosophy of Hermann Cohen*. Providence, Rhode Island: Brown Judaic Studies 324.

Zeller, Eduard. [1931] 1955. *Outlines of the History of Greek Philosophy*. Translated by L. R. Palmer. Reprint, New York: Meridian.

Zornberg, Avivah Gottlieb. 1996. *The Beginning of Desire: Reflections on Genesis*. New York: Doubleday.

Index

MODERN JEWISH PHILOSOPHY AND RELIGION
Translations and Critical Studies
Barbara E. Galli and Elliot R. Wolfson, SERIES EDITORS

Hermann Cohen
Ethics of Maimonides
Translated with commentary by Almut Sh. Bruckstein

Emil Fackenheim
An Epitaph for German Judaism: From Halle to Jerusalem

Franz Rosenzweig
On Jewish Learning